Robert Brown

The Story of Africa and its Explorers

Vol. III

Robert Brown

The Story of Africa and its Explorers
Vol. III

ISBN/EAN: 9783743418110

Manufactured in Europe, USA, Canada, Australia, Japa

Cover: Foto ©ninafisch / pixelio.de

Manufactured and distributed by brebook publishing software (www.brebook.com)

Robert Brown

The Story of Africa and its Explorers

THE EMIN PASHA RELIEF EXPEDITION: THE ADVANCE COLUMN LEAVING YAMBUYA (p. 32).
(From a sketch by Mr. Herbert Ward, an officer of the Expedition.)

THE
STORY OF AFRICA
AND ITS EXPLORERS

BY

ROBERT BROWN, M.A., Ph.D., F.L.S., F.R.G.S.

AUTHOR OF "THE COUNTRIES OF THE WORLD," "THE PEOPLES OF THE WORLD," "OUR EARTH AND ITS STORY"

VOL. III

THE LAST OF A LONG TALE—THE SAHARA—THE MISSIONARIES—
THE HUNTERS—THE INTERNATIONAL EXPLORERS

With Two Hundred Original Illustrations

CASSELL AND COMPANY, LIMITED
LONDON, PARIS & MELBOURNE

CONTENTS.

CHAPTER I.
IN A DAY OF SMALL THINGS: SOME MINOR JOURNEYS ACROSS AFRICA

CHAPTER II.
FROM THE ATLANTIC TO THE ALBERT NYANZA: A BELEAGUERED PROVINCE

CHAPTER III.
FROM THE NILE LAKES TO THE INDIAN OCEAN: AN IRRESOLUTE RULER

CHAPTER IV.
THE SAHARA: ITS EXPLORATION AND ITS EXPLOITATION

CHAPTER V.
THE MISSIONARIES: TILLING, SOWING, AND REAPING

CHAPTER VI.
THE MISSIONARIES OF UGANDA AND THE WAY THITHER: A HALF-TOLD TALE

CHAPTER VII.
THE HUNTER'S PARADISE: EARLY AND LATE: A CONTRAST

CHAPTER VIII.
BEAST AND MAN: SOME CAMPAIGNS OF A LONG WAR

CHAPTER IX.

MAN AND BEAST: THE BEGINNING OF THE END ... 200

CHAPTER X.

THE ENDING OF AN OLD ERA AND THE BEGINNING OF A NEW ONE . 221

CHAPTER XI.

THE SCIENTIFIC EXPLORERS: BEYS AND PASHAS: NACHTIGAL AND JUNKER ... 244

CHAPTER XII.

THE INTERNATIONAL EXPLORERS: "ONE TRAVELLER RETURNS" ... 266

CHAPTER XIII

INTERNATIONAL EXPLORERS: MANY MEN AND MANY MINDS: THE END OF A DREAM . 286

LIST OF ILLUSTRATIONS.

The Emin Pasha Relief Expedition: The Advance Column leaving Yambuya . . . *Frontispiece.*

	PAGE
Fort São Miguel, São Paolo de Loanda	1
Mount Mirumbi, Tanganyika	1
Lieut.-Colonel Serpa Pinto	3
Making Tethers for Oxen, Leshoma, Zambesi	4
Market, Leshoma, Zambesi	5
Map of Serpa Pinto's Route	7
Rapids of Ngambae, Upper Zambesi	8
Map showing the Density of Population in Africa	9
En route for Lialui: Preparing to Encamp	12
Mr. Blockley's Tannery, Leshoma	13
Map of Wissmann's Journeys	14
F. S. Arnot	15
"A Kid for Sale!"—Lialui	16
Traveller's Camp in the Wankonde Country, Nyassaland (North)	17
Ruga-Ruga (Bandits) employed by the Governor of Ujiji, returned from raiding	20
Cattle-House of the Wankonde Tribe	21
Major H. von Wissmann	23
Le Stanley, one of the River Steamers used by the Emin Pasha Relief Expedition	25
Makaraka Dwellings	28
Makaraka Warriors and Musicians	29
The Emin Pasha Relief Expedition Leaving Matadi, on the Congo, with Tippoo Tib and his Wives	32
Major Casati	33
Sectional Steel Boat *The Advance*	33
Arrow-heads, Arrows, and Quiver, from the Aruwhimi District	34
Map of the Route of the Emin Pasha Relief Expedition	35
Relative Sizes of Skeletons of an Akka Woman and of a Man of Ordinary Stature	36
Akka (Pigmy) Girl	37
Daylight at Last! The Advance Column of the Emin Pasha Relief Expedition emerging from the Great Forest	*to face page* 38
Weapons of the Aruwhimi District	38
Wanyoro Warriors	40
Meeting of Emin Pasha and Mr. Stanley at Kavalli's, April 29, 1888	41
Fort Dodo	44
Lango Chief with Characteristic Head-dress	45
Lango Chief	45
Mr. Ward Despatched to the Coast for Instructions: Call at Lukolela	48
Mutiny of Emin Pasha's Men at Laboreh: Beginning of the Rebellion	49
Emin Pasha	52
Unyoro Village	53
Makaraka Native	55
Officers of the Emin Pasha Relief Expedition	57
C.M.S. Station of Usambiro, where Stanley stayed with Mackay	60
Objects from Zanzibar, Mombasa, etc.	61
Dr. Carl Peters	64
Mombasa: The Road to Uganda	65
Captain F. D. Lugard	67
Dr. F. Stuhlmann	68

	PAGE
Map Showing the Zones of Vegetation in Africa	69
Akka Girl	72
Grave of Captain Nelson at Kikiyu	73
Captain Trivier and Attendants	76
Oasis near Gabes, Tunisia	77
Berber Type	78
Arab Tribesman	80
Incident in the Desert: Marauder taken Prisoner by a French Arab Outpost	81
Sir R. Lambert Playfair	83
Remains of Roman Amphitheatre at El Djem, Tunisia	84
Typical Saharan Landscape (Dakhel)	85
Arab Type	87
Young Jewess of Tunisia	88
Dr. Rohlfs' Expedition, 1873-4: Wells in the Oasis Fara'freh, Libyan Desert	89
Dr. Gerhard Rohlfs	91
Dr. Rohlfs' Expedition, 1873-4: The House of the Expedition at Gasr Dakhel, Libyan Desert	92
Dr. Rohlfs' Expedition, 1873-4: The Approach to Budchullu	93
Bedouin Women	96
St. Louis, Senegambia; Avenue de Cocotiers de Gnet-Ndar	97
Caravan at a Well in the Desert	*to face page* 99
Date-Palms on the Island of Djerba	100
Arabs Returning from a Raiding Expedition	101
Some Products of the Oases	104
Cardinal Lavigerie	105
Johann Ludwig Krapf	107
Remains of the Cisterns of Carthage, with the Byrsa Hill, the Port (Cothon), and the Gulf of Tunis, etc., in the distance	108
Map showing the Distribution of Religions and Missionary Stations in Africa	109
Marabout (Mohammedan Devotee), Gambia	112
Fetish Customs for the Dead, Little Popo, West Africa	113
Mohammedan Joloffs, Gambia	116
Images at Chief's House, Ogbomosho, Yoruba	116
Fetish Place, with Clay Idols, Porto Novo, West Africa	117
Rev. George Grenfell	119
B.M.S. Congo Steamer *Peace*	120
A.B.M.U. Congo Steamer *Henry Reed*	120
First Missionary Encampment at Holobo: Rev. G. Grenfell's Head-quarters in 1888	121
Rev. J. Holman Bentley	123
Bangala Boys	124
Evolution of a Mission-House at Lukolela, Congo	125
Rev. Thomas J. Comber	127
Street in Kuruman, showing Church built by Dr. Moffat and others	128
Field-work at Lovedale	129
Rev. Dr. James Stewart	131
Carpenters' Workshop at Lovedale	132
The *Ilala* at Matope	133
Dr. Charles F. Mackenzie, first Bishop of the Universities' Mission to Central Africa	135
Dr. C. A. Smythies, Bishop of Central Africa	135

	PAGE		PAGE
Bandawe, Mission-Station of the Free Church of Scotland	136	Group of Mashukulumbwe	225
Blantyre Church	137	Route Map of Holub's Journeys	227
Captain E. C. Hore	138	Traveller's Flotilla on the Zambesi (at Seshcke)	228
House at Mengo, Uganda, built by Natives for Bishop Tucker	140	William D. James	229
Waganda Envoys despatched by King M'tesa to England in 1879	141	Batoka Type	229
Dr. R. W. Felkin	143	F. L. James	230
Church at Karema, Lake Tanganyika, in Course of Construction by the "White Fathers": Length 150 feet	144	Group of Wakwafi	232
Church on the Hills of Namurembe, Uganda, and Houses of English Missionaries	145	Street in Lamu, East Africa	233
Alexander Mackay	148	Count Samuel Teleki (von Szek)	234
Seizure of Bishop Hannington, previous to His Murder	149	Niam-Niam Girl	236
Grave of the Mother of King M'tesa	151	Niam-Niam Wizard	237
Mumias' Village, Kavirondo, the Scene of Bishop Hannington's Murder	152	Route Map of Schweinfurth's Journey	238
Bishop Hannington	153	Georg August Schweinfurth	239
Dr. A. R. Tucker, third Bishop of East Equatorial Africa	153	Niam-Niam Musician and Warriors	240
"God's Acre," Usambiro, showing the Graves of Bishop Parker, Alexander Mackay, and others	156	Niam-Niam Farm: Visit of Traders	241
Fort at Kampala, Uganda, with Summit of Mengo and Houses of the King	157	Niam-Niam Tribesmen	243
Map of Equatorial East Africa	160	The German Consulate at Khartoum during the Egyptian Occupation of the Soudan	244
Nzoi	161	Ernst Marno	245
Game in Sight!	164	Colonel Chaillé-Long	245
Shot Buffalo	165	Slave-Boy of Darfur rescued by General Gordon	246
Two-Horned Rhinoceros	168	Map of the Actual Mean Temperature of the African Year	249
William Charles Baldwin	168	Euphorbia caudelabrum	252
A Critical Moment	169	Map of the Mean Annual Range of Temperature in Africa	253
In Search of Prey	172	Route Map of Dr. Nachtigal's Journey	254
Shot Hartebeest	173	Gustav Nachtigal	256
Mr. H. A. Bryden and Friends on Trek at Morokweng	176	Camp of Wandering Abyssinians	257
Young Cow Buffalo caught in a Python's Coils	177	Dr. Wilhelm Junker	259
Shot Grant's Gazelle (*Gazella Granti*) of East Africa	180	El Khatmich, a Suburb of Kassala	260
A Good Bag	181	Mundoo Warriors	261
The Rev. Dr. Moffat	182	Map of Dr. Junker's Routes	263
Hunting the Springbuck	185	Shooli Musicians *to face page*	264
The Kafir and the Lion	188	Shooli Village	264
Wandering Hunters (Masarwa Bushmen), North Kalahari Desert	189	Shooli Musical Instruments	264
Party of Giraffe Hunters	192	Shooli Warrior	265
At the Ford of Malikoe, Marico River	193	On the Island of Chisumulu, Lake Nyassa	268
Shooting Duiker	196	Zanzibar Beach	269
On the Maritsani River	197	Kilimanjaro from Moschi, showing Snow-clad Peak of Kibo	272
Stalking Blesbuck behind Oxen	200	Falls of Zoa on the River Ruo, a Tributary of the Shiré	273
Gorge in the Bamangwato Mountains	201	Keith Johnston	275
Twelve thousand pounds' worth of Ivory at a Trader's Store at Pandamatenka	204	Mango Fruit	276
On the Limpopo River	205	East African Water Vegetation, including the Magnificent blue Water Lily	277
Roualeyn George Gordon Cumming	208	Map of Keith Johnston's and Joseph Thomson's Route	279
Gordon Cumming's Adventure with the Hippopotamus	209	Grotesque Baobab	280
W. F. Webb	210	Ugnha People, west of Tanganyika	281
Francis Galton	212	Zanzibar	284
Carl Johan Andersson	212	Joseph Thomson	285
Cleaning Heads after an Eland Hunt	213	Karema Fort, now a Roman Catholic Mission Station	288
Frederick Courteney Selous	215	Dwellings at Acrar, Abyssinia	289
Encampment of Travellers in the Zambesi Country: Leshomas selling Native Produce	216	Abyssinia: Call to Prayer	292
Characteristic Portion of Selous' Road	217	Bateke Chief and Son	293
Native Hunters returning from the Chase	220	Lower Congo Chief in "Royal Robes" *to face page*	296
Village of Kitetu in the Kikuyu Country	221	Lower Congo Chief in "Coronation Robes"	296
Dr. Emil Holub	223	Cutting Timber in a Lower Congo Forest	297
Map showing Distribution of Languages in Africa	224	Kilimanjaro: Another View of Kibo from Moschi	300
		Mount Meru, from Moschi	301
		Lake Naivasha	302
		Lake Jipe, near Kilimanjaro	304
		The Crater Lake Chala, on Kilimanjaro	304
		Waterfall on Kilimanjaro	305
		The Kilimanjaro Range	308
		Hill of Ndara, between Kilimanjaro and the Coast	309
		El Morau (Old Men) of the Masai Tribe	311
		Masai War Party	312

FORT SÃO MIGUEL, SÃO PAOLO DE LOANDA.
(*From a Photograph supplied by H. M. Stanley.*)

THE STORY OF AFRICA.

CHAPTER I.

IN A DAY OF SMALL THINGS: SOME MINOR JOURNEYS ACROSS AFRICA.

An *annus mirabilis* in the History of African Exploration—What constitutes a Journey "across Africa"—Serpa Pinto's Expedition—Separates from Capello and Ivens at Bihé—Destroying some Goods to obtain Porters for the Remainder—Peculiarity of Rivers—New Sources Discovered—The Mucassequeres—The Mussambas Tribe and their Wanderings—The Zambesi—The Makololo Empire—Its Ruin and Extinction of the Race—The Victoria Falls—Pioneers of Civilisation met with—M. Collard—Dr. Bradshaw and Senhor Anchieta—The Kalahari and Baines Deserts—Character of the Country—Matteucci and Massari's Journey from Egypt to the Gulf of Guinea—Sultans Hospitable and Otherwise—Death of Matteucci—Wissmann's First Journey across Africa—A Great Story and a Small Lake—An Artistic People—1884 a Brisk Year for Africa—Arnot's Journey—Katanga—Confusion of Nomenclature—Two Sides to a Story—Capello and Ivens' Journey from Ocean to Ocean—Gleerup's Transit—Oskar Lenz's Travels from the Congo to the Zambesi—Changes on the Upper Congo since Stanley's First Descent—Tippoo Tib—Arab Settlements—Kasongo—Tanganyika Reached—The Stevenson Road—Nyassa—The Sea—Wissmann's Second Journey across the Continent—Ravages of Arab Raiders—The Tanganyika and Nyassa Lakes—Waning Interest in Transcontinental Journeys—Speed at which they were performed—Getting to be mere Geographical "Records."

MT. MIRUMBI, TANGANYIKA.

THE year 1877 was a notable one in the annals of African exploration. Shortly before that date Lieutenant Cameron had returned from his expedition across Africa (Vol. II., p. 266); still more recently Stanley had descended the Congo; and, above all, the journey of Livingstone—which had been finished in the Portuguese possessions—was still fresh in public memory. However, though these British travellers had reached the Atlantic within Lusitanian territory—and in those days Portugal claimed the Congo—the Portuguese themselves had done little for the exploration of the country under their flag. Their colonies extended without any determined frontiers to the east and to the west; but their boundaries, the course of the rivers and the trend of the mountains, even within the limits of these colonies, were but little known. Vague stories, we have seen, circulated regarding early Portuguese travellers (Vol. II., pp. 163–166); but few of them had left any records of their journeys, and none which could be taken without doubt.

In the meantime a difference of opinion existed as to what really constituted a journey across Africa. Livingstone, it is all but admitted, was the first traveller who successfully attempted to cross the country and preserve a description of his journey. But Gerhard Rohlfs, even before Livingstone, had penetrated from the Mediterranean to the Atlantic: and if a journey of this kind is to be signalised as one "across Africa," then Speke's famous journey (Vol. II., pp. 65–116) from the east coast to the Nile deserves that name. Colonel Grant, indeed, actually published an account of it under the title of "A Walk Across Africa." However, long before that period Clapperton (Vol. I., pp. 242-259), in the course of two journeys, had covered very much the same ground as Rohlfs. Even Caillié (Vol. I., pp. 227-238) had entered Africa at the Gulf of Guinea and left it at Tangier in Morocco.

What is a transcontinental journey?

We must, therefore, not speak of an expedition as being across Africa except on more substantial claims than these: otherwise every tourist who passed from Tangier to Tetuan may be said to have "crossed Africa." However, with the completion of Stanley's voyage down the Congo almost the last of the great problems of Africa had been solved.

A few years before these mysteries were numerous. Now the Niger had been traced from its source to the sea. The great lakes were no longer subjects of speculation. The course of the Nile and all its chief tributaries had been tracked, and finally the Congo (or the Livingstone, as Stanley, in defiance of the laws governing geographical nomenclature, had called it) was no longer one of the puzzles of geography. Nevertheless, there was still much to be done. Africa was known only in outline. Vast tracts between the rivers had not been laid down on the map and the regions on each side of the routes of the travellers across the country were still blanks. Numerous minor rivers were to be discovered and endless sheets of water, many not much less in size than the huge ones which we have described in previous chapters, remained to be traced in all their vastness. Still, no Old World mystery attached to these. The rivers were not historical streams and the lakes were the sources of no such currents as the Niger, the Congo, and the chief tributary of the Zambesi. The Portuguese, moreover, came rather late into the field. Between the utmost limits of their own colonies on the west coast and the most western extension of the British on the east coast there was a comparatively narrow strip of country remaining to be explored. Even that narrow region was being penetrated here and there by hunters and miners and traders. Hence the explorer entering from the west coast and going to the east—say to Natal—had only a short distance to travel before he came upon the trail of other civilised men. The Portuguese, nevertheless, determined not to be any longer singular among the nations in alone taking no part in the ransacking of inner Africa. The Legislature, therefore, voted a sum of over £6,000 to fit out an expedition for exploring and mapping the country immediately behind their colonies on the west coast. The officer selected for the command of this expedition was Captain (afterwards Colonel) Alexandre Alberto da Rocha Serpa Pinto (p. 3)—who, as one of the garrison of the African colonies, had already had some experience of the region to be explored—with whom were associated two naval officers, Lieutenants Menigildo de Brito Capello and Roberto Ivens. The ostensible object of the journey was to survey the great artery which, as a tributary of the Congo, runs from south to north between

A day of small things.

Serpa Pinto's expedition.

17° and 19° east of Greenwich, and is called the Kwango; and also to determine all the geographical bearings between the river and the west coast, and make a comparative survey of the hydrographic basins of the Congo and the Zambesi. Leaving São Paolo de Loanda (Vol. II., p. 216) in May, 1877, the first portion of the journey was to the settlement of Bihé, a native village on a great plateau, where several Portuguese traders had their establishments. It is known to the reader from the visit paid to it by Commander

LIEUT.-COLONEL SERPA PINTO.
(From a Photograph by Camacho, Lisbon.)

Cameron a few years earlier (Vol. II., p. 278). At this point the expedition broke up into two divisions, the travellers finding it difficult to obtain porters for the entire party. Capello and Ivens' journey to the territory of Yacca forms an interesting episode in African discovery, but from a geographical point of view it does not bulk largely in the history of the Dark Continent.* We shall, however, for the present follow Captain Pinto in his walk to the east.

Indeed, to cross the continent was not his intention when he first started out upon the journey of which these pages form a brief record. His march through the continent

* Capello and Ivens, "From Benguela to the Territory of Yacca," 2 vols. (1882); also *Proceedings of the Royal Geographical Society*, 1880, p. 647.

was almost forced upon him. Short of provisions and of men to carry them, he could not well go back; he was therefore forced to go forward, the country over which he travelled from the eastern bounds of the Portuguese colonies to the western bounds of Natal being about 500 miles in breadth, and most of it still unknown to the chartographer. Leaving Bihé in the month of May, 1878, he was for the most part alone, with a few native attendants and no white companions, as he passed across the southern limits of the Benguelan highlands. This country stands 5,000 feet above the level of the sea, and possesses great advantages in its salubrity and commercial and agricultural capabilities, which highly recommend it to European attention. Indeed, in all tropical Africa this is the territory Captain Serpa Pinto considers most suitable for European colonisation, though since that day we have learnt so much more of Central Africa that this enthusiastic dictum is too sweeping, even despite the attempts that have been made to colonise these uplands. *From Bihé eastward.*

One journey in the Zambesi country is very much like another, so that those who have followed Livingstone's and Cameron's travels will scarcely require a minute account of the campings and hardships of the explorer now under consideration. He and his party had to live solely on the product of the chase from day to day, and thus, with occasional help from friendly natives, he succeeded in accomplishing his difficult task. As a rule, all of the tribes with whom the expedition came into contact had more or less acquaintance with white men and generally, from long experience, lived in wholesome dread of their powers: so that, leaving out of account the grasping peculiarities of the little native kings, or "Sovas," the difficulty of obtaining porters to carry their baggage, and the inevitable hardships of travel, Captain Serpa Pinto encountered no great obstacles in the course of his journey. Indeed, with the exception of being so frequently compelled to destroy his baggage from the difficulty of obtaining people to carry it, we cannot learn that he met with any very serious peril. The hindrances in the way of hiring porters were largely due to the greed of the native chiefs to obtain the goods which the traveller was unable to carry. Hence his precaution in destroying them. Otherwise, the porters would never have been forthcoming. Before reaching Bihé he was surprised to find the Kubango river taking its rise to the west and not to the east of that place, as all existing maps had led him to expect. This large river receives on the east a great tributary, the Kwito, which unites its waters with those of the Kubango at a place called Darico. Within the wide fork which is formed by the two rivers the Kwanza,* as well as some of its smaller affluents, takes its source.

It was here that Pinto had occasion to remark a peculiar feature in the physical geography of this part of Africa, **River peculiarities.** namely, the dovetailing of the sources of rivers which, in the rest of their courses, run in opposite directions. Thus, close to the source of the Kwito rise three other rivers, two of which flow into the Atlantic by the Kwanza, of which they are tributaries, and one into the Indian Ocean through the Zambesi. The same feature is noticeable even beyond Lake Bemba (or Bangweolo), the Congo and Zambesi as well as their affluents having their sources and mingling their streams near to the twelfth parallel of south latitude. East of the river Kwito, the Kwando, which Livingstone calls the Chobe (Vol. II., pp. 195, 199, etc.), takes its rise. It forms a fine, large, navigable river, watering a great extent of inhabitable and fertile country, and receives several affluents as navigable as itself and all destined in future years to be enlivened by barges, boats, and steamers. In this forest-covered region, where the elephant still abounds, we meet with the Mucassequeres, a tribe of a yellowish-white colour. They are nomads and perfectly savage, spending their time continually roaming through the region between the Kwando and the Kubango. In the same country exists another nomad tribe — the Mus-

MAKING TETHERS FOR OXEN, LESHOMA, ZAMBESI.
(From a Photograph taken for the Paris Society for Evangelical Missions.)

* Also spelt Cuanza and Quanza.

sambas — who are black, and wander about towards the south, raiding the country as far as the land of the Sulatebele. These people, however, are quite distinct from the Bushmen of the Kalahari, from the pigmies of the country farther north described by

M. du Chaillu, and from those near the head-waters of the Congo and the region between it and Albert Nyanza, described by Mr. Stanley and others some years later (p. 34). The country between Bihé and the Zambesi is inhabited by three distinct races of people, the Kimbandes, the Luchares, and the Ambuellas. Another race—the Kibokwes—is now beginning to settle there, and there is a considerable emigration of these people from the north for the purpose of establishing themselves on the banks of the Kubango and the Kwando, in their search for lands more fertile than their own. In the course of his daily travel, Captain Pinto met large caravans of these emigrants, and stayed for some time in their new settlements.

Tribes and their wanderings.

All of the above-mentioned country he describes as "splendid and very fertile," and inhabited by people of docile character and susceptible of development. What struck him very much as regards their capacity for trade was that these tribes were extremely fond of dress, a disposition which should certainly not be overlooked by the "white" manufacturer. Indeed, we may consider that there is here a prospective market for the consumption of European goods.

MARKET, LESHOMA, ZAMBESI.
(*From a Photograph taken for the Paris Society for Evangelical Missions.*)

These tribes are governed in a despotic manner by independent rulers and constitute confederations, though belonging to different races. At the time of which we speak the missionaries had not reached them, nor had any European been seen amongst them until Serpa Pinto's arrival. Yet, though he claims to be the first visitor, the traveller met with a cordial reception. Travelling eastward, the Liambai—really, as

The Zambesi reached. Political changes.

Livingstone discovered, the upper waters of the Zambesi—is the first river met with beyond the Kwando.

As Livingstone has fully described the characteristics of this part of the Zambesi (Vol. II., pp. 197–234, pp. 242, 243), it is unnecessary to add any further remarks regarding it. However, since the great traveller's visit, the political geography of the Upper Zambesi has altered very considerably, the people with whom he had associated having been displaced by others of different origin. At the time the Scottish explorer first visited this part of Africa, it had recently been conquered by the genius of a really great man, the Kaffir chief Sebituane, who, having gained successive victories over the native tribes, induced them to confederate into what for a time constituted a powerful empire (Vol. II., p. 243). Six years later, during the Zambesi expedition, when he visited Seshcke, towards the end of the reign of the second Makololo monarch (Sekeletu), Livingstone, it will be remembered, foretold not merely the fall of the empire, but the extinction of the Makololo people (Vol. II., p. 194). In fact, in the course of the reign of the third sovereign of this dynasty of the conquerors, named Omboroh, the king was murdered, and the Luinas, who were the former masters of the country, again took possession of it after a sort of Sicilian Vespers, when most of the remaining Makololo were put to death. A very few, however, succeeded in escaping to Bihé, under the command of Siroca, who put himself at their head. But even these were destroyed in the beginning of 1878, close to the village of Muttambanja on the right bank of the Kwando, when they attempted to fall suddenly upon those who were at that time owners of the country.

The Makololo, as is well known, were not a single race. Sebituane (Vol. II., p. 194) was, indeed, born on the bank of the Gariep in the Basuto country, and his genius for organisation enabled him to get together an army composed of various races belonging to South Africa, with which army he conquered the country of the Upper Zambesi and gave it the name of Makololo. It was these same people, bearing the name of Makololo, who were in former times so courageous, but later were so weakened by fevers in the marsh-lands of the Kwando (Chobe) and the Zambesi, ruined by licentiousness, and enfeebled by the use of Indian hemp, as at last to be destroyed, as we have said, by the Luinas and their allies. The name "Makololo," still occasionally seen in maps, has, however, no place in geography, for the race has ceased to exist.

On the banks of the Zambesi, Machuana, who had been Livingstone's companion on his journey to Loanda, was met with. In former days he was a slave belonging to Sekeletu, but, at the time of making Captain Serpa Pinto's acquaintance, had risen to be a man of consequence among the Luinas, and through his respect for white men, owing to his esteem for Dr. Livingstone, the latest traveller received such kindness from him as to owe his life to this black man.

On the west the Zambesi receives no other tributaries of consequence, except the Lungo-é-ungo and the Nhengo, the latter being formed by the junction of three rivers, the Ninda, the Loati, and the Luanguingua. From the confluence of the Kwando, as far as the Victoria Falls, it receives only one small stream, close to the cataract, the native name of which Captain Serpa Pinto was unable to ascertain in consequence of the country being uninhabited.

Serpa Pinto's description of the Victoria Falls, or Mozi-oa-tunia, as the natives call them, which were discovered and so fully pictured by Livingstone and those who succeeded him, does not differ greatly from the accounts of which we are already in possession. Indeed, on arriving at this point, Captain Serpa Pinto's journey through unknown lands might be said to have ended. For in the course of his rambles he came upon five heaps of stones which marked the graves of five Europeans who had fallen victims to the miasma of these damp forests which they had penetrated in the pursuit of ivory or in the hunt for gold. But beyond the fact that four of them bore English names and the fifth grave was tenanted by a Swede, the history of these unfortunate wanderers was unknown at the time, and their very memory must by now be forgotten.

In a short while Patamatenka was reached, and as this was a mission station inhabited by M. Collard, of the French Evangelical Society, the journey of the Portuguese explorer, so far as unmapped country was concerned, may be said to have ended here.

The pioneers of civilisation.

In this out-of-the-way portion of Africa an English hunter of the name of Bradshaw was met with. He was an educated physician who had exchanged the pleasures of civilisation for a rough life in the midst of an African forest, habitually living on game and the proceeds of the sale of his natural history collections.

At an earlier stage in his journey Captain Serpa Pinto fell in with a Portuguese wayfarer of a different type, a gentleman who dressed for dinner in the forest, and, in evening dress, afforded a curious contrast to the English zoologist, attired in shirt and trousers. This traveller—José d'Anchieta—had been resident in Africa for eleven years and held an official position under the Portuguese Government. At the time that we make his acquaintance he was employed in preparing scientific collections for the Lisbon Museum and did not consider the fact of his living in a forest of Africa should interfere in any way with his European habits. He followed, therefore, in the ruined church where he had taken up his quarters, the ways of life which he had been accustomed to in Lisbon or in Paris. He wore a tailed coat and a white necktie in the evening and, though far from civilisation, managed to keep up his studies as though he were in Europe. One hears occasionally of luxurious travellers—even in Africa,—of men who spread table-cloths and drink champagne on the march; but the doubtful luxury of evening dress I do not remember to have met with before.

From Patamatenka Captain Serpa Pinto's journey was made in a comfortable waggon, and lay, for the most part, through the Transvaal or the British colony of Natal. Though full of interest to him, this journey can have little moment so far as geography is concerned. All of the country was, even at that date, tolerably well known, and in the course of following years not a little of the region mapped for the first time by Serpa Pinto has been the scene of busy gold-prospecting, and even of pioneer farming.

Through the entire course of his journey Serpa Pinto employs native names in speaking of places which he visited. Almost the only exception to this rule is that, when he crossed the arid country between the Botletli (which is really the Kubango) and the Zambesi, he ventured to give the name of Baines Desert to an arid track traversed by him, in honour of Thomas Baines (Vol. II., p. 238), who had for years worked laboriously in the interior of Southern Africa with scant pleasure, little fame, much toil, and no

MAP OF SERPA PINTO'S ROUTE.

pecuniary reward. This bare, arid, and cheerless plain had been crossed for the first time by Livingstone but two degrees to the west of Pinto's track, one degree farther west by Baines, and a degree more to the east by Baldwin, Chapman, Mohr, and others. It is the most sandy and inhospitable region of South Africa, the Sahara of the South, the colour. The thickness of the layer of fine white sand which formed the surface varied from four to twenty inches. Of water there was scarcely a trace, and often even in the rainy seasons very little accumulated in the depressions in the ground. After quitting it, the country was covered with forest, which went on increasing in density and luxurious-

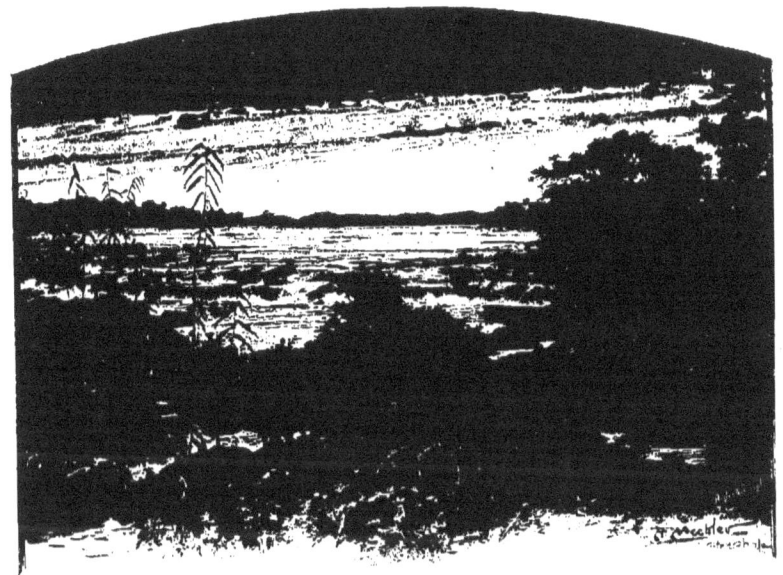

RAPIDS OF NGAMBAE, UPPER ZAMBESI.
(*From a Photograph taken for the Paris Society for Evangelical Missions.*)

northern continuation of the repulsive Kalahari (Vol. II., p. 183). The only herbage are miserable stunted thorn-trees, which, with their parched leafage, only make the bareness of the desert more perceptible. Salt-pans—the bottom of desiccated salt-lakes—(Vol. II., p. 189) are also met with, and when they are found are frequented for the sake of the salt. From the Zambesi to this point the ground was sandy, the subsoil being formed by a layer of singular plastic clay of dark chestnut

Characteristics of the country.

ness of vegetation as the route drew away to the north. The vegetation itself was distinguished by an immense variety of acacias; brilliant flowers of almost every kind met the eye on every side and filled the air with their delicious perfume. The prospect was enchanting, but travelling through it the traveller confessed was an arduous task. At times a road had to be cut through the tangled mass with a hatchet, foot by foot. At other times, say for ten miles or so together, the surface was twenty inches deep in sand, while the wheels of the waggon were literally buried, so that the wayfarers con- being visible every now and again, as the flames from the camp fires illumined the darkness.

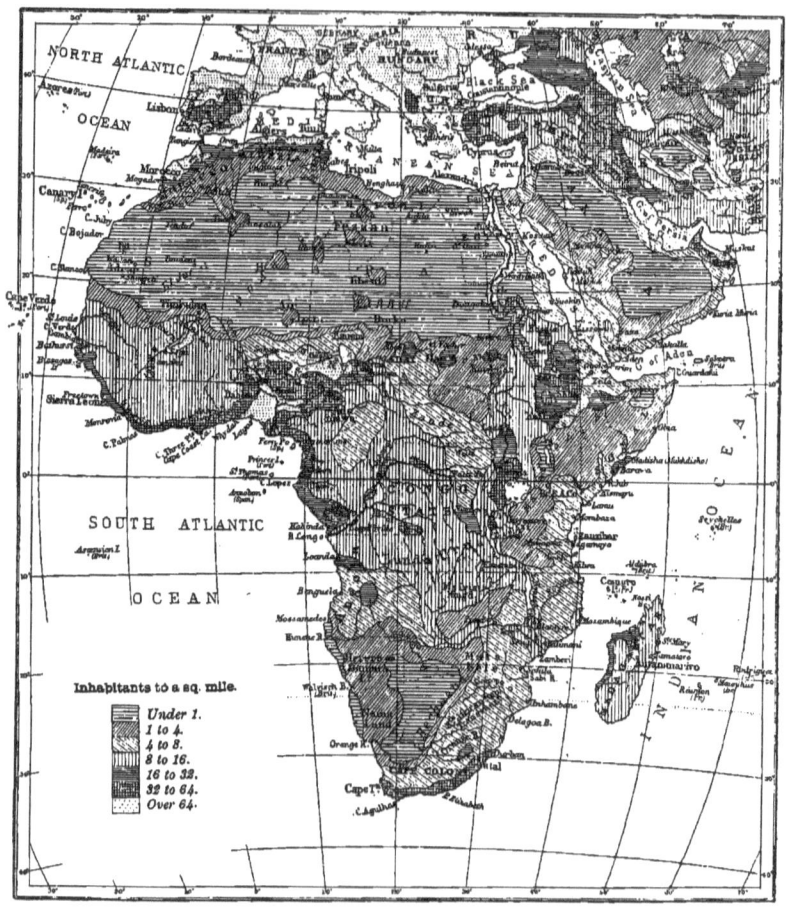

MAP SHOWING THE DENSITY OF POPULATION IN AFRICA. (By E. G. Ravenstein.)

sidered themselves fortunate if a mile was got over in forty minutes. All night long jackals and hyænas kept up an infernal concert around them, the outline of their forms being visible every now and again, as the flames from the camp fires illumined the darkness.

But beyond these facts and the personal adventures of which Captain Serpa Pinto's volumes describing his journey are full, the greater portion of the country which he traversed was at that time not unknown, and at the present moment ranks among the best-explored portions of the outer range of British colonies on the one side and of those of the Portuguese on the other.

At an earlier date Pinto's march would have ranked among one of the great explorations of Africa. Unfortunately for him, he had fallen upon a day of small things. The earlier journeys over the same region had stripped his travels of much of their novelty. Still, as almost the only Portuguese expedition worthy of the name and the first which starting from the west coast terminated on the east, the exploration of Serpa Pinto will always occupy an honourable page in the chronicles of African travel. It is, however, possible that the historian of these days does not assess it at such a high figure as did the kings and geographical societies, who bestowed medals and other awards on the author of an exploration the extent of which had been far exceeded by those of a previous date and has been cast into insignificance by less-known travellers of later years.* It necessarily touched at various points the routes of Livingstone and Cameron. Thus at Bihé it crossed Cameron's track, and from Lialui, on the Upper Zambesi, to the Victoria Falls Serpa Pinto's route was identical with that of Livingstone. At Linyanti and Shoshong also he reached familiar points in Livingstone's travels, so that it was only for a comparatively short distance that his route lay through land hitherto unfamiliar to the readers of African travels.

A year after Serpa Pinto returned to Europe, a remarkable but little-known journey across Central Africa was made by two Italians, Dr. Pellegrino Matteucci, and Lieutenant Alfonso Maria Massari, of the Italian Navy. Matteucci

Marginal note: Results of Serpa Pinto's journey.

Marginal note: Matteucci and Massari.

* "Major Serpa Pinto's Journey Across Africa" (in a letter to Lord Northbrook. President Royal Geographical Society), *Proceedings Royal Geographical Society*, 1879, pp. 481-489, the facts of which are condensed in our narrative; Serpa Pinto, "How I Crossed Africa," 2 vols. (1881). etc.

had travelled in Abyssinia and along the Blue Nile, and when they began their journey towards the Niger in March, 1880, he and Massari, like so many other Italian explorers, were residents in Khartoum, on the Nile. For a part of their journey they were accompanied by Prince Giovanni Borghese, who paid the cost of the expedition; but at Darfur he returned to more civilised regions. The route which his two companions now took led them from Suakim through Kordofan, Darfur, Dar Tama, Waday, Bornu, Kano, and Nupé, diagonally through thirty meridians of longitude, until they reached the Niger. Most of the countries mentioned have already been more or less fully described in the course of the travels of Clapperton, Caillié and Barth, and still more recently had been reached by Rohlfs and Nachtigal, and other explorers, though the Italians were the first who crossed the whole breadth of the Soudan from sea to sea. The visits of these travellers did not, however, smooth, to any appreciable extent, the path of the latest visitors to the barbarous monarchs ruling the territories in question. Indeed, the treacherous Sultan of Waday, who is believed to have murdered Vogel and who refused Rohlfs (when he came in search of his countryman's papers) entrance into his kingdom, was at times so unfriendly that the Italian explorers could only insure a moderate safety by warning this suspicious potentate that their king would avenge their deaths, but would send splendid presents if they were protected. By thus appealing at once to his fear and his avarice, they saved not only their own lives, but the lives of four hundred prisoners of war. They told him, moreover, that he could do nothing more acceptable in the eyes of the King of Italy than to spare them.

In Bornu they found an Italian named Giuseppe Valpreda, who had been left behind, at his own request, by Nachtigal, nineteen years before. He had been tempted to embrace Mohammedanism in the hope of receiving honour and profit. But during the greater part of that period he had—as is the usual lot of renegades—been kept in a condition differing very little from that of slavery. He would fain have accompanied his countrymen to civilisation and fell weeping on their necks when he found it was impossible to persuade his master to allow him to depart, but was consoled by the promise that they would endeavour to send for him.

It was originally the Italian travellers' intention to join a caravan in Waday and with it to penetrate northwards to Tripoli, by the route pursued by so many previous travellers and, still more recently, by Commandant Monteil. But to do so would have necessitated a stay of eight months in Waday for the caravan, leaving out of account the reluctance of the Sultan to permit them to travel in that direction. It was indeed fortunate for them that this plan was not carried out: for at that time all the Northern Sahara was troubled by religious broils, which would have made it perilous for Christians to travel there. The less excitable Central Soudan was free from that agitation, so that, having reached Bornu, they were really nearer the Gulf of Guinea than the Mediterranean. Indeed, considering the temper of the Sultan of Waday, his perfidious character and his infamous reputation, the wonder is that they were ever permitted to leave his territories. He kept them virtual prisoners for 113 days before allowing them to enter his kingdom and treated them throughout with the utmost suspicion. Europeans he naturally regarded as spies and it would have been in vain to attempt to make him understand the motives that induced a man who could have lived a life of ease to take so long and so dangerous a journey.

From king to king.

From first to last the time occupied by the journey from Cairo to the mouth of the Niger was sixteen months and a half, eight of which were spent in involuntary delays waiting the pleasure of the various petty kings on the route. Altogether, they travelled a distance of three thousand miles, at an average of fourteen miles a day; so that the journey of Matteucci and Massari is remarkable for the swiftness with which it was accomplished. The Sultan Ibrahim of Dar Tama, on the contrary, treated them throughout with the utmost hospitality, in his capital of Gneri, which consists merely of three hundred straw huts, the only houses built of earth being those of himself and his son. As a rule, this potentate never sees or speaks directly with strangers, but the close cross-examination to which he subjected them seemed to be satisfactory, for he gave them a friendly letter to the Sultan of Waday, though it does not seem to have been very influential in obtaining their entrance into that kingdom, since Sultan Jussuff—we have seen—kept the bearers waiting for months on the confines of his territory. He said that they came from the enemies' country, Darfur, and, as the only place in Europe that he had ever heard of was Malta, from which the new travellers did not claim to have arrived, it was difficult to persuade the suspicious negro sovereign that they were what they pretended to be. Even when he received them in his hot metropolis of Abeshr—from which the inhabitants flee in summer—they were compelled to live on the footing more of prisoners than of guests, and when finally an audience was accorded them the interview was conducted by the sovereign sitting behind a close curtain. Even the presents which they had reserved for this potentate had been pillaged before the time of their audience, and though the Sultan sent black and white ostrich feathers as gifts for the King of Italy, the Italian travellers discovered a plot against their lives during the last days of their residence in Abeshr. They were, therefore, glad to leave, under the supposed protection of the shifty king, for Bornu, the ruler and people of which have always received accredited strangers more courteously than the inferior dignitaries around them. As in Barth's day, they found the country covered with scattered villages wherever there are wells and a few palm trees, or, in most cases, luxurious vegetation. The roads are better-kept, flocks and herds abound, and there are "many sycamores, beautiful women, excellent men, and populous villages." The Sultan of another small kingdom called Midogo also received them civilly, and invited them to return. On their second visit, however, this "simpatico sultano," as is the habit of African princes, secretly asked for poison, and as it was dangerous to refuse, Matteucci presented him with a package of quinine, which might do good, and certainly could do no harm, to the King's enemies. At Kano (Vol. I., p. 264) they were well lodged and the city is described in terms of admiration of the prosperity, enterprise, and courtesy of its 50,000 inhabitants. The Sultan of Nupé received them in robes of velvet and dismissed them with a gift of a leopard's skin. But even the politeness of the most polite of African monarchs is apt to weary when the daily suspicion and endless dilatoriness of these sovereigns have to be endured. They were, therefore, glad to reach Egga, on the Niger, by way of Kano, Nupé, Zariya and Bidda, and, on board one of the trading-steamers which now churn that river, to reach the mouth at Akassa, where they received every attention, and ended a journey which, of minor value to geography, deserves more notice than it has obtained in

EN ROUTE FOR LIALUI: PREPARING TO ENCAMP.
(*From a Photograph taken for the Paris Society for Evangelical Missions.*)

England at least. But Matteucci was destined never again to see his dear Bologna, having died in London (August 8th, 1881), on his way home, at the age of twenty-nine, too soon to incorporate the results of his journeys in a fitting monument of his self-denying labours in the cause of science.*

In 1882 among the officers employed in the Congo State was Lieutenant Wissmann of the German army (pp. 14, 23). **Wissmann's** Hitherto his countrymen had **first journey** taken a comparatively small part **across Africa.** in the exploration of Africa, though the journeys of Schweinfurth, Junker, and Nachtigal were among the most distinguished of

* *Proceedings of the Royal Geographical Society*, 1880, pp. 317, 564, 597, 691, 764; 1881, pp. 560, 562, 743. Bompiani, "Italian Explorers in Africa" (1891), pp. 43-53, etc.

their order. Western Africa was, however, beginning to attract the attention of the German explorers, among whom the names of Güssfeldt, Pechuel-Loesche, Flegel, Büchner, Lenz, Falkenstein, Kund, Mechow, and the late Dr. Pögge, deserve an honourable place. It was in the company of the last-named explorer that Lieutenant Wissmann began his march across Africa. Dr. Pögge did not, however, complete the journey, for, in accordance with previous arrangements, he returned westward from Nyangwe to establish one of the Congo State stations. Already, in 1875, he had reached the capital of the renowned Central African potentate, the "Muata Yanvo" (Vol. II., p. 166), many of the great tributaries of the Congo, the country was comparatively well known, but on the 17th December, 1881, the travellers arrived at Munkamba Lake, which had been described to them as a vast sea, but which turned out a very small sheet, not more than three miles in length. It is fed by springs, is fringed by sedge and high grass, has apparently no outlet, and lies about 2,230 feet above the sea. From this point they made their way towards the Lubi, a tributary of the Sankuru or Kasai. It is a feeder of the Congo. In this country they met with the wild Bashilange and Basongo, who flocked round them by thousands; but the travellers speak of the people as friendly, laborious, and

MR. BLOCKLEY'S TANNERY, LESHOMA.
(From a Photograph taken for the Paris Society for Evangelical Missions.)

of whom he has left the best account accessible.* As far as Nyangwe, the route taking them across

* "Im Reiche des Muato Jamwo" (1880).

highly skilful in all kinds of industry, art, and weapon-making. Carved ivory, baskets, inlaid wares, and iron and copper utensils, exhibiting great artistic skill, were among the evidences of this. Leaving these interesting tribes and

The forests of the Upper Congo.
the fertile plains which they inhabit, the travellers entered the vast virgin forests, which extend as far as Lubailash, a stream of the width of the Elbe at Hamburg. This country was totally without fruit-trees and, consequently, game and birds were scarce, but elephants and a species of wild boar were met with at intervals.

Reaching Lubailash, they found, however, difficulties in the ill-will of the King of Coto, an old and much-revered "fetish-man," called Kachiche, who ruled over a number of Luba tribes, and who would not provide canoes for crossing the stream. It was, indeed, only by working on his superstitious mind by means of shots and rockets that they at last induced him to perform the required office. On the other side of the Lubailash, they entered the country of the Beneki, of whom Lieutenant Wissmann spoke very highly for their well-built, cleanly villages, surrounded by gardens and palm trees. They were a completely agricultural people, very numerous and well-to-do. Some of their villages were so large that it took four or five hours to march through them, and had one, two, or three rows of houses or streets, so that the popu-

Promising tribesmen.
lation must have numbered hundreds of thousands. From here they passed through vast prairie-lands, inhabited by the Kalebue and Mulebue tribes, which extended as far as the Lomami, also a tributary of the Congo, beyond which they crossed Cameron's track.

The travellers suffered severely from heavy rains. In fact, they could not have traversed the swamps they met with had they not been mounted on oxen—excellent animals, which jumped like English hunters, cantered and trotted, but which, unfortunately, died on reaching the east coast, the climate of which is very prejudicial to these western and central African animals.

Nyangwe (already well known to explorers) was reached on the 17th of April. From this spot eastward Lieutenant Wissmann's journey was made alone. However, the Arabs, who have always inhabited this post, furnished him with ten guns and fifteen carriers, with whom, on June 1st, he started for Lake Tanganyika, repeatedly crossing the routes of previous explorers before he arrived at "Plymouth Rock," a station of the London Missionary Society, where, on the 18th of July, the most severe portion of his journey ended : for now he had only to cross the lake to Ujiji and take the route to Saadani which had been traversed by many previous travellers.

From Nyangwe to Lake Tanganyika.

However, even at Ujiji he was not out of peril, for the people of Uhha, knowing his defenceless condition, lay in wait for him near the Malagarazi river and were preparing to put a stop to his further journeyings when he bared his arm and, pointing to a scar, shouted

From Tanganyika to the sea.

MAP OF WISSMANN'S JOURNEYS.

"Mirambo." The words acted like magic. The death of a white man with whom their dreaded chief (Vol., II., p. 275) had performed the rite of "blood-brotherhood," would speedily be avenged, and the intending plunderers, prudently remembering the fate that might befall them, desisted from further hostilities. Mirambo, whose capital Lieutenant Wissmann reached on the 31st August, is described by him as "a capital fellow." From Unyanyembe he paid a visit to the German station of Mgonga, mainly for the purpose of getting a pair of boots, and finally reached the coast by way of Mpwapwa—now a German post, well known as one of the sites of the Church Missionary Society (p. 59)—on the 15th of November, 1882, having spent twenty-two months and a half on his journey from coast to coast.*

The year 1884 opened briskly for the exploration of Africa. Thus, Lieutenant Giraud† penetrated to Lake Bangweolo in an unsuccessful attempt to cross Africa by way of the Upper Congo; Mr. Montagu Kerr crossed Matabeleland to the Zambesi, reaching, by a new route, the south-western shore of Lake Nyassa, while Mr. Richards, an American missionary, travelled from Inhambane to the Limpopo; and Messrs. Grenfell and Comber made a careful survey of the middle course of the Congo and its Bochini tributary, to the junction of the great river Kwango, on which we shall have something to say by-and-by. But **Mr. Arnot's journey across Africa.** of all the explorations which were ended or begun during that year, the journey across Africa by Mr. F. S. Arnot,

F. S. ARNOT.
(From a Photograph by John Fergus, Largs, N.B.)

though not of the highest geographical importance, excited the most attention. Mr. Arnot, like his celebrated predecessor, David Livingstone, was a Scotsman, from the vicinity of Hamilton, and when his travels brought him into notice was engaged as a missionary in South Africa without being connected with any of the recognised societies. The American missionaries stationed at Bailundu in the country to the rear of the Portuguese province of Benguela, had been expelled by order of the native king, and their colleagues at the Bihé station joining them, they retreated to the coast of Benguela, losing all their property and having their houses burned. Scarcely, however, had they been expelled, when Mr. Arnot, who, by the help of Mr. Westbeech and Mr. Blockley, two well-known traders of Patamatenka (p. 13), had been for two years established at Lialui on the Upper Zambesi (p. 10), suddenly appeared in the company of Silva Porto, the Portuguese trader, from the east at Bihé, and passed on to Bailundu. Mr. Arnot, receiving some mysterious hints of danger, had left Lialui. Soon after his departure sanguinary war broke out, and his old friend the king of the Barotse was exiled, the report which had reached Bihé of his being killed proving to be false. Mr. Arnot's unexpected appearance from the east at Bailundu astonished the chief and his people, who took advantage of his position to call a court of inquiry of all the headmen. The result was the despatch of a letter to Benguela, recalling the American missionaries; while Mr. Arnot completed his journey across Africa by going to Benguela for supplies, preparatory to penetrating to the watershed of the Congo and Zambesi, about twenty-eight degrees of longitude to the east of the Atlantic. It appears, thus, that Mr. Arnot, who had

---

* Wissmann, "Im Innern Afrikas" (1883), and *Proceedings of the Royal Geographical Society*, 1883, pp. 163-165, etc.

† "Les lacs de l'Afrique Équatoriale, Voyage d'Exploration exécuté de 1883 à 1885" (1889).

worked his way from Durban to Potchefstroom, and thence to Shoshong across the Kalahari Desert to the junction of the rivers Chobe (Kwando) and Zambesi, and thence, up the river to Lialui, and on to Bailundu (and thence to Benguela), had traversed Africa by much the same course that Serpa Pinto followed, but in an opposite direction, and somewhat farther north in crossing the Kalahari Desert. Mr. Arnot's expedition thus added comparatively little to our knowledge of the

"A KID FOR SALE!"—LIALUI.
(From a Photograph taken for the Paris Society for Evangelical Missions.)

geography of the country, though it enabled us to obtain a fuller account of the general features of a region that had hitherto been inaccessible. The journey throughout was made with the most simple appliances. Mr. Arnot carried no fire-arms, had no lethal weapons more fatal than a walking-stick, and throughout his long journey across Natal to the Portuguese colonies on the west coast was encumbered with so little baggage that the difficulties with porters, which inconvenienced his predecessors, were almost unknown to this lightly-burdened traveller.

Next year, in penetrating to Garenganze, west of Lakes Moero and Bangweolo, Mr. Arnot, among other points, had the credit of discovering that Livingstone's Liba is actually the Zambesi and not the stream which flows out of Lake Dilolo (Vol. II., p. 206), though the highest sources of the great river are in the country to the west of Lake Bangweolo, in a romantic spot which the Scottish traveller named "Border Craig."

Even more markedly than Serpa Pinto, he found the colonies from the east and west approaching each other, what had hitherto been known as an unexplored portion of the country gradually narrowing to a mere band. At Bihé, for instance, hitherto regarded as the most remote portion of the Portuguese possessions he found not only old Silva Porto, the famous trader, whose supposed journey across Africa, before the days of Livingstone, has already been noticed in these pages (Vol. II., p. 165), but several missionaries. Indeed, it was greatly owing to the assistance of this generous-minded Portuguese that Mr. Arnot was enabled to reach the west with comparative ease. At this post he met with Mr. Swan, of Sunderland, and Mr. William Faulkner, of Canada, and on Mr. Arnot's arrival in the Garenganze country in 1886, he sent his men back to Bihé, to return with these gentlemen in 1888, following the same route that Mr. Arnot had taken in travelling from Bihé to the Lualaba river.

After two years' residence in the Garenganze capital, having stayed some time to introduce Messrs. Swan and Faulkner to the chief and his people, Mr. Arnot left this region.

Katanga

Garenganze, though a familiar spot by hearsay to the Portuguese colonists in Benguela, did not until recently appear upon the maps, and was practically unknown to European geographers. It is really the chief's own designation for the kingdom which he has created, for the Arabs used the name "Katanga," and

TRAVELLER'S CAMP IN THE WANKONDE COUNTRY, NYASSALAND (NORTH)
(From a Photograph by Mr. Fred L. M. Moir, of the African Lakes Company)

by that name it is recognised on the east coast as a country abounding in copper mines. It may be remembered that it was towards Katanga and the source of the Lufira that Livingstone's steps were directed when death overtook him at Chitambo's, near Lake Bangweolo (Vol. II., p. 265).* This wide variety of nomenclature is very puzzling to the inexpert geographer. In this region, for instance, Mr. Arnot notices that the Portuguese have adopted their own orthography and the Germans theirs, while some have followed phonetic rules laid down by missionaries in other parts of Africa. Travellers, again, sometimes took their pronunciation of names from natives of different tribes, amongst which there is also a very great variation. The consonants "l," "d," and "r" are very often interchanged. Some of the tribes have a different way of pronouncing these sounds. It is thus easy to discover from names given to certain places by travellers from what district they had taken their carriers. For instance, Livingstone, travelling with Makololo men, called the Ovimbundu traders "Vambadi," a nickname, meaning in the Umbundu language "white men's slave." Nicknames have been given as tribal names, such as "Kwanguellas" (Quanguellas), east of the Kwanza (Quanza) River. The Ovimbundu give this name to the interior tribes because when they try to speak Umkendu they "ganza"—*i.e.*, stutter. Again, the "Vanyamwezi" of the Unyamwezi country east of Lake Tanganyika, means really "idle fellow," a Swahili nickname for them. Silva Porto's people, travelling with these Ovimbundu, call the Zambesi river Liambai, as also does Serpa Pinto. Lieutenant Cameron, on the other hand,

Clashing nomenclature.

* Of late several commercial expeditions organised by the Katanga Company and the Congo State have ransacked this region, the very name of which was only vaguely heard a few years ago. By one of those—that of Captain Bia, who, like Captain Stairs, died before he could return to tell his tale—a bronze tablet, sent out by Mr. Bruce, his son-in-law, has been affixed to the tree under which Livingstone breathed his last—in the district of Kalende, not of Ilala, as usually described. It had been entrusted to Mr. Arnot, but he was unable to reach the spot.

journeying west from Kasongo's country in company with Ovimbundu traders, called the Kasai River the Kassabe, which the Germans know by another native name, Sankuru —if, indeed, that river is not merely a tributary of the Kasai. Very frequently the names thus given under the notion that they are the native ones are entirely unknown to the aborigines of the country. Then, again, many wrong names have been inserted in maps, because the traveller has not understood the language of the people. An apt illustration of this is afforded by the answer given to a stranger passing Bailundu, who inquired the name of a chief's town standing on a prominent hill. The natives would immediately reply "Kombala." But this simply means "at the capital." The actual name of the town is Bailundu, from which the whole country ruled over by that chief takes its name.

At Garenganze, the chief told Mr. Arnot of the visits to his capital of the travellers Reichardt and Ivens (p. 19), in terms somewhat different from the narratives supplied by these gentlemen. Reichardt, Msiri said, did not place much confidence in him, nor received much in return. While professing to be a peace-loving traveller and not bound upon any political errand, Herr Reichardt, being impatient to leave the chief's country, offered to assist him in his war against Katapane, another petty potentate, and suggested carrying that chief's town by assault. Msiri, therefore, came to the conclusion that the German traveller's mission was not a peaceful one and he kept a secret watch round his camp night and day until at last the strain grew so great that Reichardt became alarmed and took a hasty departure.

Two sides to a story.

Lieutenant Ivens came to Garenganze from the south and requested thirty carriers from Msiri to assist him and his fellow-traveller, Lieutenant Capello, in their journey across the continent. The chief was slow to provide men for the journey to the east, as he said there was little chance of their returning.

Ivens could only remain a few days, as his companion was in poor health, and he left, as the chief thought, rather hurriedly.

On Mr. Arnot's return to England a few years later the importance of his travels in Africa was recognised by the Royal Geographical Society by the loan of a few instruments furnished him for a journey more directly geographical than the one from which he had returned, though less with the object of making exploration of new country than of determining the position of stations already formed and the exact lines of route already taken. He also received from the Society a suitable present for the chief, Chitambo, as a recognition of his services in connection with the removal of the body and personal property of Dr. Livingstone, in 1872. But with the subsequent travels of Mr. Arnot, which were not so fortunate as their more modest predecessors, we cannot charge our pages.*

We have already spoken of Lieutenants Capello and Ivens, the Portuguese travellers.

Capello and Ivens' transcontinental journey from west to east. We have met them in the early portion of Captain Serpa Pinto's journey, and have noted their meritorious survey of the country from Benguela to the territory of Yacca. They were, however, destined to cross Africa, though, unfortunately, at a period when the work of their forerunners had left for them little of the glory which fell to their former companion. This journey, during which we have seen that they passed through Garenganze, was made in 1884-85 from Mossamedes on the west coast to Quilimane, near the mouth of the Zambesi river, on the opposite shore. Hence, it necessarily followed that a large portion of it was over comparatively well-known ground ; though, as it brought to light a considerable amount of new country between the Luapula and the Zambesi, from a geographical point of view it was quite as important as that of Serpa Pinto, if, owing to much familiarity with transcontinental journeys, less sensational than that exploration. South Africa, indeed, was by this time getting so well-explored that it was difficult for any new traveller to take a route which did not cross and recross the tracks of his predecessors.

We need, therefore, occupy little space with the record of Messrs. Capello and Ivens' journey. Among the achievements which they claimed † were " the rectification of the course of the Cunene, wrongly called the Nourse river on some English maps ; the determination of the Cuarrai and its connection with the Kubango ; as also the interesting hydrography of Handa and of Upper Ovampoland and the investigation of the Kubango from fifteen degrees to seventeen degrees south latitude, and of its eastern affluents."

They had also the merit of examining the basin of the Upper Zambesi at Libonta, the upper and middle courses of the Kabampo tributary, and the discovery of the Kambai, the eastern arm of the Upper Zambesi. They studied, in addition, the source of the Lualaba, and the Luapula, also the Northern tributaries of the Zambesi, and discovered that the Loangwa and the Kafué are one and the same river. The work of these explorers likewise determined, directly or indirectly, the relations of the basins of the Congo and the Zambesi, while the information which they obtained regarding the Bangweolo region modified existing notions in favour of others indicated by former Portuguese explorations. The great Lake Bangweolo they considered to be only a marshy zone connecting two smaller lakes—the Bangweolo proper on the north and the Bemba on the south.‡

---

* "Journey from Natal to Bihé and Benguella, and thence across the Central Plateau of Africa to the sources of the Zambesi and the Congo" (*Proceedings of the Royal Geographical Society*, 1889, pp. 65-82) ; Arnot : "Garenganze, or Seven Years of Mission Work" (1890). We are also indebted to Mr. Arnot for his kindness in revising this brief sketch of his journey, and for adding various valuable notes.

† *Proceedings of the Royal Geographical Society*, 1885, p. 818.

‡ Capello and Ivens, "De Angola à Contra-costa" (1887).

This is not quite the case, though, owing to the shifting character of the lake, Messrs. Capello and Ivens' observations may have justified this conclusion. During the dry season there is no lake at latitude 11° 55′ south—only vast swamps. At that period p. 11), its level is 3,750 feet above the sea—250 below the height given by Livingstone, and 500 lower than that observed by Giraud.

Another journey across Africa, of less moment from a geographical point of view, though in earlier times it would have ranked

RUGA-RUGA (BANDITS) EMPLOYED BY THE GOVERNOR OF UJIJI, RETURNED FROM RAIDING.
(*From a Photograph by Mr. Ferd L. M. Moir, of the African Lakes Company.*)

of the year it shrinks to such dimensions that many of the islands are peninsulas, and streams which flow into it become mere tributaries of more powerful rivers. When the rains deluge this vast sponge, the lake resumes the geographical features represented on our maps, though Mr. Joseph Thomson,[*] one of its latest explorers—who regards a visit to the sources of the Nile or to Lake Bangweolo as one of the commonplaces of modern travel—considers that it does not extend so far south. According to his observation (Vol. II.,

[*] *Geographical Journal*, February, 1893, p. 109.

high among the explorations of Africa, was that of the Swedish Lieutenant, Edward Gleerup, who, leaving Stanley Falls on the 1st December, 1885, reached Bagamoyo on the east coast in the course of the next year, after a journey attended with no incidents of either a dangerous or peculiar character. For to cross Africa was now an easier task than it was when Livingstone, Cameron, and Stanley accomplished the feat. Lieutenant Gleerup was in the service of the Congo Free State, the founding of which will form the subject

Gleerup's journey from the Congo to the east coast.

of a future chapter. For a year he was in command of a remote station on the Seventh Cataract of the Stanley Falls, his neighbours being Arab slave- and ivory-hunters. Having lived here for several months without supplies, he formed a resolution to return to Europe Lieutenant Gleerup experienced the minimum amount of difficulty in reaching Tanganyika, and in pushing on from Tanganyika to his destination on the east coast, the whole journey from Stanley Falls to Bagamoyo occupying no more than six months.*

CATTLE-HOUSE OF THE WANKONDE TRIBE.†
(*From a Photograph by Mr. Fred L. M. Moir, of the African Lakes Company.*)

by crossing the continent to Zanzibar, and, thanks to the influential trader, Tippoo Tib (whose deeds and misdeeds have of late years furnished a considerable portion of the narratives of more recent travellers), was liberally furnished with the means of so doing. Armed with letters of recommendation from this generous stealer of men and women to all his stations and friends on the route,

About the same time that the Scottish missionary was travelling from Natal to Benguela, the Portuguese Capello and Ivens from Mossamedes to Quilimane, and the Swedish lieutenant from Stanley Falls to Bagamoyo, Oskar Lenz, with whom we are already acquainted as one of the few travellers who reached Timbuctoo (Vol. I., p. 309), was penetrating from the mouth of the Congo

* *Proceedings of the Royal Geog. Soc.*, 1886, p. 596.
† Down the longitudinal centre of the house there are posts of wood to support the roof. To these centre posts or to some other object firmly fastened down the centre of the house (not uncommonly an elephant's jaw-bone), the cattle are tethered, either with plaited strips of hide or ropes made of banana fibre. The people sleep on the other side of the house, sometimes (but seldom) with a partition of reeds between them and the cattle.

on the west coast to the mouth of the Zambesi on the eastern shore. This journey was completed in the years 1885–87. It was one of the most interesting, but, from the comparative ease with which it was accomplished and the frequency of similar journeys, it has occupied less of the attention of Europe than almost any similar exploration. A trans-African journey had, indeed, by the year 1885 ceased to be a novelty. Indeed, nothing shows the rapid progress of exploration in Central Africa since Stanley's memorable journey more than the fact that from every important point along the Austrian traveller's route he was able to send home letters which reached Vienna a few weeks after they had been written.

<small>Oskar Lenz's journey from the Congo to the mouth of the Zambesi.</small>

Dr. Lenz's mission was sent out under the auspices of the Vienna Geographical Society, to obtain certain news of or to reach Dr. Junker and Emin Pasha, and to solve the then perplexing problems of the hydrography of the country which lies between the Middle Congo and the Upper Nile branches.

In the year 1885 there was no great difficulty in reaching Stanley Falls on the Upper Congo, but from this point Dr. Lenz was compelled to travel without his companion, Dr. Baumann, who was forced through ill-health to turn back. Dr. Baumann's place was, however, supplied by Herr Bohndorff, an old comrade of Gordon in the Soudan. But he also was taken so seriously ill that only half of his journey was performed when he had to be carried on a litter and was, therefore, more a hindrance than a help to his companion. At Stanley Falls, which was reached in the early days of 1886, they found Tippoo Tib all-powerful and quite ready to assist the travellers so far as lay in his power. However, being unable to obtain porters for them owing to most of his men being engaged on a trading expedition to the northward, he furnished them with canoes, in which they pursued their journey by the Congo to Nyangwe.

<small>From Stanley Falls to Nyangwe.</small>

Great changes had, however, come to pass on the Upper Congo since Stanley made his famous voyage down it a few years previously. At that time the river was mostly in the hands of the natives, many of them cannibals, who, had Stanley fallen into their hands, would have left the exploration of the Congo river to other pioneers than the one who was fortunate enough to accomplish it. Now all was altered, and during the six weeks that Dr. Lenz paddled along its shores he met with little but civility. The Arabs had complete possession of the river and had taught the savages a wholesome dread of the white men. Their settlements—many of them considerable towns—stood on its banks, whilst the natives, in fear of the slave-raiders, had been driven into the forests and remote recesses of the mountains. These Muscat and Zanzibar Arab villages, surrounded with fields of rice, proved the suitability of the country for agriculture, whilst domestic animals, which could not be kept in the steaming lowlands, flourished in abundance.

On the 16th of May Nyangwe was reached. This place, it will be remembered, was the scene of a horrible tragedy enacted by the slave-traders during the time that Livingstone was resident in it (Vol. II., p. 255). It is still an important centre for caravans and the slave- and ivory-trade, though, owing to the forest in the vicinity having been destroyed, firewood is scarce. It has been also somewhat cast into the shade by Kasongo, a great Arab town some little distance to the south-east, where Tippoo and other Arab merchants made their headquarters. Leaving Nyangwe on the 20th of May, Kasongo was the next halting-place, but here, in spite of Tippoo Tib's help, the expedition was hampered by the prostration of Lenz's companion and the outbreak of small-pox among the men. However, by the end of June Tanganyika was sighted, and there, owing to the energy of the missionaries and of Mr. James Stevenson, the explorer's journey may be said to have almost terminated. For nowadays, after crossing the high plateau between the Congo and Lake Tanganyika, the explorer is welcomed at the island of Kavala

<small>Arab settlements.</small>

on the west coast, where Captain Hore, of the London Missionary Society, had been stationed for many years, who, it is needless to say, received the travellers with every hospitality.

<small>Tanganyika.</small>

Crossing the lake to Ujiji, their intentions of visiting Uganda and Emin Pasha's country were abandoned, owing to the disturbed condition of the country and the want of resources to enable them to penetrate so far. In the first week of September, therefore, Dr. Lenz and his companion left Ujiji for the southern end of the lake. Tanganyika, it may be remembered, when Cameron visited it, was emptied by the river Lukuga on the western shore. This stream had a very sluggish current, so sluggish, indeed, that it seemed to be flowing into, rather than out of, the lake. When Stanley passed that way he found that the barrier of vegetation had been swept away, and the Lukuga was flowing out of the lake, to the Lualaba-Congo. Captain Hore, who had known the lake for ten years, states that during that time its level had fallen fifteen feet, and yet the Lukuga continues to carry off the water with a more powerful current than ever. Dr. Lenz himself observed several old shore-lines as he sailed along the lake. The houses at Ujiji, which used to be close to the water's edge, are now some distance inland, and no doubt the lake will continue to fall until the level of the Lukuga river is reached, after which it will gradually rise again, to be again subjected to the changes just mentioned.

The southern coast of the lake was reached towards the end of September, and a barren and inhospitable region the travellers found it. All the villages seemed at war with each other, so that great difficulty was experienced in obtaining guides and porters for the two days' journey across the plateau between Tanganyika and Nyassa, which, since the Stevenson Road has been constructed, may now be regarded as one of the most familiar portions of Central Africa. Though this area between the two lakes is called a plateau, it is, like many other African plateaux, rather mountainous, and near its north-western end contains the sources of the Tshambezi, which, we have seen, flows into Lake Bangweolo, and may, therefore, be regarded as the ultimate source of the Congo. As the travellers approached Lake Nyassa, they met a caravan of Arabs and Zanzibaris, to the number of about three hundred, who had been to the lake to sell ivory to the Africa Lakes Company. It was clear they were reaching civilised parts, though it may be added that the Stevenson Road existed more on paper than in reality, the tropical vegetation having been allowed to choke it up, and the torrents of rain to

<small>By the Stevenson Road, Nyassa, and the Shiré to the sea.</small>

MAJOR H. VON WISSMANN.
(*From a Photograph by Schwarwachter, Berlin.*)

destroy many of the more difficult portions of it. However, after a pleasant halt at the mission and trading stations, Lake Nyassa and the Shiré river were descended in the latter part of December, 1886, and Zanzibar, the starting-place for home, was reached.*

Another journey across Africa by way of the Congo, Tanganyika, and Lake Nyassa, begun early in 1886, was soon to stir the now languid enthusiasm of the world for such travel feats. This was by Lieutenant—

---

* *Proceedings of the Royal Geographical Society*, 1886, pp. 334, 453, 596, 616; *Ibid.*, pp. 49, 114, 190, 240, 340; and *Mittheilungen* of the Vienna Geographical Society, Band XXIX., No. 12 *et seq.*

now Major—Hermann Von Wissmann (p. 23), who had accomplished a similar journey a few years earlier (p. 12). On this occasion, taking advantage of the steamers upon the Congo, Lieutenant Wissmann's journey was actually from Nyangwe, by very much the same route that Dr. Lenz had taken before him. However, in the earlier portion of his journey, both alone, and by the agency of Dr. Wolff, the Kasai river, one of the greatest of the Congo tributaries, as well as the Kwango, one of its feeders, was explored. Unfortunately, since Dr. Lenz had made his journey the differences between the Congo State and the Arabs had entirely altered the bearing of the latter towards the white travellers. Instead of friendship they met unfriendliness, and instead of help, obstruction. Provisions were difficult to obtain and the natives were everywhere wild and suspicious, while the territory of the marauding Bena Mona could only be passed by the employment of force. The ravages of the slave trade were also equally apparent. From the 28th December, 1886, to the 23rd January, 1887, the caravan marched through a region which, during his first expedition, Lieutenant Wissmann had found dotted with gigantic villages. Now the district was completely depopulated. War, small-pox, and the slave-raiders had entirely devastated the country, and the want of food was so great that Wissmann lost eighty men from hunger and small-pox on the journey from the Kasai to Nyangwe.

Wissmann's second journey across Africa.

Ravages of Arab raiders.

Here the bearing of the Arabs towards the traveller was so decidedly hostile, and the caravan so disorganised from hunger and sickness, that Wissmann found himself compelled to abandon his intention both of travelling up the Upper Lualaba and of proceeding to Lake Albert Edward. He therefore despatched the Bashilanges with his colleague, Lieutenant Le Marinel, back to Lulunberg, while he set out alone to the east coast, by way of Tanganyika, Lake Nyassa, and down the Shiré and Zambesi on the line followed by his predecessors.* Lieutenant Wissmann's journey may be said to have all but ended popular interest in these journeys across Africa. The German traveller was himself in a few years to engross a large share of international interest in his capacity of controller of the German possessions on the east coast of Africa. But, except as a feat of travel, his last journey does not occupy a large space in the annals of geographical exploration.

Waning interest in transcontinental journeys.

Livingstone, in 1854-56, took twenty months to cross Africa. Cameron, in 1873-75, occupied two years and eight months, though the whole of that time was not engaged in actual travel. Stanley, in 1874-77, was two years and nine months on his journey—also delayed by long halts. Serpa Pinto, in 1877-79, was only sixteen months doing the distance from coast to coast. Wissmann, on his first journey in 1881-82, spent twenty-two months in travelling. Arnot, in 1881-84, was three years and three months in crossing the continent, though it must be remembered that he tramped very lightly equipped, with few facilities for proceeding on his way, and that his journey was often broken by long rests. Capello and Ivens, in 1884-85, were absent during fourteen months. Gleerup, in 1884-86, was away for three years, though only a small portion of his time was spent on the actual journey with which his name is associated. Dr. Lenz might have performed his journey in an even shorter time than Capello and Ivens had he not been stopped a considerable time on the Lower Congo and at Stanley Falls, while Wissmann's second journey was completed in a still briefer period than that occupied by his first one. Finally, as a proof of the rapidity of modern African travel and its corresponding ease compared with what it was not many years ago, Joseph Thomson took just three and a half months from England to Lake Bangweolo, close to the place which Livingstone reached only to die.

Speed of later journeys.

* Wissmann, "Unter Deutscher Flagge," and "My Second Journey through Equatorial Africa in the Years 1886 and 1887." (English Translation, 1891.)

"LE STANLEY," ONE OF THE RIVER STEAMERS USED BY THE EMIN PASHA RELIEF EXPEDITION.
(Built by Yarrow and Co.)

CHAPTER II.

FROM THE ATLANTIC TO THE ALBERT NYANZA: A BELEAGUERED PROVINCE.

State of Matters in the Equatorial Province under Emin Pasha in 1886—Enthusiasm over Emin—An Expedition under Mr. Stanley Equipped for his Succour—The Members of it—Tippoo Tib—Up the Congo and Aruwhimi—A Camp Formed at Yambuya on the Aruwhimi—Plans for the Force left there in Charge of Major Barttelot—Mr. Stanley's March Eastward through the Dense Forest Country—Savage Enemies—The Dwarfs—Perils of the Jungle—Mount Pisgah and the Promised Land—Albert Nyanza—No News of Emin—Back to Fort Bodo—Improved Temper of Natives—No News of Barttelot—Tidings from Emin—His Arrival—His Irresolution—Would and Wouldn't—Return in Search of Barttelot and the Rear Column while the Pasha Made up his Mind—Banalya Camp—A Terrible Tale—Barttelot and Stanley—Return to Lake Albert—Emin Still Undecided—His Vacillation Stiffened by a Mutiny of his Troops—He, Mr. Jephson, and Captain Casati Captives—The Rebel Plot—A Court-Martial—The March to the Indian Ocean begun without waiting for Selim Bey and his Troops.

In an earlier portion of this history (Vol. II., pp. 157-162) we have had occasion to speak of Emin Pasha, the German doctor who maintained the power of Egypt in Central Africa after Khartoum had fallen and Lupton Bey and Slatin Bey were slaves of the Mahdi. Any outlet from Central Africa by way of Egypt was effectually closed by the wild hordes who followed Ahmed Mohammed, while the ferocious kings of Karagwe, Unyoro, and Uganda prevented any but a large armed force from finding a way to civilisation through their countries.

Emin in the Equatorial Province remained as the last symbol of civilised authority on the Upper Nile. It was, however, considered only a matter of months or days when he, too, should meet the fate of the other Egyptian governors. Karamallah Mohammed, the Dervish conqueror of Bahr-el-Ghazel, had, indeed, directed his march thither. However, with prudent generalship, Emin Bey (as he then was) was reported to have declined to risk his fortunes on a battle-field, "but persisted in maintaining a series of petty

Condition of Emin and the Equatorial Province.

attacks and a harassing defensive attitude, which wearied and dispirited the invaders."* For example, when the Mahdi's general advanced upon a post the garrison retreated, took up a position farther south, bravely repelling small bands, and then, on the approach of the main force, withdrew to another more remote position which they defended in like manner. But beyond the most southernly stations, where the Mahdist general reached Emin, he had still behind him a series of fortified positions which, if defended with the same courage and prudence, would have taken the Mahdi's general so far from his base that, on the least reverse, a catastrophe similar to that which befell Hicks Pasha would, in Mr. Stanley's opinion, have overtaken Karamallah. The Dervishes consequently retreated, and Emin Bey was in 1886 rumoured to have been left in comparative peace, except when disturbed by petty native outbreaks, the slackening loyalty of his troops, and the plots of the neighbouring kings.

Little was, however, known, and that imperfectly; and the position of Emin was altogether misunderstood. His interference—mild as it was—with the slave trade had not improved his popularity with a venal set of officials who, as a solace for the Mudir's plundering them of their pay, had, of old, been allowed to rob the natives to any extent. Slaves were found to figure in the accounts as oxen, asses, etc., while the money belonging to the Government was employed to buy goods which were sold for the profit of the Administration at three times the cost price. For years before Emin Pasha in the Equatorial Province, 1882-1887. Emin's arrival, no regular accounts had been kept, while the fabrication of false seals, and the forgery of receipts by their use had, as at Rumbek, become a recognised practice, in spite of the "prayer-places and fikis" with which every station abounded.

* I am quoting Mr. Stanley's Official Report (dated December 19th, 1889, and presented to Parliament February 12th, 1890), on which this narrative is based, with numerous additions and emendations from the sources duly noted and from unpublished information.

Still, up to 1883, the Equatorial Province enjoyed tolerable tranquillity: and the wild work in the North was, as yet, merely an echo in the Southern Soudan. But in that year freebooters began to enter it—a fact not remarkable, considering that the stations were largely supported by raids made on the cattle of the more or less unfriendly tribes in their vicinity. In retaliation, the Dinka of Agar (Vol. II., pp. 40, 42) surprised the garrison of Rumbek and succeeded in massacring seventy of the men, and shortly afterwards took Shambeh, where 150 soldiers fell before the savages. These disasters were afterwards in part retrieved; but what with the growing boldness of the tribes, and the disquieting news of the resistless advance of the Mahdi, the year closed in much anxiety for Emin. The arrival of Dr. Junker early in 1884 was a source of much joy to the beleaguered Governor, yearning for the society of one of his scientific countrymen. Meanwhile, the revolt of the tribes continued, and the blaze in the Bahr-el-Ghazel approached nearer and nearer Equatoria. Outlying stations had to be evacuated, and one road after another to the north—which meant to civilisation—was closed. Indeed, when the news of the surrender of Lupton Bey, the massacre of Hicks, and the siege of Khartoum reached him, Emin half resolved to surrender to the summons of Karamallah.

This, however, was only in a fit of despondency or depression; for he temporised long enough with Karamallah to make a good resistance at some stations that had to be abandoned, defeat the Dervishes at others, and to constitute his capital, Lado (Vol. II., p. 140), into a fortress, with moats, drawbridges, ramparts, bastions, etc., where he announced his intention to die a soldier's death, while hoping against hope for the arrival of a steamer from Khartoum. The fall of that city and the death of Gordon early in 1885 (Vol. II., p. 161) closed the Nile, and, for the first time, completely isolated the Equatorial Province. Amadi, after a siege during which the soldiers were for nineteen days reduced to eating cowhides and sandals, fell before Karamallah, in spite of the courage of a detachment of the garrison, who cut their way through the investing hordes, though some of the officers had intended to deliver up the town. Even then, Emin wrote, "disobedience is the order of the day : everyone seeks to protect his own interest only." In accordance with a petition of his officers—which amounted to an order—Emin had to retreat from that part of the country, concentrating his troops on the Lado-Kiri line. Among the posts abandoned were those in the Makaraka country, hitherto regarded as one of the most hopeful portions of the Soudan. The Makaraka (pp. 28, 29) are a section of the powerful Niam-Niam people, the tribe which has gained an evil celebrity as cannibals. The Makaraka are, however, good farmers, and therefore important as feeders of the garrison, and bear so excellent a reputation for courage that the best of Emin's troops belonged to that race.

The summons of Karamallah to surrender was repeated, and with it came confirmation of the rumours of Gordon's death. This resolved Emin's officers to counsel a fresh retreat and concentration by the desertion of certain stations and the despatch of the women and children to those farther to the south. By this time all luxuries were exhausted in Equatoria, so that when messengers arrived from Kabba Rega, King of Unyoro (Vol. II., p. 151), charged with messages of friendship for his old friend Emin, the sorely-pressed Governor was inclined to welcome his shifty ally as for once in earnest.

Events had now begun to move fast. The Baris (Vol. II., p. 43), incensed by the cattle raids upon them, now joined Emin's enemies, and cut all communication between Gondokoro and Lado. Detachments of troops were massacred here and there, and their captured rifles increased the peril which the hitherto imperfectly armed savages had been to the isolated Egyptians and their black followers. The immediate danger from Dervishes was now for the time being over, but the new risks from the savage Dinkas and the Baris were quite as serious, though, in attacking Rijiaf, the tribesmen were repulsed with the loss of 500 men. The Equatorial Province—so far as Emin's authority was recognised—was now reduced to a seventh of its former size, and the year ended with Lado in a state of siege, and Vita Hassan, Emin's apothecary, being despatched as a kind of envoy to the "Court" of Kabba Rega, while Dr. Junker hoped to find his way to Zanzibar through the kingdom of this supposed friendly monarch. In reality, the king was only playing a part, his pretended regard for Emin being merely a cunning device to obtain intelligence of what was going on in the Equatorial Province, and how best he might utilise the information for his own purposes. The war which in 1886 broke out between Unyoro and Uganda compelled Emin's representative at Kabba Rega's to retire to Lake Albert, and Dr. Junker to abandon his journey to the coast, through Unyoro, believing—as it turned out, rightly—that Uganda would be a safer route.

Hitherto, Emin and his troops had maintained something like the relations which soldier and officer should hold; the discipline, though possibly as severe as would have been tolerated, was no doubt loose, yet there was no actual open mutiny. But now the men began to display signs of uneasiness under even his easy sway. They were not improved in temper by learning from a despatch, which reached them by way of Zanzibar, that, as the Soudan had been abandoned, the Egyptian Government was in no way inclined to help them, and that Emin was authorised to leave the Province as best he could. A quarrel broke out between the men and officers of the First and Second Battalions—the men of the former agreeing among themselves that they would not retreat to the south. Rather than go to Wadelai, they would disband and return to their homes, which, in many cases, were in the Soudan. A plot was also discovered, by which some of the Bornu and Adamawa men from the distant Niger region intended to kill all their officers and establish a Free State; and in Dufilé, a sergeant-major fired at an officer. Add to this, the ill-will between the Egyptians and Soudanese grew daily more and more matters, always bad, did not improve. The mutinous First Battalion, though it had obeyed Emin's order to retire from Lado on Rijiaf and re-occupy Makaraka, on account of the difficulty of supplying the Northern garrisons

MAKARAKA DWELLINGS.
(From a Photograph by R. Buchta.)

acute, and the troubles beginning to throng round Emin may be conceived. At this date he was so discouraged that he meditated returning to Kabba Rega's, "and wait there until the men have recovered their senses, and will follow me—for follow me they will, sooner or later"—sentiments which aptly illustrate his frame of mind two years later (p. 50).

The war between Unyoro and Uganda having terminated, Captain Casati was sent to occupy the position at Kabba Rega's which Vita Hassan had held for a few months, and, if possible, to keep open the route to Uganda, in the hope that good relations with Mpwanga might prove useful to the Province.

In January, 1887, Dr. Junker arrived in Egypt, but seemed to consider it necessary, for the credit of his friend Emin, to put the best face upon the state of matters in the Equatorial Province. Yet soon after he left, without having this corn-yielding land open to them, was practically in open revolt. Already, indeed, some men of this battalion conspired to carry Emin away from the Province. The troops at Wadelai (which about the same time was accidentally burnt down, and a large quantity of stores lost, though the buildings were speedily re-erected), Tunguru, and Mahagi, were to have been concentrated at Gondokoro, from thence either to march back to Egypt, or, as they did not seem to have any wish to join the Mahdists, to make themselves masters of the country. Emin, who was at Kiri (Vol. II., p. 141) at the time when the plot was hatching, managed to escape to Mahagi, so that all the mutineers could do to soothe their disappointment before returning to Rijiaf was to flog the commandant soundly, and carry off a number of men belonging to the loyal Second Battalion. In short, at the very moment that

Europe, in ignorance of what was going on in Equatoria, was planning the withdrawal of the Equatorial garrison, Emin's people were strengthening their resolution to stay in a country where most of them had been long resident; and the very soldiers who afterwards caused the troubles which precipitated the departure of the beleaguered Governor were in undisguised revolt. All this time, they seem to have half discredited the story of Gordon's death and the fall of Khartoum, and regarded the accounts, like the subsequent letters from the Khedive that reached them, as mere forgeries. But in the autumn of 1886 nothing of this was known. Emin could not be for very long, and that, from his isolated position, he could not hold his own, owing to the supply of ammunition failing. That this was the state of matters Emin himself did not conceal, and, aware of the fatal results attending any renewal of hostilities by the Mahdists, he sought every opportunity to convey to Egypt and to Europe a sense of his dangerous position. The burden of the numerous letters received from him, so long as an outlet for his correspondence could be obtained, was an urgent appeal for assistance in the shape of troops or other necessaries of war, though we cannot gather from any of the Governor's communications

MAKARAKA WARRIORS AND MUSICIANS.
(From a Photograph by R. Buchta.)

was still a popular hero, at bay in Equatoria, in the midst of a loyal people.*

It was felt, however, that Emin's resistance

* Wingate, "Mahdiism and the Egyptian Sudan," pp. 31, 103, 141, 258, 293, 326, etc.

that he had the slightest desire to leave his seat of government. It was known that, besides his own officers, two travellers had for some years resided as his guests. These were, we have seen (pp. 26–28), Dr. Junker, a German engaged in a scientific exploration of the region of the Upper Nile and its tributaries, and Captain (afterwards Major) Casati, an Italian, more or less directly in the employment of the Egyptian Government. Dr. Junker, tired of inaction, resolved to try to reach the coast. At a very fortunate period he made an attempt, and succeeded in reaching Uganda, where, having nothing of which he could be robbed, he was allowed to depart in one of the missionaries' boats to the south end of Victoria Nyanza, and thence, under the protection of an Arab caravan, managed to reach the east coast in safety (p. 28). From him the latest tidings were received. In those days the newspapers were almost every day spiced with tales of Emin's courage, heroism, and self-denial. Travellers who had passed through his country in former years painted attractive pictures of the condition of the Equatorial Province.* The comparative civilisation and actual good government of the country under the doctor turned general became familiar to the readers of the daily news-sheet. The story of Emin beleaguered in the centre of Africa, surrounded on every side by hordes of fanatics and savages, appealed to the picturesque side of the English mind, and not only to the English mind, but to the imagination of most European nations. Among these, his country of Germany ought to be mentioned, where an expedition was mooted for the relief of the "Mudir" of Equatorial Africa. In short, in the autumn of 1886 Emin Bey, or Emin Pasha, to use the title which the Khedive of Egypt had bestowed upon him, filled in popular esteem very much the same place which had been occupied by Gordon in former days.

Possibly, had the world then known—what it knew later—that Emin was no hero, but a rather vacillating *savant*, whose people were anything but attached to him, being, in fact, in scarcely covert rebellion, and that the tales sent home both by himself and by Dr. Junker were, though true, not all the truth, it might have spared some of the enthusiasm that was lavished on him. But little was suspected of the real state of matters, so that when the reaction came a few years later it was almost as unjust as the admiration which it replaced had been overstrained.

Emin was not employed by the British Government; yet it was felt, considering the position of Great Britain in Egypt, that England—still angry over Gordon's tragic end—was, to a certain extent, responsible for the safety of the last of the Egyptian Governors of the Soudan, and that, if he was not to meet the fate of Lupton and Slatin Beys, and of Gordon, scanty time was to be lost in attempting his succour.

Scarcely had the project been formulated before public sympathy put ample funds at the disposal of a Committee charged with the organisation of a rescue expedition.† Mr. Stanley had only recently come back from a six years' residence in the Congo State, and was, naturally, in no way anxious to return immediately to the scene of his long labours. But when the Committee of the Emin Relief Expedition urged upon him to take command, with a self-denial characteristic of the man, he at once accepted the offer made to him.‡ It is perhaps unnecessary to say that no sooner was it announced that Mr. Stanley was on the eve of heading another venture into Central Africa than he was the recipient of hundreds of applications from volunteers anxious to accompany him on that dangerous errand. From among these volunteers his choice fell on Major Edmund Barttelot, of the 7th Fusiliers,

The Emin Pasha Relief Expedition: preliminaries.

---

* The best of these sketches is that in the *Graphic* (January, 1887), by Dr. Felkin. "Emin Pasha in Central Africa, being a Collection of his Letters and Journals," translated by Mrs. Felkin and edited by Drs. Schweinfurth, Ratzel, Felkin and Hartlaub (1888), contains the fullest account of his life and travels yet published.

† The expedition cost about £29,000, of which £14,000 was given by the Egyptian Government and £1,000 by the Royal Geographical Society.

‡ He had recommended Mr. Joseph Thomson or, failing him, Mr. H. H. Johnston, afterwards Consul-General for Portuguese East Africa and Commissioner for Nyassaland.

who had seen hard fighting in Afghanistan and in the Nile campaigns; Lieutenant W. G. Stairs, of the Royal Engineers; Captain R. H. Nelson, whose experience of Africa was won in Zululand and in the war against the Basutos; Surgeon T. H. Parke, of the Army Medical Department, who had gained great distinction for his services in Egypt; Mr. William Bonny, formerly a non-commissioned officer in the Army Medical Department; Mr. John Rose Troup, Mr. Herbert Ward, Mr. A. J. Mountcney-Jephson, and Mr. J. S. Jameson (p. 61), all gentlemen whose varied experience was considered valuable in those taking part in such an expedition. The two last, indeed, were so anxious to serve that they paid £1,000 each as a subscription to the adventure in which they shared.

But, though Mr. Stanley's pronounced opinion was that the line to be taken by the expedition should be from the Upper Congo eastward, the Committee were so decided in favour of Africa being entered by the usual route, from the east coast, that the commander abandoned his view in favour of that advocated by his official superiors. Fortunately, or unfortunately, the jealousy of the German Government of so large a force marching through or near to their recently acquired possessions in East Africa, and the still less reasonable opposition of the French authorities on the ground that Mr. Stanley's proceedings would endanger the lives of the French missionaries in Uganda, compelled the abandonment of this route in favour of that originally advocated by Mr. Stanley. The Congo, therefore, was fixed upon as the waterway along which one of the most interesting expeditions that ever entered Africa was to penetrate for over a thousand miles, until it was left to cross the continent in part through a region originally explored by Mr. Stanley, and of late years intimately connected with his reputation.

Among the members of this philanthropical expedition was included the notorious slave-trader, Tippoo Tib, who had been recommended by Mr. Stanley for the post of Belgian Governor of the Stanley Falls station, belonging to the Free State, this extraordinary utilisation of the wolf to watch the lambs being avowedly on the ground that it would be cheaper to employ him to resist the progress of the Arabs down the Congo than to drive them back when once their westerly invasion had begun—a theory doomed to woful failure. Tippoo Tib also contracted to furnish the expedition with a contingent of 600 Manyema (Vol. II., p. 255) porters to assist in the carriage of the goods and ammunition for Emin Pasha, and otherwise to do his best to expedite the objects of the mission to which he was attached. As might have been expected, the wealthy slave-trader carried out his contract with scant regard to the terms of it.

However, on the 25th February, 1887, the steamer containing the expedition sailed from the port of Zanzibar for the mouth of the Congo river. There were on board 11 English officers, 605 Zanzibari men, 12 Zanzibari boys, 62 Soudanese, 13 Somalis, and 97 people attached to Tippoo Tib; in all a force of 800 individuals armed with 524 rifles. The Congo is now so comparatively well known that the passage up this huge flood need not be described. The greater part of it was made in the steamers which now navigate its waters, and though accompanied with various interesting events, and, it may be added, not a little friction between the officers of the Free State, the missionaries, and the energetic commander of the rescue expedition, the adventurers arrived on the 16th of June, 1887, after a river voyage of 1,050 miles from Leopoldville, at Yambuya, a village on the banks of the Aruwhimi, a tributary of the Congo.

Up the Congo and Aruwhimi rivers.

Here the river journey ended and the long tramp to Albert Nyanza began. At that time it was Mr. Stanley's intention to return from Emin's province with his people and the members of his own party by the same route that he had gone eastward. Accordingly, he determined to form a fortified camp at this place to accumulate stores for the expedition on its return; or, for a rear-guard which he left here to march eastward, if necessary, for the relief of the advanced portion of the expedition. This camp he put under the charge of Major Barttelot, with Mr. Jameson, the naturalist of the expedition, as second in command, 80 men constituting its garrison. Here also Messrs. Troup, Ward, and Bonny were to remain after their arrival from Stanley Pool and Bolobo, where they were in charge of 131 men and some 600 loads of permit. If Tippoo Tib arrived with his band of porters, this duty would be comparatively light. If he did not, then the rear-guard was to proceed by double or treble stages until it met the advance column returning from Albert Nyanza. A certain lack of foresight in drafting these instructions, and a lamentable want of judgment in their interpretation, led to one of the most serious disasters which the expedition had to suffer; but of this we shall have more to say farther on.

THE EMIN PASHA RELIEF EXPEDITION LEAVING MATADI, ON THE CONGO, WITH TIPPOO TIB AND HIS WIVES.
(*From a Sketch by Mr. Herbert Ward.*)

goods stored for convenience' sake at Leopoldville. Major Barttelot's instructions, which in future days gave rise to much acrid controversy, were, in general terms, to remain at Yambuya until the contingent from Bolobo had arrived—that is, about the middle of August—after which he was to organise the rear column and march on the track of the party ahead as fast as circumstances would

On the 28th of June, the advance column, consisting of 380 men, set out from Yambuya eastward through the dense forests that cover to the extent of 400,000 square miles * the western side of tropical Africa. For five and a half months, following almost continually the course of the Aruwhimi river, they marched

From Yambuya eastward.

* Stanley, *Harper's Magazine*, April, 1893, p. 616.

SKIRMISHES WITH THE SAVAGES.

through one continuous primeval forest, which, beginning not far from the confluence of the Congo with the Aruwhimi, maintained the same unbroken density and characteristics across nearly four and a half degrees of longitude. Indeed, it was not until they were within seven days' march of the grassy region that any of the natives with whom they came in contact had ever heard of such a country. To them all the world was overgrown with one endless mass of wood. The tall, umbrageous trees grew so closely together, and with their upper branches in such close proximity, that the sun scarcely reached the depth of this vast jungle. But worse than the unknown region through which they were travelling, worse even than the gloomy and malarious character of the country, was the continual attacks of the natives who had their homes in or near this bush. In the extensive district of Yankondé the savages were so determined to accomplish the destruction of probably the first white men they had ever seen—though, unfortunately for their most recent visitors, they were only too well acquainted with the ravages of the half-caste Arab slave-traders—that they set fire to their village and attacked the party under cloud of the smoke. After a fight lasting fifteen minutes the enemy retreated, though the fact that they resisted for that length of time men armed with rifles shows the persistency of these wild tribesmen. However, they had not abandoned their attempts to intercept or kill the members of the expedition, or to pillage the boats on the river containing the greater quantity

The forest savages.

MAJOR CASATI.
(*From a Photograph by Guigoni & Bossi, Milan.*)

of the heavier baggage. At Avisibba they had another battle, in which Lieutenant Stairs was shot by a poisoned arrow, from the effects of which he recovered with difficulty. Provisions were hard to be obtained. The forest contained little game, and the banana patches were scattered at wide distances from each other. At the place called Mazamboni's—in the grass land—an even more resolute effort than any hitherto attempted was made for the destruction of

SECTIONAL STEEL BOAT "THE ADVANCE."
(*Built for the Emin Pasha Relief Expedition by Forrestt & Son.*)

the expedition. For five days in December, 1887, the savages made a succession of attacks upon it, the echoes of which reached Kabba Rega in Unyoro. For it so happened that these Mazamboni warriors were his subjects; and when the news of their defeat reached him, he imagined that his country was being invaded by a large army under a "white Pasha," summoned by his double-dealing friend Emin. He therefore immediately wreaked his vengeance on poor Casati, who was robbed and turned out of his house almost naked, to wander along the shores of Lake Albert until Emin found and rescued him; while Mohammed Biri, Emin's messenger, was killed by the incensed king (p. 28).

The story of a white Pasha devastating the Upper Nile region even reached Cairo in a strangely distorted form, and on its way

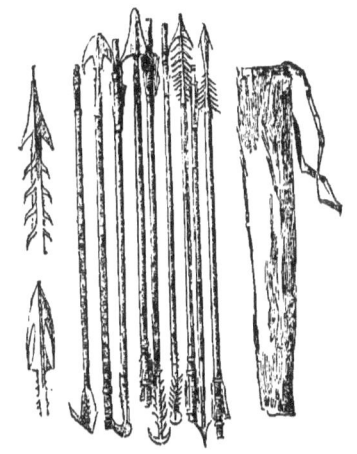

ARROW-HEADS, ARROWS, AND QUIVER, FROM THE ARUWHIMI DISTRICT.

north so alarmed the Khalifa, who had now succeeded the dead Mahdi, that he despatched troops to take possession of Equatoria and destroy the supposed intruder.

It was in this forest, and especially in the region between the Ihuru and Ituri rivers, that the expedition for the first time met with the pigmies. These dwarfs were, indeed, among the most persistent of Mr. Stanley's enemies, discharging their little poisoned arrows with great audacity. It is, however, a mistake to suppose that Mr. Stanley was, or claimed to be, the discoverer of these dwarfs of the African forest. We have seen that Speke heard of them. We know that Paul du Chaillu, in penetrating the forest behind the French possessions in West Africa, came upon a similar race of mankind. It may also be recalled that among the people whom Mr. Stanley had heard of in 1876, and Lieutenant Wissmann and Dr. Wolff met along the upper waters of the Congo, were the Watwa dwarfs not exceeding four and a half feet in height. But long before M. du Chaillu, long before the German explorer's time, dwarfs were known to inhabit the remoter portions of Africa; for does not Ptolemy, the Alexandrian geographer, speak of the fountains of the Nile, close by which a pigmy people dwelt? And, long before him, Homer, Herodotus, and Pliny had heard of these races dwelling among the marshes where the Nile rises so that unquestionably even at that early date Egyptian traders had come in contact with them, or slaves from the interior of Africa had carried into the Delta or to the remote colonies in the far north tales of a people whom it has been left for modern explorers to rediscover. Andrew Battell, it may be remembered, during his captivity in the kingdom of Loango (Vol. I., p. 118), met with the Matimbas, a kind of little people, "no bigger than Boyes of twelve yeares olde." Again, among the people whom Dapper, the Dutch geographer, who wrote in the seventeenth century, heard of from a countryman who did business along the Guinea coast, were the Bakke-Bakke: "pigmies, indeed, in stature, but with heads of prodigious bigness": and Commerson speaks of a like people in the interior of Madagascar. Dr. Krapf, the German missionary on the east coast of Africa, heard more than fifty years ago of the Doko, a race of dwarfs living among the Gallas. In 1854 tales of the Akkas, several of whom have at different times been

The Wambutti pigmies.

brought to Europe (pp. 36, 37), reached Petherick, and in 1871 they were described by Dr. Schweinfurth as the inhabitants of Monbuttu, a country which is south of the Bahr-el-Ghazel and west of the Equatorial Province to which Mr. Stanley was hastening when he met with a similar race in the depths of the Upper Congo forests.

This race he calls the Wambutti. They live farther west than the Akkas, but in disposition and general characteristics do not differ widely from that better-known people. They are brownish in colour, not exceeding four feet four inches in height, nomadic in their habits, neither keeping cattle nor tilling the ground, but subsisting solely by hunting and snaring wild animals or collecting the wild fruits and berries near their retreats. Their weapons are primitive but efficient, consisting of bows and arrows, the latter usually poisoned, not with the dried bodies of ants as at first imagined, but with the juice of various species of plants—one of which is apparently the well-known "sassy bark" (*Erythrophlœum guineense*). Another is *Palisota barteri*, a third is a species of *Strychnos* (a notoriously poisonous genus), and a fourth is *Tephrosia*, the seeds of which are used to poison fishes.*

These Wambutti have no fixed abodes and, if they build shelters at all, only construct huts of branches, with scarcely more architectural skill than the lowest of wild beasts. The explorers could, of course, obtain little information regarding their ways of life and modes of thought. They affirm, however, that the dwarfs have no government and no communities, but wander about in hordes each consisting of a few families, the necessity for finding food compelling them to be continually moving their habitations from one part of the country to another. In many cases they are dependent upon more powerful tribes of "Wasongora," as the taller savages are called, who, in return for certain services in the way of hunting and snaring animals, extend to them a small amount of protection,

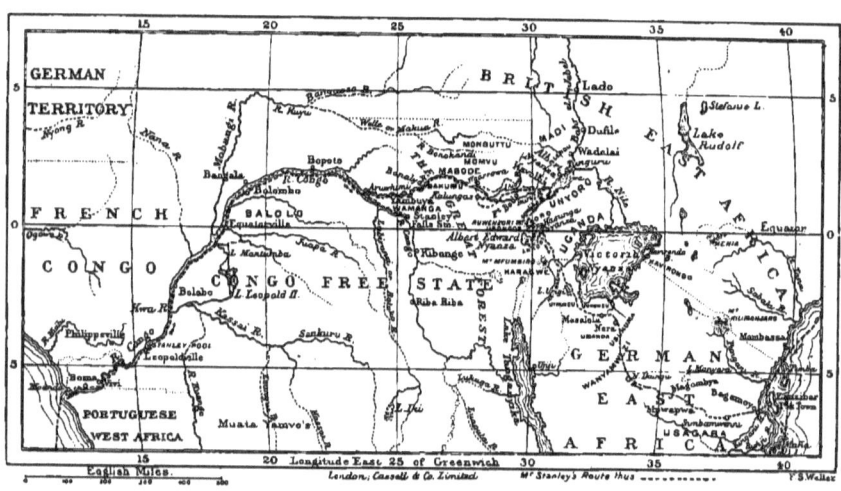

MAP OF THE ROUTE OF THE EMIN PASHA RELIEF EXPEDITION.

* Holmes and Parke, *Pharmaceutical Journal and Transactions*, 1891, p. 917; Parke, "Experiences in Equatorial Africa," pp. 308–319. Mr. Stanley (*Scribner's Magazine*, January, 1891, p. 11) seems doubtful whether the poison is not derived from the *Strophanthus hispidus*.

though, as a rule, the treatment of the thievish pigmies by their neighbours is only kept from being brutal by the latter's envenomed arrows. The Wambutti are also strongly suspected of cannibalism.

South of the Congo the tribe called Mucassequeres, living in the forests between Kubango

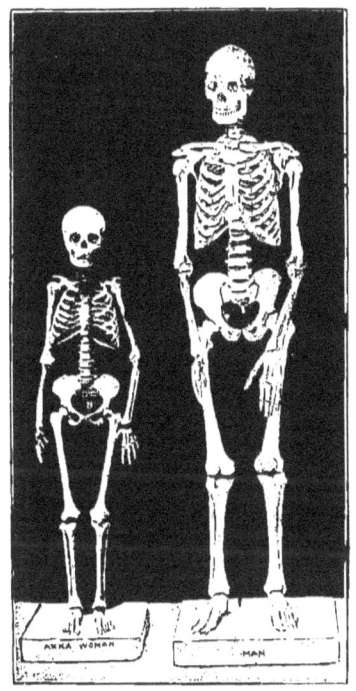

RELATIVE SIZES OF SKELETONS OF AN AKKA WOMAN AND OF A MAN OF ORDINARY STATURE.
(From a Photograph by Gambier Bolton, F.Z.S.)

and Kundo, also belong to the pigmy race; while the Massurnas whom Serpa Pinto describes as inhabiting the borders of the Zambesi sources (p. 4) are, if not a tribe of Bushmen, not very distantly allied to the peoples already mentioned. Dr. Schlichter, indeed, considers that there are four well-marked groups of African dwarfs besides others more mythical. The question, however, comes to be, who are these pigmy tribes? Are they remnants of the aborigines who inhabited Africa before the present powerful races entered and conquered it, that have been driven into the depths of the forests to escape from their persecutors? Or are they really outcasts of other tribes, who, in course of time, owing to the lack of food, to poor shelter, and much persecution, have sunk to their present degraded condition? The first theory is decidedly the more attractive, falling in as it does with the facts known regarding other inferior races. But when we examine the history of the pigmy races of Africa, there are many difficulties in the acceptance of this doctrine. In the first place, the differences between the Akkas, the Wambutti, and other pigmy races and the Bushmen are, according to Sir William Flower,[*] so radical as to preclude the possibility of regarding them as members of the same stock, as Mr. Stanley seems to imagine. Sir William lays special stress on the yellow complexion and peculiar, oblong form of the skull, characteristic of the Bushmen, and the presence of the monkey-looking profile, so characteristic of the pigmies but not of the Bushmen of South Africa. Again, there is not the least philological connection between the language of any of the pigmy races of the north and that now well known as the tongue of the southern dwarfs. Indeed, the scanty vocabularies which we possess of the tongue spoken by the pigmy tribes of the tropical forests contain so many actual and modified Bantu words as to lend strong support to the belief that these pigmies, instead of being a separate race, are really outcasts from the tribes around them; or at least, that they have had such long-continued relations with their neighbours as to have lost much of their original speech in favour of that adopted from their conquerors. It is well known that tribes of Hottentots in South Africa who had been expelled from their

[*] *Journal of the Anthropological Institute*, 1889, pp. 72–91.

tribes so very speedily retrograded as to be undistinguishable in the course of a few generations from the Bushmen around them. The origin and nature of the pigmies may, therefore, be still accepted as an open question.

It is, however, certain that they are not low in intellect. Mr. Stanley, indeed, declares that in acuteness, necessitated by their mode of life, they are vastly superior to the dull Zanzibaris, and in intellectual ability comparable with fifty per cent. of the citizens of a civilised town. Their boldness and skill in catching the elephant in pits, and in killing or trapping the various birds and beasts that contribute to their omnivorous diet, are greater than those of the taller savages around whose settlements the dwarfs form temporary hamlets. There are two types among them. One is a clear, light bronze in colour; the other is much darker, almost black. The latter is distinguished by a greater projection of the jaws and a more retreating forehead than the other variety. Some of them—but not many—are well-formed and a few are even good-looking, as African looks go. But, as a rule, the pigmies are not an attractive race. They are also imbued with some municipal instinct. The only native African road cut for more than half a mile which Mr. Stanley ever saw out of Uganda was one made for three miles between two pigmy villages. These roads when danger is apprehended are all skewered with poisonous points covered with leaves, the villagers passing meanwhile through secret parallel paths, leaving the protected way open to the unsuspecting enemy, who is generally one of a rival village, or some of the taller savages

whose banana, corn, and tobacco patches have been plundered by the dwarfs.*

Two of these Ituri River dwarfs were, in 1893, brought to Germany by Dr. Stuhlmann. That traveller seems to consider them akin to, if not identical with the Akkas. Indeed,

AKKA (PIGMY) GIRL.
(*From a Photograph by R. Buchta.*)

he expressly declares that the Wambutti bear among some of their neighbours the name of

* Stanley, "The Pigmies of the Great African Forest," *Scribner's Magazine*, January, 1891, pp. 3–17; Schlichter, "The Pigmy Tribes of Africa," *Scottish Geographical Magazine*, 1892, pp. 289–301 and 345–356 (a very exhaustive paper, though the generalisations are too sweeping for the knowledge as yet in our possession); and a useful article by Miss Werner in the *Gentleman's Magazine*, 1890, pp. 556–569. Quattrefages ("Les Pygmées," 1887) discusses what was known at the date when he wrote.

Akka, a word said to occur on an ancient Egyptian monument.

On the one hundred and fifty-fifth day of the expedition's departure from Yambuya the members were rejoiced to see from the summit of Pisgah Ridge, at the base of Pisgah Mount, the first glimpse of open country, and on the one hundred and sixty-sixth day, or the 4th of December, 1887, to emerge from the gloomy forest.

Perils of the journey to Albert Nyanza.

To the very last the natives never intermitted their harassment of the expedition. Not an hour could be passed with the certainty that a flight of arrows might not descend upon the column, and even at the time when the members were rejoicing at the thought that they would soon see Albert Nyanza gleaming before them an attack by their persistent enemies had to be driven off.

The perils, indeed, of the march through this forest before Mazamboni's was reached exceeded everything in the more recent annals of African exploration. For weeks the sky could not be seen for the thick foliage overhead, and every bush swarmed with wild people sunk in the last depths of savagery, dwarfish, ape-like, and altogether repulsive. During their long march the members of the expedition had neither seen nor heard of any open place in the bosom of the forest, with the exception of the clearings that had been laboriously made by the natives, though, as Mr. Stanley tells us, at the season of planting these patches had to be subjected to laborious cutting, lest the forest should usurp the place from which it had been previously expelled. "Take," he tells us, "a thick Scottish copse, dripping with rain; imagine this copse to be a mere undergrowth, nourished under the impenetrable shade of ancient trees, ranging from 100 to 180 feet high; briars and thorns abundant; lazy creeks, meandering through the depth of the jungle, and sometimes a deep affluent of a great river. Imagine this forest and jungle in all stages of decay and growth—old trees falling, leaning perilously over, fallen prostrate; ants and insects of all kinds, sizes, and colours, murmuring around; monkeys and chimpanzees above, queer noises of birds and animals, crashes in the jungle as troops of elephants rush away; dwarfs, with poisoned arrows, securely hidden behind some buttress or some dark recess; strong, brown-bodied aborigines, with terribly sharp spears, standing poised, still as dead stumps; rain pattering down upon you every other day in the year; an impure atmosphere, with its dread consequences, fever and dysentery; gloom throughout the day, and darkness almost palpable throughout the night; and then if you will imagine such a forest extending the entire distance from Plymouth to Peterhead, you will have a fair idea of some of the inconveniences endured by us from June 28th to December 5th, 1887." *

The great forest.

When the expedition issued out of the gloomy depth of these primeval woods it numbered 173 men all told. It had, however, dropped on the way thirty or forty men, whom excessive sickness had weakened or grievous

WEAPONS OF THE ARUWHIMI DISTRICT.

* Stanley's "Letters" (1890), pp. 63-64.

DAYLIGHT AT LAST! THE ADVANCE COLUMN OF THE EMIN PASHA RELIEF EXPEDITION EMERGING FROM THE GREAT FOREST (p. 38).

ulcers had crippled. These they had been obliged to shelter with the Arabs whose stations had been passed. Such calamities had thinned the ranks grievously. Many of the invalids had died and others were too feeble to be likely ever to be of much use to the party. A sort of epidemic of dreadful ulcers raged throughout the camp, and anæmia, engendered by poor diet or semi-starvation, had reduced others to a condition of decrepitude. Poisoned arrows had caused a great many deaths, in most cases, except where the poison was fresh, preceded by hours of intense agony. But, apart from sickness and fatal casualties, desertion accounted for the absence of so large a number from the effective force that had left Yambuya five and a half months before. "There are no circumstances under which the Zanzibari will not desert—excessive feasting, extreme famine, a heavy or a light load, a hot or a cold day, going from or approaching home, it makes little difference. When the fit takes him he will immediately march to certain death to escape the tyranny of work. The worst of it is that he even marches away with rifle, equipment, and load, and wrecks the expedition, or reduces it to a dangerous state of destitution and weakness. At Kilonga-Longa's, where there is an Arab settlement at which thirty-three men had been left, the entire force sold its ammunition, so that we lost three thousand rounds. Over thirty men sold their Remington rifles; others sold their ramrods and equipment. They entered our tents by night, and stole our bedding. Surgeon Parke lost his entire kit of clothing. Captain Nelson lost his blankets, and I lost my cutlery and spoons. During August, September, October, and November, the people were demoralised by sufferings. Whatever we said to them was disbelieved; they hooted at and jeered at our assurances that a few energetic marches would take us far beyond our suffering. It required an infinite patience to bear against this wolfish feature of human nature. They might have proceeded to extremities, but they did not: considering their sufferings, I call this a virtue. When we finally issued out of darkness into daylight and bright sunshine, and the lucent atmosphere, its virtue expanded, and every soul of the 173 men who witnessed the sight and joined with us became inflamed with zeal to do the best he could, and we never had any trouble with them afterwards;" though, it ought to be added that, as a warning to others, Mr. Stanley considered it necessary more than once to inflict severe punishment upon those who had bartered away the arms with which they had been entrusted.

The "promised land" into which the expedition entered on the 5th of December, after leaving the great forest behind, was exquisitely lovely in character, and remarkably fertile and populous. Yet the commander would have been glad if by any means he could have avoided the necessity of marching through it, for the population was so dense and unfriendly, and the band of sorely-tried men who had to oppose them so few in number, that for a time it seemed to be utter madness to press onward through a region swarming with enemies so numerous and powerful. The nearer the lake was approached, the more obstinately determined were the natives in resisting the advance. Skirmish after skirmish had to be faced, until, on December 13th, the long journey seemed to have come to an end, when, from a lofty precipice, Albert Nyanza lay gleaming below. *The grassy country.*

Reaching its edge, close to a village of the natives who had hitherto been so unfriendly, the first question, naturally, was as to any white men being in the vicinity of the lake. No steamer had, however, been seen since Mason Bey's in 1877 (Vol. II., p. 137), and no information regarding the whereabouts of Emin Pasha could be obtained. What little they could elicit from the natives in answer to their inquiries seemed at first like arrant nonsense. It was only in after days that they ascertained the reason of the tribesmen's ignorance. For Emin, though residing for so many years at the northern end of the lake, and on the river which ran out of it, had never visited the southern end, and up to this period had never been heard of by the fishermen in that vicinity.

In these circumstances, it seemed idle to remain any longer in this position. It was, therefore, resolved to return to the forest

WANYORO WARRIORS.
(From a Photograph by R. Buchta.)

region as the least dangerous, select some promising spot for occupation, build a fort, store the extra goods, and march back again to the lake with the boat *Advance*, reluctantly left behind at Kilonga-Longa's, but without which it would not be easy to communicate with Wadelai. The extensive clearing of Ibwiri was selected for the first-named purpose, and here on the 8th of January, 1888, some 190 miles from the lake, Fort Bodo was begun, and seven acres of corn were planted in its vicinity. Meanwhile,

Lieutenant Stairs had been despatched to Kilonga-Longa's for the boat, and afterwards to Ugarrowa's* station for such of the convalescents as could march, in the hope also that he would meet with Major Barttelot and the rear column on their way to the lake. On the 2nd of April Mr. Stanley was so far recovered from a painful attack of gastritis and the prevailing abscess malady as to be able to move again towards Albert Nyanza. Mr. Stairs, however, had not yet returned from his second mission, though he had obtained the boat which on their first journey had been abandoned through sheer inability to carry it. Mr. Mounteney-Jephson and Dr. Parke accompanied the commander, Captain Nelson remaining as commandant at Fort Bodo. In travelling through the district which, a few months earlier, had proved so dangerous to the expedition the travellers were pleased to observe a marked change in the disposition of the natives. Instead of flying at them with spears, they entered into friendly overtures to assist the white men against their common enemy—the Wanyoro, subjects of the King of Unyoro, who were found to be raiding, murdering, and conquering on both sides of the lake. Wherever the white men came the natives now eagerly brought to the camp gifts of plantains, corn, goats, and cattle, and continued these supplies of gratuitous provisions as long as they remained in their vicinity.

When about one day's march from Albert Nyanza, letters from Emin were delivered to Mr. Stanley. Two months after Mr. Stanley's descent to the lake, Emin had heard of the arrival of the expedition and left these notes for the information of his friends. Mr. Jephson, accordingly, set out in the boat now launched on the lake to search for the Pasha, and on the second day came to Mswa station, the southernmost in the Equatorial Province.

At last, on the 29th of April, 1888, the Expedition were gratified to see the Khedive's

* Ugarrowa, or Uledi Balyuz, was a tent-boy of Speke's, but at the time Mr. Stanley met him was a very great man in the slave-raiding line.

steamer on the lake and in the evening to welcome Emin Pasha, Captain Casati, and a number of Egyptian officers who had come with them. For more

Emin arrives.

Contrary to expectations—unwarranted, however, considering his previous declarations—he and his friends displayed no anxiety to take that step. As he had repeatedly

MEETING OF EMIN PASHA AND MR. STANLEY AT KAVALLI'S, APRIL 29, 1888.

than three weeks Emin and his friends stayed with Stanley in camp at Nsabé. The latter occupied most of the time in trying to persuade the Pasha to return to Egypt with his followers.

asserted in his letters to Europe, he had the utmost reluctance to desert his post. He declared that the soldiers had no inclination to evacuate the Soudan. The few

Europeanised officials — Vita Hassan the apothecary, and Marco the Greek, for example — might desire this course; but even the Egyptians of considerable rank in the military service had by this time begun to regard the Equatorial Province as their home. They had wives and children and gardens, and they held a position and enjoyed an ease which could not be expected in Cairo and on the Lower Nile.

Nor was Emin himself, or his companion Captain Casati, any more inclined to seek civilisation. Mr. Stanley, indeed, declares that they seemed quite content to remain where they were. They praised the country for its fertility and its equable climate. They even loved the natives, and were tireless in their praise of everything connected with that region. All that these two cultivated men seemed to care for was the means of defence against invasion or accidental disturbance. The land yielded abundance of food, and Emin had accumulated sufficient ivory to supply himself, if necessary, with all commodities that the Arab caravans passing through Equatoria were able to dispose of. Extensive gardens and plantations supplied all native and many European vegetables, and, though the aborigines had not yet learned to weave woollen fabrics, they manufactured, as the clothes worn by the officers proved, a coarse though substantial cotton cloth out of a plant grown in the country.

What the Governor chiefly desired was ammunition. The greater part of their supplies of this important material was now gone, and originally it had not been of the best quality, the corrupt officials in Cairo, in order to conceal their peculations from the Government, sending to the Soudan all the worthless rubbish which they could find in the magazines. Even that brought by Mr. Stanley for the use of Emin was found to be of less value than had been hoped, as it had been supplied to them from the Egyptian stores. In short, Emin reasserted his oft-expressed resolution to remain by the Equatorial Province for better or worse.

In vain Mr. Stanley tried to impress upon him "the hopelessness of his situation, the almost certainty of the Mahdi reaching him and overwhelming his small force by dint of numbers; that the powerful Kings of Unyoro and Uganda would always be a bar to safe communication with the east coast; that caravans would never venture by Masailand and Lango, to be decimated by famine and thirst, for the uncertain profits to be derived from the dangerous risks of the journey; that no body of philanthropists would repeat these expensive outlays on behalf of a province so remote from the sea as Emin Pasha's when there were thousands of square miles of equally fertile soils lying close to the ocean." These and similar arguments (which, it appears, lost their pristine virility in the arguments for the retention of Uganda) seemed for a time to have considerable weight with the vacillating Pasha. But Emin was seldom for many hours in the same mind. Now he was willing to leave; now he affirmed he would stay. One day he declared he would go if the Egyptians wished to go; then the Egyptians were willing to go if Emin would go; and, finally, Captain Casati would join the caravan to the sea if Emin and the Egyptians were of the same mind. In the course of his long stay in the tropics, wearied by continual anxieties, the resolution of the Pasha, if, indeed, he ever possessed much, seemed to have entirely vanished. For undoubtedly the impression which his visitors derived of his character during the three weeks spent by the shore of Albert Nyanza was entirely different from that which the accounts they had read in the European papers before their departure had led them to entertain.

Finally, believing that Emin had been persuaded to take what, in the opinion of his friends, was the best course, Mr. Stanley sent Mr. Jephson and thirteen Soudanese soldiers to assist Emin in collecting his scattered troops with a view to commence the march eastwards, while he himself resolved to return westwards again in the hope of meeting

Major Barttelot's rear-guard, or ascertaining the reasons for its long-delayed arrival.

Emin prepares to leave, and Stanley returns in search of the rear-guard. Every day for many weeks past the weary eyes of their companions had been turned in the direction in which Major Barttelot and his column were expected to come. They imagined they heard the looked-for signal shots. They even dreamed that the column was approaching, and that they saw the Major at the head of quite an army of carriers. But the days passed away and no news was heard either of him or of the volunteer couriers who had left Fort Bodo on the 16th of February in search of the rear-guard. Accordingly, Mr. Stanley, having prepared sufficient food to last him for the return journey through the dreadful wilderness that had well-nigh proved fatal to him and his companions on their first journey towards the lake, departed on the 16th of June from Fort Bodo on a search for the rear-column, leaving Lieutenant Stairs, Captain Nelson, and Surgeon Parke behind with a garrison of fifty-nine men.

Long and wearisome though this return tramp through the dense forest undoubtedly was, it was much lighter than the former journey had been. The natives seemed to have learned a lesson of prudence, and seldom molested the travellers, while the Arab slave-traders at whose settlements they halted had acquired a higher respect for the white man than that with which they had been formerly inspired. At Ugarrowa's, they were glad to find the surviving couriers who had been despatched from Fort Bodo on the 16th of February in search of Major Barttelot's column, though only five had escaped grievous arrow wounds.

Every day on the tramp through the forest Mr. Stanley and his caravan expected to meet with Major Barttelot. At every turn in the forest path they eagerly strained their eyes through the gloomy bush in the hope *Barttelot's camp.* that the next few steps would bring them in sight of his long-hoped-for caravan. But no such hope was gratified until on the 17th of August, at ten o'clock in the morning, they sighted a camp which could be no other than that of their long-lost companions. This was at a place called Banalya, 90 miles from Yambuya, 592 from Lake Albert, 63 from Fort Bodo, and the eighty-fifth day from the Nyanza plain. True enough, it was the rear-column, or, at least, the wreck of the 271 men all told of which it consisted when last seen at Yambuya. Instead of five white men to welcome them, only one, emaciated by fevers and anxiety, made his appearance. This was Mr. Bonny. Major Barttelot was dead; he had been shot in a quarrel with one of Tippoo Tib's Manyemas less than a month ago. Mr. Jameson had started two days later for Stanley Falls in the hope of obtaining more men from Tippoo Tib, whose dilatoriness in fulfilling his contract had been the cause of the long delay in the column starting for the east, and, to some extent, for the disasters that had so early overtaken it. Indeed, at that moment—though Mr. Stanley was not aware of the fact—Mr. Jameson was dead. Mr. Troup had been sent home to England in an invalid condition, and Mr. Ward had left for the mouth of the Congo in order to telegraph to London for the instructions of the Rescue Expedition Committee as to the course to be taken by the rear-column. Deserters had been continually arriving at the camp with well-concocted stories of the misfortunes which had happened to Mr. Stanley's advance party. Indeed, so frequently had these tales reached Major Barttelot, and so long had the rear-guard been without intelligence from the commander, that it was thoroughly believed that he and his party were dead, imprisoned, or otherwise beyond the reach of their companions. In Europe much the same opinion had begun to gain ground, an experienced African traveller demonstrating in the most conclusive manner that the long lack of news from the expedition was to be explained in no way more agreeable.

Hence it was that no one was left with the rear-column except Mr. Bonny. His tale was a disastrous one. Not only was Major Barttelot dead, but 100 Soudanese, Zanzibaris and Somalis had been buried at Yambuya; 33 men were left at that camp helpless and dying, and 14 of these expired later, while 26 had deserted. Accordingly, writes Mr. Stanley, "when I saw Bonny and his people, the rear-

FORT BODO.

column—Zanzibaris, Somalis, and Soudanese —numbered 102 all told out of 271, and only one officer out of five! Besides this deplorable record, the condition of the stores was just as bad. Out of 660 loads of 65 lbs. each there remained only 230 loads of 65 lbs. weight. All my personal clothing, except hats, boots, one flannel jacket, a cap, and three pairs of drawers, had been sent down to Bangala [on the Congo], because rumour had stated I was dead and the advance party gone to the dogs; a remnant of thirty had, however, managed to escape to Ujiji!"*

In all the annals of African exploration, no more pitiful sight was ever witnessed than in the palisaded hamlet where the remnant of the rear-guard was encamped when Mr. Stanley arrived. It was crowded with dead and dying, and a very pesthouse to the living. Small-pox was raging, and there were six bodies lying unburied in the village, the stench of which was overpowering. Dozens of disease-disfigured beings passed constantly before the newcomers, and when any member of the rear-guard presented himself, it was difficult to recognise in the living skeleton the robust negro who had been left behind twelve months before. A poor creature stricken with anæmia, or a wretched man whose pitiful state of mind and body was too painfully expressed upon his hollow cheeks, woebegone face, and eyes brimful of grief or anxiety, was the too-apt representative of the column in charge of which Mr. Bonny had for a time been left. "I shall not forget readily," Mr. Stanley wrote when the facts were fresh in his mind,

* Letter to Mr. Jephson in the latter's "Emin Pasba, and the Rebellion at the Equator" (1890), p. 391; Casati, "Ten Years in Equatoria, and the Return with Emin Pasha," Vol. II., 212. This work ought to be read with Stanley's "In Darkest Africa," 2 Vols. (1890).

"that terrible story which told of the destruction of the rear-column, and the shocking

LANGO CHIEF WITH CHARACTERISTIC HEAD-DRESS.
(From a Photograph by R. Buchta.)

effects the sights seen that day had on us."

The long delay of the rear-column and the consequent disasters which befell it were largely due to the breach of contract by Tippoo Tib and to his prevarication and dissimulation. He had repeatedly promised to provide a large contingent of porters to convey their baggage eastwards. These did finally arrive eleven months after date, but meanwhile Major Barttelot's force, consisting of Zanzibaris and Soudanese, had lost more than half of their number from disease, anæmia, and the poisonous cassava or manioc meal* which forms a large portion of the food. Nor can it be affirmed, looking at the whole matter in the light of all the information obtained since then, that Major Barttelot and

Major Bart- telot and Mr. Stanley.

* Prepared from the tubers of *Manihot utilissima*.

his companions were altogether innocent of blame for the troubles which overtook them, and which, in the case of the commander himself, led to his melancholy death. The question of how far Major Barttelot was justified in interpreting his instructions in the sense that he did, has, it is almost unnecessary to remind the reader, been the subject of much heated controversy, and the theme of quite a little literature in itself. Mr. Stanley has repeatedly contended that Major Barttelot and his companions were culpably negligent in not attending to the letter of the instructions which were left them. He blames them for apathy in remaining in Yambuya camp, and for sending, after nine months' stay at that spot, Mr. Ward to the west coast to cable for instructions to the Relief Committee, only to receive as his reply a request to read the instructions which they received from Mr. Stanley before he left them on his march to the east. He, furthermore—somewhat unreasonably, we think—considers that these young and inexperienced officers ought not to have so readily accepted the repeated promises and prevarications of Tippoo Tib. But it must be remembered that

LANGO CHIEF.
(From a Photograph by R. Buchta.)

without Tippoo Tib there was no possibility of their advancing with advantage from the camp where Mr. Stanley had left them. For without a supply of porters the baggage could not be carried any great distance, or without a delay that was out of the question, and without baggage the party could not subsist. Indeed, there would have been little use for their arriving on the shores of Albert Nyanza unless as the guardians of the large supply of stores which had been left in their charge.

Again, though Mr. Stanley's instructions provided for a move, it was to be made only in two circumstances. The first of these was if Tippoo Tib should have sent the stipulated number of porters. The contingency of the Arab Governor of Stanley Falls not sending any porters at all was not even alluded to, such a neglect of duty never seeming to have entered the minds of any of the party. Indeed, it is remarkable, if the young officers ought to have been so aware of the wiles of the veteran slave-trader—who, it is said, had an old grudge against Mr. Stanley, by whose influence he had been appointed to the post which he was so incapable of filling,—that so experienced a traveller as Mr. Stanley made no allusion to the possibility of his treachery wrecking an important part of the expedition.

At the same time, it must be admitted that Major Barttelot was ill-fitted, both by previous training and natural disposition, for the important post to which he had been appointed. He was a young man of generous impulses, but of violent temper, noted for his intense dislike of the natives of Africa with whom he had daily to deal, and so imbued with the otherwise commendable instincts of a soldier that at the time when, in the changed condition of affairs, the exercise of private judgment was necessary, he felt it treason to his commander to transgress in any way the instructions laid down for him.

The truth is, that at the date when Mr. Stanley wrote his letter for the guidance of his second in command, neither he nor any of the party had the remotest idea of how events would turn out. When the advanced column left the Yambuya camp, it was Mr. Stanley's full intention to return by the same route. He naturally believed that his journey eastwards would be made more rapidly than it really was, that Emin and his force would gladly leave their beleaguered province, and that in a few months the expedition would be united on the banks of the Aruwhimi. Unfortunately, the story of the expedition took a very different turn; so that it is idle to stigmatise those in a subordinate position for not seeing what they could not possibly have foreseen, and for not altering their plans in accordance with the altered position of affairs 600 miles distant.* Even Mr. Stanley himself found that his persuasiveness had little effect upon the temper of Tippoo Tib. In vain he invited the wealthy trader to accompany him to the east. But neither Mr. Stanley's eloquence nor Tippoo's cupidity had any effect upon his desire to live at ease in his camp on the Upper Congo.

<small>Mr. Stanley again marches to Albert Nyanza.</small>

Accordingly, on the 31st of August, Mr. Stanley had again to turn eastwards without the escort of the chief from whom so much had been expected by him and so little by everyone else at all acquainted with the character of the dignitary in question. At first, Mr. Stanley's marches on his return to Albert Nyanza were slow and short, in order to give Mr. Jameson (of whose death they were not aware) and Mr. Ward (who was still far down the Congo) an opportunity to follow them. However, the route was now so well known that the latter portion of the journey was made with comparative ease, though not without peril, and with such remarkable accuracy as to time, that on the 20th of December, 1888, two days before the expiration of their term of absence, Mr. Stanley and his caravan arrived at Fort Bodo (p. 44).

Here disagreeable news met him. The officers were well, though they had suffered many hardships in the interval from disease

---

* "Life of Major Barttelot," etc. (1890), pp. 143 *et seq.*; Jameson, "Story of the Rear Column" (1890), pp. 60, *et seq.*; Ward, "My Life with Stanley's Rear-guard" (1891); Troup, "With Stanley's Rear-guard" (1890), etc., with correspondence in the London and other newspapers during 1890 and 1891.

and other concomitants of African travel. But no tidings had arrived from Emin Pasha and Mr. Jephson, though both had promised to be at Fort Bodo with the Egyptians belonging to Emin Pasha's force, in order, if necessary, to begin the march to the west coast as soon as Mr. Stanley had returned. A move was therefore again made to the shores of Albert Nyanza with the large quantity of stores that had accumulated in Fort Bodo.

Arrival at Albert Nyanza, and unpleasant news.

No trouble was now found so far as the natives were concerned. All of them welcomed the white men. Chief after chief arrived with armies of followers conveying contributions of corn, plantains, and small herds of cattle, as gifts to those whom they now began to look upon either as kindly guests whom it was their duty to treat well or as powerful enemies whom it would be imprudent to oppose.

While engaged in this work letters reached them from Mr. Jephson and Emin Pasha. It now appeared that, whatever Emin's vacillation might have been hitherto, he had scarcely any other choice left him than to accept Mr. Stanley's offer to leave the province for which he had hitherto expressed so decided a love. For, on Mr. Jephson and Emin returning to intimate to the different garrisons the instructions of which Mr. Stanley was the bearer, the long, almost unconcealed and sometimes open discontent which had been gathering among the troops burst into open mutiny (p. 49), the first signal of which was that Emin, Jephson, and Casati were held prisoners by the rebellious officers. Indeed, though these mutineers belonged to the second battalion, the first had resolved, in the event of his reaching Rijiaf, to seize him and carry out the old idea of setting out for Khartoum, which they believed to be still in existence. There cannot be much doubt that the arrival of Mr. Stanley had a large share in precipitating this revolt. But, possibly, had not the Mahdi's troops captured Lado and the three most northerly stations, though the attack on Duffilé failed, and thus led the Egyptian officers to believe that before long they would be at the mercy of the Dervishes, matters might have gone on for a long time just as they were when the Relief Expedition arrived. Indeed, had Mr. Stanley's force been as large as the Egyptian officers had believed it would be, they might have readily rallied round the new arrivals. But when they saw that it consisted of a mere handful of men, many of them sick, and most of them little able to take part in the arduous toil of battle —if, indeed, many of them had been soldiers by training,—furnished with an insufficient amount of ammunition, they saw that little was to be expected from a force so feeble. Finally, when the instructions from the Egyptian Government, which Mr. Stanley had brought to Emin, were read out to the different garrisons, the resolutions of the subordinate officers were soon taken. Stanley was pronounced a mere adventurer, his letters forgeries, and his intention to be to hand over the people of Equatoria as slaves to the English. The news of the Mahdists having reached Lado was confirmed by three messengers from Omar Saleh with a demand for Emin's surrender and the promise of a free pardon to all. This embassy the mutineers treated by torturing and then killing the envoys. When the news of Rijiaf being in the Dervishes' hands came to Laboreh, dissension ensued among the rebels, but when the panic-stricken garrison arrived with tales of fighting and massacre, Emin and his companions were permitted to retreat to Wadelai; and, when this was abandoned at the news of the Mahdists' approach, to Tonguru. Thus the year 1888 ended with the deposition of Emin and the falling of the province from Rijiaf northwards into the Mahdists' hands, while from Rijiaf southwards to Wadelai the garrisons were in a ferment of mutinous disorder and confusion. This was the state of matters when Mr. Stanley arrived for the third time at Lake Albert, only to hear of Emin and his friends being at Tonguru.

The mutiny of Emin's troops.

So far as the men were concerned, their situation could not be improved by any such move as that which Mr. Stanley tried to persuade them to take. The Egyptian authorities intimated in the most decided manner that Emin must withdraw with as many troops as chose to follow him from the Equatorial Province. If these orders were obeyed, all of the officers and men were guaranteed their arrears of pay and the continuance of the rank which they had held in the Soudan. But, if they did not choose to accept the offer then made them, it was the Khedive's orders that for the future they should have no claims whatever upon his Government. However, it was well known that for months past envoys from Omar Saleh, general of the Mahdi's forces, had been sowing the seeds of dissension among the Mohammedan troops under the command of Emin Pasha. A letter demanding the surrender of "The Honoured Mohammed Emin, Mudir of Khat el Istiwa"—"the Middle Line"—was also sent. Moreover, many of the officers were "broken" men who, as was not uncommonly the case, had been sent to the Soudan as a punishment for military and other misdeeds, and very few could be relied upon in an emergency such as that they were now called upon to face. Long experience having taught them the worthlessness of Turkish promises, the words of the Khedive's letter had very little effect on their minds. On the other hand, the emissaries of the Mahdists promised great things—high rank, great pecuniary rewards, and, above all, a "free hand with the natives," which Emin's abolition of the slave trade had no longer rendered lucrative—if they would desert to the Khalifa or deliver over the European officers to work in chains in the streets of El Obeid with Slatin Bey or Lupton Bey, who had met the fate which it now seemed certain Emin could not long avoid (Vol. II., p. 159). The capture of Emin, Casati, and Jephson was, however,

MR. WARD DESPATCHED TO THE COAST FOR INSTRUCTIONS: CALL AT LUKOLELA.
(From a Photograph by the Rev. R. D. Darby, Baptist Missionary Society.)

MR. JEPHSON IN CAPTIVITY.

the preliminary step to carrying out this plot. The letters which reached Mr. Stanley intimated that Mr. Jephson's captivity was not so rigid as that of his brother prisoners. Couriers were accordingly sent by canoes with letters to Mr. Jephson ordering him to take advantage of the first opportunity of leaving the Tonguru station, where he was then a partial prisoner. It seems that no great difficulty presented itself in carrying out this wish, for within a few days the ex-captive arrived in Mr. Stanley's camp. Mr. Jephson was, naturally, able to give the most complete account of matters amongst the revolted soldiery.* But, to the astonishment of all concerned, he was also the bearer of information that, notwithstanding all that

* In Mr. Jephson's "Emin Pasha and the Rebellion at the Equator," and Major Casati's "Ten Years in Equatoria," an exhaustive history of these events will be found.

44

had occurred, Emin Pasha and Captain Casati had not, any more than before, made up their minds to leave a country where, unquestionably, ere long they would have no power of action one way or the other.

This was an irritating situation for men who had risked their lives and undergone so many hardships to free Emin and his com-

MUTINY OF EMIN PASHA'S MEN AT LABOREH. BEGINNING OF THE REBELLION.
(From a Sketch by Mr. A. J. Mounteney-Jephson, one of Stanley's officers and the companion of Emin Pasha at the time.)

panions. Mr. Stanley, however, as we think, was somewhat unjust to the Governor of the Equatorial Province, and still more so to his companion, an Italian officer of high rank and unspotted reputation. It was somewhat ungenerous to affirm that the chief reason which prevented them from leaving Central Africa was that the Governor was "wedded to the life where he had kinged it so long, wedded to its courteous ceremonies and amenities in the same way as Captain Casati loved its gross pleasures and large licence."

It was, nevertheless, very necessary that a

resolution should be arrived at without any further loss of time; for, whether Emin chose to go or to remain, it was imperative that the expedition, which had been much longer in Africa than had been expected, should now take the first steps on its homeward journey. The action of the rebels had unconsciously hastened the solution of the problem which had for months kept the Pasha and his friends in a state of irresolution. Emin, it has been affirmed by the members of the Relief Expedition, had not even then, in spite of his imprisonment and the mutiny of his soldiers, any complete realisation of the situation. He seemed to the last to be of the belief that, with a few exceptions, his men were faithful to him, just as they had been in days gone by, and that the personal affection which he had won by his mild rule and self-denying exertions for their welfare would, in the end, result in their return to allegiance. He seemed not to be aware, as one so well acquainted with the Oriental character ought to have been, that the people with whom he had to deal were only faithful so long as their own interests justified them in being so, and that in the East personal affection weighs very little in the balance against the necessity for self-sacrifice. Indeed, long after Emin had left Equatoria, he insisted, in his conversation with personal friends, that had not Mr. Stanley "forced" him to return he could with some time at his disposal have brought perfectly loyal troops from outlying stations to overpower those who had mutinied against his authority. Emin had even the audacity to declare to Dr. Peters that Stanley did not come to him, but he to Stanley; that the latter never reached the Equatorial Province, and but for the provisions and clothing brought, his men would have been destroyed.*

A rebel conspiracy.

No such illusions affected Mr. Stanley. A man of more robust mind, and possibly not so innocent of the ways of the wicked world, he speedily saw, or believed that he saw, not only that the rebellious soldiers were preparing

* "New Light on Dark Africa," p. 518.

to deliver Emin and the other European officers into the Khalifa's hands, but that they were planning a plot by which Mr. Stanley and all his men should meet the same fate.

He was, therefore, resolved at once to prevent so disastrous a *coup*. To carry out this conspiracy it was necessary to affect regret for past conduct, and, in the guise of remorseful rebels, to produce Emin and the other officers in Mr. Stanley's camp before the suspicions of the latter should gain ground. This plan was so far carried out that Lieutenant-Colonel Selim Bey Matera, the least objectionable of the officers concerned in the mutiny, with twelve others more or less acceptable to Emin Pasha, proceeded to Tonguru, the place of the Pasha's captivity, to implore forgiveness for the past and to reinstate him in his honours and position. So far as Emin was concerned, the wily words of the mutineers were successful. He believed in their sorrow, and gladly gave them forgiveness and promised to intercede with Mr. Stanley on their behalf. The result was that the Pasha and a deputation of mutineers arrived in Mr. Stanley's camp, the latter armed with a document signed by all the principal officers regretting their hasty and wicked action in deposing their master, and expressing loyalty and gratitude to the Khedive of Egypt, the Government of the Soudan represented by Emin, and the Relief Expedition for the part the members had individually performed for the beleaguered garrisons. A hope was also expressed that a reasonable time would be allowed for the officers to collect the troops and their families and bring them to the place of rendezvous, which was at Kavalli's, near the southern end of Albert Nyanza. Three weeks were considered reasonable time for performing this necessary duty, and, full of Oriental compliments and professions of esteem, the rebel officers left for their respective garrisons, ostensibly with the intention of bringing them into Mr. Stanley's camp: actually, it was then believed, with the object of surrounding and capturing the entire expedition.

But when one month expired without any sign of the arrival of the troops, who numbered about 1,500 Regulars and 3,000 Irregulars, with their families, suspicion began to gain ground in the minds of everyone, except Emin Pasha, that something was wrong. It was known that almost daily communications passed between Emin's and Stanley's men, and the nominally loyal Egyptians in his camp and the rebels in Wadelai and other stations. Then it was whispered that secret meetings were being held, and it was evident to all that symptoms of unrest were spreading among the refugees. Still, Emin would not listen to any imputations of disloyalty, far less of mutiny, among the friends around him. Indeed, after an attempt to steal several rifles was frustrated and a report of the plot was brought to Mr. Stanley, the Pasha showed such an unwillingness to crush the mutinous designs of his people that Mr. Stanley was obliged to take matters into his own hands.

At last, information reached the commander which left no doubt that not one out of the 570 refugees in the camp had any intention of leaving with the Pasha on the day fixed for their departure for the coast. In itself this was not remarkable. Time to an African is as nothing, and an Oriental has no idea of punctuality. But both were becoming very essential to Mr. Stanley. Accordingly, on the date fixed, namely, the 10th of April, the expedition, escorting the Egyptians and their followers, and assisted by 400 native warriors, set out for the southern end of Lake Albert on their way to the Indian Ocean, the route first planned having necessarily been adopted for its return; the great forest, without a depôt to fall back upon after emerging from it, being no longer regarded as feasible for so large a caravan. But, though Mr. Stanley had not waited for the promised return of the officers with the troops under their command, the machinations among the disguised rebels in camp did not abate. Almost every day rifles, equipments, and ammunition were disappearing, and every face, in spite of the ready dissemblance of the Oriental, expressed hatred, sullenness, and discontent. Then little parties of four or five began to vanish, until, finally, a troop of twenty deserted with what arms and ammunition they could seize, as the forerunners of a still larger detachment, who, it appeared, had intended to take the same course.

Still, in spite of suspicion and native gossip, it was impossible to say for certain that any untoward conduct towards the expedition was intended by these ex-subjects of Emin, until a native chief who had been entrusted with the dispatch of mails to Wadelai brought, through ignorance, a large packet of letters addressed to the mutineers at that station. Some of these were opened, and in one of them Ibrahim Elhem Effendi, an Egyptian captain, at that moment in Mr. Stanley's camp, wrote to Selim Bey in something like these words: "For God's sake, send as soon as you receive this fifty soldiers to our aid; with their help we may at least delay the march of the expedition until you arrive with your force. Had we 200 we could effect immediately what you and I wish."

There was no misunderstanding these words, and, for the safety of all concerned, it was necessary to take severe measures. Power seems by this time to have passed out of the hands of Emin Pasha. He neither could nor would act and, having, during his long governorship of the Equatorial Province, never inflicted the extreme penalty of martial law, it was hopeless now to attempt to persuade him to perform a duty so imperative as that which Mr. Stanley, after trying Rehan, an old servant of his, but now the principal ringleader among the conspirators and deserters, proceeded to carry out. The finding of the Court being that he was guilty of murder, theft, and of a plot against his superior officers and the expedition generally, and of having, by disseminating lies about Mr. Stanley's conduct during the march to and from the Aruwhimi, done his best to prevent the troops and people from going with him, he was sentenced to death, and forthwith hanged and his corpse left to the hyænas.

This necessary severity had a most desirable effect upon the future discipline of the motley company which Mr. Stanley was convoying to the Indian Ocean. During the early years of his government Emin was a model governor. So long as communication was open with the rest of the Soudan a harsh disciplinarian was not necessary. Emin accordingly devoted most of this time to improving the social condition of the people and developing the resources of the country he had been sent to govern. But when the Equatorial Province got closed-in in the manner described in the early part of this chapter, Emin's hand was no longer strong enough for its government. Month by month, as it became more and more evident to the Egyptians that they were isolated from the world at large, their discipline grew laxer and laxer, until at the time Mr. Stanley arrived he was amazed to see the very unmilitary freedom which Emin permitted his officers. Instead of promptly obeying every order transmitted to them, they would actually discuss its merits and carry it out or not as it suited their own purpose best. Some of Arabi's officers were amongst them, and since Gordon's death they had lived in an almost unchecked licence. They were, we have seen, even in mutiny more than once. But from that day forward the march of the expedition to the sea was one of absolutely unbroken peacefulness, so far as Emin's people were concerned.

Emin as a governor.

EMIN PASHA.
(From a Photograph.)

UNYORO VILLAGE.
(*From a Photograph by R. Buchta.*)

CHAPTER III.

FROM THE NILE LAKES TO THE INDIAN OCEAN: AN IRRESOLUTE RULER.

Emin's Motives for Leaving the Equatorial Province—The March Begun—Fadl el Mulla and Selim Bey—Attack by Kabba Rega's Men—The Semliki River—The "Mountains of the Moon"—Lake Albert Edward—Beatrice Gulf—The Salt Lake—A Grateful People—New Prolongation of Victoria Nyanza—Mackay's Mission—Unfriendly Folk—Prejudice Against the Blacks—Pot and Kettle—Arms and Civilisation—Mpwapwa—French Missionaries—Dr. Peters—Sore News for Him—Wars and Rumours of War—Champagne and Hams at Simbamwenni—American Newspaper Correspondents—Scenes in Camp and on the March—At Bagamoyo—The Roll-call—Losses—Gains—Drummond's "Africa" and Stanley—Geographical Discoveries—The Great Forest—New Nile Source—More Accurate Outline of the Nile Lakes—Ruwenzori—It and its Fellow Peaks—The "Mountains of the Moon" Question—A Qualified Failure—An Apology for Selim Bey—His After Conduct—What Befell Emin at Bagamoyo and Beyond—His Travels—His Rumoured Death—A Comedy of Errors—The Aftermath of the Expedition—The Last of the Equatorial Province—Captain Trivier's Journey.

THE motives which eventually decided Emin Pasha to abandon his much-loved Province have been frequently canvassed, and our means for arriving at an opinion on the subject are not helped by the very contradictory reasons which the Pasha has himself given for leaving after he declared he would not leave. He assured Dr. Peters, for instance, that he did not go of his own free will, but was absolutely forced by Mr. Stanley to take the step which he did. On the other hand, he informed the correspondent of an American newspaper,* who met him at Bagamoyo, that he relinquished his position in Equatorial Africa solely because this was the order of his liege lord, the Khedive of Egypt. Then, a few minutes later, forgetting the reasons he had assigned for entering upon

* Stevens, "Scouting for Stanley in East Africa." p. 275.

so important a step, he explained that it was simply the desire to put his daughter, Ferida (a child of five years, by an Abyssinian mother), in a family where she could receive a suitable education that prompted him to leave Equatoria for the ocean. In truth, Emin could not help himself; and, in spite of his various reasons for leaving and not desiring to leave, Lieutenant Stairs was probably right when he declared that the Pasha—who was a charming companion round the camp fire, where he unburdened himself freely—quite realised the necessity for evacuating Equatoria. He had done so just in time, though he always felt keen regret at being compelled to take such a step, since all his work would consequently go for nothing.*

The march of so large a caravan was necessarily slow, and enabled laggers or deserters from Emin's stations to overtake it on the way. Among those who joined it were several couriers from Selim Bey, and a Coptic clerk, who gave terrible news of the disorder and strife created by rival leaders among the rebels. Fadl el Mulla "Bey," an officer not of such high rank as Selim Bey, but, seemingly, of greater alacrity, had seized the opportunity of the latter being asleep at Wadelai to take possession of all the stores, assume a higher military rank, and depart to the Makaraka country, with fully half the troops and the greater portion of the ammunition. It appeared, however, though now and then stragglers from Wadelai and the neighbouring stations overtook the caravan, that Mr. Stanley had seen the last of Emin Pasha's rebel officers.

<small>Fadl el Mulla and Selim Bey.</small>

Indeed, as they approached the territories of Kabba Rega, King of Unyoro, neither Selim Bey nor his rival would care to follow the caravan into so dangerous a region. The first day the expedition entered that country they were attacked by a band of the Wara-Sura, or soldiers of Unyoro, many of them armed with excellent breech-loaders, Remingtons,

<small>Attack by Kabba Rega's people.</small>

Sharps, Winchesters, Sniders, and Martini-Henrys, and double-barrelled, large-bore game rifles, which they had obtained from the Arab traders, who had for the last fourteen or fifteen years frequented the country in large numbers for the purchase of ivory, slaves, and other commodities, which the king refused to sell for any other articles of barter than lethal weapons. The sharp defeat that this horde experienced cleared the country in advance for some distance. Until the Semliki, the river which unites Albert Edward and Albert Lakes, was reached, very little was seen of these marauding guerillas.

Here, however, an attack was made upon Mr. Stanley's people as they were being ferried across the river, though without any other effect than causing the robbers again to flee from the presence of their new enemies.

After crossing the Semliki, the expedition entered the Awamba region, and each day's march led them through an almost entirely new country, with which Emin, notwithstanding his long residence in the vicinity of Albert Nyanza, was utterly unacquainted, and which Mr. Stanley, on his former expedition, had equally missed exploring. In the country between the two lakes a splendid range of snow-capped mountains, called the Ruwenzori or Ruwenjura, rising to a height of from 17,000 to 19,000 feet above the sea, burst upon their view as the mist surrounding their summits cleared away. From this range of mountains endless streams flow into the river Semliki, bearing down mud from the volcanic sides of the range, which mud again is fast shoaling up the lakes into which it is carried. This range of mountains was perhaps the most interesting of all the discoveries made by Mr. Stanley during this expedition. He himself, indeed, claims for it a high place among his discoveries. He is enthusiastic as regards the scene of this snow-capped range of mountains in equatorial lands. The snow mountains were, however, very coy and hard to see. "On most days," he tells us, "it loomed up,

<small>"The Mountains of the Moon."</small>

---

* "From Albert Nyanza to the Indian Ocean" (*Nineteenth Century*, 1891, p. 962).

impending over us like a storm-cloud, ready to dissolve in rain and ruin on us. Near sunset a peak or two here, a crest there, a ridge beyond, white with snow, shot into view— jagged clouds whirling and eddying round them, and then the darkness of night. Often at sunrise, too, Ruwenzori would appear, fresh, clean, brightly pure; profound blue voids above and around it; every line and dent, knoll and turret-like crag deeply marked and clearly visible; but presently all would be buried under mass upon mass of mist, until the immense mountain was no more visible than if we were thousands of miles away. And then, also, the Snow Mountain being set deeply in the range, the nearer we approached the base of the range the less we saw of it, for higher ridges obtruded themselves and barred the view."*

In the valley of the river Semliki the natives build their huts at a considerable elevation— dwellings of these tribes, known as the Wakonju, being seen as high as 8,000 feet above the sea. After tramping so long through steaming lowlands and dank tropical forests, an eager desire seemed to seize Mr. Stanley's officers to climb these African Alps. Even Emin Pasha—who did not usually waste much time over such frivolities as Alpinism, being more intent on examining the plants and animals of the country, and the habits and customs of the natives among whom they travelled—was attacked by the prevailing mania. He did not, however, manage to get higher than 1,000 feet above the camp; but Lieutenant Stairs reached a height of 10,677 feet above the sea, only to have the

* Stanley's "Letters," p. 132.

MAKARAKA NATIVE.
(From a Photograph by R. Buchta.)

mortification of finding two deep gulfs between him and the snowy peak. He was, nevertheless, at this lofty elevation, surprised to find himself among Alpine plants. Among the specimens collected by him, Mr. Stanley speaks of giant heather (*Erica arborea*), blackberries (*Rubus*), and blaeberries (*Vaccinium*).

By-and-by, after passing a grassy plain, the very duplicate of that which is seen at the extremity of Albert Nyanza, the expedition reached the lake which Mr. Stanley had discovered in 1877. This, out of compliment to the Prince of Wales, had been named Albert Edward Nyanza. Compared with Victoria, Tanganyika, and Nyassa, it is a small sheet of water, the importance of which lies in the fact that it is the recipient of all the streams at the extremity of the south-western or left Nile basins, and discharges these waters by one river, the Semliki, into Albert Nyanza, just as Victoria Nyanza is the recipient of all the streams at the extremity of the south-eastern, or right Nile basin, and, in its turn, pours its waters by the Victoria Nile through the northern end of Albert Nyanza. Some still more recent discoveries, with which the name of Emin Pasha is linked, show that even Albert Edward Nyanza is not the ultimate source of the Nile in this direction, but that to a stream flowing into its southern end must be accorded that distinction (Vol. II., p. 6). A western prolongation of the lake—Beatrice Gulf—may, indeed, be described as a separate lake joined to Albert Edward by a narrow neck or river. It is known to the natives as the Rusango, Ruisambe, Kafuru, or

Ransakara, while the main lake is called the Mwutan-nzigé (or "Barrier to Locusts"). At one time the Beatrice Gulf must have spread to a great distance. Mr. Stanley describes the plain as perfectly flat and far-stretching, with tongues of water projecting far inland, until the hills of Toro come in view. Except at the north-west end of Albert Edward, there is no swamp. Here dense jungle and impenetrable bush afford, according to Captain Lugard's observations, a home for great herds of elephants. It is at this point that the rivers Wami and Mpanga, into which the countless streams from Ruwenzori flow, discharge their waters into the lake. The gorge through which the latter flows is very picturesque, especially during the rainy seasons, the great body of water confined within its rocky walls boiling and eddying over the sunken rocks below. The gorge itself is about 700 feet deep, and full of tropical vegetation—orchids, ferns, and mosses being found in all the luxuriance of a huge natural forcing-house, always enveloped in a damp, hot atmosphere.*

Though the native name of Albert Edward Nyanza is usually given as Mwutan-nzigé, the same name is applied to various lakes in this part of the country (Vol. II., p. 5); so that, for the sake of distinction, this sheet of water is likely to bear the name bestowed upon it by its discoverer.

Mr. Stanley now marched round the northern half of this lake through Usongora. Close to Albert Edward Nyanza he discovered Katwé, a salt lake two miles long and three-quarters of a mile wide, containing brine of a pinky colour, which deposits salt in solid crystals upon every object in its vicinity. The collection and sale of this salt is a lucrative business to the tribes near it, since caravans come from far and near for this most valued commodity in African life.

Salt lake.

The advance of Mr. Stanley's caravan into Usongora was therefore incidentally of great importance to the salt collectors; for it drove

* Lugard. *Proceedings Royal Geographical Society,* December, 1892, p. 836.

the Unyoro raiders from this region, which, previous to his arrival, they had dominated in a ruthless manner. The tribes of Ukonju, Usongora Toro, Uhaiyana, and Unyampaka and Ankori, were, indeed, so conscious of this service rendered to them, that the march of the expedition through these countries was a triumph, during which endless courtesies were extended to them by old and young, by king, chief, and peasant, all anxious to express their gratitude to the white men for ridding them of the robbers whom they had so long feared. This was fortunate for the travellers; for, had so populous a country as Ankori been unfriendly, their journey might have been seriously impeded; but with the removal of the obstructions placed by the Wanyoro around the valuable salt deposits of the salt lakes near Albert Edward Nyanza, these deposits were opened up to all comers. Hence, while Mr. Stanley's party slowly tramped through the land, flotillas were hastily despatched by the tribes round Albert Nyanza to be freighted with valuable cargoes of salt—an article much needed by the pastoral people of the lake, on account of their immense herds of cattle. Even as far as Karagwe this relief from the presence of the Wanyoro was felt with equally happy effect on the fortunes of the travellers, for on the south-west frontier of the kingdom the expedition was supplied with grain, bananas, and cattle, voluntarily contributed by a grateful king and people. When it is remembered that Mr. Stanley's party consisted of 800 souls, who, in ordinary circumstances, would have needed forty bales of cloth and twenty sacks of beads as currency to buy food for a single day, the value of these gifts may be readily appreciated.

On the 28th of August, after a long march over grassy plains, they arrived at Usambiro (p. 60), Mr. Mackay's mission station at the south end of Victoria Nyanza, after a journey which Mr. Stanley characterises as one of the most peaceful and happy any expedition ever made in Africa. Eight days before, they had sighted

Mr. Mackay's mission station.

OFFICERS OF THE EMIN PASHA RELIEF EXPEDITION.

Victoria Nyanza, glittering in the morning sunlight, its island-dotted expanse reminding those who had seen them of the Canadian lakes. Here it was found that the Nyanza stretched into a deep bay, which brought it thirty miles nearer Tanganyika than had been hitherto known. At this hospitable oasis of civilisation in the heart of pagandom, the expedition halted until the invalids of the party had sufficiently recovered to proceed, the march of 720 miles to the coast not being resumed till the 16th of September. Their three weeks' stay was a time of pleasant intercourse with the kindly inmates of the mission, one of whom death was soon to claim. All day the members of the expedition, long severed from civilisation, revelled in books and in the news of the busy world. They heard of dead kings and of governments which had gone in and come out since last they had received tidings from the land of light, and, what concerned them more, of the Germans fighting with the Arabs in the newly-acquired domains along the Zanzibar coast. But, best of all, they obtained from Mr. Mackay a few pairs of those hobnailed boots of which all of them had been for some time past in sore need.

Led by one of the mission people, the road through Nera was taken; but, unfortunately, the friendliness of the people was less marked than that of the tribes among whom they had already travelled. Only four days from the mission station there were tussles Unfriendly folk: the Usukuma. with the Usukuma, who objected to the small amount of "hongo," customs, black-mail, or tribute —call it what you will—which the expedition offered to pay for passing through their country. Being now provided with firearms, the attacks of these surly savages put the caravan in a critical position, as the region was an open, sandy desert, in which a defensive position was difficult to take up: for the women and children had to be placed in the centre of a square, which offered an easy mark for the enemy. Another cause for the hostility shown was sufficiently amusing. The natives, it is said, took such an unaccountable prejudice to the Soudanese of the Equatorial Province for their intense black colour and the ugly scars on their cheeks, that out of mere spite they attacked the column on its arrival near the king's village.

Usukuma is exceedingly populous and the people are warlike and courageous. They are also accustomed to caravans, though, as their demands are generally complied with, there is seldom much trouble with them. However, one Arab caravan had been recently massacred because the chief refused to yield to the extortionate demands made on him. Still more recently, two missionaries—Messrs. Ashe and Walker—were imprisoned until they were ransomed by their friends. With these experiences in their memories, the Usukuma probably imagined that all they had to do was to rush on Mr. Stanley's expedition and see it collapse. In this expectation they were speedily disappointed, for the attack was promptly resented, though for five days the incensed tribesmen gathered in immense numbers and disputed every mile of advance through their territory. Not unfrequently they rushed by hundreds on either flank of the column, to within 120 yards of the riflemen; but, though wonderfully active, the breech-loaders restrained them from reaching the line of march. Nevertheless, with the exception of one man killed with a spear during a brief parley, no casualties occurred to the caravan; and, after seeing the hopelessness of struggling with the new-comers—and with the Maxim gun—they made off, amid the derision of the Soudanese women, and the column, entering a friendly territory, arrived at the German station of Mpwapwa without any other incident of a notable character, save the frequent want of water. Lieutenant Stairs noted that since the strange social revolution which had taken place in Africa of late years, the weapons of the natives are undergoing an equally remarkable transformation. Most of them have obtained firearms from the traders, and, in spite of the agreement among the European nations not to permit the importation of gunpowder, are still obtaining them; while those who have to depend on weapons less lethal are discarding the light throwing-spear or assegai for the heavier stabbing one. This has entirely altered the fighting tactics of these tribes, just as the adoption of the magazine rifle must alter those of civilised armies.

On arriving in Southern Usukuma the expedition had been overtaken by couriers from the French mission of Bukumbi, on Lake Victoria, who bore a letter from the Bishop, Mgr. Livinhac, who solicited protection and escort to the coast for two sick missionaries, Fathers Girault and Schynze, a favour which was immediately granted,* and the column slackened its marches to allow the new-comers to overtake them at Ikungu. Then its somewhat motley character was increased by the addition of two Algerian Fathers to its number. Already it included representatives of England, Germany, France, Italy, and Egypt, and from almost every district between Usukuma and Mpwapwa accessions of Africans who were afraid to travel to the coast by themselves, or dreaded oppression by the way, solicited permission to join the expedition, until it amounted to upwards of 1,000 people.

At Mpwapwa, also, the expedition fell in with Dr. Carl Peters, who had been engaged, though less successfully, on a mission somewhat similar to that from which Mr. Stanley was now returning triumphant. For while the leader of the German Emin Pasha Rescue party had been unable even to reach the Pasha's country, he learned at this point from the mouth of his countryman the indubitable fact that not only had Emin left Equatoria, but that the treaties the German traveller had been making so industriously with the chiefs through whose country he passed were, owing to the arrangements for the division of East Africa between Germany and Great Britain, of no more value than waste paper. These facts ought to be taken into account in assessing the unfriendly criticisms of Dr. Peters at their true value.

During Mr. Stanley's three years' absence in "Darkest Africa" many events had been happening. Among these were the frictions between the whites and the natives of Zanzibar coast territory consequent on a change of masters, and the alterations in manners which they had introduced. On their way to the interior, gossip regarding these incidents had naturally considerably altered. Hence, long before reaching Mpwapwa, rumour, much exaggerated, was busy with events in progress nearer the coast. Stories of missionaries murdered and mission houses burned, of German officers killed, and seaside towns levelled to the ground in retaliation, were the burden of the tales brought by every passing caravan, until, Mr. Stanley tells us, it seemed to the returning travellers that the savagedom of the wild interior of the continent was more acceptable, judging from the tidings related to them, than the barbarism of the semi-civilised coast. Yet at Mpwapwa, they had unfortunately before their eyes tangible results of the war of which the echoes had reached them, in the ruined house of the Church Missionary Society and the dilapidated fort of the bankrupt German East Africa Company, which the German officers had arrived to rebuild. So that, in spite of exaggerations which the news had assumed in travelling from east to west, there could be little doubt that the stories told them were not mere fabrications.

Near Sinbamwenni their journey might almost be said to have come to an end, for here the expedition was met with a supply of European comforts—hams, champagne, and cigars—despatched to them by Major Wissmann, familiar to us as a traveller across Africa, but then German Imperial Commissioner; and from this point the returning travellers were almost daily gladdened with

---

* Father Schynze, a German, repaid the kindness extended to him by a book—"Journal de voyage: À travers l'Afrique avec Stanley et Emin-Pacha," 1890—of extremely ill-natured and, it seems to us, quite unjustifiable criticism of Mr. Stanley and all his works.

kindly notes and friendly gifts from their friends in Zanzibar and Bagamoyo.

At this place also Mr. Stanley was met by the ubiquitous American newspaper correspondents, bearing goodwill-offerings of tooth-brushes, soap, and Florida water. One of these, in his eagerness to tap the news with which Mr. Stanley was laden, had been far

Approaching the journey's end: appearance of the caravan.

belonged figured on some member of the party, and not a few of them were clad in the nakedness which is the daily garb of the greater number of the African people. Thirty or forty men of the expedition had been rewarded with flaming red blankets as robes of honour for good service, and had been promoted by Mr. Stanley to the office of carrying his tent and personal effects. The commander him-

C.M.S. STATION OF USAMBIRO, WHERE STANLEY STAYED WITH MACKAY.*
(From a sketch by Bishop Tucker, made from the door of the room where Mackay died.)

into the Masai country, expecting that the return column would have taken that route. Mr. Stevens—the enterprising gentleman in question—describes the expedition, as he saw it just before its breaking up, as extremely picturesque. Out of the disorder of the start,† good order had long ago been evolved. Nearly one thousand people defiled along the winding African path in Indian file. Every costume seen in those parts of Africa to which they

self rode a very good donkey, which was in charge of a young man with a red turban, red knee-breeches, and a red shirt, and who seemed fully conscious of the exalted position to which he had, by his personal merits, attained. Behind the donkey streamed the great explorer's special corps, with boxes, tents, and other articles on their heads, and each with a red blanket proudly trailing at his heels. This scarlet brigade—

* The shed to the right was Mackay's workshop; the door to the left leads to the dining-room and library.
† Stairs, l.c., p. 956.

with Mr. Stanley and his donkey—hurried along, passing the others as a fast train passes a slow one, and easily reached the camp in advance. If the sun were shining, Mr. Stanley hoisted up a greenish umbrella. The plucky surgeon had, indeed, never ridden a step of the way across Africa. Two steady servants carried Emin Pasha's little girl in a litter; and among the Egyptian and mongrel women, some rode donkeys,

OBJECTS FROM ZANZIBAR, MOMBASA, ETC.
(Collected by Miss Mary A. Wardlaw Ramsay. Photographed by Dr. Felkin, Edinburgh.)

The rest of the folk were divided into companies, over one of which an officer had command and was responsible for certain goods.

Of the Europeans—besides Mr. Stanley—Emin Pasha, Captain Casati, Mr. Jephson, and Mr. Bonny rode donkeys, but Captain Nelson, Lieutenant Stairs, and Dr. Parke walked. some walked, and some were conveyed on stretchers. Men and women bore infants on their shoulders, though not always, for one of the saddest sights of the whole march was poor little children, of six or seven years old, footsore and weary, hobbling along and crying all the time to be carried. Thirsty, hungry and tired, limping, as thorns ran into their feet, they wailed piteously as they now and then lost sight of their mothers. Jostled and pushed by rude, brutish men, who wished them dead and out of the way, the lot of these little travellers from the Equatorial Province deserved the deepest pity.

Every person seemed to be carrying something, though much had been thrown away in the course of the long tramp, and a great deal more had been left behind at the rendezvous on Albert Nyanza. The people, indeed, seemed to have had the most primitive ideas of the necessities of travel; for, if Mr. Stanley had permitted them to carry one-half of the rubbish with which they came laden to his camp, he would have required thousands of porters to carry the baggage of his refugees. Then, in addition to the numbers of his caravan proper, there were Wanyamwezi porters bringing ivory. They had joined the caravan for safety. Emin's Egyptian officers formed a prominent portion of this strangely-assorted caravan; for all of them were accompanied by their families (when they had any), and by their native wives belonging to numerous tribes and of every degree of blackness. Many of these ladies were in the primitive dresses of their countries and tribes, while others, more coquettish, wore an approach to the Egyptian costume.

At the Kingani Ferry the expedition was met by a deputation of Europeans from Bagamoyo, and there, for the first time for nearly three years, did any member of the party—and indeed not for a much longer period had the greater number of them been able to—sit down to a table furnished with the luxuries to which they had hitherto been strangers. In a few hours more Bagamoyo, on the coast, was reached and the responsibilities of Mr. Stanley were at an end.

The Zanzibaris were now in their own homes, and the Soudanese soldiers would in due time be mustered into their regiments in Egypt. The Egyptians would at the same time reach their homes and be assigned to other duties than those which they had fulfilled for so many years, while the Europeans would, in the course of the next few days, separate to every point of the compass. According to the roll-call at Kavalli's on the 15th April, 1889, 570 refugees from the Equatorial Province had placed themselves under Mr. Stanley's protection for convoy to the sea. By July 2nd this number had been reduced by desertions to 555; by August 15th, to 414; by October 1st to 311; and now, on the 4th of December, only 290 souls answered "Here" in Bagamoyo. Thus the loss on the journey from Albert Nyanza to the sea was 280, nearly one-half, during the journey of 1,400 miles. Of these 280 missing people the commander calculated that about 200 had been cared for by various native chiefs through whose territories they passed, and at whose villages they felt too sick, with the prevalent ulcers, to proceed. It did not, however, necessarily follow that the whole of the 200 were invalids. For when the head of a family could not travel any farther, his wife, children, and servants preferred to stay with him. The remainder died from fevers, ulcers, fatigue, and debility; and one old lady, the mother of the vakeel of the Equatorial Province, expired from sheer old age. When she began her last journey she was eighty years of age, so that it is not improbable she has the distinction of having been the oldest civilised traveller in Africa.

The journey ended: the roll-call.

Of the thirteen Somalis engaged by Major Barttelot at Aden only one survived the journey; of the sixty Soudanese enlisted at Cairo no more than twelve returned to the coast, seven having already been sent back from Yambuya: of the remainder two suffered the death-penalty for mutiny and murder, and one deserted. Of the 620 Zanzibaris, 225 were all that were welcomed by their friends at home. Fifty-five of them had been killed in the skirmishes between Yambuya and Albert Nyanza. Two suffered capital punishment for selling their rifles and ammunition to the enemy, 202 died of starvation, ulcers, dysentery, and exhaustion, and the rest of this lamentable tale of loss is made up by desertions.

Altogether, the last of Mr. Stanley's expeditions in Africa was the greatest in which he had taken part. It was accomplished with an energy and a skill which cannot be too highly praised, though, unfortunately, its end was not attained without a loss of life unknown in the annals of African exploration. Organised for purposes entirely apart from geographical exploration, the discoveries which it was fortunate enough to make will compare with those of any previous expedition. In the first place, it passed over about 1,200 miles of unknown region, and proved that east to north and north to east of the Congo there exists—as might have been expected—an immense area (p. 32) covered by one unbroken, dense forest, very different from any of the wooded country found in most other parts of the continent. A popular writer, who has himself visited Africa, namely, Professor Drummond, describing the general features of the scenery of the region about the Zambesi and Shiré, which he examined, remarks:—"The fairy labyrinth of ferns and palms, the festoons of climbing-plants blocking the paths and scenting the forests with their resplendent flowers, the gorgeous cloud of insects, the gaily-plumaged birds, the paroquets, the monkey swinging from his trapeze in the shady bowers—these are unknown in Africa."* Mr. Stanley, in criticising this passage, takes complete exception to its accuracy, so far as that great area which he traversed for thirteen months is concerned; for the progress of the expedition was through a dense undergrowth of bush and ambitious young trees which choked the space beneath the impervious shade of the forest giants. Here almost every open space was matted by arums, phrynia, and amoma, interlaced by endless lines of calamus, and still further blocked by great cable-like convolvuli, so that not unfrequently it was difficult to make 400 yards

margin: The gains and losses of the expedition; the forest.

* "Tropical Africa" (1888), p. 54.

in an hour. A way for the column to pass had actually to be tunnelled through this dense mass of vegetation. The Amazon Valley cannot boast a more impervious or more umbrageous forest than this vast tangle of the Upper Congo, nourished as it is by eleven months of tropical showers.

Another discovery of the greatest interest was the source of the south-western branch of the White Nile. We now know that the White Nile is formed by the surplus waters of two lakes, Victoria and Albert Edward to the south-east and south-west respectively, which are received by Lake Albert and discharged northwards towards the Mediterranean by the great Bahr-el-Abiad, or White River. Hitherto, the source of the water of Lake Albert was a puzzle, as no great river was known to pour into it; the Semliki not having been detected even by Mason Bey, the lake was still open to be regarded as a backwater (Vol. II., pp. 5, 115).

margin: Nile lakes and new Nile source.

To Mr. Stanley's explorations we are also indebted for the exact definition of the Albert and Albert Edward Lakes, both of them contained within the Nile basin and constituting sources of that famous river.

Finally, the discovery of the snowy Ruwenzori—possibly the Mount Gordon Bennett of his former expedition—which furnishes the waters that flow into the Semliki River and Albert Edward Lake, is a discovery of the first importance to geography. At the same time, it is open to doubt whether Mr. Stanley's conclusion that these were the "Mountains of the Moon." known to Ptolemy and the early chartographers as situated near the source of the Nile where the pigmies lived, and which derived their name from their semi-lunar shape, is well sustained. It must at the same time be allowed that the discoverer of Ruwenzori has made out an excellent case for the theory which he adopts. On the old maps they were generally figured as a high range crossing the entire continent from Abyssinia to the Gulf of Guinea. As

margin: Ruwenzori and the "Mountains of the Moon."

modern enterprise has opened up Africa, this mythical range had to disappear, and the Mountains of the Moon were then identified in Abyssinia, in the snow-capped Kenia, and Kilimanjaro, or as the so-called Kong Mountains inland from the Gulf of Guinea. The latest claimant has, on the whole, the most plausible facts in support of it. Dr. Peters and other explorers, however, place no moment by Mr. Stanley's conclusion, though, on the other hand, the German traveller's rival theory is even less acceptable. Dr. Peters affirms that the ancient maps reproduced by Mr. Stanley*

DR. CARL PETERS.
(From a Photograph by W. Hoffert, Dresden.)

"flatly contradict his hypothesis, as they one and all place the Mountains of the Moon south of Lake Victoria."† Unyamwezi is the "Land of the Moon," and, as the mountains of the country, as seen from the east, are crescent-shaped, it is, he thinks, possible that the name may be derived from this circumstance. At all events, he is not quite convinced of the magnitude of Mr. Stanley's researches in ancient history. Dr. Baumann, a later traveller, entertains a kindred theory. According to him, the real Mountains of the Moon are in Urundi, within the German sphere of influence—in the shape of the precipitous and wooded hills which form the water-shed between the basin of the Rufizi and the Kagera (Alexandra Nile)—the latter river not rising in a lake, but at the base of the hills in question. This chain is known to the natives as "The Mountains of the Moon," and is held in peculiar reverence by them, owing to a pious tradition attaching to it. Their kings are regarded as descendants of the moon, and return to it. One of these monarchs—Mwezi ‡—was killed in battle about a generation ago, and a large share of Dr. Baumann's welcome was due to the simple natives believing him a descendant of this lunar potentate. Their respect extended even to the white donkey of the white man, who, they had come to the conclusion, was a visitor from the moon. In an ancient wood close by the Mountains of the Moon the Warundi (or natives of Urundi) used to celebrate the funeral rites of the Mwezi, whom they buried upon the summit of the Ganzo Kulu, or peak which rises above the rest of the range.

Mr. Ravenstein, a geographer whose eminence even those who differ from him on questions of Ptolemaic geography must admit, is quite as certain as Dr. Peters that Ruwenzori has nothing to do with Ptolemy's Mountains of the Moon, and that no mountains answering to their description are to be found in the locality indicated by the old Alexandrian geographer. To apply that name to those discovered by Mr. Stanley "is really asking too much." §

Mr. Cooley, a geographical commentator of greater boldness than success, went even so far as to suggest that the Mountains of the Moon are described in a passage which is an interpolation of later date and forms no part

* "In Darkest Africa," Vol. II., pp. 267-288.
† "New Light on Dark Africa," p. 419.

‡ "Mwezi," or "Moon," is mentioned by Burton, Journal Royal Geographical Society, 1859, p. 278; Geographical Journal, 1893, p. 228. The hypothesis advocated by Peters is, however, by no means his own; it is a suggestion from Beke, who broached it as early as 1846, though at a later date he looked for the Mountains of the Moon on the eastern edge of the African plateau and assumed that the Nile had its origin on their inward slopes.
§ Scottish Geographical Magazine, 1891, p. 306.

THE MOUNTAINS OF THE MOON.

of the genuine text of Ptolemy.* This is, perhaps, too sweeping a criticism. For though many of his immediate followers are silent with regard to the "Montes Lunae," nearly all of the Arab geographers have something to say about a Jebel Komr (Gumr), or El Kamar—the Green or Lunar Mountain—shadowing the head-waters of the Nile. But none of these writers knew the exact position of the Nile lakes, and Ptolemy did not possess any itineraries to guide him. He wrote merely from descriptions or from the rumours that reached him through traders or through slaves from the interior. In short, considering the vagueness of Ptolemy's geography and the necessity for admitting that in the second century of the Christian era Sir Samuel Baker and Mr. Stanley himself were anticipated by unknown travellers, it is, on the whole, safer to accept the conclusion that the Ruwenzori range is the Mountains of the Moon simply as the pious belief of its modern discoverer.

The tribes with whom Mr. Stanley came in contact during the expedition thus happily ended were of such interest that unavailing regret must be entertained at the absence from his party of any scientific men capable of studying the languages and other points of interest connected with these people. The light-bronze-coloured aborigines of the forest region, the various tribes of dwarfs found in the same jungle, the high-featured people of the pastoral regions (sprung, it is believed, from the Amharic of Abyssinia), and the

The tribes seen.

MOMBASA: THE ROAD TO UGANDA.
(From a Photograph taken for the Imperial British East Africa Company.)

aboriginal races among whom they are settled as masters, open up questions of prime importance, from an ethnological point of view.†

Unfortunately, however, the object for

* "Claudius Ptolemy and the Nile" (1854), pp. 77–98.

† Stanley, "Geographical Results of the Emin Pasha Relief Expedition" (*Proceedings of the Royal Geographical Society*, 1890, pp. 313 *et seqq.*).

which Mr. Stanley's expedition was fitted out, and in accomplishing which such fearful sacrifices were endured, was the least successful portion of his great adventure. Emin, no doubt, was brought to the coast, with a certain portion of his officers and people; but more than half of the Egyptian troops and officers were abandoned in the Equatorial Province. How far Mr. Stanley was justified in leaving Selim Bey and his friends behind is a point still capable of being debated. From the facts, which at the time seemed to him perfectly conclusive, Mr. Stanley considered the safety of the expedition dependent on his not waiting any longer for Emin's second in command and the troops and camp-followers whom he had returned to Wadelai for the purpose of collecting, and insisted that these laggards had no intention of joining the convoy to the coast. Indeed, Mr. Stanley stated, in the most positive manner, that the sole intention of Selim Bey and his fellow-conspirators was to capture and, if possible, deliver into the hands of the Mahdists, the whole of the expedition, with those whom it had come to rescue (p. 50).

A successful failure.

The data presented to us by Mr. Stanley go far to substantiate this grave conclusion. At the same time, we cannot learn that Emin Pasha—who was better acquainted with the suspected officers than Mr. Stanley, and fully as familiar with all the facts of the case—ever withdrew from the opinion that Selim Bey and his friends had been hardly used; though some of the officers had, no doubt, been in communication with the Mahdi's general. The subsequent fate of the troops thus left behind justifies, to a certain extent, Emin's optimist conclusions. For in June, 1892, a portion of the old Equatorial garrison arrived in Cairo, having travelled under the ægis of the Imperial British East Africa Company from Uganda to Mombasa. They stated that Selim Bey, whose arrival had been delayed by the loss of a steamer, finding that the rescue expedition had gone, settled down with his followers at Kavalli's; while Fadl el Mullah, who had separated from his commander and was avowedly not loyal, remained in the neighbourhood of Wadelai. This place was afterwards attacked by the Dervishes, who were driven off; but most of the garrison, fearing that they could not trust Fadl el Mullah, who was known to have been in communication with Omar Saleh, the Mahdi's general, deserted to Selim Bey.

In 1891 Captain Lugard arrived at Kavalli's from Uganda and, after long debate with Selim Bey, the chief subject of which was who was to be master, took the entire force into Uganda and Unyoro, where most of it afterwards garrisoned the military posts temporarily under the control of the British East Africa Company. Selim was found, even in his isolated position, by no means easy to deal with. He knew his worth, and valued himself accordingly. A man of resolute will, his power over the remains of Emin's troops was absolute, and this absolute power he wished to retain if they accompanied Captain Lugard on the service offered them; and, as the force under Selim was armed with Remingtons and had plenty of ammunition,* it is evident that the Bey had the best of the argument. At last Captain Lugard carried the point. Nothing like treachery was attempted, though Selim's troops largely outnumbered the guard of the English officer. This scarcely bears out Mr. Stanley's description of Selim's character, while the fact that neither he nor his followers had gone over to the Mahdists is still less in keeping with the deep-laid plot to join those fanatics which was in 1890 laid to their charge. "To all appearance, they were intensely loyal to the Khedive; and Selim Bey, pointing to his snow-white hair, said it was not age—for he was not much over forty—which had turned his hair white, but the war and the troubles of the Soudan, through which he had loyally upheld the Effendina's [Khedive's] flag through good repute and ill repute. He would not consent to pledge himself in any

* They had accidentally discovered the boxes of ammunition which Mr. Stanley had buried when it was necessary to make for the coast.

way to me till the Khedive should have given him permission to transfer his allegiance ; nor would he change his flag until the Khedive should himself dispense with his services. ' From a boy till now in my old age,' he said, ' I have served under this flag, and exposed my life many times; nothing in the world shall make me give it up unless the Effendina tells me to.' And if his tale be true, he has, indeed, fought bravely and suffered loyally for it; having been imprisoned by the disloyal rebels and expelled from the country.

CAPTAIN F. D. LUGARD.
(From a Photograph by Elliott and Fry.)

It was a thrilling sight to see the remnant of the troops of the old Equatorial Province march past. Less than half, I was told, were there; the rest had died fighting for their flag. Many had honourable wounds to show. Their banners and flags were tattered and torn; they were clad in long coats made of skins, and their band made strange music with bugles, and drums, and trumpets."* Once under Captain Lugard's authority, with his promise passed that he would ask the Khedive's permission for them to remain permanently in the British service, no men could

* Lugard. *Scottish Geographical Magazine*, 1892, p. 638;
Proceedings of the Royal Geographical Society, 1892, p. 838.
Selim had been with Baker in 1869.

have been braver than this "refuse of the Soudan." They hailed Lugard as their friend, who had delivered them from living among savages to their status as the soldiers of a civilised Power. Though these people do not know what hurry is, they were ready to march, with their wives, children, and slaves— a caravan of not less than 9,000, nearly ten times that of Mr. Stanley—punctually on the day fixed; and ever afterwards, during the long journey through hostile countries and in Uganda, these once rebel troops remained loyal to their new master. Even when the Christian sects in Uganda were cutting each other's throats, they refused to listen to the suggestions of the Mohammedans that now was their time. " No," they replied, " Captain Lugard has saved us in our trouble and when we knew not where to turn, and we will not fight against him. We are his people, and if you fight against us we will attack you in the rear." Yet these Egyptians and Soudanese had been deserted by the Government to which they were now so faithful and denied their back pay by those who spoke in the Khedive's name. Selim Bey, nevertheless, died in the summer of 1893, a prisoner on the way to Mombasa, to answer for his share in a futile Mohammedan insurrection in Uganda, though the Soudanese remained loyal to King M'wanga and his suzerain Queen Victoria.

This brings us to speak of the after conduct of Emin Pasha. "The quest, rescue, and retreat of the Governor of Equatoria" was almost grotesque in the results to which it led. At an enormous sacrifice in men, money, time and toil, an English expedition had penetrated to the heart of Africa for the purpose of succouring the beleaguered ruler of the last of the Egyptian Provinces that had maintained its independence in the Soudan, only to find that neither Emin nor many of his friends had the least desire to be the recipients of the kindnesses thus heaped upon them. So far from being distressed for food or raiment, they were found living in rude plenty, and instead of being either fed or clothed by the expedition which

What befell Emin Pasha.

with such difficulty had reached them, they were able to assist their rescuers out of the abundance at their disposal. Even after Emin and a certain number of his officers had been reluctantly persuaded to make for the coast, a large portion of the force had to be left behind. Indeed, there is nothing more extraordinary in the history of theoretical philanthropy than the fact that Mr. Stanley had to march to the sea in fear lest those he had come to relieve should murder his party or, failing this, deliver them into the cruel slavery

DR. F. STUHLMANN.
(From a Photograph by F. Mewke, Cobourg.)

of the Dervishes from whom they were supposed to be in peril of life and liberty.

Nor did the strangeness between fact and theory end here. For Emin, who for many years of his life had lived scatheless from wild men, fanatics, climate, diseases, and a score of other perils, had scarcely arrived among his countrymen at Bagamoyo before he all but ended his career. On the evening devoted to a banquet in his honour and that of his companions, a grievous accident, owing to his stepping out of an open window, kept him for months lying between death and life. And lastly, Emin, who had been brought to the coast by Britons, and at the cost of British people, instead of expressing any gratitude for the favours thus heaped upon him, no sooner recovered from his accident than he prepared to return whence he had been conveyed with so much dolour.

It was, indeed, difficult to get him past Mr. Mackay's mission station: he seemed to have a morbid dread of approaching civilisation. At Bagamoyo Mr. Stanley and his companions were forgotten, and the people and the nation from whom he had received so much kindness—even admitting his version of the "quest, rescue, and retreat"—were, among his countrymen, the favourite theme of his least friendly criticisms. Once out of their sight, he ceased all correspondence with his 'rescuers": even the good Doctor did not receive the courtesy of one of his many letters. Nor were his "dear people" any more the object of his solicitude. His own accumulated pay was not neglected, though the Khedive—to whom he was so loyal (p. 53) —was treated with something very like insolence by his late servant, and his old comrades were told that, so far as he was concerned, they would have to shift for themselves. For after first agreeing to enter the British service, and then changing his mind, only finally to offer his services once more to the nation which, indeed, he had at one time wished to take the Equatorial Province (p. 74), he accepted a post under the rival German Administration of East Africa. This was not unnatural considering the influence under which Emin now fell; but this last specimen of his irresolution and ingratitude shut the mouths of his friends in Britain.

Then, at the head of an expedition—the exact objects of which have never been explained —he set off for the region from which, according to his gloss of the story, thus briefly recorded, he was **The last travels of Emin Pasha.** taken by Mr. Stanley so entirely against his will. Accompanied for part of the journey by Dr. Stuhlmann, he reached and explored the south end of Lake Albert Edward, the rivers running into which flow through plains dotted with lofty volcanic cones—Kisigali, the highest, being 13,000 feet above the sea—

the most distant of them (Virunyo Viagongo) being reported to be still active. The whole region, swarming with rhinoceroses, affords a splendid field for future exploration. The most southern part of the lake lies at the present time at 0° 45′ south latitude, but it varies much according to the wetness or dryness of the season; and the natives declare, as is evident from the flats around it (p. 56), that Lake Albert Edward is, like so many of the African sheets of water, gradually diminishing in size.

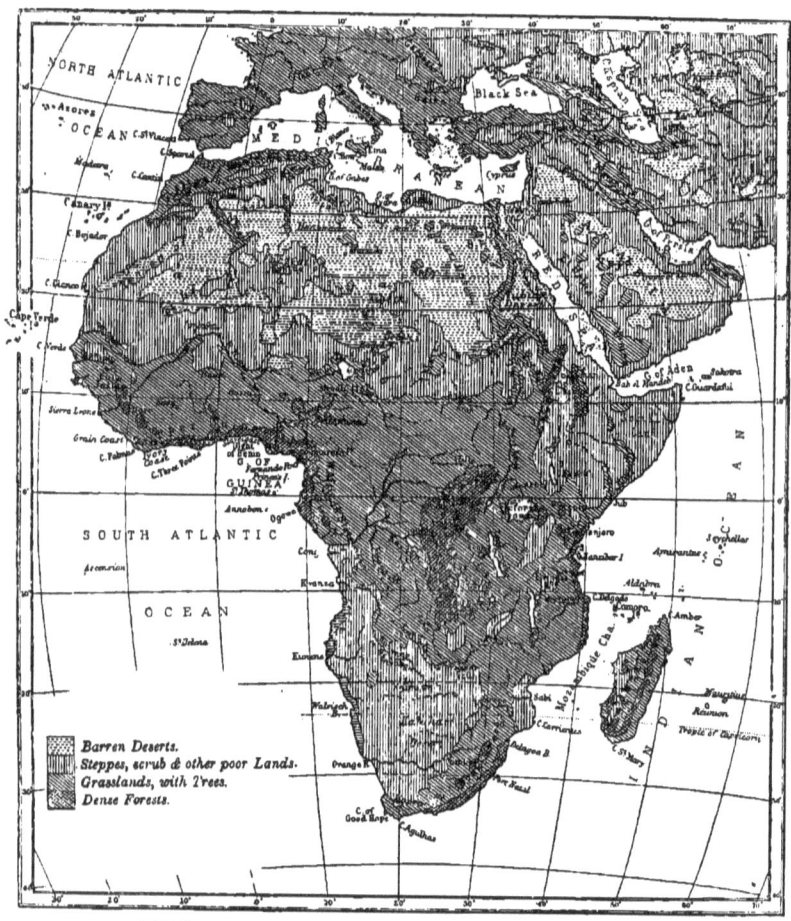

MAP SHOWING THE ZONES OF VEGETATION IN AFRICA. (By E. G. Ravenstein.)

The Semliki, when it leaves the lake, is known as the Isango, and for some distance flows amid virgin forests. On the steppe beyond the forest, elephants, not seen since leaving the coast, were found—a proof of the rapidity with which this animal is disappearing. An examination of Ruwenzori —the splendid Snowy Mountain at the base of which is Karevia—occupied some of the time of the expedition. The following zones of vegetation were made out:— (1) bananas, high grasses, 3,850 to 5,350 feet; (2) colocasia and beans cultivated, high grass, upper limit of settlements, 5,350 to 6,700 feet; (3) deciduous forest, in its upper part heaths, mixed with bamboos, 6,700 to 8,530 feet; (4) heath forest, with bogs, whortleberries, 8,530 to 11,800 feet; (5) bushy heath, *Rhynchopetalum* (6,700 to 12,800 feet), tree ferns, *Senecio* (10,200 to 12,500 feet), *Helichrysum*, a little grass moss, and lichens, 11,800 to 12,500 feet; the snow-line commencing at about 13,000 feet. The Lu or Lulu, which on Mr. Stanley's map is traced to the Ituri, is said to flow into the Semliki, and is therefore a tributary of the Nile. In this region the expedition had, like their predecessors, to encounter some of Kabba Rega's marauders. At Kavalli's Emin tried to persuade his former followers to join him. But when they heard that their "Mudir" had entered the German service, very few of them would go with him, and he had to abandon the notion of entering the Equatorial Province.

After this unsatisfactory meeting with his old soldiers, Emin and his companions explored the Wambuba territory into the grass region of Lendu, and finally to the north through a country watered by numerous deeply-bedded streams, which unite to form the Abumbi, an important source of the Ituri. Finding the Momvu country laid waste by Manyema slave-hunters, they were forced to turn back, in spite of attractive tales of the "great river Tsili" three days' march farther on, of the district of Moba, said to contain much cattle, and then, two or three days yet farther, of "the River Andemari," which must

be the Bomokandi, the head-waters of which are north of those of the Ituri.

The return journey was made through Lenduland to the slope of the table-land of the same name, and then south until the party crossed the Duki at Bilippi, and Undusuma was again reached on the 12th of November, 1891. Here the caravan, exhausted by hunger, wounds, and small-pox, halted for some time. It may be remembered that it consisted, besides Emin's original party, of 126 Soudanese, including women and children, who were among the people who had joined their old master at Undusuma—that is to say, on the Lendu table-land close to Kavalli's, near Lake Albert, a rolling upland from 4,000 to 5,000 feet high, with rounded hills and ridges rising from it, with very steep slopes to the east and west.

Albert Nyanza was found to have continued the shrinking formerly noticed (Vol. II., p. 137) to such an extent that Kassenya and Nyamsasi had become peninsulas, and a number of sand-banks had made their appearance. It was also found that the Semliki flows into the lake much farther to the west than is shown on Stanley's map.

By this time the caravan was in a woful plight. Emin's imperfect eyesight had grown worse and worse, until he was almost blind, and his people were in a dreadful condition from small-pox. They therefore decided to remain in the camp at Undusuma, while Dr. Stuhlmann marched on to Kinyawanga, near the left bank of the Semliki, close to the great forest, and almost on the Equator, there to await Emin's arrival. No tidings of the hapless Pasha being obtainable by the 15th of January, 1892, Dr. Stuhlmann, acting on his instructions, pushed on as fast as possible in the direction of Bukoba, which was reached a month later by the south end of Lake Albert Edward, and a southerly and more difficult route than on the outward journey.

Bantu tribes, distinguished by filing their teeth to a point, inhabit the country as far north as the Ituri river. Non-Bantus, or "negroes" proper, occupy a still larger area, under many tribal names. Finally, the Pigmies inhabit the forests of the Upper Ituri and to the south or west of the Wakonjo, under the various names of Efe (Walese and Momvu), Baiswa (Wavera), Akka (Walumbi), Watua (Wanyoro), Wasumbo (Wakonjo), as well as Wambutti, etc.* Thus Emin's later work as an explorer was more important than any in his long previous career. But since that date no accurate tidings have been obtained regarding him. He became, indeed, almost as sore a trouble to his new masters as he had been to Mr. Stanley.

Vague tales reached us of the Pasha, blind and weary, wandering about with the remnant of his force, making his way westward to the Congo or the Cameroons. But more likely information affirmed that on the 9th of March, 1892—so ran the tidings brought by Arwad Effendi, one of the Kavalli people who had joined him—Emin marched in the direction of the west coast, after having concluded blood-brotherhood with an Arab named Bivana. On the same day Arwad left him to return to Kampala, and stayed twenty-eight days with Kituntzi, a potentate of higher rank than the chieftain Kavalli. On the 1st of April he received from a brother of Masamboni, known from Stanley's description (p. 33), news that some Manyemas, who had bought ivory in his village, had stated that the Pasha and all his people had been murdered and eaten by Manyemas " under Ismail, a Vali of Seyid bin Abid." The same news reached the Tanganyika missionaries, though the dates differed. One of the accounts indicates the murder as having taken place as late as February 26th, 1893, while information obtained by the Congo State expedition against Nyangwe fixes the place of the tragedy near the Lualaba River, between Tanganyika and Nyangwe.

In short, one of the most remarkable results of Mr. Stanley's expedition for "the quest and rescue" of Emin Pasha was the complete change which popular opinion as to

* Stuhlmann, Petermann's *Geographische Mittheilungen*, June, 1892; *Proceedings of the Royal Geographical Society*, August, 1892 (with map).

this famous man underwent. Instead of being distinguished by firmness, he proved himself a miracle of irresolution; and, in lieu of an honest German, frank and straight-forward, all the facts which we possess regarding the late Governor of the Equatorial Province compel us to accept in his place a man who, if originally permeated by a strain of Teutonic truthfulness, must, during his long residence with Orientals, have imbibed something of their duplicity and a great deal of their desire to say to everyone what may please him best. Indeed, if we are to believe Romolo Gessi, Emin was never much better; for that outspoken Italian described him in 1880 as "full of deceit, and without character—pretentious, jealous; a German Jew, he passes for a Turk; a hypocritical person, ridiculously complimentary and cringing in his manner, and capable of deceiving the acutest man in the world." It was this subservience and readiness to obey orders without showing any outward sign of offence for plain language that won Gordon's favour in a country where capable men were few and every man liked to be master. When Vakeel of Lado under Gessi, then Governor of Bahr-el-Ghazel, the Egyptian officers laughed at him for his exaggerated affectation of being a Mussulman. The demoralisation in his province reached such a point that he was reprimanded for permitting the most outrageous abuses, lest he might, as a suspected Christian, be blamed for punishing Mohammedans. Capital punishment was unknown (p. 51). An officer murdered four natives with impunity, and another fiend bound a female slave to a tree, smeared her with honey, and left her to be eaten alive by flies and ants. Yet, as it was not fitting that the life of a Mussulman should be sacrificed for having killed a few unbelieving savages, Emin quashed all inquiry. In short, his abilities as a linguist were amazing; his theoretical notions of government good, but his practice was deplorable: he was physically courageous, but morally a coward.

Mr. Stanley's reception in England was like

the progress of a Royal personage. City after city conferred its freedom upon him. One learned society after another enrolled him among its honorary members, and four universities dubbed him doctor. After being the guest of municipalities, kings, and great private persons, his triumph was fittingly ended by his marriage in Westminster Abbey. The prince—as always happens in the fairytales—wedded the princess, and it is the hope of unnumbered admirers that they may live

AKKA GIRL.
(From a Photograph by R. Buchta.)

happy all their days—but not in Africa. It has, however, always been the fortune of Mr. Stanley, on returning from his African adventures, to be assailed by a legion of rancorous critics. The publication of the narrative of this expedition was the signal for that aftermath of adverse opinion to be reaped. Indeed, so long and so bitterly did the controversy regarding certain crucial questions discussed in the pages of these volumes rage, that the literature of the Stanley expedition before many months grew into a little library. It is not necessary to rehearse the points then at stake. Most of them have already

The aftermath of controversy.

been settled or have been incidentally dismissed in the course of the preceding pages. However, it is essential for the completion of this brief history that one or two of the more prominent should receive some notice before we close this chapter. It may be remembered that when Mr. Stanley returned from his expedition in search of Livingstone, the chief place where he laid himself open to attack was in the acridity with which he assailed the reputation of those differing from him. On this occasion the somewhat ungenerous treatment which he bestowed on the memory of Major Barttelot roused the friends of that officer to combat. This we have already touched upon.

A question of still wider import was Mr. Stanley's treatment of the natives through whose country he had been marching. After his famous descent of the Congo in 1877, it was affirmed by the critics of his conduct on that expedition that by his slaughter of the natives on the river-bank he had introduced a "revolverism" into African exploration which would be bitterly paid for by those who were so unfortunate as to follow in his steps. This, however, was not the case: the savages were taught a lesson. Again, on his return from the Emin Pasha expedition, it was pointed out that no traveller had ever entered Africa with so many followers and no one had ever left it with so few. The distinguished traveller was not only blamed for the carelessness with which he treated the lives of his own companions, but he was loudly stigmatised as a "filibuster," who had marched, shooting and hanging, through the territories of independent princes, and, what was still more serious, through territories under the control of the Congo Free State and of the East Africa Company.

It is impossible to deny that Mr. Stanley's progress had been attended with heavy loss of life, and that some of his proceedings might be described as high-handed. But it must be remembered that no commander, no matter how philanthropic, can be responsible for the climate or for diseases which dog his steps, and that it would have been both foolish and fiendish recklessly to throw away the lives of any of his party and thus leave his expedition stranded in the midst of a savage waste. Nor could it be expected that any men endowed with the most ordinary sense exploration, travellers passed and repassed through the midst of the wildest tribesmen without lifting their hand or having a hand raised against them. The long list of explorers who have fallen before finishing their allotted work is the best answer to this

GRAVE OF CAPTAIN NELSON AT KIKIYU (p. 75).

of self-preservation would calmly hold their hands while their savage enemies were assailing them with poisoned arrows, assegais, and other weapons. If there was to be a reign of peace, it was for *messieurs les sauvages* to begin. Nor is it quite correct to affirm, as has been done more than once, that, previous to Mr. Stanley's advent on the field of African assertion. In the course of these pages we have had again and again to record the death of eminent travellers, from the days of Mungo Park downwards, besides the hostile treatment in the aborigines' country of other explorers more fortunate in returning alive. Even the title of Mr. Stanley's narrative was as suggestive of strictures as that of his earlier volume (Vol. II., p. 260); for there could be no "quest" for a man whose whereabouts was never in doubt, while Emin, not without reason, loudly protested against his return to the coast being regarded as akin to a "rescue and retreat."

Lastly, among the other charges brought, not so much against Mr. Stanley himself as against the promoters of the expedition which he had commanded, was that, under the guise of philanthropy, it had been sent less to succour Emin Pasha, or to rescue his forces from the thrall of the Mahdists, than to secure his services for the British Imperial East Africa Company. It is undeniable that the rescue expedition was organised, and in the main supported, by those who, a few months later, became the leading members of this corporation, and that among the proposals Mr. Stanley laid before Emin Pasha was—if he did not choose to return to Egypt, there to await the orders of the Khedive—that a post would be provided for him as an official of the East Africa Company. The King of the Belgians had also offered Emin a similar position for the purpose of preserving the continuity of his labours in the Equatorial Province, and, by temporarily administering it under the flag of the Congo Free State, to prevent the work of civilisation reared by Emin from falling to wreck and ruin should he leave the country to itself. But the proposal to enter the service of the East Africa Company, Mr. Stanley declares, was entirely on his own initiative; that he had no mandate from the Company to make any such offer, though, at the same time, he had no doubt that, when the facts of the case were communicated to the directors, they would acquiesce in what he had done on their behalf. Emin, on the other hand, if we may believe the conversations reported by his German friends, received offers more positive than those Mr. Stanley admits to have laid before him. Indeed, so far from acting on his own initiative, the commander of the Relief Expedition, according to this account, brought with him from London an agreement signed by the founders of the British East Africa Company, officially drawn up and with seals attached, at the foot of which agreement Emin had only to sign his name to conclude the bargain. Mr. Stanley, if we are to credit this story —and the only facts before us are the rival assertions of the different parties concerned—suggested that Emin should march with all his troops round Victoria Nyanza to Kavirondo. There they would seek out a suitable island, on which the force could intrench itself. Then the commander of the rescue expedition would hasten back to Mombasa to bring up reinforcements. Every one of Emin Pasha's officers and men would, on entering the service of the British East Africa Company, receive the same pay as he had had from the Egyptian Government, Emin's own stipend being the subject of future negotiations with the directors of the Company. It would seem from Emin's fretful complaints that it was his intention to accept this offer; for in his conversation with Dr. Peters he declares that when they arrived upon the shores of Victoria Nyanza Mr. Stanley suddenly found that he did not care to march as far as Kavirondo, from whence, as had been expressly agreed, Emin was to conquer the territory of Unyoro and Uganda with the reinforcements Stanley was to bring up. On the contrary, the latter suddenly declared that Emin must go with him to the coast to complete the affair they had partly discussed. He said that, without the express command of the Queen of England, he could not mix himself up with troubles in Uganda. "In this manner"—we are quoting the report of a conversation Emin is affirmed to have had with Dr. Peters at Mpwapwa—"I have been compelled to march with him to the coast, whereas originally the question was only that of the transfer of my capital from Lake Albert to Lake Victoria." So far there is no great clashing of evidence between the witnesses before us, the main difficulty being that while Mr. Stanley asserts that, in making this offer to Emin, he was acting on his own responsibility, Emin is quite as positive in saying that he was merely carrying out the plans formed by the founders of the East Africa Company before the so-called Relief Expedition had left England. Nor, if Emin's conversation was not the outcome of a serious misunderstanding, does Mr. Stanley explain in his narrative the reasons why he departed from the arrangement he had entered into with the Pasha, and compelled him to leave a region in which it was the sole desire of his life he should be permitted to remain and, as far as possible, carry on the work of civilisation he had so vigorously begun. The rest we know (pp. 67–71). It may be added that about the last glimpse we had of Emin Pasha was when Captain Lugard, hearing of him wandering about in search of his scattered forces on the shores of Albert Nyanza, sent him a letter, which in all likelihood was never delivered, protesting against his encroachment with armed men on territory under the British flag, and, as the natives declared, planting the ensign of German authority at Ruwenzori, which showed that, even as an official of the German Government, Emin acted with as free a hand as not unlikely he would have acted had he been enrolled in the British service. Lastly, to complete this extraordinary comedy of errors —which was not without a tragic touch— Mr. Stanley entered an action against Tippoo Tib for not doing, in his capacity of a Christian Governor, what few people ever imagined the Moslem slave-trader would attempt.

After Mr. Stanley's return he took unto himself a wife, as we have seen, and, for the time at least, occupied himself in politics and other fields of interest. But three members of his party did not long survive the expedition. Dr. Parke died on the 10th of September, 1893, while on a visit to the Duke of St. Albans, at Altnacraig, near Ardrishaig. Lieutenant Stairs, after again rejoining the army—exchanging from the Engineers to the Line—so wearied for Africa that he took the command of an expedition sent for commercial purposes into the Katanga country, and, unhappily, died of fever on the 8th of June, 1892, at Chinde, near the mouth of the Zambesi, while on his way home from that successful mission.* Captain Nelson also soon found his way back to East Africa as an official of the British East Africa Company, but died of an attack of dysentery caught in Kikiyu, on the 26th of December, 1892 (p. 73).

What became of Emin's Province after it had been deserted by all the even moderately loyal portion of his troops can only be conjectured. Fadl el Mullah was said to have made common cause at Wadelai with the Mahdists in Makaraka. The steamers were sunk and the country of the Lur was wasted and the inhabitants were harassed by slave-raiders from the Congo country.

The last of Equatoria.

Vague rumours—originated how, it is difficult to say, though, as a rule, these echoes from the Soudan have generally some bases of truth—reached Egypt that Captain Van den Kerckhoven (afterwards accidentally killed), in command of one of the posts of the Congo Free State, which in 1891 started for the purpose of reaching the Upper Nile, most likely by the route that Mr. Stanley took, arrived at Emin's old station at Lado, and there, with a considerable force—variously estimated at from 3,000 to 5,000—intrenched himself, and gained some successes over the Mahdists sent to attack him in force. But though strange tidings may be expected from that region at any moment, there is not, at present, any means of refuting or confirming this last development of the story of Equatoria. The chances are that the Mahdists, with no one to oppose them, have taken possession of all the remnants of civilisation deserted by Emin and his officers, and are now, so far as such a barbarous horde possesses any solidarity, masters of most of Equatoria, as they have been of the other Egyptian provinces in the Soudan.

How long this can continue is doubtful.

* Moloney, "With Captain Stairs in Katanga" (1893).

for not only did the Mahdists split up into rival fragments, but the sect of the Senoussi, more fanatical even than the Mahdists, though not the less unfriendly towards their co-religionists, were pressing on them from the Sahara desert, and may, before long, come into collision with the latter in the Southern Soudan. Still more recently, a rival Mahdi arose in Kordofan, and is said to have attracted many of the old Mahdists, among others the troops sent against him. If so, anarchy, in which a civilised force will easily make itself master, cannot be far off.

Mr. Stanley's march from the Congo to Bagamoyo was the last of the great journeys across Africa. In all likelihood it will be the last journey of the kind likely to invite the energy of explorers; for now all the great routes from sea to sea have been so often traversed that no district of sufficient extent to contain any large lake or important river is left for the exploration of future travellers. Indeed, had it not been for the numerous picturesque incidents connected with Mr. Stanley's last tramp across Africa, as a mere crossing of the continent it would have excited comparatively little attention. Actually at the same time that he was marching from the Upper Congo to Albert Nyanza, a Frenchman, Captain E. Trivier, was passing from Loango, through French Congo and up the river by a well-known route, to Tanganyika and thence by Nyassa to Quilimane, which he reached in the end of 1889, having taken just about a year on the journey. It is, however, not necessary to occupy much space with a narrative of this officer's experiences; for in reality, with the exception of a few patches here and there, he journeyed over or in the vicinity of regions familiar from the explorations of earlier and more unfortunate travellers.* Captain Trivier's trip was a mere African tour of no importance geographically.

Trivier's journey.

* Trivier, "Mon Voyage au Continent Noir" (1891).

CAPTAIN TRIVIER AND ATTENDANTS.
(*From a Photograph by G. Godefroy, Rochefort.*)

OASIS NEAR GABES, TUNISIA.
(*From a Photograph in the Paris-Tunis Collection.*)

CHAPTER IV.

THE SAHARA: ITS EXPLORATION AND ITS EXPLOITATION.

The International Travellers—The Sahara Area—Erroneous Notions of its Nature—French Work in Making it Better Known—Varied Character of Africa—The Different Divisions of the Sahara—The Erg—Ahaggar—Hamada—Oases—Caravans—Inaccurate Pictures of the Desert—Not the Bottom of an Ancient Sea—Desiccation since the Roman Period—Microscopic Appearance of the Sand—A Saharan Volcano—Underground Water—Bahrs or Gouffres—Zibau and Other Artificial Oases—Artificial Wells—Origin of the Saharan Sand—Unequal Temperature—Sand-storms—Saharan Sand in the Atlantic—Locusts—Perils of Caravans from these—Plants and Animals—Inhabitants—Tonaregs—Arabs—Tibboos—Jews—Products—Caravan Routes—Explorers—Rohlfs, Douls, and Others—" Inland Seas "—Shotts—Artesian Wells of Sahara—French Colonial Aims—The Trans-Saharan Railway—Flatters' Expedition—Its Massacre by the Touaregs—Rolland's Labours—Renewal of the Work—Oases and the Date Palm—More Railway Surveys—Wargla—Traffic—Soudan Resources—" Armed Brethren of the Sahara "—French Rule and its Effect—Rapid Progress of French Influence.

SHORTLY before Mr. Stanley started on his latest expedition, a Russo-German traveller, Dr. Junker, had left the Pasha in order to reach the coast by a journey through Uganda (p. 27); and it may be remembered that among those who came from Equatoria with Emin was Major Casati, an Italian officer who had for ten years been sharing the fortunes of the beleaguered Governor. In the course of Mr. Stanley's journey, also, he not infrequently either came in contact with or heard of travellers belonging to different nationalities engaged in the exploration of Africa. These explorers may be termed members of the International Corps; for they had entered Africa by arrangement between different European countries. What part remained to be explored in the Dark Continent was to be allotted to the expeditions organised under international auspices. The only work that these explorers had left them to perform was really to fill in the blanks in the labours of their predecessors.

Before Africa attracted the great attention

that it has done during the last twenty years, nearly all of the leading problems of its geography had been almost completely solved. However, the new travellers who began the work which is now nearly finished were, as a rule—if occasionally little fitted by physique for the duties they had undertaken—men of scientific accomplishments far beyond those of most of their predecessors. Hence their expeditions, if not of the first moment geographically, have added not a little to our minute acquaintance with the plants, animals, geology, and ethnology of the country.

But before sketching the main facts ascertained by those international explorers, it may be useful if we turn for a brief space **The Sahara.** to the vast dry country in the north of Africa, along the borders or even through the centre of which some of the earlier travellers penetrated. This is the well-known Sahara. We say well-known, because it was one of the earliest portions of Africa that attracted the attention of the world, and, until recently, was regarded as a typical section of that continent. But even the Sahara has of late yielded up secrets which the early geographers little suspected. They generally believed that it was a vast sandy waste, the bed of some ancient dried-up sea that stretched from one side of Africa to the other. In reality it has been found, since the explorations of the Sahara have been carried on with the earnestness of the last few years, that this rainless expanse is in few places below the level of the Atlantic; that the greater portion of it is not covered with sand, but is stony waste, and that sometimes it rises to the height of considerable hills, and in one spot, at least, into mountains attaining an altitude of 8,000 feet.

Still more recently the energetic efforts of the French Government to unite their colonies on the west coast of Africa with those in the northern part of it have led to surveys being made across this barren stretch with the purpose of building a light railway which will connect Algeria and Tunis with Timbuctoo—now "within the sphere" of French influence—or some other commercial centre, with branches to the Atlantic. These interesting aspirations have vastly increased our knowledge of the Sahara; so that a brief sketch of what has been accomplished may form a useful interlude to the travels of African pioneers in the wetter and more umbrageous regions farther south. This will, at least, show how varied **Varied** Africa is. A **character of** traveller **Africa.** whose acquaintance with the vast continent is limited, let us say, to Morocco and Algeria will see little in this comparatively fertile region differing from the neighbouring countries of Europe. Indeed, in riding through some of the valleys of Northern Africa, it is only an occasional palm-tree shading the white tomb of a holy marabout, or a clump of palmetto, among which the tortoises squeak unintermittently, or a long string of camels, with their turbaned drivers, that recalls the fact that one is not in some of the valleys of southern Scotland.

Across the Atlas, however, we enter an entirely different region, the area we are now about to describe; and, as we have seen,

BERBER TYPE.

this dry section graduates into the wetter tropics, where we have almost to bore our way through dense forests of tangled vegetation. Again, on approaching the southern extremity of the continent, we are in another region, not throughout so dry as the Sahara, but less rainy than the country we have just left, and here and there dotted with deserts which in their appalling barrenness may well be compared with the arid track to which even the Arabs, familiar as they are with barren lands, have applied the name of "Zahra," or desert.

Africa is, indeed, a country in geographical features very different from Europe, and, by contrast, scarcely less remarkable than Asia or America, with this distinction, that the alternation of desert and fertile plain, steaming forest and dry upland, is more sudden than in any of the continents mentioned. In short, as Mr. Stanley remarks, in criticising some descriptions of Africa written by travellers whose experience of the continent was limited to only a small section of it, the man who knows Nyassaland alone has a personal acquaintance alone with Nyassaland. Nor can we call the wilderness of Masailand, or the scrub-covered deserts of Kalahari, or the grass land of Usukuma, or the thin forests of Unyamwezi, or the ochreous acacia-covered area of Ugogo, anything but sections of a continent that is made up of many zones. Africa, as the explorer who knows it so well reminds us, is about three times greater than Europe in its extent, and its topography is, unfortunately, more varied. In the Sahara, for instance, there are deserts of deserts. In Masailand and parts of South Africa you have counterparts of the steppes of eastern Russia, and the Castilian uplands are well represented in Unyamwezi and parts of Barbary. The best part of France finds a fitting counterpart in Egypt, while the Switzerland of Africa may, without stretch of language, be pointed out as existing in Ukonga and Toro, the Alps being Ruwenzori, Kilimanjaro, and Kenia. Finally, there is an African Brazil in the Congo basin, and an African Amazon in the Congo river, the immense forests of the great American flood being rivalled by the central African jungles through which the relief expedition to Emin Pasha marched for so many days (p. 32, and Map, p. 69), the entire area of this dense tree-covered track being estimated by the pioneers who first entered it at upwards of 400,000 square miles.

The Sahara may, in general terms, be said to stretch right across Africa in the shape of an arid belt; for, though the Libyan desert (pp. 85, 89, 92, 93), lying between Egypt, the Central Soudan, and Tripoli, is sometimes regarded as a separate division, it is, in reality, only a smaller detached portion of the vast tract we are describing. The old opinion that the Sahara was one unbroken expanse of drifting sand was no doubt derived by glimpses obtained of it on the Atlantic shore, where a vast semicircle of sand-hills stretches from Cape Blanco round the northern side of the Sahara to Fezzan, skirting the Atlas and the mountains of Algeria. These "dunes" rise to a height of from 70 to even 1,000 feet; but as they are subject to be broken up and rebuilt by the desert winds, they vary both in position and altitude. They are composed of quartz-sand, reddish-brown in colour, and though naturally entirely without water, the fact of a few plants maintaining a stunted existence in the more sheltered places proves that at times showers of rain refresh the surface; and it is seldom that a well sunk for a few feet in one of the hollows does not reach a small accumulation of water. This dreaded country of sand-hills is known to the Arabs as the "Erg," or "Areg." *Extent and character of the Sahara: the Erg.*

On the other side of it is the lofty plateau of Ahaggar, which constitutes the middle part of the Soudan, and, so far from carrying out the popular notion of the Sahara, rises to an average height of 4,000 feet, where the winters are so severe that for three months at a time snow whitens the surfaces of this portion of the desert. From this section the country *The Ahaggar plateau.*

falls gently towards the basin of the Niger and Lake Tchad, though Mount Tusside, in the Tibboo country, attains a height of 8,000 feet, and the oasis of Aïr, or Asben, is in reality a clump of hills which, in one place at least, attain a height of 6,500 feet.

These hilly portions of the Soudan are hollowed into many deep valleys, seamed with the dry beds, or "wadys," of ancient rivers, which, though empty for the greater

ARAB TRIBESMAN.

part of the year, and sometimes for years together, will occasionally after heavy rains or the melting of the upland snows course in a foaming current towards the "shotts," or salt lakes without outlet, which form so remarkable a feature in the geography of Tunisia and the neighbouring region. Even the Draa, except when the Atlas snows are melting, seldom sends its waters to the sea. These valleys are nearly all inhabited, for if water is not found on the surface or in the water-courses, enough can easily be obtained for the sheep, cattle, camels, and horses of the wandering tribesmen by sinking shallow wells.

The Hamada is another variety of Saharan surface. It consists of low plateaux, strewn with blocks of granite and other rocks, alternating with tracts of bare sand, broad marshes covered with thin layers of salt, or of flats littered with small rounded stones. These Hamadas are invariably barren, and, unless where wells exist, are uninhabited. The Hamada-el-Homra, on the borders of Tripoli—and the Sahara almost reaches the walls of the city of Tripoli—is one of the best-known of these tracts, lying, as it does, on the caravan route southward by way of the mountain region of Ghurian (Vol. I., p. 240). But on the route from Timbuctoo to Morocco also there are Hamadas and hills of about 2,000 feet alternating with rolling sands (Vol. I., pp. 304, 309). *The Hamada, or elevated stony tracts.*

However, scattered all through the Sahara, in even its sandiest and most repulsive sections, are oases (p. 77), or green islets in the midst, it may be, of a dry, sandy region, where palm-trees grow and gushing springs support vegetation sufficient for the feeding of the flocks and cattle of the tribesmen who gather hither during certain months of the year. Indeed, without these oases it would be almost impossible to cross some parts of the Sahara; and it is certain that its roaming population would necessarily be confined to the very few fertile parts were it not for these verdure-covered spots that link together long stretches of barren waste. The great caravan routes between the Central Soudan and the Barbary states along the shores of the Mediterranean are marked out by the occurrence of inhabited oases on the line of travel. *The oases.*

Those popular pictures, in which the Sahara is painted as an immense plain of moving sand, dotted here and there with fertile oases, are thus strangely inaccurate. Yet even to this day—so hard do old impressions die—the simile of the panther-skin is with many an article of geographical faith. Even so near as Algeria, the Sahara consists of a region widely different from what is generally

INCIDENT IN THE DESERT: MARAUDER TAKEN PRISONER BY A FRENCH ARAB OUTPOST.

supposed to be the case. Sir Lambert Playfair* (p. 83) divides it, in his admirable description of that French colony, into two distinct regions, the lower and the upper Sahara; the one consisting of a vast depression of sand and clay, stretching in the east as far as the frontier of Tunis, the other of a rocky plateau, frequently attaining considerable elevation, extending on the west to the borders of Morocco.†

Altogether, though the boundaries of the Sahara are naturally rather vague, its area may be estimated at something less than 3,566,000 square miles—that is, nearly as large as Europe, without the Scandinavian Peninsula and Iceland. But while Europe supports a population of 327,000,000 people, it is doubtful if the whole Sahara contains much more than a million and a half. Yet even these figures prove that a large portion of the country, generally supposed to be a mass of barren sand, is actually capable either of cultivation or of growing fodder for cattle and sheep.

Area and capabilities: geology.

But perhaps the most interesting discovery that has been made by the explorers of late years is that the Sahara is not the bed of any ocean within recent geological periods, and that its drifting sands are not due to causes similar to those which have formed those beaches that are the familiar features of sea-shores. Water, indeed, has exercised very little

Desiccation of the Sahara.

* Lieut.-Colonel Sir R. Lambert Playfair, K.C.M.G., one of a family of soldiers and savants, bears a name very familiar to all African travellers. As Political Resident at Aden and Zanzibar it was his lot to see the coming and going of many of the most famous explorers, to send them forth on their missions, and to welcome them when they returned to these "jumping-off places" of a then little-known continent. At a later date—from the year 1867—as Consul-General for Algeria, and for a time for Tunisia also, Sir Lambert has not only been the guide and friend of the multitudes of his countrymen who seek health and sunshine in the French colony, but by his long journeys through the vast region with which he is, or has been, officially connected, and his many works, reports, and papers descriptive of it, he takes a high place among those who have shed light on the dark places of Northern Africa.

† See also, Dumas, "Le Grand Désert" (1848), and "Le Sahara Algérien" (1845); Pomel, "Le Sahara" (1872), etc.

influence on the Sahara since the beginning of the Tertiary period, though previous to that epoch it was, in all likelihood, if not a vast territory dotted with lakes and permeated by rivers, much damper than it has been at any time since that geological era. There are, indeed, good reasons for believing that the desiccation of the Sahara has been going on steadily during the last two thousand years, if not, in all probability, long before the Christian era.

We say two thousand years, because before that date there was nothing in the shape of history to enable us to arrive at accurate conclusion regarding the condition of the desert. But we know that the Romans had colonies or military posts a long way southwards in what are now uninhabited deserts. The remains of their gateways, fortresses, and other monuments now stand bare and lonely in a sandy tract where no man lives, or where the only resources of the country could never tempt so practical a people as the conquerors of the world to rear buildings that indicate permanent residence (p. 95, and Vol. I., p. 240). Less dependence is to be placed on the historical remarks of Herodotus and Pliny to the effect that the rhinoceros, crocodile, and elephant—all animals to which an abundant supply of water is essential—were common in parts of northern Africa where none are at present to be found, nor have existed for many centuries, though the presence of the elephant north of the Sahara less than two thousand years ago is, we think, indubitable (Vol. II., p. 227).‡

Another curious fact which shows that the Sahara was not always so arid a region as that known to us is afforded by the Egyptian inscriptions and animal sculptures: for in none of these do we find the camel represented or referred to. Nor do the Roman historians mention this animal, now so

‡ The Egyptian kings also obtained them from their own territory (Floyer, *Geographical Journal*, 1893, p. 411; and Andersson, "The Lion and the Elephant," p. 382). The remains of a hippopotamus were found at Duvivier, in Algeria (*Bull. de l'Acad. Hippone*, No. 13 (1878), p. 25).

essential to the desert wanderers, as an inhabitant of any part of northern Africa. It was, we know, introduced by the Arabs, in post-Pharaonic, possibly post-Mohammedan, times,* and did not spread northwards from the Sahara until some centuries after the Christian era.

The inference from these facts, however, is that the drying-up of the Sahara must have gone on more rapidly during the last twenty centuries than previously. The desiccation of all North Africa has, indeed, been marked since the Roman period. Dr. Lenz considered much of the desert character of the Sahara to have been caused by the hewing down of the forests on the Atlas, and the consequent drying-up of the streams which there took their rise (Vol. I., p. 310). Mr. Floyer attributes the ruin of some of the Egyptian valleys to a similar reckless rural economy—the trees having been cut to supply fodder to the camels; and in parts of Tunisia and other districts of Barbary vast tracts are almost desert and capable of supporting a mere handful of people where the remains of Roman oil-mills and towns show that before the forests were destroyed there was a thriving population.†

We find in many places the distinct marks of ancient rivers and lakes, and in the less arid portions of the Sahara there are "shotts," or "sebkas,"—salt, marshy lakes without outlet, which may reasonably be regarded as remnants of greater accumulations of water during earlier days. An examination of the Sahara sands is also inimical to the theory of their being portions of a comparatively recent sea-bottom: for on applying the microscope to the component materials of any of the drifting dunes, we find that those minute shells, the rhizopoda, so abundant in sea-sand, are strikingly absent. Indeed, according to the observations of Erwin von Bary, there is a distinct volcanic crater in the isolated mountain

* Floyer, *Kew Bulletin*. No. 72. p. 290.
† Playfair, "Travels in the Footsteps of Bruce," pp. 31, 153, 191, 212, 226; and Playfair and Brown's "Bibliography of Morocco" (*It. G. S.*), Introduction, pp. 203–9.

mass of Aïr, with a vast lava stream down its side.‡ In short, all the geological and topographical features of the Sahara go to prove that, while it must, like a great portion of Africa, have been under water at one time, this period was probably not later than the Cretaceous epoch. Even then there would have been isolated masses, or islands, above the surface of the sea.

One of the most remarkable facts about the Sahara is the comparatively small depth at which water is found. In the Algerian "souf" the water actually circulates close to the surface of the soil, so that a well can be sunk almost any- *Underground water: gouffres.*

SIR R. LAMBERT PLAYFAIR.
(*From a Photograph by H. J. Whitlock, Birmingham.*)

where with comparative ease by simply penetrating the layer of gypsum that covers the sandy substratum in which the water is contained. In Algeria, indeed, all the way from Biskra—an oasis in the Sahara—to Timassin, throughout the whole extent of the Wady Ghoir, and even to the south of it, depressions known to the natives as *Bahr* (sea, lake), and to the French as *Gouffres*, are found full of water. They appear to be the spiracles of a vast subterranean sheet of water. All of these apertures, Sir Lambert Playfair tells us, are inhabited by numbers of

‡ *Zeitschrift für Erdkunde*, 1880.

fishes (*Cyprinodontidæ* and *Chromidæ*), which live freely exposed to the air and light, and breed under normal conditions. Their underground life "is merely an episode, and, as it were, an incident in the voyages which they undertake between one *bahr* and another. When they reach the neighbourhood of a well, they are forced up with the water, or obey an instinct to mount to the surface." Accordingly, when it is intended to plant a date-grove, the industrious "Souafa" remove the entire course of gypsum, and plant their palms in the water-bearing sand beneath. Then, to use the words of Sir Lambert Playfair, "their green summits rise above the plain around, thus forming orchards excavated like ants' nests, sometimes 8 metres [24 to 25 feet] beneath the level of the ground."*

By utilising this water in the best part of

* "Handbook to Algeria and Tunis," p. 18.

the Sahara, oases, called "Ziban," are formed by building dams across little running streams and obstructing water in canals. Water absorbed by permeable beds constitutes the oases with shallow wells; in other cases, oases with artesian wells; and, finally, there are the excavated oases so characteristic of the Souf. But wherever an artificial oasis is formed—wherever, in brief, water reaches the sand—fertility in this warm, equable climate

REMAINS OF ROMAN AMPHITHEATRE AT EL DJEM, TUNISIA.
(*From a Photograph in the Paris-Tunis Collection.*)

is the certain result. In a few weeks what seemed the acme of barrenness is covered with verdure. Palms are planted and, before long, bear the dates that are the all-in-all of the desert wanderer's food. Other crops soon follow, and from far and near the news of the new paradise spreads to the nomad tribes, until the spot, which a year or two before was entirely uninhabited, or, at best, only supported a few thirsty families, becomes a

Artificial oases.

thickly inhabited and prosperous district. These artesian wells, which are being formed by the French Government in the portion of the Sahara under their government, will be sunk still more extensively in the future, if much more practical, and serve every purpose which the other project could possibly accomplish. Of this scheme we shall presently speak.

However, we may return for the moment

TYPICAL SAHARAN LANDSCAPE (DAKHEL).
(From a Photograph by Dr. Gerhard Rohlfs.)

the projected railway through the Sahara is carried out. For it is needless to say that, without large watering-places and centres of civilisation, it would be extremely difficult for any line to be constructed through such a region. The artesian wells may, indeed, not bulk so largely in popular imagination as inland seas, which at one time there was a dream of making; but, in reality, they are to the causes that have formed the sand so characteristic of the Sahara, which, according to popular belief, covers the greater part of the region. The sand, it does not require a very extensive study of the Sahara to see, is merely the ground-down dust of the granite, gneiss, and cretaceous, or other rocks that underlie the Sahara. The Sahara necessarily enjoys an

Origin of the Saharan sand.

exceedingly dry climate, though one of extreme inequality. During sunshine the thermometer will frequently rise to 100, and even 130 degrees, and at night fall so far below the freezing-point that ice forms in the travellers' water-skins. The result of this is that in the course of the day the rocks expand under the action of heat, and at night, owing to the sudden drop in the temperature, split, crack, and break into pieces. Then the violent winds that so often sweep across the Sahara toss these comminuted fragments against each other. So that, acting after the fashion of files, or sand-blasts, they grind together not only on each other, but on the still unbroken rocks over which they are carried backwards and forwards.

In this way layers of sand have been gradually formed wherever rocks unprotected by vegetation protruded above the surface; and, being swept together by the prevailing winds, have formed the dreaded sand-hills characteristic of some portions of the region we are now describing. The sand in these hills is, however, so dry that travellers describe the tread of the camel or of a man making the hill thunder as a vast quantity of it slips down to a lower level.

Climate of the Sahara. The climate of the Sahara, especially where it is under the influence of the westerly and north-westerly winds, which are the prevailing breezes, is extremely healthy. Yet the terrors of the sand-storms which sometimes overtake the wayfarers have formed a favourite picture in the works of explorers, and have furnished many legends of a more or less apocryphal character to Arab mythology. On a clear day objects can be seen for a great distance, and at times the deceitful mirage buoys up the traveller with hopes of green oases and refreshing lakes a few miles distant. Then suddenly a dark pillar is seen advancing in the direction of the caravan, and, before the wayfarers can prepare for the coming storm, they are involved in a dense cloud of drifting sand—though, perhaps, not quite buried, according to the undying tale of the story-books. So violent are the winds that at times sweep across the Sahara that at a considerable distance from the African coast the dredgings brought up by the *Challenger* showed that the sea-bottom was covered somewhat thickly with the sand blown seawards from the neighbouring continent. At times, also, the verdure of the oases is eaten up by vast clouds of locusts, which appear and disappear with equal rapidity. It is then fortunate for the Arabs and other dwellers in the Sahara if a westerly wind begins to blow, for in that case, to use their own expression, "the army of the Most High" is swept into the Atlantic. At times such enormous quantities of these ravenous insects have been drowned in the sea that the tide has deposited whole banks of them for miles along the coast, causing fevers among the villagers within the influence of the fetid smell which the rotting mass diffused far and near.

But of all dangers that overtake the Saharan travellers the worst is the fear that the water-places may be without that most essential necessary of life in that region. They may have filled their skins at one well in a particular oasis, hoping that by the time the supply is exhausted they will have arrived at another green spot in the desert from which their vessels may be filled again, only to find that, owing to unusual drought or other causes, the springs have dried up, and the wells yield nothing. The Arab traders who pass through the worst portion of the Sahara—namely, that between Morocco and Timbuctoo—have many stories to tell of such mishaps. Thus a caravan proceeding from Timbuctoo to Tafilet not finding water in one of the customary wells, perished to the number, it is said, of 2,000 people, besides 1,800 camels—animals that are capable of enduring thirst longer than their masters. Accidents of this sort account for the many human and other bones that lie mingled together in various parts of the desert.

The plants and animals of this vast region are naturally, like the human inhabitants,

THE INHABITANTS OF THE SAHARA.

largely confined to the oases.* In those fertile spots the date-palm grows, and in some more civilised districts oranges, lemons, peaches, figs, pomegranates, and similar fruits, and rice, millet, durra, and other food crops are grown. Outside the narrow limits of such verdure-covered spots, tamarisks, prickly acacias, and smaller drought-

Plants and animals.

ARAB TYPE.

loving shrubs are about the only vegetation to be seen, unless we except some coarse grasses, and one or two other peculiarly desert plants. In nearly every portion of the southern Sahara not altogether deprived of water or of vegetation, the giraffe, now so narrowed in its range, was at one time common. It is now much less frequent, though the ostrich may be detected at intervals, with two or three species of antelope and some wild cattle. The wild ass and jackal are to be seen, with crows, desert larks, the horned viper, and a few

* Tristram's "The Great Sahara" (1860) is an excellent popular work on the natural history of the region adjoining Algeria, then little, now well known.

other reptiles; but the lion never penetrates the desert proper.

The various tribes of Touaregs are the true inhabitants of the Sahara. These people belong to the Berber stock (p. 78), so widely scattered over the whole of northern Africa. They constitute, though civilised enough to possess an ancient alphabet, the wildest and least tractable of the Saharan nomads, coursing about on their camels from one oasis to another, intercepting caravans for the purpose either of robbing or of blackmailing them; or, when the travellers are too strong for the "desert pirates" to pillage them, of hiring camels to the traders engaged in conveying goods to the sea from the Soudan. The appearance of these Touaregs, who are now fanatical Moslems, is somewhat singular, the men wearing a cloth round the lower portion of their faces, which gives them a semblance to Mohammedan women. In most cases the outrages on travellers who have attempted to penetrate the desert have been due to these wild wanderers.

Inhabitants.

In addition to these Touaregs there are a number of Arabs (pp. 80, 81, 87, etc.) who follow a life not unlike that of their rivals, though most of the inhabitants of the oases belong to the latter. Some Tibboos and negroes inhabit the southern portion of the Sahara, and there is a peculiar tribe either of Jews or of Judaised Touaregs whose home is in one of the oases between Morocco and Timbuctoo, and who are extensively employed as guides through the sand-hills by the caravans using that route. Jews, also, whose settlement in the country is of very ancient date, may be found in almost all the oases, and, as we have seen, some of these living in Akka have established themselves as traders in the once exclusive and still fanatical city of Timbuctoo, while it is needless reminding the reader they thrive amazingly in Morocco, Tunis (p. 88), Algeria, and Tripoli. But the Touaregs, when semi-civilised, are the great native traders of the Sahara, and, if less inclined for peaceful pursuits, are the

THE STORY OF AFRICA.

dreaded robbers who control all the lines of traffic.

Beyond dates and salt—the latter collected in one or two places—there are few products of any value to be obtained from the Sahara itself. A few horses are occasionally hired in the larger oases—the celebrated "horse of the Sahara"* being really that of Algeria—and soda and some saltpetre generally form part of the lading of most caravans passing through the country.

But it is not for the wealth of the Sahara that the traders traverse its dreary wastes. From time immemorial it has been the only line of travel between the rich and comparatively civilised countries of northern Africa and the **Products of the Sahara** wealthy **Caravan routes.** Soudan and Niger States to the south of it. In this region, ivory, ostrich feathers, spices, gums, musk, indigo, cotton, palm-oil, gold-dust, kola-nuts, and other articles, are trafficked by the negroes and Tibboos for weapons, gunpowder, and other goods of European countries. We have also seen that there is still a considerable slave trade between Morocco and the Soudan; the number of captives carried by the Timbuctoo caravans to Mogador increasing since the other outlets for these human wares were closed.

YOUNG JEWESS OF TUNISIA.
(From a Photograph in the Paris-Tunis Collection.)

The chief trade routes still used in the Sahara are those from Morocco to Cairo by Insalah and Ghadames, which is followed by the West African pilgrims bound for Mecca: that is to say, when the devout Moslems are not carried to Jeddah by English steamers, which pick them up at their villages, and convey them to and from the latter port at a small sum per head. Then there is the route, less used, from Kukawa to Murzuk and Tripoli. There is a third line of travel from Tripoli to Air and Ghat. From Timbuctoo to Insalah, and thence to Algeria and Tunis, is another once well - frequented caravan track; and lastly, that from Timbuctoo to Morocco is used even more extensively than in former times.

Although the Sahara has not been minutely examined, until within the last twenty or thirty years it formed the field of travel to many of the early adventurers whose discoveries have formed the subject **Exploration** of previous chapters. Those among **of the Sahara.** the earliest explorers of the Sahara were Mungo Park, Lyon, Laing, Caillié, Clapperton, Denham, and Oudney; Panet, who in 1850 traversed the region from St. Louis to Morocco, though without passing very much eastwards; Richardson and Barth; Vincent, who in 1860 travelled also from St. Louis northwards as far as Adrar; Si Bou el-

* Dumas, "The Horses of the Sahara": translated by James Hutton (1863); Schirmer, "Le Sahara" (1893).

Moghdad, who travelled from the same Senegal town to Mogador; Mordokhaï; Gerhard Rohlfs (p. 91); Duveyrier (who between 1860–4 made some most important journeys for scientific purposes into the Touareg country); Soleillet, Largeau (1875); Dourneaux and Dupère and Joubert, who lost their lives in circumstances still little known; Nachtigal, who, minor explorers of the Sahara; and a melancholy interest will always attach to Camille Douls, who, after some adventurous but, geographically, rather useless journeys in the coast region (Vol. I., p. 282), so very thinly disguised as a Mohammedan that his nominal renegadism served him little with the fierce tribes in the neighbourhood, lost his life in

DR. ROHLFS' EXPEDITION, 1873–4: WELLS IN THE OASIS FARA'FREH, LIBYAN DESERT.
(*From a Photograph taken by Ph. Remelé.*)

in the course of his meritorious travels from Egypt westwards by Lake Tchad, was enabled to obtain considerable information regarding the more outlying portions of the Sahara; Lenz; and, still more recently, Captain Berger and Commandant Monteil, who, though he has not travelled over any new ground, is the first Frenchman who has visited Bornu, which he reached from the French colonies on the west coast, returning to Tripoli over the route traversed by so many previous explorers. Cervera (1860) may be mentioned among the 1890, when attempting in a like futile mask to penetrate from Morocco southwards by Lenz's route to Timbuctoo and the Niger. The particulars of the fate of this young and enthusiastic explorer will probably never be fully known. When rumours of his death reached Algeria, the Governor-General of that colony sent emissaries in various directions to inquire into the matter, and, if possible, to recover his remains. In July, 1891, one of the search parties returned with a body which they had found buried in the sand to the east of Taourirt, half-way between Aoulef and Akabli, places somewhere near Touat. The desert sand seems to have mummified the remains of the unfortunate traveller. The face, notwithstanding the fact that the body must have lain where it was found for several months, was quite susceptible of recognition; but several of the members were wanting. Probably they had been devoured by birds or beasts of prey. There was every appearance of his having been strangled—most probably either by his treacherous guides or by some of the marauders with whom he fell in alone and unprotected.*

Most of the other journeys of much moment we have already described in greater or less detail, and the minor ones it would be tedious to rehearse. One march through the Sahara is extremely like another. The travellers, unlike their fellow-explorers in tropical Africa, are in little dread of nearing the villages of hostile tribes, and, from the entire absence of bush, are in no peril of poisoned arrows or spearmen in concealment. They may travel for weeks without meeting any of the nomads of the desert, and, indeed, may be troubled with no fear so much as falling in with the roving band of marauding Touaregs. The mirage and the sand-storm, the hot sun during the day and the coolness of the night, the water, abundant in one oasis or wanting in another, form the chief items in the somewhat monotonous journeys. It is, however, unnecessary to narrate these travels at any length. We have contented ourselves by giving in an abstract form the chief results arrived at by the laborious researches thus shortly dismissed.

Of all the modern explorers of the Sahara, the most indefatigable was probably the German traveller Gerhard Rohlfs (p. 91), a native of Vegesack, near Bremen, where he was born in 1832. He studied medicine, and in 1855, with the direct purpose of being able to penetrate some portions of French Africa not

* For these particulars I am indebted to Sir Lambert Playfair, who has kindly enriched this chapter with many valuable emendations.

then opened to all travellers, enlisted in the Foreign Legion serving in Algeria. Here he made himself familiar with Moslem customs and the Arabic language, and after arriving in Morocco was appointed physician to the then Sultan of that country. Claiming to be a renegade, he travelled through a great portion of Morocco, reaching the Wady Draa, on the northern borders of the Sahara. Here he was attacked by his own guides, plundered, and left for dead in the desert; and had not two marabouts conveyed him to Algeria, he must inevitably have ended his explorations at this point. In 1864 he succeeded in getting as far as Touat and Ghadames, in the Sahara, and next year reached Fezzan and Tibesti. In 1866, starting on a journey for the purpose of recovering the papers of his countryman, Dr. Vogel (who, it may be remembered, was murdered by the Sultan of Waday—Vol. I., p. 302), he reached Bornu: and though he failed to gain an entrance to Waday, penetrated by way of the Niger to the British colony of Lagos, on the Guinea Coast. After visiting Abyssinia with Lord Napier's expedition, and Bornu a second time as an envoy from the King of Prussia, he explored in 1873-4 the oasis of Siva in the Libyan desert (pp. 85, 89, 92, 93). Four years later the German Government sent him to carry gifts from the Emperor to the Sultan of Waday, but his expedition being attacked and driven back by the Arabs inhabiting the oasis of Kufra, the intrepid explorer never reached the surly sovereign to whom he was accredited, and with whom MM. Matteucci and Massari (pp. 10-12) had such uncertain intercourse.

Nevertheless, in spite of the many travellers who had visited its borders, or had penetrated by the trade routes, the Sahara might still have remained only partially known had it not been for the political interest which the French attached to it, and the schemes for utilising it devised by different engineers belonging to that nation. At first these projects took the shape of trying by various scientific means to modify the drought of the Sahara, so as to **The Inland Sea of Africa.**

constitute its desert wastes "inland seas." It was fully believed in those days that the region which we have described had actually been at no very distant date the bottom of a sea, and that, as the greater portion of it must lie under the level of the Atlantic, all that needed be done was to cut an entrance by which the ocean could be permitted to flood the desiccated region. It was then argued that, apart from the convenience of reaching all parts of what had once been desert by means of ships, the few portions that might rise above the surface of the waters would have a climate so altered as to become fertile instead of waste. It was, no doubt, pointed out that the enormous evaporation from such a great sheet of water in so hot a region must necessarily demand a continual supply of water from the ocean, and that the drifting sands when the canal from the Atlantic was cut would more than likely entirely close the inlet. Moreover, if the desiccation of the Sahara is due to continental changes of elevation, as has been mentioned, it is certain that nothing in the way of changing its climate can be accomplished. Lastly, it was exceedingly doubtful whether the loss of the date-trees of the Sahara by the damp climate, in which they could not subsist, would be counterbalanced by the other supposed advantages of creating an inland sea or seas.

However, though the plan has been frequently discussed, it has never gone further: and, owing to the different directions which French interest in the Sahara has of late taken, it is extremely doubtful if any attempt will ever be made to carry this muchtalked-of project into execution. Westward from the Gulf of Gabes (p. 77), in Tunisia, stretching for a distance of 250 miles, is a chain of salt lakes, or "shotts," all of which are below the level of the sea. The two isthmi that separate them are of varying heights, though in both cases considerably above the level of the Mediterranean. The entire area is divided from the sea by a third isthmus, also above the level of the adjacent sea. Some geographers contend that this depression is the site of the ancient Lake Triton; that it communicated with the Mediterranean down to a very recent period; and that partly by the upheaval of its bottom, and partly owing to the difference between the quantity of water which entered and the amount of evaporation and absorption, the sea gradually disappeared, leaving the existing shotts as the only evidence of a former condition of things.*

On the other hand, many geographers affirm that there never was any inland sea

DR. GERHARD ROHLFS.
(*From a Photograph by Reichard and Lindner, Berlin.*)

here at all, and that the Tunisian "shotts" are identical with the more elevated "sebkhas" of Algeria and Eastern Morocco, the salt in them being due to the washing of the higher ground by the rain, which has no means of exit except by evaporation. However, Captain Roudaire proposed in 1874 to flood this undoubted depression by cutting through a ridge thirteen miles wide and 150 feet high,

* Playfair, "Algeria and Tunis," p. 321, and *Proceedings of the Royal Geographical Society* (1890), p. 625. Roudaire. "Rapport à M. le Ministre de l'Instruction publique sur la Mission des Chotts. Études relatives au projet de Mer Intérieure" (1877), and "Une Mer Intérieure en Algérie" (*Revue des Deux Mondes*, May 15th, 1874); Rouire, "La Découverte du bassin Hydrographique de la Tunisie Centrale et l'emplacement de l'ancien lac Triton (ancienne mer intérieure d'Afrique)" (1887); Paty de Clam. "Le Triton dans l'Antiquité et à l'Époque actuelle; Réponse a la brochure de M. Rouire" (1887), etc.

and so forming an artificial inland sea of some 3,100 square miles in area, with an average depth of close upon eighty feet.

From an engineering point of view, there is no difficulty whatever in this project. The difficulty of obtaining the capital is the only obstacle which as yet the projectors of this grandiose scheme have been unable to overcome; and though M. de Lesseps, in the days when the name of the "Grand Français" was one to conjure with, interested himself in the scheme, the French investor was supremely sceptical regarding the advantages which would accrue to him from the formation of this new sea in an old land. Some slight modification of climate might possibly be the result of this flooded area, but, as Sir Lambert Playfair points out, the new sea would occupy a space hardly larger in proportion to the rest of the Sahara than a single spot on the traditional panther-skin: so that Captain Roudaire's scheme, even if carried out, would scarcely result in the regeneration of the Sahara. But, considering that the Sea of Aral and the Caspian do not modify the climate, and, through the climate, the soil of the regions in their vicinity, it is far from certain that the country adjoining the flooded shotts would be in any way altered in the direction promised by the projectors of the scheme—a scheme, however, now very unlikely to be carried out.

Mr. Donald Mackenzie's still more ambitious project of flooding the Western Sahara* by letting the waters of the Atlantic into the district called El-Juf was found quite as pronouncedly to be impracticable: first, by the fact that most of the Sahara is above the level of the Atlantic; and secondly, by Lenz showing that El-Juf was not a vast depression, but only a small valley.

Meanwhile, the artesian wells sunk by Captain Roudaire have unconsciously solved the problem of the inland seas. For by bringing the means of irrigation to 1,500 acres, and

* "The Flooding of the Sahara." (1877).

DR. ROHLFS' EXPEDITION, 1873-4: THE HOUSE OF THE EXPEDITION AT GASR DAKHEL, LIBYAN DESERT.
(From a Photograph by Ph. Remelé.)

DR. ROHLFS' EXPEDITION, 1873-4: THE APPROACH TO BUDCHULLU.
(From a Photograph by Ph. Remelé.)

enabling 60,000 palm-trees to be grown in land hitherto sterile, all the advantages which could result from any inland sea have been thus practically accomplished.

The success obtained in sinking these artesian wells very soon diverted public attention in another channel. It was felt that while the inland sea was problematical, and at best could only utilise a limited portion of the desert, the building of a great line of railway across the Sahara from oasis to oasis, made by the formation of irrigated spots, would open up a vast extent of country, both to the south and to the north, which hitherto could only be approached by caravans of camels. Such a scheme, however, necessarily left the hands of private individuals for those of the State, since the policy thus inaugurated had a deeper political than mere utilitarian significance. The losses France had suffered at home during the war of 1870-1 made her still more eager to recoup herself by acquiring territory beyond the seas, or by making more of the colonies she already possessed in different parts of the world. Africa, as the

The Saharan artesian wells: Political projects.

nearest continent to work upon, naturally roused most attention. Algeria had always been a bottomless sink for French money, without the nation receiving much in return for the enormous expenditure of which that disappointing country had been the object. In 1880, indeed, Algeria had only been partially conquered, for recurrent outbreaks of the native tribes warned France of the slender tenure by which she held the colony, first taken possession of more than fifty years before. Then the protectorate extended over Tunis has still further increased the virtual area of French territory in northern Africa. On the west she controls the colony of Senegambia, as well as the outlying country of Futa-Djallon, the "Rivers of the South," and the French Soudan, not to mention the still more extensive, though somewhat shadowy, "hinterland" which she acquired by the international compact of 1884. The vast, but still almost undeveloped, French Congo largely increased the interests of France in that part of the world. The leading aim of the colonial authorities was now to connect these scattered colonies, and make one Algeria from the Senegal to the Congo by way of the Sahara. This ambitious project was materially assisted by the Anglo-French Convention of August, 1890, by which the protectorate of France in Madagascar was recognised, and the consent of Great Britain obtained to the extension of French influence south of Algeria and Tunis to the line from Say, on the Niger, to Barrua, on Lake Tchad.

The advantages obtained by France from this Convention have been bitterly and most unjustly attacked, just as the supposed feebleness of Great Britain in granting so much in return for so little has been equally a subject of party animadversion. France, however, seeing that there was little likelihood of her obtaining any further territory in that particular part of Africa, now wisely concentrated her efforts to constitute her colonies on the west and on the north one consolidated block. Accordingly, of recent years nearly all of the French expeditions, whether nominally geographical, scientific, or otherwise, have had this end almost solely in view. Crampel, who lost his life; Mizon, who was more fortunate; Dybowski, who followed up the explorations so gallantly begun by Crampel; and Monteil, who in 1892 completed the first journey made by a Frenchman across that part of the Sahara between Lake Tchad and Tripoli—undertook their expeditions for this purpose alone. The object they aimed at was to investigate the resources that might possibly be found in this outlying territory, and the best method of tapping the country so that no other nation should be able to obtain a footing for commercial purposes in any of the country between the Soudan and Barbary.

The reports of the officers employed in these expeditions pointed out that the Sahara might be divided into four zones. There is the oases region, from which come dates and camels for caravan use; secondly, there is the desert region, in which palms are few, and vast plains of sand, stones, and salt, over which roam nomadic tribes, ever on the watch for caravans to pillage; then there is the gum-tree belt, in which cattle, sheep, and horses thrive; and lastly, and most southerly of all, there is a zone where running water and tropical vegetation appear. This, properly speaking, comes under the head of the Soudan. The caravan routes from Algeria to this part of Africa pass through the sterile country in which, sometimes for six or eight days at a time, the traders traverse a region without vegetation, wood, or water, and, in addition, suffer from the hostility of the native tribes. For these reasons this route has not been used by Europeans, so that unless the trade between northern Africa and the French possessions in the Soudan should continue to remain in native hands, a railway, it would seem, was absolutely necessary.

But a railway of such extent, built through a country so entirely unprotected over the greatest portion of its area, is an even more gigantic enterprise than threading the American prairies with iron roads, Central Asia with a railway which the Russians have built, or crossing Siberia by the rails that are now being fast laid from the Urals to the Pacific. Accordingly, when M. Duponchel first mooted this scheme, his proposals did not meet with a very enthusiastic reception. However, in 1879 a commission was appointed for the purpose of examining all questions relating to the building of this railway through the desert. As the result of their deliberations, three plans were taken into consideration, the starting-point for the three routes which were to be examined being the Algerian provinces—Oran, Algiers, and Constantine. In 1883, accordingly, three

The Trans-Saharan railway.

expeditions were sent to these provinces; two of them being over country already well known, do not demand any extended notice. But the eastern party, namely, that starting from Constantine, undertook the most dangerous and difficult part of the work; for it was directed to reach the Soudan by way of Rhat, one of the villages of the Hoggar-Touaregs, in the great desert.

Railway exploring expedition: Flatters' evil fortune.

The command of this expedition was entrusted to Colonel Flatters (Vol. I., p. 282). His first attempt to reach the point indicated was attended with an entire want of success, for, owing to the scarcity of provisions and the hostility of the Touaregs, he and his companions had to return without having reached Rhat. It was, however, not entirely without important results, for the expedition discovered the great pass of Igharghar, through which runs the Igharghar, a "wady" which, after a course of 700 miles, ends in the Mebuhr Shott. Its valley, in places fifteen miles broad, offers an easy road towards the Niger.

Colonel Flatters also beguiled himself into the belief that he had established amicable relations with the Touaregs, which would enable him on a future occasion to reach the Soudan without any of the difficulties apprehended from the hostility of these savage tribesmen, who naturally dreaded a loss of their caravan trade by the construction or such a road as that which the survey parties had begun the first step in building.

Full of confidence in this belief, the hapless enthusiast obtained permission to start for the second time. On the 18th of November, 1880, he and his party left Wargla, never to return. Besides the commanding officer, it consisted of two civil engineers, a captain of the artillery corps, and a surgeon, all of whom had served in the first expedition. In addition, the party numbered two other scientific members, as well as several soldiers, camel-drivers, and the usual swarm of attendants on a desert caravan. In all, this ill-fated expedition comprised eighty-eight persons, including a priest of the Mohammedan Order of Tedjini, who was expected to be of much use to the expedition by giving the sanctity of religion to the enterprise in which he had agreed to take part, since members of his brotherhood are scattered over the Soudan, constituting secret societies, having initiation ceremonies, signs, pass-words, and secret codes. Hence the Khouan, or brethren of these Mohammedan sects, have affiliations that carry them in a fraternal manner all through Morocco, Algeria, Tunisia, Tripoli, Egypt, Syria, Persia, Central Asia, India—in short, through the most distant parts of Islam. Unfortunately, on the present occasion the presence of this holy man failed to protect the "infidels" with whom he was associated. After a three months' journey in a leisurely fashion, not attended by any remarkable incident, the expedition, passing through Amguid, reached the Sebkha, with its salt-marshes, which was the most southern point occupied by the Roman colonists of Africa; for here Cornelius Balbo reared, in the year 44 B.C., a monument, of which the ruins can still be seen. Yet never before in recent times had a European penetrated so far in this direction into the great African desert, proving, what we have already discussed, the improbability of the country being during Roman times so arid as it is at present (p. 82).

Hitherto all had gone well, and the expedition was about to enter the Au country, 870 miles on the route intended to be taken by the railway, when, on the 16th of February, 1881, Colonel Flatters, Captain Masson, the engineers Beringer and Roche, and Dr. Guiard were killed near the wells of Bir el-Gharama by Touaregs, who for several days had followed the party, biding their time. These implacable tribesmen also murdered M. Deverny, the commissary of the expedition, and thirty of the camel-drivers, who had been leading their beasts to water, and captured all the camels. The murderers were, however, afraid to attack the main camp, their victims having been

The massacre of the Flatters' Expedition, and retreat of the survivors.

surprised when engaged at a distance from the party. No sooner was the disaster known than it was necessary to discuss the situation. With so serious a loss both in men and beasts of burden, there was no alternative but to retreat to Wargla. Yet the situation was a desperate one, for between them and the base lay a sixty days' march without

BEDOUIN WOMEN.
(From a Photograph in the Paris-Tunis Collection.)

camels, and, further, only with such water and food as could be carried by the retreating members of the expedition through a region of such forbidding aspect that even to the desert wanderers it is known as "the land of thirst." Nor could the remnants of the expedition conceal from themselves the extreme likelihood that they would be followed by the murderers of Colonel Flatters and his companions, and be compelled to defend themselves in circumstances of the least favourable character. In short, to use an apt simile of M. Napoléon Ney,

who has written so admirable a sketch of the Saharan railway surveys, these unfortunates were "shipwrecked in the desert." Still, as no time was to be lost, the survivors started the very night that news of the catastrophe to their companions reached them. The baggage was broken up, and a division made of the money, food, and ammunition which it contained. The water-skins were intrusted to the strongest men, but every member of the fifty castaways carried a certain amount of the common baggage. Then step by step they trudged wearily over the desert which they had passed so recently in such high hopes. Harassed night and day by the Touaregs, they suffered greatly from hunger and thirst. By-and-by their provisions gave out, and they vainly imagined that their troubles were approaching an end when their hitherto relentless enemies offered to sell them some dates. These they eagerly purchased, only to learn, when it was too late, that the dates had been poisoned with the powder of a plant growing in the oases of the Sahara, and known to the Arabs as El-Bettina, and to the Touaregs as Falezlez. Its botanical name is *Hyoscyamus Falezlez*. No sooner had the famished men eaten the dates thus treacherously put in their way than they rushed about screaming like madmen. Some of them fired off their guns; others, running off, tried to strangle themselves in the vain attempt to keep out the air, which seemed to burn their lungs at every inhalation. Others tore off their clothes, springing backwards and forwards like caged beasts, shouting out words without any meaning. One of the officers fired upon his men, and had to be disarmed by the sharpshooters and the guides, who, fortunately for themselves, had eaten few or no dates. After a time, those on whom the poison had worked less violently begged for hot water, which, acting as an emetic, relieved their stomachs of the *Hyoscyamus*.

Meanwhile, the Arabs belonging to the party were seized by something like a panic, and the few men of the expedition who remained calm had great difficulty in preventing them from trying to escape. Some, indeed, did actually desert. The dreadful scene has been likened to the classic story that tells how the companions of Ulysses were transformed into swine by Circe, the Ææan sorceress. But the castaways of the Sahara had no good Mercury to counsel them when, next day, the retreat was continued. At Amguid their troubles were renewed, for the wells were found in the possession of a strong band of Touaregs, who were only driven away after a fight, in which four officers and twelve sharpshooters were killed.

The commissary Pobeguin was by this time the only Frenchman of the party left. Filling their water-skins with the fluid that had cost them so dearly, the thinned party of retreating explorers continued the march, until by-and-by the Touaregs, reaching the limits of their own country, gave up the pursuit.

But while harassment from their enemies stopped, the miseries of hunger again came upon them. Several of the men succumbed,

ST. LOUIS, SENEGAMBIA: AVENUE DE COCOTIERS DE GNET-NDAR.
(*From a Photograph taken for the Paris Society for Evangelical Missions.*)

some to lack of food and fatigue; but others, horrible to relate, crazed with sufferings, slew their companions and fought over the bloody remains. The commissary officer was eaten on the 31st of March, in circumstances so horrible that the historians of the expedition prefer by common consent to draw the veil over this portion of the lurid picture. Suffice it to say that on the 2nd of April four sharpshooters, barely alive, reached Wargla, and three others were picked up on the road—these seven men being the sole survivors of the eighty-eight persons who, less than five months before, had left the desert town at which they now found succour.

The horrible fate of the Flatters expedition, instigated, it is now known, by Abd-el-Kader ebn Ba-Djonda, of In-Salah—though the worst facts connected with it were not told for many years afterwards, and, indeed, until M. Ney put them into print* were not generally known even in France—naturally prevented any immediate repetition of the experiment that had resulted so pitifully. Not only was little heard for eight years regarding the trans-Saharan railway—though, in 1886, another explorer, Lieutenant Palat, was assassinated—but, what is more remarkable, no efforts were made to punish the murderers of Colonel Flatters and his companions. This apathy doubtless reacted with evil effects upon the prestige of France among the Saharan tribes. The credit of reviving the long-dormant idea of such a railway belongs to M. Georges Rolland, a young civil engineer, who had established in the Sahara of Constantine an excellent colony, and in the arid regions of Wad-Rir between Biskra and Touggourt introduced a system of irrigation by which the desert had been transformed into a rich and profitable oasis by means of artesian wells. M. Rolland, in his efforts to rearouse public enthusiasm in the scheme which for a time had gone to rest, was powerfully supported by General Philibert, a retired Algerian officer.

Rolland's labours.

The result was that in 1890–91 the Algerians evincing most interest in the revival of the project voted an appropriation for the completion of surveys, and through their Chambers of Commerce pronounced distinctly in favour of the scheme. A Parliamentary Committee having declared in the same sense, a trans-Saharan railway became once more one of the colonial schemes of France. Surveys were again undertaken, and, though the first sleeper in the line, which is to end at Timbuctoo and at St. Louis, has

* *Scribner's Magazine*, November, 1891.

yet to be laid, we can scarcely doubt but that the railway is simply a matter of time. During the year 1892 MM. Foureau and Méry succeeded in reaching the country of the Touaregs—properly "Touâreg," the plural of "Targui"—which had not been visited since the Flatters mission was massacred, and induced the chiefs to acknowledge French supremacy and "protection."

Before, however, speaking of the explorations which have resulted so happily, we may describe more fully the means by which this remarkable public work is to be built. The line will naturally start from Algiers, which is already connected with Tunis by means of an iron road; and, as Algiers is only a twenty-four hours' voyage from Marseilles, the projected railway may be said to be continuous from Paris, with the exception of a single day's voyage. Algeria furnishes abundance of iron, and for some distance the route would not run far from the extensive forests of that country; while water, we have seen, is found plentifully under the whole Sahara along the line of the proposed road. These circumstances will not only facilitate the work, but make the territory through which it runs of marked value in the near future; for "with sand and water one accomplishes wonders in Africa."

As the Arab proverb runs, " Plant a stick in the sand, water it, and you will have a tree;" and the tree which is to be the Arab the tree of all trees is the date-palm. **Artificial oases and the date-palm.** for dates are to him what wheat is to Europe, and rice to India and China. They are the staple of life, and the chief wealth and commodity of barter to millions of people, by whom they are exported to every country in the world. In eight years after being planted the date bears fruit, and sometimes in favourable situations it returns a revenue within an even shorter period. Thus, with two hundred trees upon two and a half acres of ground, an income of £40 a year is secured to the capitalist, so that, in reality, a palm-orchard is as profitable to the Saharan Arab as the vineyard is to the toiler in the

CARAVAN AT A WELL IN THE DESERT (p. 90).

south of France. For if his fruit is slower in coming, there is no phylloxera to be feared. The date was, no doubt, the lotus of Homer, and on Djerba, an island off the coast of Tunis, which is now generally admitted to have been the home of the Lotophagi, whose palm-wine made the sailors of Ulysses forget "wife and child and slave," the date grows thickly to this day (p. 100). All that this beneficent tree wants is water, and this water can almost everywhere be obtained by sinking an artesian well.

One of the most striking evidences not only of the advantages which the native Algerians have derived from the French possession of their country, but of the ease with which large areas can be rendered productive by means of artesian wells, is seen in the oasis on which the ancient town of Touggourt is built. In 1856 this, like many other oases in the desert, had become more or less uninhabitable, owing to the old wells having become filled up, and the water necessary for the irrigation of the gardens reduced in amount. The consequence was that the people began to migrate in search of more hospitable quarters. These facts being brought before the Algerian authorities, an attempt was made to tap the supplies of water which were known to underlie so large a portion of northern Africa. After five weeks of persevering labour, the confidence of the engineer was rewarded by a water deposit being reached at a depth of less than 200 feet from the surface, and immediately afterwards a river rushed forth yielding 888 gallons a minute—double the quantity poured out by the famous well of Grenelle at Paris. The joy and gratitude of the inhabitants can be understood.

When the engineers first began to sink in the sand the village grey-beards shook their heads over the likelihood of their trials bringing forth what to them was the greatest necessary of life. With true Moslem fatalism they considered that the filling up of the old wells was an act of God, and that it was useless for men to oppose the ways of Providence. "Our children are weak," said one of the chiefs, "if Allah, the worker of miracles, does not help us. In ten years the Wad-Rir will be deserted, and our gardens buried in the sand." The people would then perish of thirst. But when this unexpected river foamed over the parched ground the joyful occasion was celebrated by singing, dancing, and Arab "fantasias" of every description, and "The Fountain of Peace" was the name given by general consent to the first artificial well bored in this oasis.

Since that date numerous other wells have been sunk in the same region, with equal success, if possible, with a greater amount of astonishment, and with no less rejoicing. Thus, in October, 1885, there were in this irrigated district 114 artesian wells belonging to the French settlers and 492 belonging to the natives. Including the few natural supplies of water, these wells yield over 56,000 gallons of water a minute, or about 141 cubic feet a second—equivalent, M. Ney calculates, to one-tenth of the flow of the Seine in summer.

The result of this remarkable transformation is that the oases round Touggourt have become a most fertile portion of the Sahara. The forty-three oases in the Wad-Rir are said to support 520,000 date-palms in bearing, 140,000 palms less than seven years old, and about 100,000 other fruit-trees, the annual crop of dates being valued at more than one hundred thousand pounds. The wealth of the people in gardens, wells, houses, and other sources of riches, has, in the thirty years that have elapsed since the first well was drilled, increased fully five-fold. In seven years M. Rolland and his associates have "created" three oases and three villages, the existence of which depends entirely upon the artesian wells sunk in their midst. Indeed, the amazing success that has attended the beneficent efforts of the irrigating engineers justifies the remark of one of their number, that "The conquest of the land has been achieved by first conquering what is under the land."

With these encouraging results before them, the Parliamentary Committee began afresh the surveys for the trans-Saharan railway. Three routes were examined, but that proceeding from central Algeria—that is to say, by way of Philippeville, Constantine, Biskra, Wargla, and Amguid—was unanimously selected as the most favourable. Amguid must therefore be the central point in the line whenever it is built. From this place it can be extended, as

More railway explorations.

the trade of the country from finding its way down the Niger to the English trading-posts, if only a branch extending from Senegal meets that from the north. At present the Saharan railway does not extend farther than the oasis of Biskra, already a favourite winter haunt of the invalids who crowd Algeria for some months in the year. It is hoped that before long it will be extended to Touggourt

DATE-PALMS IN THE ISLAND OF DJERBA.
(*From a Photograph in the Paris-Tunis Collection.*)

circumstances may render advisable, to all parts of the Sahara.

But though the fertile Soudan will necessarily supply the chief traffic to the Saharan line, it will not be alone dependent on the produce of the country, for, leaving out of account Bornu, part of which at least extends into the Sahara, Damergou, near the Au mountains, in the pass of which Colonel Flatters was killed, contains some excellent land. Under the influence of irrigation this tract would equally respond to the sinking of artesian wells, since almost no portion of that region is naturally sterile. By this line the French hope to tap the Soudan, and to divert

and Wargla. The latter place, 220 miles south of Biskra, affords sufficient freight to render the line moderately profitable, since it is fed by the products of the oases already described. For the present, Wargla is the most southern outpost of the Algerian Government, its garrison consisting of a camel corps of 250 sharpshooters, led by French infantry officers mounted on dromedaries; so that the police force of the desert (p. 81) is capable of making long and rapid journeys. Wargla is as yet essentially a Saharan town, untouched by those evidences of civilisation which have destroyed the interest of so many other places farther north. The streets are narrow and tortuous, and blocked by arcades, in which a horseman can barely pass; and most of the houses are of one storey, and, like the early hours of the morning is, however, a busy quarter, the shops being, for the most part, in the hands of the Mozabites, natives

ARABS RETURNING FROM A RAIDING EXPEDITION.

every building in the town, whitewashed. The streets, it is needless to say, are extremely dirty, and the few reasonably well-built houses, of unbaked brick, are inhabited by the officials of greater wealth than the rest of the community. The market-place in of the M'zab, a district of oases very recently annexed to Algeria.

After leaving Wargla the line is intended to follow the bed of the Wady Igharghar by way of Mokhanza, a kind of glen free of sand that runs through the drifting dunes.

From this spot to Amguid, and, indeed, over the first thousand miles south of Wargla, there are said to be no engineering difficulties. Water can be found by sinking at almost any portion of the route selected. Tinassin seems especially favourable for forming an irrigating colony, and when Amguid is reached a commercial and agricultural centre 435 miles south of Wargla will be established right in the middle of the Sahara. From this point it is believed that the desert races will be easily controlled, and the central and western Soudan will be open to commercial conquest. For when the tribesmen discover that not only are the new arrivals too powerful to yield to their depredations, but that there is a lucrative market for their wheat, salt, textile fabrics, and cattle, their natural shrewdness will speedily enable them to come to the conclusion that it is cheaper to trade honestly with white men than to try to rob them with so little chance of success.

Route of the trans-Saharan railway.

It is possible that the termination of the line may remain for a long time at Amguid, a central position of sufficient importance to justify its being regarded as a point from which branch lines may extend in different directions. But at present the best line for the second section of the trans-Saharan railway has not been fully decided upon, though its extension to Kukawa, the capital of Bornu, on the shore of Lake Tchad, 1,906 miles from Philippeville, is a settled point.

So far the plans are fixed for the 653 miles between Biskra and Amguid, and the country has been generally surveyed from Amguid to Kukawa, 1,242 miles. But the financial future of the Saharan railway is still unsettled. Accepting the estimate of £40,000 per kilometre—6⅖ths of a mile—the total cost of the Saharan railway would be 337 millions of francs, or, in round numbers, not much short of the expenditure on the Suez Canal. It is hoped that the funds will be provided by a great company with privileges in the way of taking up irrigated land on each side, though probably the scandals connected with the Panama Canal may, for a time at least, impede the formation of this joint-stock enterprise. At the same time, one can hardly doubt but that before many years the railway will stretch not only to Lake Tchad, but to Timbuctoo, and from thence south-westward to the Niger and the French colonies on the west coast of Africa.

The traffic that is to support this line will consist of two sections. The first may be described as a local trade, namely, that between oasis and oasis. The second kind of business is between the extreme ends of the line, that is to say, between Algeria and France and the Central Soudan, though as irrigating wells are sunk, depôts and little settlements with markets will spring up along the line, since the route intended to be followed crosses in several places the line taken by the caravans that at present carry on the commerce of the desert. Grain from Algeria for the use of the Touaregs and the people of the Au country will always form a considerable import, which at present cannot be carried by means of caravans. Then the export of salt, which is found in the Soudan, will render the salt wells of Amadrhor places of considerable importance. It is also quite certain that as soon as the railway is completed and the desert tribes gain confidence, there will be a steady stream of visitors from the south pouring into Algeria, Tunis, and other portions of North Africa for the purpose of selling their hides and leather-work.

Traffic of the railway.

The Central Soudan must, however, form the chief support of such a railway. Its soil is of surpassing richness, and its natural resources, even rudely developed as they are at the present time, can furnish no small amount of traffic to any railway if the goods carried, as they have been for ages, by means of caravans, are taken as any criterion of what will eventually gravitate from the more expensive mode of carriage to the less expensive. At present the great difficulty is to find an entrance into that portion of the Soudan which will be crossed by this line. Hence it is hard to say with any accuracy what development certain sources of wealth could take under more energetic management than that which has so long controlled them. There are, for instance, great quantities of gold in the Soudan, but it is washed from the sands in the most primitive manner possible, and then only to very small extent. Gold quartz doubtless exists, but as no geologist has been able to spend his time in seeking for it, the question of its presence is purely speculative. Spices, ostrich feathers, indigo, hides, leather, various cereals and fruits, cotton, ebony, gums, and dye-stuffs either grow there or can be grown with the slightest encouragement when they can be carried to market without costing more in freight than their intrinsic value. Palm-oil is reckoned among the most important articles that will be carried by the Saharan railway. But the oil-palm never flourishes far out of the influence of the sea-breezes, and, therefore, if the greasy substance which is extracted from its fruit is to be produced in much greater quantities than at the present, by means of the stimulus which the new line will impart, it must be after a branch is extended to the west coast.

Wealth of the Soudan.

Still, for a long time to come the trans-Saharan railway must be regarded in the light more of a political lever than a mere commercial speculation. In other words, it must be looked upon as a great iron band with which to unite the French colonies in Western and Northern Africa, and—there is the consoling fact for France—as a means of preventing the vigorous Niger Company and the British colonies along the west coast from tapping what trade still finds its way across the Soudan to Algeria and Morocco.

As early as 1875, the missionary outposts of Cardinal Lavigerie (p. 105) were fully two hundred miles beyond the French frontier, and the incumbents of these stations so confident of success that three of them started to cross the desert to the Niger, intending to collect information about the country and its folk.

But before they had proceeded far on their way, the three young priests were beheaded and their followers plundered and dispersed by the ferocious tribesmen of the Sahara.* In these circumstances the "Armed Brethren of the Sahara," founded by Cardinal Lavigerie shortly before his death, who were to dig wells, establish oases, and form centres of civilisation, could scarcely have expected any better fate than for this romantic scheme to die almost as soon as it lived.

At the same time, while theory would lead us to suppose that the Arabs and other inhabitants of the desert would flock to the oases thus formed, and in time abandon their wandering life, the facts of the case point to a somewhat contrary state of matters. For instance, M. Dybowski, the companion of M. Crampel, in his unfortunate journey towards Lake Tchad, while reporting the success which has attended the irrigation schemes, and the possibility that before a great many years have elapsed some portion of the Sahara will be converted into green pastures, tells us that the oases are being neglected by the Arabs as soon as French authority becomes firmly established. An example of this is afforded by Biskra, at present the terminus of the Saharan railway. Hotels have been built here for the winter visitors, and a town, more French than Arab, has grown up in this secluded spot, but the native commerce has declined *pari passu* with the growth of foreign enterprise.

Biskra was formerly a busy commercial centre, but, like Touggourt and Wargla, its trade is rapidly on the decline. The reason for this is that the caravans avoid the oases under French rule, and turn aside to Morocco and Tripoli, not only because the Arabs prefer to deal with their co-religionists, but owing to the slave trade being suppressed in French territory.

The declining cultivation in the larger swampy oases M. Dybowski also attributed to the abolition of slavery. During the summer months these spots are hotbeds of

* Clarke, "Cardinal Lavigerie and the African Slave Trade." (1889), pp. 99, 100.

malarial fever.* But as soon as the disease appears the Arabs pack up and desert them, leaving their negro slaves, who are not subject to attacks of fever, to water the palms throughout the rest of the year. This system has naturally come to a close, or at least cannot be followed with the ease with which it was when the supply of slaves could be renewed by any caravan coming from the Soudan.

The traveller whom we quote, however, believes that colonies of free negroes might be established in less healthy spots with the best results. El-Golea he considers to be a site peculiarly favourable for agricultural industry. Water is abundant, and proofs of former fertility are to be found in the shape of numerous vestiges of human habitation and the remains of animals now extinct. Already, the sands are—as at Aïn Sefra—becoming bound together by the vegetation which irrigation permits to grow.† The jealousy of the powers that be will, however, eventually die away. It is mentioned just now simply as an illustration of the growth of civilisation in the Sahara and the stubbornness with which the old-time life is dying away.‡

Meanwhile, the sole reliance of the trans-Saharan railway is not upon the route from Biskra southward. In the opinion of many, the western line, which after crossing the Tell and the High Plateaux ends for the present among the sand dunes of Aïn Sefra in the Sahara, is preferable.§ For the line, it is hoped, will in time approach the fine oasis of Figuig, with its 15,000 inhabitants, and the collection of oases known as Touat. Both of these are claimed to be either in Morocco or within the influence of the Sultan of that country. But in neither is his authority well established, and, so far as the latter is concerned, it is disputed by the French, while the seizure of Figuig would be less apt to occasion a European broil than if a piece of Morocco nearer the sea was "protected." In any case, the possession of Figuig would render a march on Fez an easy act of aggression. For the present, however, the line is worked at a loss of about £5,000 a month, and the traffic is not infrequently simply the stores for the military stations in the vicinity of it. The occupants of these advanced posts of civilisa-

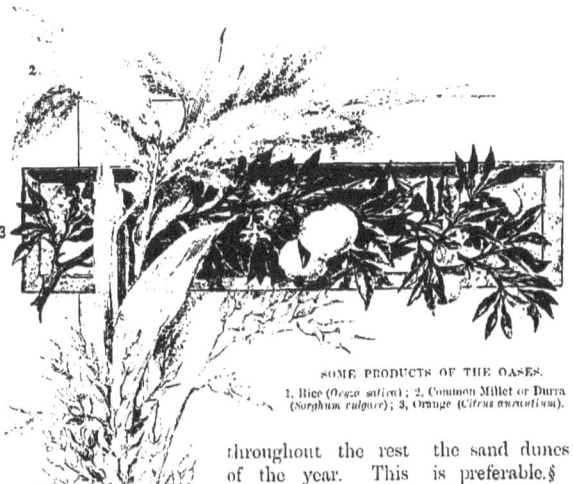

SOME PRODUCTS OF THE OASES.
1. Rice (*Oryza sativa*); 2. Common Millet or Durra (*Sorghum vulgare*); 3, Orange (*Citrus aurantium*).

* For an excellent account of the diseases and climatology of Africa, the reader is referred to a paper by Dr. Felkin in the *Proceedings of the Royal Physical Society*, Edinburgh, 1891-92, pp. 198-215.

† *La Dépêche Algérienne*, May 17th, 1893.
‡ *Bulletin de la Soc. de Géographie Com. de Paris*, Tome 12, No. 2.
§ Guy, "La Vérité sur le Transaharien" (1892), where the relative merits of the different routes are discussed.

tion are members of the Foreign Legion, soldiers of fortune belonging to many nationalities, whose careers have often been strangely chequered. But in the sands of Aïn Sefra, now getting green, or in the mountains north and south of the Arab town, they are permitted to atone for and, it may be, forget the past, since not a word is ever officially asked regarding their antecedents. The railway as surveyed would pass by Touat and Mor'ar Fokania to Bou Resq. The first of these places is an Arab village in a pretty oasis where a stream tumbles over ledges of rocks. Just outside the oasis is a high rock, on which are sculptured figures of warriors, marriage ceremonies, and animals, such as ostriches, elephants, and oxen, which, M. Jacquot thinks, are probably the work of Egyptians long before the Arab invasion. But before Figuig is within striking distance many things will happen, among which are the Arab disturbances already showing signs of beginning.*

* Bissuel. "Le Sahara Français" (1891) and "Les Touareg de l'ouest" (1888); Vivarez. "Alger, Wargla, Lac Tchad" (1891); Foureau, "Une Mission au Tademayt (Territoire d'In-Salah) en 1890" (1890); Deporter. "Extrême-sud de l'Algérie" (1890) and "La Question du Touat" (1891); Duveyier, "Les Touaregs du Nord" (1884); Vatonne. "Mission du Ghadames"; Rohlfs, "Kufra" (1881), "Quer Durch Afrika" (1874), and other books; Derrecagaix, "Exploration du Sahara: Les Deux Missions du Lieut.-Col. Flatters" (*Bulletin de la Soc. de Géographie* (1862); Zittel. "Die Sahara" (1884); Alis, "À la Conquête du Tchad" (1891)—a work which must be accepted with care, so far as its statements regarding Great Britain are concerned, etc.

CARDINAL LAVIGERIE.
(*From a Photograph by Cepelle, Paris.*)

CHAPTER V.

THE MISSIONARIES: TILLING, SOWING, AND REAPING.

The African Missionary seldom an Explorer in the Strict Sense of the Term—Exceptions to the Rule—Africa one of the Oldest Mission Fields in the World—Great Language Groups and Religions of Africa—The Proselytising Faiths—The Jews of Ancient Origin in Africa—Their Creed Perhaps the Oldest of its Foreign Faiths—How the African Hebrews Live—The Romans in North Africa—What Remains of Their Civilisation—The Christian Churches of North Africa—Arrival of the Moslem—The Rapid Advance of Mohammedanism with the Conquests of the Arabs—Mohammedanism *c.* Christianity—The Extirpation of Christianity and its Reintroduction—Modern Missions—West Africa—Yoruba and Others—The Congo Missions—The Explorations of Comber and Grenfell—South Africa—North-East Africa—Abyssinia and the Troubles of the Missionaries There—East Africa—Krapf and Rebmann—Kilimanjaro and Kenia—Nyassaland and the Services of the Scottish and other Missionaries in Opening-up that Country—Dr. Stewart—Strange Races—The Zambesi Industrial Mission—Other Smaller Missionary Enterprises—Central Africa—Occupation of Tanganyika—Services of Captain Hore to Geography, etc.

BEFORE describing the journeys of the African hunters, and those whom we have called the international travellers, who filled up the great outlines made by the explorers whose journeys have been narrated in previous volumes, some account is called for of a class of self-denying men who, though not explorers in the ordinary sense of the term, have, in several cases, done more to open up Africa to commerce and civilisation than many whose names are more intimately connected with this enterprise. We refer to the missionaries.

These religious teachers went to Africa for a purpose, and for this object it was necessary for them to settle down in an appointed place—generally on the borders of civilisation, or in touch with it. Hence their labours, valuable though they have been in the development of Africa, do not show largely on the maps of that continent. This is the rule, and may be stated without any discredit to the pioneers of Christianity. On the other hand, many of the most famous of African travellers have been missionaries. Livingstone, it is needless recalling, spent the earlier years of his life as a South African missionary, and the most extensive of all his journeys were made in that capacity. Krapf and Rebmann were missionaries, and New (Vol. II., p. 263), who by following in their steps did so much to extend our knowledge of Eastern Africa

Missionary explorers.

gained his reputation as an explorer while engaged as a teacher of Christianity to the tribesmen. In more recent times Arnot, one of the latest crossers of Africa, undertook his travels solely in the interests of his work among the natives: and Grenfell and Comber, both Baptist missionaries on the Congo, like several of their colleagues, took ample advantage of the fact of their stations lying in close proximity to the unexplored country Nor must we forget the circumstances of Lake Nyassa being virtually taken possession of for Great Britain by the Scottish missionaries, as Tanganyika was seised of civilisation through the Protestants and Roman Catholics combined. The missionaries of Uganda—unfortunate though the relations of that country afterwards became—penetrated into the interior of Africa within a year of Mr. Stanley describing the field that was ready for them to reap. And lastly, the heroic labours of the Austrian missionaries on the Upper Nile (Vol. II., pp. 111-114) cannot be forgotten when the contributions to geography of these single-minded men are recalled.

However, in the pages that we propose to devote to the chief incidents connected with missionary efforts in Africa, we must of necessity limit ourselves to the features of these enterprises that were more or less connected with geographical exploration. The modern African missions have naturally of late years occupied a large space in the public eye.

But it is not to be forgotten that Africa was the scene of the earliest missionary labours of which we have any record; and that there have been religions other than Christianity which fiery zealots have advanced less by the book than by the sword. In the introduction to this work we sketched briefly the great divisions of the African peoples and the broad partitions which divide the languages (Map, p. 224) spoken by these numerous tribes. When we glance at the map of the religions of Africa (p. 109), we find their sects very numerous, though, broadly speaking, the faiths professed in the "Dark Continent" are only four — Paganism, Mohammedanism, Christianity, and Judaism, the last embracing only a small number of the inhabitants. To these may be added about a million of Hindoos, who in comparatively recent times have settled on the east coast. The Pagans—that is, the people professing none of the great book religions—are more abundant in Africa than in any other part of the world. The races practising Paganism are, as a rule, sunk in the lowest depths of barbarism. The deities whom they worship and the spirits whom they fear are revengeful demons rather than beneficent gods. Witchcraft in various forms exercises a baneful control over their lives, and the fetish-men, taking advantage of this superstition, are even more powerful than the chiefs themselves. Human sacrifice is prevalent among almost all of the African tribes: and, though there are heights and depths in the degradation of the heathen races, among few of them is there any clear idea of a future life. "When a man was born he was born," replied one of these black materialists, when approached on the subject,

The oldest missions in the world: African religions.

"and when he died he was dead, and there was an end to the palaver." Mohammedanism is one of the introduced religions in Africa. Paganism, indeed, is the only native one. Islam appeared in northern Africa in the seventh century, and in an incredibly short space of time carried the faith of the Koran over a vast extent of country; and, unless we except Christianity, is the only African religion that is steadily extending its bounds.

Judaism need not be referred to, for it is not a missionary religion. It does not attempt to make proselytes, and is professed by no people except the ancient race who regard it as the faith transmitted to them by their fathers, and as such to be cherished by their children.

As for Hindooism, it is simply the religion of the Banians, or emigrants, who come from Bombay mainly into Zanzibar and what were recently the Sultan of Zanzibar's dominions as merchants, usurers, and petty traders of all sorts. But they ignore alike Christian, Jew, Pagan, and Moslem; they practise their own worship, but display no desire to convert others from theirs. The same may, indeed, be said for the Mohammedan Malays who were settled by the Dutch, in some cases as slaves, in the Cape Colony.

Christianity and Mohammedanism are, therefore, the only two faiths that come within the scope of this chapter. Yet it is doubtful whether Judaism was not the first foreign faith known in Africa. Most of the Jews now living in the Barbary States, or in the European colonies, are comparatively new-comers—inhabitants of Spain, Portugal, and other European countries, who were driven to take refuge in the Moslem countries of northern Africa at the time the

Judaism in ancient Africa.

JOHANN LUDWIG KRAPF.
(*From a Print.*)

Christian sovereigns and their subjects set so poor an example of toleration by persecuting the Mohammedans, whom they despised as followers of the false prophet.

The advent of the greater number of these refugees does not date more than four hundred years back, and most of the Jews settled in the British colonies, and many even in Algeria, Tunis, Tripoli, and Morocco, have might readily be taken for the other inhabitants of the country. It is also not uncommon to come upon little tribes of so-called Arabs, who in features and by the gossiping legends of the natives seemed well established as the descendants of Jews who adopted the faith of Islam at some time in the remote past. It is also affirmed that, covered by the sands of the desert, are

REMAINS OF THE CISTERNS OF CARTHAGE, WITH THE BYRSA HILL, THE PORT (COTHON), AND THE GULF OF TUNIS, ETC., IN THE DISTANCE.
(*From a Photograph in the Paris-Tunis Collection.*)

been attracted thither within this century. But in the interior of Morocco, in the Atlas Mountains, in the depth of the province of Sus, and in the oases along the route from Morocco to Timbuctoo, there have been, from time beyond which the memory of man does not extend, little colonies of Jews (Vol. I., p. 306) who speak no other language than Arabic, or, in some cases, no tongue except Berber, and who, except for their marked features and the religious fervour which they have maintained throughout all persecutions, tombstones with inscriptions in Hebrew characters, the remains of settlements of which the legend no longer exists.

These early colonies of Jews must have been founded by emigrants from Palestine, and one can hardly doubt that, arriving as they did long before the Arabs entered the country as conquerors, their Jewish monotheism and elaborate ritual must have influenced the then Pagan Berbers, among whom they settled as merchants or as agriculturists.

However, leaving the Jews out of the

THE EARLY AFRICAN CHURCHES.

question, Christianity was very early introduced into northern Africa, and the African and Morocco were, long before the Christian era, flourishing colonies of the Roman Empire.

MAP SHOWING THE DISTRIBUTION OF RELIGIONS AND MISSIONARY STATIONS IN AFRICA. (By E. G. Ravenstein.)

Church shared in all the triumphs and schisms of early Christianity. Tripoli, Tunis, Algeria, All over the country, but especially in Tunis, are found memorials of these early colonists of Africa. Amphitheatres (p. 84), temples, churches, tombs, and fortresses, besides numerous private houses, in spite of twelve centuries of Arab vandalism, still remain in massive ruins to attest the prosperity and the enterprise of a race who occupied parts of the country now uninhabited, or, under better climatic conditions, were able to grow the vine and the olive in regions now absolutely arid (p. 82). Christianity was, however, not generally adopted by the African colonists until a comparatively late period, and was still regarded simply as an Eastern faith long after it had passed the persecuting stage in Europe. As Gibbon observes: "While the Roman Empire was invaded by open violence or undermined by slow decay, a pure and humble religion gently insinuated itself into the minds of men; grew up in silence and obscurity, derived new vigour from opposition, and finally erected the triumphant banner of the Cross on the ruins of the Capitol."

The early Christian Church of Africa.

Little is known of the African Church until the end of the second century, but during the following century Christianity in that part of the world experienced its period of greatest trial and greatest glory. Fervour and devotion permeated the converts, and martyrdom was almost eagerly sought for by the professors of the new creed. The names of 580 sees between Cyrene and the Atlantic have been preserved in the records of that period; and among the most illustrious ornaments of this missionary church were Tertullian in the second century, Cyprian in the third, and Augustine in the fourth. The schism of the Donatists wrecked the African Church grievously, just at the time when the mountaineers were descending with eager ferocity to attack the settlements near the coast. The result of this Donatist division was civil war, which lasted for the better part of a century. And even after the quarrel seemed partially settled some of the wilder spirits of the Donatists joined with Genseric, King of the Vandals in Spain, and some of the native tribesmen, to devastate the colonies then in that condition of anarchy and confusion which before long afforded an inlet for the enemies who broke up that portion of the empire.*

For in the year 647 arrived the fiercest and most successful enemies of the Roman colonies in North Africa, and, in their train, the missionaries who rooted Christianity out of the country which they had conquered. When the Arabs invaded the Barbary States, eager to spread the faith of the Prophet by fire and sword, the greater portion of the colonists of Africa must have been Christians. The old faith had died out among the Roman settlers, and the "Mauri"—hence the term "Moors"—now semi-civilised, might also have adopted the religion which we may fondly believe to have been brought for the first time into Africa by those Hellenist Jews who heard Peter preach on the day of Pentecost. Yet at the present time there are no more fiercely fanatical Moslems in all Africa than the Berbers who constituted the native races with whom the Romans had to deal. As for the colonists themselves, many of them were murdered by the invaders. Others left for more peaceful homes, and some, it is possible, sought freedom from persecution by nominally accepting the creed of the newcomers. Many of the Christian churches were converted into mosques, and those which were not so utilised were destroyed out of fanatical hatred towards Christianity. Statues, symbols, and inscriptions alike fell victims to the fury of these bigoted barbarians; and, as this iconoclasm continued for ages, the wonder is that so many memorials of the past still remain to attest the greatness of the Roman colonies and the hold which

Introduction of Mohammedanism.

---

* The works on the African Church form quite a library by themselves. Those of Schelshate, Leydecker, Morcelli, Münter, Sebour, Barges, Yanoski, Godard, Hirschfeld, Marshall, Angele, Fabre, Guis, Sainte-Marie, and Ramsay need alone be mentioned as almost exhaustive from a historical point of view. See also Playfair's "Bibliographies" of Algeria and Tripoli, Playfair and Brown's "Bibliography of Morocco," and Ashbee's "Bibliography of Tunis," for references to other works.

Christianity had obtained upon them. In Tunisia—nearly equivalent to the Roman province of "Africa"—the ruin was so thorough that the population has fallen from eighteen millions to less than two millions; and, instead of eighty towns, it is now difficult to enumerate seven or eight, and none of them—with scarcely the exception of Tunis—of any importance. After the fall of Carthage (p. 108) the massacre of the Christians began afresh, and up to a very recent date slavery or martyrdom was the lot of all who professed the abjured faith.*

But it is certain that before long Christianity was completely exterminated—the only instance on record in which after it has been introduced into a country it has been subsequently eradicated. Yet the Mohammedanism of some of the mountain Berbers is still somewhat corrupt and their ritual defective. They eat the wild boar and drink the juice of the grapes which they cultivate, but they yield nothing in fanaticism to the rest of their coreligionists, and hold the very name of Nazarene in holy abhorrence. Nevertheless, it is said that the sign of the Cross may be sometimes detected among the ornamentation of the Morocco Berbers, and that the women in their sorest hour of trial will be heard crying, "Oh, Marie!"—thus echoing a traditional prayer which their ancestors were taught twelve centuries ago. At the same time, it is needless to say, the phrase has lost to them every trace of its true meaning. It is also affirmed, on less substantial authority, that, shoaled up by drifted sand, the remains of Christian churches still exist in the remoter parts of the Sus province; and it is suspected that some of the older tombs to which pilgrimages are made may be really the graves of early Christian Fathers.†

Islam, ever since its entrance into Africa,

has been a missionary creed. It has never contracted its bounds to any appreciable extent. Paganism has never crowded it out of any region where it has obtained a footing, nor has Christianity ever curbed its bounds. On the contrary, it has been making proselytes for twelve hundred years, and it is making proselytes still. A curious instance of this may be adduced from a British colony on the west coast of Africa, namely, that of Lagos. The Niger has been, and continues to be, the high-road from the north and east of Mohammedan people, and their active pioneers towards the western coast of Africa have been the Fulahs (Vol. I., p. 223) and the Kambaris, who in the past overran each country, and have succeeded in contracting the area of Yorubaland. Mohammedanism was introduced to Lagos in the year 1816. About 1836, when civil war broke out, the Moslems fled to the town of Ibi, where they remained until they were invited back to Lagos about four years later. Since that day they have increased rapidly, and are now characterised by Sir Alfred Moloney, at one time Governor of the colony, as a most orderly, intellectual, and respectable class of citizens, comprising members of all the tribes of Yoruba, though the prominent men among them are of the Houssa and Bornu peoples. The present Mussulman population of the colony is estimated at 15,000. Yet when Sir Richard Burton made his estimate in 1863‡ they did not number more than 800. In short, notwithstanding the fact of a Christian mission having been established in the Yoruba country for more than fifty years, the gain in converts has been infinitely greater on the side of the Mohammedans than on that of their rivals.§

---

* Sainte-Marie. "La Tunisie Chrétienne" (1878): Tissot, "La Province Romaine d'Afrique" (1884-88), etc. There is an excellent sketch of the African Church and early missions in Walker's "Missions in Western Africa," pp. 88-177.

† The Moors sometimes reverse this. Thus in M. Charant's day in the middle of the seventeenth century—

there was a monument at a place called "Gomet" in Morocco (probably Aghmat) which was thought to be the grave of St. Augustine, whom the Arabs called Sidi Belabech. Everyone who has visited the site (p. 108) of Carthage must also remember the native village of Sidi Bou-Saned, from the tomb of a saint of Islam whose name the Arabs affirm to have been St. Louis, who on his deathbed became a convert to Al-Islam!

‡ "Wanderings in West Africa" (1863).

§ Moloney, *Proceedings of the Royal Geographical Society*, 1890, p. 599.

The Moslems' teachings have ever had greater attractions for the African negroes than Christianity. The formal ritual of Islam appeals to their crude intellect. It saves the trouble of thinking to embrace a faith that does not appeal to sentiments which many of them are incapable of understanding. In Islam no doubt the weeds and the corn grow up with equal luxuriance; but, on the other hand, by

Moham-medanism v. Christianity.

MARABOUT (MOHAMMEDAN DEVOTEE), GAMBIA.
(*From a Photograph by the Rev. J. T. F. Halligey.*)

the negro the weeds are looked upon as of as much value as the grain, and are cultivated with equal care. To perform such and such like motions when they pray, in the direction of Mecca; to mention the name of Allah unendingly in every hackneyed phrase; and to dress in robes that have been prescribed by their religion is far less confusing to the African intellect than to be permitted any choice in the matter. For the same reason it is soothing to the negro to learn that in "The Book" both the moral law and the civil code are to be found. He is not puzzled by contradictory acts of the local legislature. The Koran simply says so-and-so, and there is an end of the matter. Nor is it to be denied that the influence of Mohammedanism upon Africa has, on the whole, been for good. To pass, say in West Africa, from the Pagan negro village, with its filth, its fetishmen, its human sacrifices, its Mumbo-Jumbo, and its half-naked, ape-like inhabitants, to one of exactly the same race professing Mohammedanism, affords a contrast which at once strikes the least observant traveller. So shrewd a critic as Mr. Joseph Thomson particularly notes this. In his journey up the Niger river he tells us, as others have told us before him, of the large, well-built towns of the Soudan (Vol. I., p. 287), of the people clothed in decent, and sometimes sumptuous raiment, behaving with self-possessed dignity and exhibiting signs on every hand of opulence and industry. Here the stranger is treated with hospitality, and his hosts, in spite of their black faces, conduct themselves in every essential respect like well-bred gentlemen. If the veriest rascals, they do not display their rascality. Yet these people were not many years ago simply negro savages who lived in dread of the fetish and the fetishman (p.113), whose only faith was a set of grovelling superstitions and whose hope of a future life was either non-existent or vague and shadowy. The teaching of the Koran had formed semi-civilised nations out of these degraded barbarians. Once within the pale of Islam all men are, theoretically at least, equal; and the negro who had lived in daily dread of being captured as a slave by the white-robed traders, learned that once he became one of their coreligionists, "The Book" forbade him to be taken as a bondman, whatever might be the Arab or the Fulah's interpretation of the Prophet's command. Mohammedanism, it is said, and said with truth, does not admit of any great progress. The Koran is the Alpha and the Omega of the pious Moslem, so that a confused farrago of

FETISH CUSTOMS FOR THE DEAD, LITTLE POPO, WEST AFRICA.
(From a Photograph by the Rev. B. gan Bey, Lagos.)

three faiths compounded by an epileptic camel-driver 1,300 years ago must be the code of laws by which men of the nineteenth century have to govern their daily lives. It is therefore undeniable that advances in modern civilisation are impossible to Mohammedan people who obey the Koran in its strict integrity. Turkey has progressed, Egypt has grown greater, Persia has taken on the gloss of Europe, and India has outlived its ancient ways, in spite of their faiths; but it must be remembered that the points in which they have progressed have been just those that are inimical to the letter of the Koran. Countries, indeed, like Morocco and the Soudan look upon Turkey and Egypt as little better than lands of the infidel.

Mohammedans are also accused of religious intolerance, expressed in the most brutal manner to dependents who are not of their faith. This religious *hauteur*, this actual or implied claim that the members of their faith are alone to be chosen, is, however, so far as Africa goes, not confined to the Moslems. It is a racial trait which the higher is apt to display to the lower stock; and, servant of servants as the African has ever been, he has had to bear the brunt of this feeling more than any other race, or is more apt to display it when taught that in Islam alone is there a chance of Paradise.

But still, after all has been said that can be said against Mohammedanism as a faith and as a missionary power, it is undeniable, as Dr. Blyden—himself an African—acknowledges, that "between Sierra Leone and Egypt the Mussulmans are the only great intellectual, moral, and commercial power. The tribes intervening have for more than three hundred years been in the hands of Islam. It has taken possession of and has shaped the social, political, and religious life of the most intelligent of the tribes. Its adherents control the politics and commerce of nearly all Africa north of the equator."* Since the decay of Egyptian civilisation and the fall of Carthage, the greatest city that Africa has ever seen,

* "Christianity, Islam, and the Negro Race." p. 28.

the rise and spread of Mohammedanism has been the greatest factor in the civilisation of Africa. It is unquestionable that the displacement of Paganism by this form of monotheism has been to the advantage of the negro. Its apostles have been as self-denying, as single-hearted, as any of the Christian missionaries, and, unlike the Christian missionaries, the Mussulman teachers have assimilated with the people. For, as M. Reclus remarks, the European is in Africa necessarily an alien. He cannot give his daughter in marriage to a native Christian, any more than he can, with self-respect, take to wife a daughter of the land. Moreover, the Arabs spread their faith and their civilisation gradually; and hence, wherever they go, they speak the language and understand the habits of the people they desire to influence.

At the same time it would be idle to claim for Mohammedanism a high place in abstract ethics. Morality, as Europe looks upon personal morals, is strange to the greater number of the African professors of the religion of Mohammed. It is simply when contrasted with Paganism that praise can be given to adherents of the faith of the Arabian prophet. Compared with Christianity, it is a stationary, a retrograde, form of worship. Be that as it may, the future religion of the greater portion of Africa on the northern side the Atlas will be Islamic. But that of the vast majority of the people of tropical Africa, not taking the west coast into account, bids fair to be Christian.

Christianity, we have seen, at one time was more or less the creed of the greater portion of northern Africa. Of this early church not a remnant is left except the Copts of Egypt and its daughter church in Abyssinia, both lingering "in a sadly depressed and corrupted state." Elsewhere, the flood of Mohammedanism has washed away the traces of the faith implanted in the first seven centuries of the Christian era. At almost no period in its history has the Coptic Church ever proselytised; and now, surrounded as it is by Moslems, its very existence depends on not attempting to bring converts into its fold. It has never been a missionary church, and, so far as the subject of this chapter is concerned, is a negligible quantity.

The reintroduction of Christianity into Africa. For eight centuries no serious attempt was made to reintroduce Christianity into Pagan Africa. Yet it died hard, for as far back as 853 we hear of a Christian martyr in Morocco. Among the Berber mountaineers in that country traces of Christianity, we have seen, long survived the Islamic conquest; and as late as 1550, when Diego de Torres traversed the Atlas, he saw various Christian rites among the tribesmen, and heard of a bell kept, with certain books dating from Christian times, in a cave, and regarded with superstitious veneration by those who had access to them.* As early as the eleventh century attempts were made to reintroduce Christianity into the Barbary States, and during the pontificate of Gregory VII. there were two Bishops of Africa.† These, however, were probably only *in partibus infidelium*.

It was only when Portugal became a great exploring and a great colonising Power that— as was always the custom with the mediæval conquerors—the priests followed in the soldiers' train, and speedily established themselves with such courage and self-denial on the north, the west, and the east of Africa, that flourishing Christian settlements grew in the midst of Paganism. Roman Catholic churches and cathedrals rose in Abyssinia alongside those of the older Greek form of Christianity, until the just jealousy of the "Negus," or sovereign, regarding the political intentions of the Jesuits, compelled them to withdraw from that kingdom.

In Loango, Angola, Congo, and the Mozambique country the success of the missionaries

* "Histoire des Chérifs" (D'Angoulême's Trans.). p. 151.
† Godard, "Maroc." p. 318. The various modern missions to the Berbers and other Mohammedans in North Africa, do not, in common with those to the Jews, come within our survey, which takes cognisance solely of those to the Pagan, or uncivilised, portion of the continent.

was more marked than has been the case at any other period in the history of Christianity in Africa. All over the country, which constituted in the sixteenth and seventeenth centuries what was known as the Congo Empire, may be seen ruined churches or cathedrals, long fallen from their ancient grandeur, which attest the success of the Fathers at that period. Yet, as we shall see presently (p. 120), outside the Portuguese colonies scarcely a tangible trace can now be found of the Christianity which two hundred years ago was supposed to have tinctured the whole population of the vast area of country mentioned. There are plenty of Christians, in name at least, though, in reality, they practise the worst features of Paganism. Nor are the priests who attend to their spiritual wants, in all cases, well fitted to set an example to their degraded flocks—people who have fallen from the position their ancestors attained under a more intellectual and zealous class of missionaries. The truth is, that baptism was administered wholesale, and Christian observances were too freely accommodated to heathenish superstitions and customs. The young were not educated, and the hold of the Church upon the older savages was fostered by an exercise of so-called miracles. To these explanations of the decay of Christianity in the Portuguese territories may be added the cruel punishments inflicted for the slightest deviation from the rules of the Church, and the demoralisation caused by the slave trade. This made it almost impossible for any teacher to impress those who daily practised, and who were asked to practise, most abominable acts of cruelty and dishonesty. Natives whose children or whose relatives had just been locked up in a slaver's barracoon, could scarcely look with much kindness upon a church whose bishop had a marble chair placed upon the pier—as might be recently seen in Loanda— from which to bless the slave-ships lying in the roads.

We are speaking at present simply of the Roman Catholic missions as seen in the Portuguese territories. In other parts of Africa

THE STORY OF AFRICA.

MOHAMMEDAN JOLOFFS, GAMBIA.
(From a Photograph by the Rev. J. T. F. Halligey.)

they have been more successful. In many cases the efforts of the priests for the civilisation of the natives deserve the utmost praise; and in the Barbary States they were sometimes enrolled in the noble army of martyrs (p. 115).

The Protestants did not enter on the missionary field until comparatively late after the Reformation. It could scarcely be expected that the Guinea traders would receive missionaries with any great warmth, since, if they preached honestly, the tenor of their discourses must necessarily have been inimical to the staple trade of the country around them. However, in 1736, the Moravians began work on the Gold Coast. But after thirty years' struggle with the climate and the depressing influences against which they had daily to contend, the enterprise was entirely abandoned. About the middle of the eighteenth century the Society for the Propagation of the Gospel sent a missionary to the Guinea Coast, and in 1765 an ordained negro; but we cannot learn that any permanent work was accomplished. Towards the close of the same century the Baptist Society and the Glasgow Society despatched evangelists to Sierra Leone. The Scottish (Edinburgh) Society, and the London Society also entered the field, and for a time several American societies maintained missions on the coast, mainly in what is now Liberia; while the Quakers were not behind in trying to accomplish good among the Joloffs and other tribes. But the historian on whom we are depending for these facts remarks : " Some proved unfit men, one or two died, and there were none left when the Church Missionary Society began its now world-wide mission by sending two men to the Susu country, near Sierra Leone. The Wesleyans soon followed, and the extension of their work along the coast to Yoruba and the Niger has gone on nearly *pari passu* with that of the Church Missionary Society. These two societies now divide between them the large majority of the native Christians in northern and West

Protestant missions: West Africa.

IMAGES AT CHIEF'S HOUSE, OGBOMOSHO, YORUBA.
(From a Photograph by the Rev. J. T. F. Halligey.)

Africa." The United Presbyterians have long had stations on the old Calabar River. "Other important missions on the coast are those of the American Societies in Liberia, and the Basle Society on the Gold Coast (and in Ashantee). The English Baptists had a mission at the Cameroons, but they have

The outcome of this laudable zeal is that almost the entire coast-line of West Africa, and part of the interior, is studded with missions. The best-known of these is that of Yoruba. It originated in 1844, with missionaries sent from the Sierra Leone stations, and has extended its operations coastwise into

FETISH PLACE, WITH CLAY IDOLS, PORTO NOVO, WEST AFRICA.
(From a Photograph by the Rev. J. T. F. Halligey.)

been obliged to abandon it since the Germans annexed that territory. In West Africa, south of the equator, the Protestant missions are of recent date. Since the determination of the course of the Congo, the Baptists, English and American, have made the river their special field. Bishop Taylor, of the American Episcopal Methodist Church, has led a party to Angola, and the American Board (Congregationalists) has a mission in Benguela." (p. 118).*

* "Church Missionary Atlas" (7th Ed.), p. 35, from which excellent work many of these data have been obtained.

the region which is now the British colony of Lagos, though, in reality, the first missionaries to the Yoruba country landed at Badagry, now in the same dependency. Threatened more than once with destruction from Dahomeyan invaders, expelled from Abeokuta as the representatives of the nation with whom the chiefs were at feud, and at times in peril from native quarrels, the mission has established itself all over the Yoruba country † (Vol. I., pp. 256, 260, 261 ; Vol. III., pp. 113, 116, 117).

† Pinnock, "The Yoruba Country" (1893).

The Niger Mission, which, by aid of their steamer *Henry Venn*, is extending up the river to the confines of, and even into, the Mohammedan states, will always possess an interest from the fact of the first bishop of that diocese being the late Dr. Crowther, a native Yoruban.

The influence of these Christian teachers settled in the midst of the most degraded races of all Africa cannot but be admitted as conducive in the highest degree to a civilised life. In this chapter, however, we must confine ourselves almost entirely to the services of the missionaries in opening up the country, and in exploring the regions in the vicinity of their stations, thus aiding, consciously or unconsciously, in the development of Africa.

Accordingly, before leaving West Africa, a few words are demanded for the important explorations of the Baptist missionaries on the Congo. No sooner had Mr. Stanley descended this great river, and the Association out of which subsequently grew the Congo Free State been established, than the missionaries of different sects and nationalities formed stations along its banks, until at present there are numerous growing centres of civilisation for hundreds of miles to the eastward. The Roman Catholics —Belgian priests, and members of the Société d'Alger (French), and the Société du St. Esprit; though, in most cases, the French missionaries are withdrawing to French territory—are working at Boma, Kwamouth, New Antwerp, in the Bangala country, and New Bruges, at the confluence of the Kwango and Kasai, and at New Ghent, nearly opposite Bangala. The American Baptist Missionary Union have their establishments at Palaballa, Banza, Mantcka, Lukungu, Leopoldville, Chumbiri, Mossembo, Irebu, and Equatorville. The Evangelical Alliance is at work at Ngangelo, the Swedes at Mukinbungu, and Bishop Taylor's mission, under the American Episcopal Methodists (who have stations in Angola and Benguela, where Mr. Arnot and his friends also have missions, p. 117) is represented by settlements at Vivi, Ntombé, and Kimpoko.

The Congo Mission.

But the earliest and perhaps the most energetic of all the Congo missions are those of the English Baptists. They have steamers on the river, and, in spite of the loss of many valuable lives, are constantly extending the sphere of their operations. At present their stations are at Ngombe, Ntundwa, Kinshassa, Lukolela, Bolobo, Lutete's, Lukungu, Bangala, and Upoto, while the Congo Bololo Mission, under the East London Missionary Institute, labours at Molongo and three other stations in Bolololand.[*] There is also, at Colwyn Bay, in Wales, a Training Institute at which native Congo boys are instructed as Protestant missionaries, schoolmasters, and craftsmen.

When the Congo was first opened up, the zeal of good men bade fair to do mischief where good only was intended, by an overlapping of missionary effort. Two English missions established themselves at Leopoldville, on Stanley Pool—the one on the right and the other on the left of the Government station. The establishment on Leopold Hill belonged to the English Baptists, and, from a munificent Leeds patron, was known as the Arthington Mission. The other, which was unsectarian, had been founded by Mr. Grattan Guinness and was known as the Livingstone Inland Congo Mission. Mr. T. J. Comber (p. 127) was the head of the Baptist Mission, and Dr. Sims presided over the other. Both were remarkably energetic, and for a time this energy was largely devoted to trying which should reach Stanley Pool first. Dr. Sims was the first to navigate any portion of the Upper Congo ; but the Baptists anticipated their friendly rivals in first occupying a station above Stanley Pool, though soon afterwards the Livingstone Mission arranged for a station as far inland as the equator. The Baptists were the first to launch a steamer, the *Peace*, which did such excellent service in exploration ; but the Livingstone Mission began building one at the same date that the other was ready.[†] By-and-by,

[*] Stanley, *Harper's Magazine*, 1893. p. 623.
[†] Stanley, "The Congo," Vol. I. (1885). p. 496.

however, this surplusage of labour, this rivalry which the natives misapprehended, these shades of religious doctrine which puzzled them, ended, so far as the Livingstone Mission was concerned, by its stations and property being made over to the American Baptist Missionary Union—the "A.B.M.U."—of the Congo residents. It would be ungracious and might be unjust, to attempt anything like an appraisement of the good accomplished by these twenty missions, manned by about one hundred clergy, not including native catechists—all volunteers for the often depressing, and, in the Congo country, perilous work on which they are engaged. Mr. Stanley and the officers of the Free State bear willing witness to the value of their labours in transforming the negro into a semblance of civilised man, by enlarging his intellectual horizon, and refining feelings brutalised by unnumbered ages of savagery.

However, this aspect of missionary life, interesting and, of course, all-important though it undoubtedly is, does not come specially within the limits we have assigned to these pages. We therefore turn to the services in opening up Africa that have been performed by two missionaries of the English Baptists, who in the course of a few years did work well worthy of comparison with that of some of their fellow-labourers already noticed (pp. 115–118).

Before reaching Stanley Pool by the river banks, Messrs. Comber, Grenfell, and their colleagues had made some extremely interesting attempts to do so by leaving the lower river for the old capital of the Congo kingdom, and thence trying to strike eastwards and northwards by Makuta, and thus come upon the Congo higher up. Mr. Comber, like his future colleague in exploration, had been a missionary in the Cameroons, part of which country—that back from the Cameroon Peak —he had travelled over.* When the Baptist Missionary Society selected the Congo River as the scene of their missionary efforts, the first aim of Mr. Comber and Mr. Grenfell was, we have seen, to reach Stanley Pool, in case the Jesuit priests might anticipate them. Before doing so, however, the two missionaries were directed to visit the capital of the old Congo kingdom, the greatness of which had been so exaggerated by the Portuguese and Italian padres of an earlier day.† The capital of this country, which is south of the Congo River, was Ambassi, which, on the facile conversion of the king to Christianity at the beginning of the sixteenth century, was changed by the Portuguese to San Salvador. Proselytes are affirmed

Explorations of the Baptist missionaries: San Salvador and the old Congo kingdom.

REV. GEORGE GRENFELL.
(From a Photograph by T. Lewis, Birmingham.)

to have increased so rapidly that in 1534 there were a cathedral and several churches in the town, and a bishop presiding over the faithful. Thirty-six years later, in the incursions of the Jaggas, Giagas, or Yakas (Vol. I., p. 116), probably wandering Zulus, who murdered and destroyed everything, the city of San Salvador was ruined, and the king, court, and clergy had to take refuge on one of the islands in the Congo, from which

* *Proceedings, Royal Geog. Society*, 1879, p. 225.

† Pigafetta, "Relatione del Reaume di Congo et delle circonvicaine contrade, etc." (1591); Odoardo Lopez, "Report of the Kingdome of Congo, a Region of Africa, etc.," translated by Abraham Hartwell (1597); De Tovar, "Mission Evangelica al Regno de Congo" (1649), etc.

B.M.S. CONGO STEAMER "PEACE."
(From a Photograph by the Rev. R. D. Darby.)

San Salvador is about one hundred miles distant.

The Giagas being expelled from the country, the town was rebuilt, and most of the kingdom ceded to the Portuguese. This arrangement did not last long; for early in the seventeenth century the mission establishment at San Salvador was broken up, owing to the hostility of the natives, and the bishop's seat transferred to São Paolo de Loanda (Vol. II., p. 216). In 1781—about a century and a half after the expulsion of the Portuguese—an attempt, also frustrated owing to civil war, was made to reopen the mission work at San Salvador; but we hear little more of the half-mythical town until 1857, when Dr. Bastian visited it, and found that this "city" was "only an ordinary native town, with a few scattered monuments of other days."* In 1873 the late Lieutenant Grandy, R.N.† (Vol. II., p. 281), passed through the town on a somewhat futile search for Dr. Livingstone, in case he reached the Congo country. He, like his predecessor, saw little except barbarism. A few of the leaders of the coast caravans spoke a little corrupt Portuguese; but the people, as a whole, had sunk into barbarism, if ever they had been raised above it, and offered no welcome to the white man: they had evidently no very pleasant legends of his ways towards the black one. Messrs. Comber and Grenfell were not more impressed in 1878. The king, it is true, still kept up a semblance of dignity under the lofty title of

* Bastian. "Afrikanische Reisen," etc. (1859); "Die Deutsche Expedition an der Loango-Kuste," etc. (1874-75).
† Grandy, Journal of the Royal Geographical Society, 1876, p. 428; Proceedings of the Royal Geographical Society, Vol. XIX., p. 78.

A.B.M.U. CONGO STEAMER "HENRY REED."
(From a Photograph by the Rev. A. Billington.)

H.M. Dom Pedro V., and flew a dark-blue flag with a golden star in the centre. But he proved to be an unimportant person, and was little able or willing to help them to reach Stanley Pool. They visited, however, Makuta, a country farther to the east, and nearer their destination. Tungwa, the capital of the region, had also been essayed by Grenfell on not only permitting them to enter his really pretty town, but according them a "grand reception, with much dinning of music." Makuta being a great ivory market, the king seemed richer than his neighbour of San Salvador. But it was in vain that the missionaries asked permission to make his town the interior base of their proposed operations

FIRST MISSIONARY ENCAMPMENT AT BOLOBO : REV. G. GRENFELL'S HEAD-QUARTERS IN 1888.
(From a Photograph by the Rev. R. D. Darby.)

the "search expedition," which Dr. Young, of Kelly, had so liberally subsidised. But the king, who is quite independent of the San Salvador dignitary, declined to see him, and, still more extraordinary, to receive his presents. "He wanted nothing to do with white men. What do they want, coming every day to my country?" was the pleasant speech of this Congo-land potentate. He was, however, much more complaisant to the Baptist missionaries, on the Congo River, or to give them carriers to that goal. He was afraid of the consequences if a white man was permitted to live in his country; for he knew that if any misfortune befell the neighbouring tribes they would blame him for the calamity, and go to war in consequence. Messrs. Comber and Grenfell were, therefore, forced to retire, lest they should bring any such evil fortune on their royal host.

The Falls of the Congo, round which a railway will one day run, were the great obstacles that had hitherto prevented the missionaries from reaching their goal on the Stanley Pool. A small steamer in sections was now sent out from England, and in due time launched on the Middle Congo. Meanwhile, Mr. Comber left England in advance of his vessel, with the intention of again reaching Makuta, and thence the Congo, by a march across the intervening country. This expedition was so far successful that in 1879 the party arrived with a sufficient number of carriers at San Salvador. But at Makuta the party met with a rebuff, though at Sunda, about two days' journey from Makuta, Mr. Crudington, one of the party, received a very civil reception.* But in the object of the expedition they were disappointed; for, being entrapped into visiting Makuta by an invitation from the treacherous king, Messrs. Comber and Hartland † were savagely attacked, and both injured by gunshot wounds while escaping to the friendly town of Sunda, where Mr. Crudington extracted the "bullet" from Mr. Comber's wound: it proved to be a square piece of ironstone. So far, therefore, the efforts of the missionaries had been futile: Stanley Pool was not to be reached by way of Makuta. Their long stay in San Salvador had, however, not been fruitless for geography. Among other interesting discoveries was that of the fine Arthington Fall, on the Brije River, in the Zombo Mountains, which formed one of the most striking views from the missionaries' house in San Salvador.

Makuta: an unfriendly king.

Mr. Comber was, however, not dismayed by the failure of his previous attempts to reach Stanley Pool by a journey across country from Makuta, or by the repeated desertions of the Kroomen, who, though admirably suited for work on board ship, are worthless on land, owing to the novelty of the duties and their consequent timidity. The Makuta people had a "big palaver" over the former hostile reception,

The Upper Congo reached.

and, learning that it had been decided in his favour, Mr. Comber resolved to make another trial. But again the Kroomen deserted on hearing of danger ahead, so that he and Mr. Hartland had once more to return to San Salvador. From this town they made for the Lower Congo, to assist Messrs. Crudington and Bentley, who eventually, by keeping along the river banks, reached the longed-for Stanley Pool, thus anticipating the arrival of a Jesuit mission which had set out with a view to strike the upper river by the route the Baptist missionaries had so frequently tried in vain. The Jesuits, it is said, were escorted to San Salvador by Portuguese officers and marines, and carried, as the most appropriate gifts to the negro "Dom Pedro V." a piano, large silver tankards and cups, "several kegs of rum, large cases of gin, gold cloth, etc." This notable journey in the annals of missionary effort took place in February, 1881.‡ The steamer, which afterwards did such admirable service on the river, having been constructed, the struggles to reach Stanley Pool came to an end, so far as the Baptist explorers were concerned. Their travels, of which the merest outline can be given in this place, deserve a fuller record than has yet been published, for in many respects they rank with the most romantic of African explorations: and if they had been undertaken in times not so crowded with journeys hither and thither on the continent which has ceased for ever to be "dark," would have obtained for the courageous missionaries an even higher reputation than they have so deservedly won.§ All of the African missionaries have been more or less explorers, and it is only the necessity of space that has compelled us to pass over with simple mention the travels, for example, of the Yoruba clergy and others, which, though of inferior importance to those of the Congo Baptists, were not without interest for geography, and for the opening up of the regions examined.‖

* *Proceedings, Royal Geog. Society,* 1880, p. 366.
† *Ibid.*, p. 765 ; *Ibid.*, 1881, p. 20 (Map).
‡ *Proceedings, Royal Geog. Society,* 1881, p. 353.
§ Bentley, "Life on the Congo" (1887).
‖ Milum, "Notes of a Journey up the River Niger to Bida, the Capital of Nupe, and Ilorin, in the Yoruba

One of the first explorations accomplished by Mr. Comber* after establishing his station at Stanley Pool was to make a boat voyage round that lake-like enlargement of the Congo. Nowadays this section of the river is so well known that a journey no farther into the interior of Africa scarcely merits a line in any geographical publication. But in 1883 it was still a novelty: even Mr. Stanley had not circumnavigated the piece of water to which his name had been given. Mr. Comber's trip was, therefore, an addition to our knowledge of the river. For, instead of finding it from two to seven miles broad and about nine miles long, his survey gave it a length of twenty-three miles, a breadth of about equal amount, and an area of 350 square miles, in place of the "fifty-five or thereabouts" assigned to this now notable water by its discoverer. Even then, as the natives were still divided in opinion regarding the white men, prudence compelled the explorers to hug the shore and thread the narrow channels inside the sandy and grassy islands which line it, so as to minimise the chance of a successful attack from the savages. "Dover Cliffs," about two hundred feet in height, and cut in the most fantastic way by the floods of the rainy season, were found to be neither chalk, as Mr. Stanley had imagined, nor pipeclay, according to a later legend, but the whitest silver sand, varied occasionally by an admixture of brown sand, and here and there by black masses of forest, which, by contrast, add to the beauty of the cliffs. The great island of Manyanga, in the middle of the Pool, was uninhabited save by elephants, buffaloes, and other game. Hippopotami were so abundant in this part of the Congo that hundreds were seen, sometimes in herds of from ten to twenty—apparently so little familiar with man that it generally required a second shot before they would put themselves out of danger. But though the "hippos" did not attempt hostilities, a huge crocodile made a savage rush at the boat, which it evidently mistook for the carcass of some animal floating down the current. Wild ducks abounded, and the tall adjutant stalked about the sandbanks in its stately, solitary, soldierly fashion. This bird is among the most voracious of its order. Nothing comes amiss to an adjutant; even a dead monkey goes down its capacious gullet whole—only the tail, in a case of this description recorded by Mr. Comber, causing inconvenience as it hung outside the bill. Pelicans in V-shaped flocks of twenty or thirty are also frequent, and

REV. J. HOLMAN BENTLEY.
(*From a Photograph by J. H. Killick, Holloway Road, N.*)

the coral-beaked and footed scissor-bills are found in flocks of one or two hundred.

An alternation of low hills, generally covered with umbrageous forest and long wooded reaches, imparts a certain picturesque beauty to the country, while the scenery at the entrance to the Pool is absolutely "grand." Villages and people are few: only one or two canoes were seen until Nshasha was approached on the party's return to their station of Arthington, which is built on the hill, at Leopoldville, close to the native village of Kintano.†

Country, 1879–80," *Proceedings of the Royal Geographical Society*, 1881, p. 26.
* Accompanied by Mr. Bentley and Dr. Sims.

† Comber, *Proceedings of the Royal Geographical Society*, 1889, pp. 71–75 (with Map).

Shortly after this expedition (1884), Mr. Comber was joined by Mr. George Grenfell (p. 119), who had already made some explorations of the Cameroon district from Victoria, the then Baptist Mission station there,* and, we have seen, had shared in various adventurous journeys in the country south of the Congo (pp. 119-121). The steamer *Peace* (p. 120)

The Bochini or Kasai River.

It is formed by the junction of several large streams, the most important of which is the Kasai; and, accordingly, in the latest maps it bears that name. Up this large tributary the missionaries steamed for fully seventy-five miles, until they arrived at the spot where the Mfini, flowing out of Lake Leopold (in reality, a tributary of the Kasai), joins with what is, no doubt, the Kwango. This proved to be a

BANGALA BOYS.
(From a Photograph by the Rev. R. D. Darby.)

being now put together, the river was explored above the Pool more accurately than had been possible on its first hurried reconnaissance. Keeping to the south side of the current, the mouth of the Bochini was entered. This important tributary of the Congo was described by Stanley as the Kwa (hence the station of Kwamouth), and has since received the name of the Ibari Nkutu, Wabuma, and Bochini, according to the various theories of its character or the different native nomenclature.

* *Proceedings, Royal Geog. Society*, 1882, p. 585.

fine stream, four hundred to five hundred yards broad (about twice that of the Thames at London Bridge), with a mean depth of twelve feet, and a current averaging one mile and a half an hour.†

† *Proceedings of the Royal Geographical Society*, 1884, p. 742, and 1885, p. 353 (Map). In the same volume there are two other admirable papers on the Congo below Stanley Pool—one by Sir F. J. Goldsmid (p. 177), and another by Mr. Delmar Morgan (p. 183). Sir H. H. Johnston gives his observations (as far as Bolobo) in "The River Congo" (1884), one of the earliest of the many books on that subject, but still one of the most valuable for its scientific remarks.

Between Stanley Pool and the Bochini mouth the banks of the river seemed uninhabited, and for a long distance up which its tributary penetrated, the country appeared equally desolate, though it looked fruitful. At places its borders were fringed by great grassy plains, with here and there a *Hyphæne* palm, but no other vegetation, the forest being far from the river. But on other stretches the scenery —wooded sand-hills, with the river ever contracting and expanding—looked almost picturesque. On some of the sand-banks were little clusters of huts, inhabited by Ba-buma people. "We asked them what they were doing, and found that they kept beer-shops, and also caught fish. Their beer was made from sugar-cane growing on the mainland: brought in large stone jars and calabashes, and stored in the little huts, it was sold to the *bona-fide* travellers passing constantly to and fro on their business—trading or otherwise." Nga-Nkabe, Queen of the Ba-buma, was a most interesting woman. She had a husband, but this prince consort knew his place, and kept it; so that, instead of interfering in the high affairs of state, Nchielo—that was his name—sat meekly smoking his pipe and philosophising, while his wife ruled. The queen was a tall, stalwart woman, muscular and brawny, about fifty years of age, with a fine, dignified air, and a great deal of authority about her firmly set mouth. She spoke little, but very much to the purpose; though making so little pretension to ceremony that she did not consider it out of place to paddle herself to the nearest plantain patch to cut a bunch for her guests.

Entering the main river again, the missionaries ascended it as far as Bangala, then a part of the river little known, but now a familiar mission-station (p. 124).

Another voyage by Mr. Grenfell in the *Peace* added greatly to our knowledge of the northern tributaries of the Congo. The Lefini River (the Lawson of

EVOLUTION OF A MISSION-HOUSE AT LUKOLELA, CONGO.
No. 1 (a Native Hut); 2 and 3 were successively utilised as kitchen, stores, etc.; No. 4, final stage.
(*From Photographs by the Rev. R. D. Darby.*)

Stanley) was found to be only navigable for two or three miles, when it became a torrent. The Nkenye, or Nkië, is a small, tortuous stream, with a mean breadth of sixty yards, a depth of twelve feet, and a current of 220 or 250 feet per minute. The Mobangi (Oubangi) is, however, one of the noblest of Congo tributaries. After following it from the spot where it forms a delta between twenty-six and forty-two miles south of the equator to 4° 30′ N., nearly 400 miles from its mouth, where Mr. Grenfell left it, just below the second rapids, it was still an open waterway, about 670 yards broad, with a mean depth of twenty-five feet, and carrying an immense volume of water, which it collected by endless tributaries rising in the Niam-Niam country and the watershed between the Nile and the west coast rivers. On this voyage, which occupied five months, Mr. Grenfell also entered the Ukere, the Lomami (Lubilash), the Mbura, the Mangala, and the Ruki for some distance. This was early in 1885.* In the autumn of the same year, Mr. Grenfell utilised the *Peace* for another few weeks' exploration of the Congo tributaries. On this occasion he ascended the Lulanga and Boruki, or Ruki† (that is, Black River), the only two of the great Congo tributaries on the southern bank between the Kasai and Lomami, still unexamined. The Lulanga runs nearly parallel to the main stream, but the Boruki is a still more promising waterway. It is formed by the union of three streams. The one which is properly so called is not navigable for more than six or eight miles; but of the other two the Juapa, which was ascended for 350 miles, was, when left, still an open waterway, 100 yards broad, twelve feet deep, and rolling along with a current of nearly 200 feet per minute.

Mobangi River.

The Lulanga and the Boru-ki Rivers.

* Grenfell and Comber, *Proceedings of the Royal Geographical Society*, 1885, p. 353; and Grenfell, *Ibid.*, p. 455.

† Grenfell, *Proceedings of the Royal Geographical Society*, 1886, p. 627 (Map). See, in the same number, Sir Francis de Winton's paper on the Congo Free State (p. 627) and the German Explorations (p. 634).

Still more recently — namely, in 1887 — Mr. Grenfell, in company with Mr. Bentley, ascended the Kwango as far as the Kikunji Falls, the point at which Major von Mechow, one of the many explorers who flocked to this region after Mr. Stanley's famous descent of the Congo, was obliged to turn back in 1880. About six miles above the junction of the Kasai with the Kwango, the Djuma, another large tributary, is reported to enter the river from the east. The Kikunji Falls are, however, scarcely worthy of the name, being only about three feet high, though insurmountable by the *Peace*.‡

Kwango River.

This brilliant series of explorations may be said to have ended in 1887. By that time the missionaries had selected the stations in search of which their many voyages had recently been made, and the Congo basin was getting well known, thanks to the travels of the officers belonging to the Free State and the many adventurous travellers who had been attracted to one of the few great areas of Africa until then virgin to the pioneer. Admirable work has been done since Mr. Grenfell and his colleagues began theirs; and though, possibly, exploration in a steamer is more comfortable than exploration on foot, the missionaries had a good deal of that also. Mr. Grenfell alone, before he undertook his survey of the Congo, travelled in the Cameroons country between the years 1874–78, some 1,300 miles on foot, and more than 5,000 in canoes. In, therefore, receiving from the Royal Geographical Society the patrons' medal as a mark of esteem for the extensive explorations recorded in the "Proceedings" of that distinguished body, Mr. Grenfell was awarded nothing more than his due. For though, perhaps, neither of the calibre of, nor with the opportunities of, Livingstone, he had acquitted himself with a zeal and a success worthy of the greatest of African travellers.

When we turn to South Africa we find that the Moravians were there also the pioneers

‡ *Proceedings, Royal Geog. Society*, 1887, p. 239

During the Dutch occupation of Cape Colony missionaries to the Kaffirs were not encouraged. George Schmidt, who went in 1736 to Genadendal, then known as Bavian's Kloof (the Baboon's Glen), was banished by the Dutch Government, for the crime of being "a great Hottentot converter." Slavery prevailed there, as it did in all the African colonies, and the farmers, though extremely pious, were more apt to look upon the children of Ham in the light of servants than as converts to the faith which they themselves professed. However, in 1799, the London Missionary Society began its beneficent campaign against ignorance and heathenism; and, had it done nothing more than bring to Africa men like Vanderkemp, Kichener, Campbell, Moffat, and Livingstone, it would have performed a great work for the regeneration—and, even in those early days, for the exploration — of Africa.* Twenty-three years later the Scottish mission, now under the auspices of the Free Church, began its operations, and still continues it from the well-known Lovedale Institution as the centre.

This admirable establishment (founded in 1841), where the results of missionary enterprise are seen to the best advantage, is situated about 650 miles N.E. of Cape Town, and about 40 W. of King William's Town. Kaffir children and young people are educated there, and teachers trained for native schools. At Lovedale also, the arts of civilised life—printing, bookbinding, telegraphy, blacksmithing, carpentering, tinsmithing, and the like—are taught, so that in almost every tribe there are now good workmen capable of instructing the others. On an average, as many as 700 native Africans are under tuition, and of more than 2,000 native "graduates" of Lovedale, of whom the after history could be traced, the majority proved highly creditable to the Institution. Though generously supported by the Free Church of Scotland, Lovedale, like Blythswood, its offshoot, 120 miles distant in the

* Moffat. "Missionary Labours and Scenes in South Africa." (Ed. 1846.) This is still an admirable book.

Transkei, is unsectarian. But so highly appreciated is the institution that about £2,000 per annum is paid by the natives for the privilege of being educated there.

The name of the Rev. Dr. James Stewart (p. 131) is now almost as familiarly associated with this establishment as those of the men already quoted. We shall, however, have again to meet him in another part of Africa, more as a pioneer than he could become in so comparatively well-known a part of the world as South Africa.

The French Evangelical mission has established several stations among the Basuto

REV. THOMAS J. COMBER.
(From a Photograph by Debenham & Gould, Bournemouth.)

tribes. The Rhenish Society, the Berlin Society, the Hermansburger Society, the Dutch Reformed Church, the Norwegian Society, the Finnish Lutheran Society—in addition to some Roman Catholic stations—all have missions dotting the country from Damaraland on the west to Zululand on the east; and in 1837 the Church of England sent a mission into Zululand under the Rev. F. Owen, who was, however, compelled to leave after a year or two's struggle with the cruelty and barbarism of Dingaan, one of the predecessors of Cetywayo. His work was never resumed, but under the auspices of the Society for the Propagation of the Gospel there are still flourishing missions in Kaffraria, Natal, the

Orange Free State, Mashonaland, and, in short, all over southern Africa, the religious influences of which are now controlled by ten bishops. The South African missionaries, though they contributed largely to our knowledge of the natives, did not, as a rule, take any notable part in the work of geographical exploration—Livingstone, a name which overshadows all the others, so far as travel is concerned, being, of course, a notable exception.

the heels of the discoverer, and, in several cases, has actually himself been the explorer of the region where his labours were in future to lie. **North-Eastern Africa: Abyssinian troubles.**

The Church Missionary Society opened work in Egypt in the year 1826, and four years later extended its operations to Abyssinia, with results which have been no more successful than could have been expected.

STREET IN KURUMAN, SHOWING CHURCH BUILT BY DR. MOFFAT AND OTHERS.
(From a Photograph by the Rev. Alfred J. Wookey.)

Yet it is safe to say that the early pioneers, the hunters, and the travellers whose names are connected with the mapping of the regions just outside the limits of the Cape Colony could never have been so successful in their work had it not been for the mission-stations which afforded these pioneers welcome asylums at periods when a civilised shelter was of the utmost moment to them.

It is, however, in North-East, Central, and East Africa that the missionary's work has linked itself most markedly with that of the geographical explorer ; for, in not a few instances, the missionary has followed very closely on

More than thirty years subsequently, the imprisonment of the German lay missionaries by Theodore led, among many other causes, to Sir Robert (afterwards Lord) Napier's expedition of 1868, which ended in the capture of Magdala and the death of the high-handed monarch whose despotism it was intended to curb. In days when the tale of Prester John (Vol. I., p. 110) set layman and clerk alike searching for his mythical kingdom, the Portuguese padres arrived in Abyssinia towards the close of the fifteenth century, and prospered so well that they managed to divide the people in a sect who followed them and

MISSIONS IN ABYSSINIA.

a sect who still clung to the Greek form of Christianity, which had been introduced by Frumentius as early as 330. At length a demand by the Jesuits, who had by this time found their way into the kingdom, that the Negus, or king, should embrace Roman Catholicism led to a rupture. The result was that in 1633 they were expelled, though the remnants of their churches and the many public works which they completed bear evidence to the energy of these remarkable men. Until the year 1829, when Messrs. Gobat (afterwards Bishop of Jerusalem), and Krugler, of the Church Missionary Society, made an attempt to gain a footing, no further efforts were made to send missionaries to Abyssinia.

The Church Missionary Society's agents were, however, compelled to leave as early as 1842. At a later date an industrial mission, consisting mainly of Germans, was started by Bishop Gobat. This came to a close with the fall of Theodore, and the missionaries still in that country are supported by Swedish and Norwegian societies. The Italians have, it is understood, again begun a Roman Catholic propaganda, though both in Shoa and Abyssinia there have been priests for many years, whose influence was not exerted in favour of the Protestant teachers; while the American United Presbyterians and the Church Missionary Society occupy the limited area that is open to proselytism in Egypt.

The efforts of one branch of the Christian Church to compete with another, which have produced such deplorable results in Uganda, ought never to have been repeated in Abyssinia; and happily, so far as the Church Missionary Society is concerned, the first mistake which led to the expulsion of their teachers has not again been made.

In 1844, soon after the English clergy were

FIELD-WORK AT LOVEDALE.
(From a Photograph supplied by the Rev. Dr. Stewart.)

ordered to leave Abyssinia, they established themselves on the east coast of Africa, where, if the prevailing faith of the more civilised portion of the population was Mohammedanism, the number of Pagans, pure and unadulterated, was large enough to afford room for the most zealous of missionaries. This mission still exists. The labours of two members of it to advance our knowledge of Central Africa has shed such lustre on the East African mission as to make the names of John Ludwig Krapf (p. 107) and John Rebmann, both of them of German nationality, among the most familiar in the history of African exploration. Krapf,* after being compelled to abandon his attempts to plant Protestantism in Abyssinia and Shoa, settled at Mombasa, under the auspices of Seyid-Saïd, then Sultan of Zanzibar, who commended him to his people as "a good man who wishes to convert the world to Allah." Two years afterwards Krapf was joined by Rebmann, with whose assistance the mission-station at Kisulutini was established in the Rabai district, fifteen miles inland; and it was from this centre that these two devout men began the series of remarkable journeys which did so much to open up the "hinterland" of East Africa. Krapf, for instance, visited Usambara and Ukamba, and made himself familiar with the whole coast as far south as Cape Delgado, while Rebmann penetrated into Chagga, a mountainous region of East Africa.

But the most remarkable discovery made by the members of this mission was Kilimanjaro, a mountain-mass now ascertained to be about 19,680 feet high, which Rebmann first sighted on the 11th of May, 1848. In the following year Krapf made known the scarcely less extraordinary snow-capped Mount Kenia, between 18,000 and 19,000 feet in height. So extraordinary, indeed, to the geographers of fifty years ago was the intimation that almost within the African tropics there were mountains furrowed by glaciers and capped by eternal snow,† that there were not wanting commentators of no small eminence who ventured to solve the difficulty which troubled their theoretical minds by declaring that the good missionaries had promulgated a fable.

But the East African Switzerland was no more a fable than was the Central African one which the travels of Stanley brought to light forty years later, or the great inland lake of Africa which Krapf and Rebmann heard of before Speke and Burton had started on the journey which enabled the world to

* Krapf, "Travels, Researches, and Missionary Labours," etc. (1860).
† Cooley, "Inner Africa Laid Open" (1852), pp. 89-102.

learn that the foundation for this Arab story was the existence of Nyassa, Tanganyika, and Victoria Nyanza, and not unlikely also Albert Nyanza, Albert Edward Nyanza, and Lake Rudolph still farther to the north (Vol. II., p. 54).

The enthusiasm aroused by the discoveries of the two German missionaries induced the society to form extensive plans for founding institutions still farther in the interior. These efforts were, however, completely unsuccessful, Krapf, who superintended them, barely escaping with his life as a starving fugitive in a hostile country. He afterwards returned home, where he died in 1881, after gaining among philologists a name almost as brilliant as his pioneer journeys in Africa had obtained among geographers.

Rebmann remained in Africa for twenty-nine years without ever paying a visit to Europe. In 1856 an invasion by the wild Masai drove him from Kisulutini to the coast, where he remained for two years. But when matters quieted down again the devoted old missionary returned to the scene of his labours, rebuilt the mission-house, and gathered about him the scattered converts, among whom, in 1873, Sir Bartle Frere found him living, quite alone and stone-blind, immersed in dictionaries and translations, his philological labours being carried on with the help of a native attendant, the son of the first convert to the mission. At last he, too, returned to Germany, and died in 1876, not far from the home of his lifelong colleague, Dr. Krapf.‡ Mr. New, a missionary of the United Methodists, distinguished himself (in 1871) by ascending Kilimanjaro higher than it had ever previously been climbed and acquiring so extensive a knowledge of East Africa and its languages that he was selected as one of the members of an expedition of succour that was at one time on the eve of being sent to Livingstone (Vol. II., pp. 259, 263).

When Mombasa was constituted a station for the reception of liberated slaves, the East African mission assumed greater proportions

‡ "Church Missionary Atlas," Part I., pp. 55, et seq.

than at any former period of its history, and the settlement named Freretown, in honour of Sir Bartle Frere, who had originally suggested the formation of this freedman's colony, rose on the eminence opposite the town. Some of these people have since then been transferred to the old station of Kisulutini, where the soil is better, but a number still live in a civilised condition on the coast. Stations still farther in the interior have been formed; and, now that the slave trade has received a permanent blow from the partition of the coast-line and of the back-lying country among different European Powers, it is expected that Mombasa and its scattered annexes will become important centres of civilisation.

The United Free Methodists have also a mission-station near Mombasa, with some outlying posts, and, it may be added, one establishment in Golbanti, in Gallaland, which was maintained with such extreme peril that in 1887 the missionary, his wife, and many of the native Christians were massacred by the fanatical people among whom they were settled.

The Universities' Mission to Central East Africa was, we have already seen, the outcome of Livingstone's Oxford lectures in 1857 on his return to England from his first great Zambesi and Nyassaland expedition across the continent. It began its work on the Zambesi in 1859;* but five years later, after the death of Bishop Mackenzie (p. 135) and the prostration of the greater number of his clergy, its headquarters were transferred to Zanzibar, though it sent branches far into the mainland, for the most part into the country now under German control. It has also several stations on the east shore of Lake Nyassa, the waters of which are now churned by a steamer belonging to the mission.† There are also a German steamer and some German missions on the lake.

* In 1892 the Universities' Mission cost nearly £20,000; £11,200 was received for the Nyassa stations.
† Masasi, like some of the others, has never recovered the Magwangwara raid of 1881 (Von Behr, *Mittheilungen aus den Deutschen Schutzgebieten*, Vol. VI., No. 1).

But Nyassaland is essentially the field of the Established and Free Churches of Scotland. The Free Church was the first in the field. As early as 1862–63 the Rev. Dr. Stewart,‡ of Lovedale College, in South Africa (pp. 129, 131, 132), came to reside at the Universities' Mission station on the Shiré as a commissioner from the Free Church of Scotland, his object being to examine the country with a view to opening up mission work in the most favourable portions of it. He had escorted Mrs. Livingstone to the Zambesi, and travelled with her and Dr. Livingstone

REV. DR. JAMES STEWART.
(*From a Photograph by E. Lindner, King William's Town, S. Africa.*)

up that river (Vol. II., p. 244), and helped to lay the devoted wife of the great missionary in her grave at Shupanga (Vol. II., p. 245). Dr. Stewart's report on the country was laid before the Free Church, but the establishment of the Universities' Mission, and the disasters that overtook it, caused the Church to hesitate about undertaking a fresh enterprise in the country which before long was to be one of the most notable fields of the Scottish missionaries. Meanwhile, in 1866, Dr. Stewart was put in charge of Lovedale, claiming, when the old plans of taking possession of the Nyassa region were again mooted,

‡ Born at Edinburgh, February 14th, 1831; M.D., Edinburgh; D.D., Glasgow.

the well-earned right of being the pioneer of that notable venture.*

It was, however, 1874 before Dr. Stewart's schemes for the renewal of missionary work on the Shiré and Lake Nyassa obtained shape. And it was not until 1875 that Mr. E. D. Young, R.N.—who had already been on Lake Nyassa to inquire into the tale brought by Moosa regarding the death of Livingstone— was sent in command of the *Ilala* (p. 133), the first steamer ever launched on any of the African lakes, with the Scottish missionaries for this field of action. The pioneer establishment of the new mission was built on a projecting point of land at the eastern end of the lake, and there for some years Livingstonia —as it was called in memory of the missionary-traveller whose most suitable monument

up the lake. The Livingstone Mission is on the lines of Lovedale and has been eminently successful. It supports nine missionaries—six of them medical men—and thirteen teachers and artisans, at an expense (1893) of £7,000 a year. Trades are taught and over four hundred children are at school. The New Testament has been translated and many school-books are in the native tongue. It may be added that, though a Free Church institution, it works in connection with the United Presbyterian Church and the Dutch Reformed Church in the Cape Colony, each of these Churches supplying one ordained clergyman. The great services rendered by this mission to African civilisation cannot, indeed, be well exaggerated; for to it and the sister one of the Established

CARPENTERS' WORKSHOP AT LOVEDALE.
(*From a Photograph supplied by Dr. Stewart.*)

it is—remained. But, a more healthy situation being deemed advisable, the head-quarters were removed to Bandawe (p. 136), farther

* Blaikie. "Personal Life of Dr. Livingstone," p. 289; Hughes' "Livingstone," pp. 106–199.

Church of Scotland is due the formation of the Africa Lakes Company. This Scottish enterprise was the primary cause of the British Government extending its flag over the whole of Nyassaland. Long, however, before the Government took this important step, the Glasgow traders and planters, in collaboration with their countrymen the missionaries, held their own on the shores of this distant lake, and, for the first time by force of arms, checked the inroads of the Arab slave-raiders in the country along its borders. Many an explorer has found these mission-stations and trading-posts welcome centres from which to depart for the unknown. But the missionaries themselves have rendered a by no means unimportant service to the cause of opening up Africa by means of exploration. For instance, the first voyage of the *Ilala** round the north end of Nyassa, under the direction of Mr. Young and Dr. Laws, showed that, instead of the lake being 150 miles long, as had been supposed, it was really 350 miles from one end to the other, and of a breadth varying from sixteen to nearly fifty miles (Vol. II., pp. 49, 241). They did not, however, land anywhere. But the voyages and other journeys of Drs.

THE "ILALA" AT MATOPÉ.
(*From a Photograph by Mr. Fred Moir.*)

Stewart and Laws a little later also added extensively to our knowledge of the country on the shores of the sheet which they and other friends have made a British lake. They circumnavigated Nyassa, landing on the east and west sides and north end, at many places every day, while Dr. Stewart came down the west side by land, for ten days accompanied by natives only, and rejoined the steamer at Kota-Kota. In 1878 a journey of more than 400 miles was carried out by Dr. Laws and the late Mr. James Stewart (a Civil Engineer who had come to Nyassa from India for the purpose of spending a furlough in the society of his cousin) along the southern and western sides of the lake and the country beyond.

* Young, "Nyassa: A Journal of Adventures whilst exploring Lake Nyassa, Central Africa, and establishing 'Livingstonia.'"

At a later date Mr. Stewart crossed from the north end of Nyassa to the south end of Tanganyika, arriving the day after Mr. Joseph Thomson, of the Geographical Society's expedition, had reached this point. At last, in 1882, Mr. Stewart completed the survey of Lake Nyassa.*

These explorations by the missionaries and their lay colleagues have brought to light the fact of iron-mines in several places, of coal cropping out on the surface, and the existence of copper close to the lake. Referring more particularly to scientific work, their researches have revealed the fact that in the territory lying immediately to the west we have at least fifteen different tribes, speaking as many different languages, besides dialects of these languages. Finally, instead of Nyassaland being a desert country inhabited only by wild beasts, as all Central Africa was not long ago supposed to be, the shores of the lake are now known to be dotted with numerous villages, or even towns, containing from 200 to 10,000 people: while in the pastoral districts of the cool western highlands the population is much larger than in many of the corresponding districts of South Africa.† Nor must it be forgotten that, though the missionaries did not actually make the "Stevenson Road" between Nyassa and Tanganyika, that first rude attempt at a European highway ever made in Central Africa—which, when renewed, promises to constitute Nyassa and Tanganyika important links in the great waterway through Africa—was surveyed by Mr. James Stewart and constructed at the cost of Mr. Stevenson, mainly at the prompting of the Scottish missionaries.

* *Proceedings of the Royal Geographical Society*, 1883, p. 689. See also, for various notes and papers, *Proceedings*, 1879, pp. 289 (Dr. Stewart), 305 (Dr. Laws), and 1880, pp. 44, 122, 247 (James Stewart's Journey to Tanganyika), 337 (Waller), 350 (chiefly on Masasi and Rovuma district by Mr. Chauncy Maples, of the Universities' Mission), 428 (James Stewart), etc. I have to thank Dr. Stewart for much assistance in obtaining the materials for this sketch.

† Waller, "Nyassaland" (1890), pp. 24-26; Mrs. Moir, "A Lady's Letters from Central Africa," etc.

The Established Church of Scotland, by an arrangement with the Free Church, in founding its missions stopped short of the lake, and, with the help of Dr. Stewart, began operations in 1875 at a healthy spot on the Shiré hills, about half-way between two former stations of the Universities' Mission, namely—Chibisa's and Magomero. Blantyre, as this spot was called in honour of the birthplace of Livingstone, is close to the salt Lake Shirwa, and outlying stations were built afterwards. The mission being intended as an industrial as well as an evangelical agency, a medical missionary, five artisans, and a gardener were among its earliest officers. It is at present in a flourishing condition, in spite of some ups and downs that were experienced at the beginning of its career, mainly through injudicious management on the part of some who, with the best intentions in the world, did the most imprudent acts imaginable.

As Blantyre is on the road round the falls from Katunga's on the Lower Shiré to Matopé on the Upper navigation of the Shiré, every traveller from Nyassa must pass through that settlement. This road extends for sixty miles, and when the debt of Europe to the missionaries comes to be placed in black and white, it may be well to remember that the cost was borne equally by the Established Church of Scotland and the Livingstonia Mission, under the direction of the Free Church. Already the influence of the settlement is admitted, even by the least friendly critics of such enterprises, to be for the good of Africa. The missionaries have taught the natives to respect the British name to such an extent that the mere request of one of them was enough to prevent two chiefs, on the eve of going to war, from opening hostilities. Altogether the Church of Scotland has expended over £50,000 on her work in the Shiré highlands, with an annual outlay estimated at £4,000. Education is spreading, large numbers of the young people being able to write and read in English and their own language, and all kinds of labour are tending to flourish. Excellent brick buildings, including a church, have been erected by the natives (p. 137); and, in places where a few years ago the unbroken wilderness extended, coffee plantations, maize-patches, and wheat-fields wave with luxuriant crops. In this connection it may be noted that in April, 1893, three missionaries—two of them with their wives—set out to establish the "Zambesi Industrial Mission," an English unsectarian enterprise, in the cool, healthy Shiré highlands. It is to be conducted on the most practical lines and each station is expected to be self-supporting before many years elapse.

Besides the great missions already mentioned, others conceived on a smaller scale are at work in Eastern Africa. There is, in the first place, the Neukirchen Mission, supported by contributions mainly from the Rhine Provinces.

German and other missions in East Africa.

In addition to its station at Ngao, in Gallaland, on the north bank of the river Tana, its basis is at Witu, in the midst of the Wa-Pokomo. The Bavarian Mission from Nurenburg is situated at Mbanqu, near Mombasa, and at Chimba in the same district.

DR. CHARLES F. MACKENZIE, FIRST BISHOP OF THE UNIVERSITIES' MISSION TO CENTRAL AFRICA.

Its field of work is intended to be among the Wa-Kamba. The Berlin Mission is stationed at Zanzibar and Dar-es-Salaam. The German Roman Catholic Mission is, like the last two mentioned, quite a new enterprise. Its chief establishment is at Dar-es-Salaam, and is apparently intended to counteract the political influence of the long-established and

DR. C. A. SMYTHIES, BISHOP OF CENTRAL AFRICA.
(From a Photograph by Samuel A. Walker, 230, Regent St., W.)

most meritorious French Roman Catholic Mission at Bagamoyo.

We have just spoken of the Universities' Mission and of the beginning of its labours in the Zambesi country (p. 131). Since 1880 this enterprise has taken an entirely new life. From its head-quarters at Zanzibar, its stations have extended from Lindi on the coast, not far from the Rovuma river, to Nyassa Lake, and have therefore, to a certain extent, occupied the field that had to be abandoned in the early career of the project. Now, by a good understanding with the Scottish missionaries already at work in the same quarter, it has the superintendence of a considerable area of the lake shore, and, under the control of Dr. Smythies, Bishop of Central Africa, is doing excellent service to civilisation, not only by teaching the natives, but by taking charge of the slaves captured and set free by British cruisers.

Among these *protégés* of the Universities' Mission are the inhabitants of some extinct settlements of veritable "Lake - dwellers." These people, as is not uncommon in other parts of Africa, have built their huts of collections of long poles driven into the bottom of the lake, so as to escape their enemies more easily. At different dates one of their mission-stations has suffered from the incursions of the Magwangwara, a powerful race of Kaffir origin, who from time to time carry fire and sword throughout Nyassaland and even as far as the coast. These people are notoriously bloodthirsty and for ages have been the scourge of hundreds of villages in the Yao and Maku countries. As yet all efforts to influence them for good have been unavailing. The Machingas, another even more powerful and devastating tribe, whose range is farther to the north, up to the present time have shown themselves equally unimpressionable by the agents of the mission that have visited them. To reach the lake station from Lindi along the Rovuma river, which, it may be remembered, was first explored by Livingstone, demands a weary tramp of four hundred miles as the crow flies, but at least half as much again as African travel necessarily entails. Hence the Shiré and Zambesi water-road down to Quilimane is generally adopted as an alternative route.

Altogether the Universities' Mission have expended on their labours in the Nyassa country a sum considerably exceeding £60,000, and at present support in this region a staff which comprises nine clergymen, two ladies, and eight laymen.

The London Missionary Society's labours lay until comparatively recently in the Cape Colony and the neighbouring Kaffir territory. But soon after the discovery of Lake Tanganyika, the society's operations were extended to the very centre of Africa. The year 1876 was a memorable one in the history of the inland missions of Africa. The *Ilala* had just been launched on Lake Nyassa. Bishop Steere and his party were exploring in the direction of Nyassa for the purpose of selecting sites for the Universities' Mission; and the Church Missionary Society had dispatched a pioneer party to commence operations on Victoria Nyanza. Stimulated by the munificent gifts of £5,000 by Mr. Arthington, of Leeds (p. 118), for the purchase of a suitable steamer and the establishment of a mission at some eligible place by the shores of Lake Tanganyika, the London Society determined to break ground on the border of a sheet of water which seventeen years before was not to be found on the maps of Africa. The pioneer party consisted of four clergymen and two laymen; and for the first time in the history of Central

Occupation of Tanganyika.

BANDAWE, MISSION-STATION OF THE FREE CHURCH OF SCOTLAND.
(*From a Photograph by Mr. Fred Moir.*)

THE TANGANYIKA MISSIONS.

African exploration it was determined to utilise, as far as possible, the Cape bullock waggon for the purpose of travel.* Two waggons and fourteen carriers laden with tools of all kinds—besides implements, household and camp outfit, and provisions, as well as rope, canvas, and gear for rigging a boat for use on the lake—set out at the beginning of

Mkali, Unyanyembe, Unyamwezi (where, at Uyui there was afterwards a station of the Church Missionary Society), Urambo (now a post of the London Missionary Society), Uhha and Uvinza, to the well-known Arab settlement of Ujiji (Vol. II., p. 260). Their progress was necessarily slow, and not unchequered by misfortunes, among which the

BLANTYRE CHURCH.
(*From a Photograph by Mr. Fred Moir.*)

the travelling season of 1877 on an adventure almost unprecedented in the annals of missionary enterprise. Starting on June the 11th, 1877, it was not until August the 23rd in the following year that the cumbersome caravan arrived on the shores of Lake Tanganyika. They had proceeded from Saadani, through Useguha, Usagara—where at Mwpwapwa, one of the stations of the Church Missionary Society (p. 58), they received welcome succour—through Ugogo, Magunda

* Hore, "Tanganyika" (1892), pp. 1-64.

"seasoning fevers" of Africa were not the least prominent. Cattle died and waggons broke down, while, in spite of the familiarity the tribes along the route to the lake had gained with the white men, the temptation to steal from them was not always resisted.

Still this peaceable journey proves not so much the change that this part of Africa had undergone since Speke and Burton travelled across it, or even since Stanley witnessed its savagery, when he went on his expedition of

succour to Livingstone, as the influence of just treatment on the natives. Their new masters and the new men who carry out their policy are again so maddening the tribes that the "road" to Ujiji is more difficult than it was in Livingstone's day; for Africa is pretty much what Europe has made it. But since 1888 the London Missionary Society have never lost their hold on this region, and, indeed, have been extending their operations very considerably. They have a steamer on the lake, and, until lately, a station at Kavala Island, on the western shore of the lake; another at Fambo, thirty miles up in the hills; a third at Niamkolo, on the southern coast (Vol. II., pp. 237, 256), and some temporary outposts. But now the missionaries are all concentrated at the two last-named localities. These spots form, with the mission-stations on Lake Nyassa, links in the chain of civilisation that have gradually extended across Africa from the Cape by the Zambesi on to Victoria Nyanza: and by-and-by, when the Soudan gets again opened up, the chain will be continued, by means of the Nile, down to the Mediterranean. The London Missionary Society, notwithstanding the comparatively concentrated character of its mission, is in the peculiar position of having two bases for access to Urambo, which is situated in the Unyamwezi country, at a considerable distance from the lake. Supplies must, therefore, be obtained from Zanzibar, through the German Sphere of Influence. This is the best and healthiest route, provided there is a steamer on Tanganyika. But, owing to obstacles put in their way by the Germans, to reach the stations on Lake Tanganyika it is necessary to pass circuitously up the rivers Zambesi and Shiré, along the whole length of Lake Nyassa and across the fast-disappearing Stevenson Road—now little more than native tracks—which, as we have seen, connects the north-west corner of the lake with the southern shore of Lake Tanganyika. The missionaries of Lake Tanganyika have not hitherto been of such pre-eminent service to geographical science as those of the Congo. Instead of exploring themselves, they have been content to aid the various explorers who have found succour at their hands; but the minute surveys made by Captain Hore of the lake on the shores of which he resided for eleven years deserve the highest praise.*
Thanks, indeed, to this energetic master mariner—who, though there was no fighting to be done, played in the Tanganyika Mission something of the same part as that which Miles Standish, the Puritan Captain, did among the Pilgrim Fathers —we now know the character of Tanganyika almost as well as that of Nyassa. And the devoted men to whose labours this is due have taken possession of their appointed field of action with a courage not less conspicuous than that of those who, in a different way, occupied for civilisation another heritage across the Atlantic.†

CAPTAIN E. C. HORE.
(*From a Photograph by Russell & Sons, Baker St., W.*)

* Hore. "Lake Tanganyika" (1892), and *Proceedings of the Royal Geographical Society*, 1889, p. 581; Mrs. Hore, "To Lake Tanganyika in a Sedan Chair" (1887); and, among numerous other papers already referred to, or which will be touched upon subsequently—Sharpe, "Journey from Karonga (Nyassa) to Katanga (Msidi's Country), *viâ* the Northern Shore of Lake Mwero"; *Proc. Roy. Geog. Soc.*, 1891, p. 423; and "A Journey from the Shiré River to Lake Mweru, and the Upper Luapula," *Geog. Journal*, 1893, p. 524; Buchanan. "Journey along the Southern Frontier of Nyassaland," *Proc. Roy. Geog. Soc.*, 1891, p. 265; Cross, "Notes on the Country lying between Lakes Nyassa and Tanganyika," *Ibid.*, 1891, p. 86; Robertson. "Martyrs of Blantyre," etc.

† We are indebted to Captain Hore for kindly giving us the benefit of his unique knowledge of the Tanganyika region, and to Dr. Stewart for reading our sketch of the missionary work in the country with which he is so familiar.

CHAPTER VI.

THE MISSIONARIES OF UGANDA AND THE WAY THITHER: A HALF-TOLD TALE.*

Henry Venn's Dictum—Stanley's Letter and the Church Missionary Society—The M'tesa of Stanley's Day—First Missionary Expedition to Uganda—Early Days and Coming Trouble—Second Mission Party—Journeys by Way of the Nile—Disappointments—M'tesa no longer Unsophisticated—Mackay's Opinion of Him—Arrival of the Roman Catholic Missionaries—Their Missions in East Africa—A New Enterprise—Dissensions—"Many Religions"—Rival Christians—Arabs Troublesome—Vacillation of M'tesa—Paganism Again—Return of Envoys from England and Rise of British Influence—Priests Leave—M'tesa a Nominal Roman Catholic—M'tesa's Mother—Death of M'tesa—The "Great Zanzibar Doctor"—Missionaries in Peril—The New King M'wanga—Political Changes—Evil Days—Roman Catholic Missionaries Recalled—Suspicion Aroused by Joseph Thomson's Expedition—Troubles—First Uganda Martyrs—Conspiracy against the King—Assassination of Bishop Hannington—Persecution of the "Readers"—Arrival and Departure of Dr. Junker—Ruin of the Mission—M'wanga Driven from the Throne—King Kiwera—Dawn again Followed by Darkness—Murder of Kiwera—The Puppet King Kalema—Restoration of M'wanga—Rebuilding of the Mission-Station—A New Power in the Land—Foreign Politics—Anarchy again, and the Arrival of Captain Lugard with the British Imperial East Africa Company's Troops—The East African Scottish Mission.

ONE of the most remarkable departures in the history of opening up Africa was that by which the Church Missionary Society took possession of the shores of Victoria Nyanza less than twenty years after the date at which Spoke first saw it. This was the culmination of a long hope; for, in the instructions delivered to Dr. Krapf, on the 2nd of January, 1851, Henry Venn, speaking in the name of the Church Missionary Society, uttered these words: "If Africa is to be penetrated by European missionaries, it must be from the east coast."

At that time no travellers, except the missionaries Krapf and Rebmann, had attempted to reach the interior from the eastern shores of the continent. What followed in the course of the next twenty years has already been the theme of some of the preceding chapters. But it was not until the remarkable journey of Stanley to Uganda that any efforts were made to carry the teachings of Christianity to the populous country of which the Welsh-American traveller gave so graphic an account. On the 15th of November, 1875, a letter from that famous explorer appeared in the *Daily Telegraph* (Vol. II., pp. 287, 297), describing his conversations with King M'tesa, the eagerness of that potentate to learn, and

_{Stanley's letter, and its first-fruits.}

the duty which devolved upon civilisation to send Christian missionaries to the African monarch. How far the cunning king hoodwinked Mr. Stanley it is not necessary to discuss in this place. It is not improbable that, had all been known that was afterwards learned in the bitter school of experience, M'tesa and his Waganda might have remained for some years longer without being acquainted with the teachers who, amid much good, wrought so much evil to the empire misgoverned by his son until the patience of his people and of his suzerain got exhausted.

However, in the dull days of the winter of 1875, hope burned bright in the bosoms of many generous Englishmen. Three days after the now historical letter appeared in the London newspaper a sum of £5,000 was offered to the Church Missionary Society towards the establishment of an Uganda Mission. Another £5,000 quickly followed, and before a few months elapsed no less than £24,000 was actually contributed for the same purpose. The enterprise was confessedly arduous, and, in the opinion of those who knew the character of the people to be dealt with, by no means hopeful. M'tesa was an extraordinary man, wayward in character,

_{The M'tesa of Stanley's day.}

* Revised by Robert W. Felkin, M.D., F.R.S.E., formerly of Uganda.

and reared in the worst practices of the savage kingdom which he ruled: but his ability, and even his generosity, were scarcely less remarkable. To the last he remained capricious, double-dealing, and self-indulgent; but only those embittered by disappointment can deny him the possession of some of the kingly qualities. Eager for novelty, anxious to please, and ready to follow desired the traveller, on departing, to leave with him a young African who had been at the Universities' Mission School at Zanzibar, in order to read to him the Scriptures in Swahili, a language understood by the king and his chiefs.

Still, whatever might be the dangers and the discouragements of the new mission to the centre of Africa, the enthusiasm of those

HOUSE AT MENGO, UGANDA, BUILT BY NATIVES FOR BISHOP TUCKER.
(From a Sketch by Bishop Tucker.)

the influence of any mind superior to his own, more especially when the mind was that of a foreign visitor, M'tesa, between the visit of Speke and that of Stanley, had become nominally a Mussulman, and was so far captivated with the new faith which he had learned from the Arab traders, who since Speke's visit had frequented the place more and more, that he sent to Gordon, begging him to despatch a Mohammedan teacher capable of instructing him in the Koran. Equally facile in the hands of Mr. Stanley, he professed to be convinced of the superior merits of Christianity (Vol. II., pp. 287, 297), and, as we have seen, eager to go was equal to the munificence of those who had provided the means to defray the cost of this great adventure. In June, 1876, seven months from the time the society had resolved to undertake the work, a well-equipped party, eight in number, were at Zanzibar preparing for their march to Victoria Nyanza. But three of them—the engineer and artisans—did not reach the goal to which the expedition was bound. One died on the coast, and the other two returned home invalided. The remaining five were Lieutenant G. Shergold Smith, R.N.; the Rev. C. T.

The first missionary expedition to Uganda.

Wilson; Mr. T. O'Neill, architect; Dr. John Smith, of the Edinburgh Medical Mission; and Alexander Mackay, a Scotsman, previously engaged in engineering work in Berlin. Mr. Mackay was detained near the coast for a time by sickness, so that of the pioneer party only four arrived together at the lake. The number was still further decreased by the death of Dr. Smith at its southern end. Finally, on the receipt of the letter written by M'tesa, by means of the boy already mentioned, Lieutenant Smith and Mr. Wilson sailed across Victoria Nyanza in a boat that had been brought from England in sections, and on the 30th of June, 1877, reached Rubaga, the then capital of Uganda.

At first all went well. It was one of the amiable ways of M'tesa to receive all newcomers with profuse hospitality, mainly, as was afterwards found, for the purpose of gratifying his vanity by standing well in the eyes of foreigners. He gave the missionaries a warm welcome, and professed himself a believer in Christianity and eager for further instruction. Regular Christian services were begun in the "palace," and the first letters received from the Uganda missionaries were enthusiastic regarding the prospect generally. It was not long before less favourable news reached London. Meanwhile, Lieutenant Smith returned to the south end of the lake for Mr. O'Neill, who had remained there with

WAGANDA ENVOYS DESPATCHED BY KING M'TESA TO ENGLAND IN 1879.
(From a Photograph by Elliot & Fry, Baker St., W.)

the stores, and, while the latter was engaged in building a large boat for their conveyance, he explored some of the rivers, bays, and creeks not then known to geographers. A quarrel arising between the king of Ukerewe—an island at the south-east arm of the lake—and the Arab traders, the latter fled for protection to the mission-camp. This was forthwith attacked, with the lamentable result that Smith, O'Neill, and all their native followers but one were killed on Wezi Island (Vol. II., p. 289), on or about the 30th of December, 1877. Mr. Wilson was now left alone in the centre of Africa, but the arrival of Mr. Mackay from the coast, and, a few weeks later, of reinforcements from England, strengthened him to persevere in the work now begun, in spite of the deplorable misfortunes which the mission had so early suffered—disasters that might well have discouraged him.

Early days, and coming troubles.

The new-comers were the Rev. G. Litchfield, Mr. C. W. Pearson, and Dr. R. W. Felkin, a medical missionary (p. 143). At first it was intended that these gentlemen should take the eastern road; but, on Gordon Pasha promising every assistance, it was eventually resolved that they should reach Uganda by way of the Nile, then open to almost any traveller. Landing at Suakim, they crossed the desert on camels to Berber, and proceeded by steamer up the river to Khartoum. Here they were received with every kindness by Gordon, who not only sped them on their way, but spent large sums out of his private funds to provide them with the necessaries which he considered proper for travellers undertaking such a journey as that on which they were bound. It was, moreover, in Government steamers that the missionaries ascended the river to Albert Nyanza, and it was under the escort of Government officers that they reached the Uganda frontier.

A journey by the Nile.

However, notwithstanding the facilities which the authority of Gordon put in their way, the journey was even in those days not made without great difficulties. The intense heat—98 and 100 degrees in the shade—struck down one of their number, Mr. Hall, who was compelled, very reluctantly, to return home from Suakim. The Bahr-el-Abiad was much encumbered with floating islands composed of immense masses of vegetation that had been detached by the floods and carried northward. These so retarded their progress that the voyage from Khartoum to Shambeh, which usually took fourteen or fifteen days, occupied sixty-eight, with the result that they were seriously inconvenienced from want of food. On leaving Gondokoro, the travellers had to take to small boats capable of passing through the rapids, and, the current being very strong and the river high, the voyagers were for a time in imminent hazard. From Bedden to Dufli they had to march overland. From the latter point a steamer conveyed them, as we have already mentioned, across the lower end of Albert Nyanza to Magungo, where the Murchison Rapids break the continuity of the river.

The next stretch of road was at times exceedingly difficult. It lay through stiff, high grass which, when one man passed through, swung back on the next with such violence as to prostrate him if he were not careful. At other times the path led across fallen timber, or through places encumbered by creepers, and often the pedestrians were compelled to tramp through malarious marshes. The consequence of this exposure was that Mr. Litchfield and the young interpreter of the party were both attacked with fever, to which the latter succumbed. To this the fact must be added that, in spite of the severe measures taken by Baker, Gordon, and other officials of Egypt in the Soudan, the natives were very threatening, and, as always happens in African expeditions the porters proved an uncertain element in the travellers' calculations. From Foweera to Mrooli, the last of the stations then under the Egyptian Government, the journey was made by boat, in the company of Mr. Wilson, who had set forward to meet his colleagues when he heard the news of their being on the way.

At Mrooli M'tesa's messengers met them, so that until their arrival in his capital on the 14th of February, 1879, further perils were obviated.*

Later in the year—we may so far anticipate our narrative—Messrs. Wilson and Felkin returned to Europe in charge of the envoys whom M'tesa desired to send to England in order to ascertain whether the stories of that country being more powerful than his own were well-founded or merely the fictions of the latest of the white men (p. 141). They again took the northern route, diverging, however, to the west and coming through Darfur.†

By this time the missionaries had been forced to abandon many of the sanguine hopes with which they had come to Uganda. M'tesa, they soon found, was vacillating in the extreme. He had professed to be a Christian, while in reality he followed out all of his old heathen practices, and was particularly angry when told that there was no truth in "lubari," or witchcraft. Another day he would declare that he was a Mohammedan, and for a time be under the influence of a motley crowd of Arab traders, deserters from the Egyptian army, and other questionable characters, who crowded his "Court," flattered him, and generally pandered to his worst vices He was also no longer so unsophisticated as Speke and Grant, and even Stanley, had found him. He had assimilated more evil than good from his visitors : while the inordinate opinion he possessed of his own greatness was daily inflated by the flattery that was poured into his ear. Soon after Stanley's stay Colonel Chaillé Long, one of Gordon's officers, had visited him,‡ and was honoured by the slaughter, in his presence, of a large number of slaves, without the Egyptian envoy having the power to prevent so diabolical an act. During Emin Pasha's embassy to M'tesa, which took place six months after the arrival of the first missionaries, the king swaggered about in a frock-coat and bare feet, under the belief that he was dressed and demeaned himself exactly like the German Emperor. He is even said to have tried the effect of a tall hat in heightening his dignity.

DR. R. W. FELKIN.
(*From a Photograph by J. Moffat, Princes St., Edinburgh.*)

The missionaries were soon fain to confess that Mr. Stanley had, to no small extent, been deceived by the cunning young savage, though to stigmatise that traveller's account of Uganda and its monarch as "utter falsehoods"— as the French priests did at a later date —is a misuse of words which his narrative in no way deserves. He simply told what he saw, and repeated what the king had told him. The reception of Colonel Chaillé Long, and many of the subsequent proceedings of M'tesa, showed clearly enough that his character still left ample room for improvement. Yet the fact is undeniable—we state it on the authority of Mr. Mackay—that the people of Uganda themselves date from Mr. Stanley's arrival the commencement

Disappointment; M'tesa in a new light.

---
* Miss Stock. "The Story of Uganda and the Victoria Nyanza Mission" (1892), p. 69, from which excellent work many of the facts in this chapter have been derived ; and "The Victoria Nyanza and Bishop Hannington" (Church Missionary Society).

† A full account of this interesting journey will be found in Messrs. Wilson and Felkin's "Uganda and the Egyptian Soudan," 2 vols. (1882). Dr. Felkin's diary of his first journey appeared in the *Church Missionary Gleaner* for 1879.

‡ "Central Africa" (1876), p. 106.

of leniency in place of the previous bloodshed and terror. "As soon as Stanley came, they say, the king no more slaughters innocent people as he did before. He no more disowns and disinherits in a moment an old and powerful chief and sets up a puppet of having no decided religion rather than professing any one in particular. He was, in truth, a strange anomaly. Capable of lying when lying served his purpose, impregnated with low cunning, hatred, pride, conceit, jealousy, cruelty, and ignorance of the value

CHURCH AT KAREMA, LAKE TANGANYIKA, IN COURSE OF CONSTRUCTION BY THE "WHITE FATHERS": LENGTH, 150 FEET.
(From a Photograph by Mr. Fred Moir.)

his own who was before only a slave." In short, compared with what Uganda was in Speke's time, the government witnessed by the missionaries was mild in the extreme: but, undoubtedly, M'tesa was a pagan, and if he died with this paganism somewhat modified, it was a modification in the direction of of human life, he was capable at times of what seemed inordinate generosity; but those who know his disposition best affirm that this seeming generosity, or any other virtue of a redeeming nature, was merely for the glorification of himself in the eyes of the foreigners, or as a bait to gather more into his net. His vanity was extreme, his desire for notoriety almost monomaniacal. His greed was also inordinate, while his absolute want of control when the gratification of his animal propensities was at stake rendered it impossible to say what enormity he would next commit. Yet, if guilty of almost every vice—a robber, a tyrant, a murderer, and a fratricide—this strange character in the history of Central Africa displayed an extraordinary affection for some of his young children, and at times a real sense of justice without respect of persons. Thus, for instance, he would punish a powerful chief when the latter was complained of by even the humblest of his subjects. Indeed, one of

CHURCH ON THE HILLS OF NAMUREMBE, UGANDA, AND HOUSES OF ENGLISH MISSIONARIES.
(From a Sketch by the Rev. Frederick Smith.)

the most curious features of Uganda, as in contrast with surrounding states, was its lawlessness combined with a ceaseless succession of trials at law. Every chief was a judge in his own land, with, of course, the power of life and death, and every minor chief and petty officer had also frequently cases brought before him, and the same suit was often heard by many such judges in succession before it was settled. At the capital the common people from different districts had their causes tried by three judges, who exacted a small fee for their services, while the chiefs, in their turn, had all their differences settled by an old chief called Mungobya, who was said to be very just in his decisions. From him appeal could be had to the prime minister, or katikiro, who was, however, a very young man, elevated to a position for which he was unfitted from the humble post of being cook to the king. This man, according to Mr. Mackay, was an utter time-server, and always gave his decision in favour of the litigant who had bribed him most heavily in slaves and cattle. Finally, the king settled disputes without a fee, and was generally regarded as fair in his judgments. A poor man, however, could bring no case against a richer man, for, if he did, spoliation and death would be the certain doom of the peasant, even should his plaint get a hearing at all. In a former chapter (Vol. II., pp. 282-312) an account was given by Dr. Felkin of the political condition of the country at the time when he and his colleagues arrived in Uganda, and it will, therefore, be unnecessary to dwell upon this aspect of the great Central African kingdom. What has been said may, however, enable the reader to grasp the situation when a new factor in the history of Uganda had to be taken into account.

This was the arrival of the Roman Catholic missionaries. The Arab traders had never been friendly. At times, indeed, they were almost openly hostile; for, in addition to their fear that the white men who had arrived might be only the forerunners of rivals to them in business, their Moslem fanaticism was aroused at the possible spread of the Christian religion in a country where, until the advent of the English missionaries, they had been making rapid progress in proselytism. The English missionaries had

Arrival of the Roman Catholic missionaries; their missions in Africa.

not, however, calculated on meeting any difficulty from a quarter whence it now came; yet on the 23rd of February, 1879, when there were seven Protestant missionaries in the country, a party of French Jesuit priests arrived from Algiers avowedly to oppose the Protestants by promulgating "the truth," as understood by the members of their creed.

The Roman Catholic Mission at Dar-es-Salaam, which is now under German control, and the French one at Bagamoyo, have already been mentioned. In addition to these there is the Saint Esprit et Cœur de Marie, a Paris mission, organised by the late Father Horner, the principal station of which is at Bagamoyo. There is also a similar station at Mhonda, in Uguna, and several outposts. The Jesuits, some of whom come from a training college in North Wales, have a station at Tete on the Zambesi river within the limits of the Portuguese colony of Mozambique, and several others of less importance.

But the Fathers in these districts are not aggressive and have not mixed themselves up in political affairs. The missionaries who now made their appearance in Uganda belonged to a newer, more militant and, as subsequent events proved, less judicious organisation than any of those mentioned. Their order was Notre Dame d'Afrique, with its head-quarters in Algeria and Tunis. It was one of the creations of Cardinal Lavigerie, Archbishop of Carthage (p. 105)—on the site of which is the chief school of the mission—and, apart from its religious objects, is notoriously portion of an ambitious political plan to extend French influence in Central Africa. It is perhaps not uncharitable—because it is true—to say that the Cardinal's crusade against slavery was not entirely without an eye to the accomplishment of a purpose which gained for the new organisation the powerful influence of politicians who did not usually feel an absorbing interest in a purely sectarian scheme. The Central African missions of these "White Fathers" were planned so as to form four districts—the provicariates of Unyamyembe and the Upper

Congo, and the two Apostolic vicariates of Tanganyika and Victoria Nyanza.*

But, instead of permitting the mission-field to be divided up among the adherents of the different Christian creeds, the "White Fathers" would admit of no compromise. They seemed to believe it was better that the natives should remain in Paganism than imbibe a heretical form of Christianity. Hence, with all wide Africa to choose from, instead of selecting a post at a distance from the Protestant missionaries, with an indiscretion of which, unfortunately, the latter have not been always innocent themselves, they planted their stations alongside of those already established, and never concealed their avowed enmity, if not to the Englishmen personally, at all events to their teachings.

The first detachment of the Tanganyika White Fathers arrived at Ujiji on the 24th of January, 1879. They now occupy the station of Karema (p. 144), originally established by the African International Association and for some time held by the French Pontifical Zouave, M. Joubert, on whose assistance in his enterprise against the slave trade and his ulterior political objects Cardinal Lavigerie laid much stress in his addresses—not so much in England as in capitals where his plans might be received more sympathetically. Ruwewa, on the western shore, near the northern extremity of the lake, is another of the White Fathers' stations, and at Mpala, also an old station of the African International Association, a third party of priests have their quarters.

As yet, probably owing to the fact that it has not been convenient to settle in the immediate vicinity of the London Missionary Society's stations, we hear little there of the rivalry that has made the Uganda Mission so notorious. Indeed, either for this reason, or because the men selected for the Tanganyika scheme have been more judicious than their brethren on the great lake to the north, the Protestants and the Roman

* Clarke, "Cardinal Lavigerie and Slavery in Africa" (1889), p. 165.

Catholics seem to live in Tanganyika on terms of tolerable friendship.

M'tesa, always eager to see new faces, especially if his visitors did not come empty-handed, received the first detachment of priests with profuse pro- **The rival Christians.** fessions of friendship. Nor was his amiability decreased when he found that the preachers of the gospel of peace had brought to him—as their predecessors had to a smaller extent—those presents of guns, swords, and gunpowder which his heart hankered after. This agreeable impression was not long in being disturbed; for the priests immediately took up a position hostile to the Protestant missionaries, refusing to kneel for prayer at their Sunday services and denouncing them to the king as liars who taught a foreign religion. Then the Protestants retaliated and the two Christian sects were at open enmity. Naturally, this attitude of opposition to those whom he had begun to regard as his friends struck M'tesa with astonishment. He had till then believed that the new teachers were friends of the old ones, and, to use his own expression, "that the white men had not two religions." Whatever might have been his ideas hitherto, he was not long kept in ignorance of the fact that the French party recognised what he had been taught hitherto in the light of untruth. At an interview with the king, in the presence of Mr. Mackay, M. Lourdel declared in an excited manner, "We do not join in that religion because it is not the true. We do not know that book [the Prayer Book], because it is a book of lies. If we joined in that, it would mean that we were not Catholics but Protestants, who have rejected the truth for hundreds of years. They were with us, but now they believe and teach only lies."

The mischief soon took such deep root that it was impossible to eradicate it. In vain was the king instructed in the minor points of difference between the two creeds; all the explanations left him more sorely perplexed than ever, and chiefs who had stood listening to the explanation turned away sadly with the remark that "every white man has a different religion." The Arabs, who had hitherto remained either neutral or passively unfriendly, now saw their chance to take a more decisive attitude by sowing dissension in the king's Court. This opportunity occurred on the receipt of a friendly letter to the king from Sir John Kirk, then British Consul-General at Zanzibar, which the Arabs were ordered to

<small>Arab op-
position.</small>

ALEXANDER MACKAY.
(*From a Photograph.*)

translate for the benefit of M'tesa. But either because they were too ignorant to understand the import of it, or, more likely, because they scented an opportunity of casting reflections upon the missionaries, they rendered the communication in a sense inimical to the character of the Englishmen and their honesty of purpose.

British influence, and no doubt the influence of the Europeans generally, now reached a very low ebb. The king's demeanour towards the missionaries changed, and sometimes he refused to see them altogether. To some extent the king was even more incensed against the Frenchmen. So far did

this feeling go that when the English missionaries went with some medicine for one of the sick priests, they were stopped by a number of armed natives, acting, as it seemed, by the orders of the king. Perhaps, however, owing to his gratitude for medical services rendered to him by Dr. Felkin, the old friendliness of the king began to return soon after the departure of this gentleman and Mr. Wilson with the Uganda envoys for England. His desire for information bearing on the character of England prevented him from changing his mind regarding this embassy. This love of knowledge was displayed in other directions also. By means of a small printing-press, reading-sheets were supplied, and remarkable eagerness for instruction manifested itself among the chiefs and people, a large number of them learning to read, and the public services which had been stopped for a time were resumed.

Towards the close of 1879 another change came over the fickle king. He now fell under the thrall of a "sorceress," who claimed to be possessed of the "lubari" of the Nyanza, and under her influence he and his chiefs prohibited both Christianity and Mohammedanism, and returned to their old Pagan practices. The year 1880 was a period of sore trial for European influence. Only a few lads remained among Messrs. Mackay and Pearson's pupils, but even they deserted the school, and the lives of the missionaries were placed in imminent peril, owing to an absurd story circulated by the Arabs to the effect that Mr. Mackay was an insane murderer who had escaped from his own country.

<small>Vacillation
of the king.</small>

Once more, however, the king's attitude towards the missionaries altered for the better. The return of the Uganda envoys from Europe, full of what they had seen of the populous cities of England and of the greatness of its Queen, to whom they had been presented at Buckingham Palace, raised British influence in Uganda to a level not hitherto attained. The pupils came back to school

SEIZURE OF BISHOP HANNINGTON, PREVIOUS TO HIS MURDER.

and several converts presented themselves for baptism. Building, carpentering, blacksmithing, and other industrial pursuits were learned by numbers of the intelligent people of the country, while various new books were translated into the language, in which the missionaries were now proficient. Another event that relieved the mission of frequent embarrassment was the departure, in November, 1882, of the French priests to one of their other stations,* after a residence of three and a half years in Rubaga. Their absence was, however, only temporary.

Without following the mission in its encouragements and discouragements from year to year, it may be enough to say that its success suffered little check until the 10th of October, 1884. Up to that time the English Church in Uganda claimed eighty-eight members among the natives of the country, and several relays of missionaries had come and gone without any of the hostile demonstrations that greeted some of the pioneers in passing from the lake to the sea. One of the converts was M'tesa's daughter, whose baptism aroused the king's anger, in spite of the fact that he himself had at different times professed Christianity. Then for a time the mission was in real danger; but, as usual, the storm blew over and the vacillating king restored the missionaries to all their old favour. On the whole, M'tesa had been friendly to the teachers sent him in response to his request through Mr. Stanley. Naturally unstable, however, anything like steady friendship, or progress in any particular direction, was impossible to the king. First a Mohammedan, then ostensibly a Protestant, he became nominally a Roman Catholic, while at heart, and according to his practices, essentially a Pagan, his favourite excuse for any act of a particularly atrocious character was that he was puzzled how to act amid the dictates of such various religions.

His mother predeceased him by some months. This was the lady of whose affability

Halcyon days.

* They have stations on the Victoria Nyanza at Rubaga and Bukumbi, and at Sweru in Unyamwezi.

Speke gives so lively a description. M'tesa determined to do her honour after his barbarous fashion, tinctured with some of the civilisation which he had acquired by his intercourse with the white man. Thus he asked Mackay to make her a huge copper coffin, and such an enormous quantity of costly clothes were thrown into her grave that it is said they were valued at £15,000. At last— on the 10th of October, 1884— M'tesa died, and affairs in Uganda assumed an entirely new aspect.

Death of M'tesa.

The king had long been ailing, and seemed to grow daily worse and worse in spite of the medical advice which he received from the missionaries. The Arabs, however, assured him that there were some traders from Zanzibar now in the Unyamwezi country who possessed a marvellous medicine that would cure him. Messengers were immediately despatched to bring these great doctors to the Uganda Court. They duly arrived, and issued orders that no one was to see the king while the drug was working. He was ordered a particular diet and forbidden to eat salt—black people, as a rule, seldom eating salt while they are ill. For a time the king endured this regimen: but, as usual, he soon tired of the monotony of any particular course, and refused any longer to follow the advice of the "great doctors" from Zanzibar. The condition of the king was kept a profound secret from his subjects; and, even when he died, the event was not made known for some time afterwards. Nor is it yet known, with accuracy, what was the manner of M'tesa's "taking off." As usually happens in such cases, it was whispered about that the king had been poisoned by the foreign doctors. More likely was the rumour which affirmed that he was smothered by his wives. Murder in this fashion is not unknown.

But when the king's death could no longer be concealed, it was evident that the position of the Europeans was not so safe as it had been the day before. In the interregnum there might be an outburst of anarchy, and it was well understood that the heir to the

AN INTERREGNUM IN UGANDA.

throne was by no means friendly to the missionaries. It is now known that when the chiefs met in council over the state of affairs precipitated by the death of the king it was debated whether the strangers—that is to say, the Arabs and the Europeans—should be attacked, and the proposal only fell to the ground when it was explained that any such proceedings would discourage the visits of strangers and the development of trade.

Nor were the Arabs very confident. They, too, expected an attack, and spent the night armed to the teeth. They also distributed muskets and ammunition among their slaves, and so serious were the prospects of all concerned that the missionaries launched their boat at once and made ready for sailing, in case the missionhouse should be destroyed and the inmates be compelled to seek refuge on the lake.

The character of the new sovereign was not such as to inspire confidence in the minds of the threatened Europeans. M'wanga was a lad only eighteen years of age, and, though not the oldest son of the late king, had, for reasons of state, been chosen by the nobles to succeed him. He had often visited the missionaries, and learned something from his intercourse with them, though unable to concentrate his attention for any length of time. In addition to being as unstable as his father, he was endowed with few of his virtues, but with most of his vices. His accession to the throne was, however, marked by the absence of many of the hideous customs which, until the teachings of the missionaries

The new king.

were listened to, had been part of the ceremonial on such occasions. His brothers, for instance, were spared the usual fate of the Waganda princes, who, on the accession of the heir-apparent, had hitherto been killed, in case they might in any way endanger his tenure of power. What also was almost unprecedented in the political annals of Uganda, the katikiro, or prime minister, was continued in office; but the king, influenced, no doubt, by the customary superstition connected with inhabiting the residence of his predecessor, changed the royal quarters from Rubaga to Nabulagala.

M'wanga, however, very speedily treated the missionaries with scant courtesy, ordering them at one of his first audiences to go to the south of the lake and bring more white men, his idea being that white men could be had by "ordering" them, like so much cloth or so many muskets.

Evil days.

GRAVE OF THE MOTHER OF KING M'TESA.
(From a Sketch by the Rev. Frederick Smith.)

However, some reinforcements for the British mission being expected from England, Mr. Mackay went in the direction indicated in the hopes of escorting them to head-quarters; but, on his return without them, M'wanga was so disappointed that he immediately resolved to supply their places by others, and sent to Bukumbi for some of the French priests who had retired to that station (p. 150).

This was the beginning of no small trouble both for himself and for his kingdom. As time went on the suspicions of the king towards the white men were increased rather than lessened. At that period Mr. Joseph Thomson was engaged on his successful journey through Masailand to Victoria Nyanza, and had arrived in

Busoga,* a tributary state to the east of Uganda and separated from it by the Nile. The king immediately jumped to the conclusion, when he heard of the advent of this traveller, that he and his companions were the white men whom Mackay ought to have brought from the south end of the lake and that they had taken another route. And of all routes which they could have taken, that by way of Busoga was the least pleasing to him; for the come as usual with his yearly tribute of ivory, an unpardonable remissness on his part, which was attributed to the presence of strangers who had excited him to rebel against his liege lord. Ever on the watch for any circumstances that might prejudice the Court against the white men, the Arabs immediately put into circulation evil rumours to the effect that the missionaries were harbouring malefactors, solely from the accidental circumstance

MUMIAS' VILLAGE, KAVIRONDO, THE SCENE OF BISHOP HANNINGTON'S MURDER.
(From a Sketch by Bishop Tucker.)

Waganda are jealous of any strangers reaching their country by that state—mainly, no doubt, lest the new arrivals should reach Uganda empty-handed, but partly because of an old prophecy that Uganda was to be conquered by people coming from the east. This superstition was so strong even in M'tesa that on one occasion he told Mackay—"I know you white men want very much to see what is beyond Busoga, but I will never let you do it." It unfortunately happened also that, coincidently with the rumour of white men being in Busoga, the king of that country failed to

* Or Usoga, the "B" being indifferently added or omitted—*e.g.*, Uganda and Buganda.

of a man who had committed some offence having been found in the house of a Christian convert. The anger of the king was also fanned by the fanatical Mujasi, head of his body-guard, who was friendly to 'the Arabs and correspondingly unfriendly to the Christians.

In January, 1885, the long-feared troubles began to break out openly. The missionaries were insulted, and their lives even threatened, while their followers were seized and their property was sacked by the Moslem and Pagan mobs. Three boys, the eldest aged fifteen, were destined to be

The first Waganda martyrs.

the first martyrs of the persecution that was now on the eve of beginning. In the midst of a mocking crowd, a rough scaffold was erected and heaped with firewood, on

BISHOP HANNINGTON.
(From a Photograph by Fradelle and Young, Regent Street, W.)

which, after the most savage torture had been applied to them, the youths were burned; but the insensate hate of the enemies of the new faith was to be wreaked on even more important persons than those unfortunate children. The tyranny of the king had by this time incensed against him a large portion of the Christian and even of the heathen population. Accustomed latterly to the comparatively mild rule of M'tesa, they dreaded, when they saw such vengeance vented on unoffending boys, that they were on the return to the hideous old days before the arrival of the Christians. A rebellion and the assassination of the king were therefore planned. This plot was also favoured by the old chiefs, who feared that M'wanga, like his father, was on the point of adopting the new customs, and, from his unstable character, of even rewarding those who had brought these innovations into the country. This conspiracy, happily for the whites, who, no doubt, would have been the first sufferers by its success, was discovered

before the persons concerned in it had time to carry out their intentions. The result was that the shifty king immediately swung over to the whites, and, as a mark of his regard, gave the adherents both of the French and English missionaries high offices at his Court.

But M'wanga's new mood did not last long. His innate suspicion of everyone was soon again directed against the Europeans, with results of the most deplorable description. Dr. James Hannington (p. 153), who had been for some time engaged as a missionary in Africa, had been appointed in the summer of 1884 to proceed to Uganda as the first Bishop of Equatorial Africa. He was now on his way to his distant diocese, and, journeying by the new route from the coast, was heard of in "fair Kavirondo" (Vol. II., pp. 80, 92). The king was acquainted with the fact that there was a prospect of early receiving a distinguished Englishman in his capital; but at the time the missionaries had no idea that

Assassination of Bishop Hannington.

DR. A. R. TUCKER, THIRD BISHOP OF EAST EQUATORIAL AFRICA.
(From a Photograph by Elliott and Fry, Baker Street. W.)

the Bishop was going on to Busoga, and had, indeed, been intending to send a boat to Kavirondo to bring him to the capital by way of the lake.

In those years events began to thicken in Central Africa, and among these the report of the Germans' activity in Zanzibar and on the mainland gave renewed uneasiness to the fickle king. The Arabs, jealous of those whom they recognised as being their trade rivals in the near future, had repeatedly impressed upon M'tesa the danger that he was running by encouraging so many white men in his kingdom. "They will eat up your country," the Moslems used to tell him; "that is their only object in coming here." To a certain extent, though possibly not to the extent they imagined, the Arabs were right in their forebodings; but the easy-going king, fond of visitors, and still fonder of the gifts they brought him, laughed at these warnings. "Let the Bazungu alone," he would say. "If they mean to eat the country, surely they won't begin at the inside of it. When I begin to see them eat the coast, then I shall believe your words to be true." But now there could be no doubt about the Bazungu (Europeans) having begun to eat the coast. It was vain for the missionaries to point out to him that the Germans and the English were not the same people. The chiefs told him differently—the white men were exactly the same, and all bad. "When you see running water," they said, in the proverbial style of their countrymen, "you expect more to follow," and the general opinion of the king's Council was that the new white men should not be allowed to enter through the back-door of Busoga. When the news reached his countrymen that messengers had been despatched by M'wanga to kill Bishop Hannington, both they and the French missionaries implored the king not to bring trouble on himself by killing white men, but rather, if he disapproved of their coming, to order them to turn back. Gossip travels quickly in Africa, in spite of the want of posts and telegraphs and telephones, and the news that came to Uganda day by day recording the position of the Bishop was of the very worst. At last the tidings arrived that on the 29th of October, 1885, the Bishop and several of his attendants had been speared by executioners whom M'wanga had despatched for that purpose.*

Encouraged by the audacity of this act, and, perhaps, also rendered desperate by the dangerous course he had entered upon, M'wanga now openly _{persecution.} ^{A time of} proclaimed himself a persecutor. The friends of the missionaries were continually bringing them secret warnings of the dangers they were running. Among these well-wishers was the "princess," who sent word that, if ever they wished to propitiate M'wanga, now was the time, since, when he killed anyone, the friends of the dead man were regarded as his enemies unless they made the king a present to show they were not actuated by revengeful feelings. A gift was accordingly brought to the murderer; but, unexpectedly, it seemed to act upon him in quite a different way from what had been expected. He was, indeed, for a time extremely angry with the missionaries and considered he had done nothing that required propitiation. He even threatened to kill his visitors. "What if I kill you?" he shouted. "What could Queeni [Queen Victoria] do? What could she and all Europe do?" And when Father Lourdel attempted to interpose a word of explanation he was at once overwhelmed by more abuse. "If I kill them, do you think I should spare you?" Then, calming down just as suddenly as he had flared up, he ended the audience by ordering his attendants to give his visitors two cows "to quiet their minds." Strict orders were, nevertheless, issued forbidding any natives to go near the missionaries' premises.

In February, 1886, M'wanga's anger was roused by a fresh and equally imaginary grievance; for the collection of wattle-and-daub huts that constituted the royal apartments was burned to the ground, the fire originating in his gunpowder store. In terror for his life, the king took refuge on the shores

* In 1893 his remains were disinterred by Bishop Tucker (p. 153)—who succeeded to the brief episcopate of Bishop Parker, who died at Usambiro (p. 156) before reaching Uganda—and laid in the "Cathedral" of Uganda; Dawson, "Lion-Hearted: The Story of Bishop Hannington," and "Last Journals."

of the creek, and there became, as Mr. Ashe writes, "gradually disagreeable again." And when M'wanga became disagreeable his unamiability generally took the shape of accusing somebody of doing something for which they had to be punished forthwith. He did not claim that the white men had actually kindled the fire by which he had been rendered houseless; but he loudly announced that, after the fire, they had bewitched him, and would be the death of him some day, and even went so far as to issue orders that Mackay should be caught and beheaded for his share in this deplorable plot against the royal person and property. The missionary was, however, warned in time, and kept away from the place until the king's wrath abated.

By May dark days began to fall on Uganda. The Pagan party was once more triumphant, and the special objects of their wrath were the "readers," that is to say, the converts or pupils of the missionaries who had learned to read the books which they had translated into the Waganda language, and printed for the use of the people, many of whom bought them with remarkable eagerness. The fury of M'wanga against all who were known or suspected to be "readers," passed all reasonable bounds. Those who did not manage to escape to a place of safety, or were not concealed by their friends, were seized, tortured, or killed on the plea of being disloyal and seditious. But as the missionaries were isolated, no one being allowed to go near their quarters, it was only long after that the full extent of the persecution reached their ears. No form of atrocity was lacking in the scenes which ensued. "Readers" were not only killed, but were tortured in the most inhuman manner. One man, whose turpitude had been increased in the eyes of the king by having been a friend of the murdered Bishop, was put to death with exceptional cruelty, one limb after another being cut off and flung into the fire, before the trunk of the still living victim was committed to the flames.

While the persecution was at its height— on the 2nd of June, 1886—Dr Junker, the Russo-German traveller, arrived at the mission-house, in despair of being able to leave Emin Pasha's province by any other route (pp. 26, 27) than that through Uganda to the east coast. He brought a terrible account of the mutilated bodies of M'wanga's victims lying by the wayside. A wholesale butchery had been enacted, not only in the vicinity of the mission, but over all parts of the country—many of the victims being only suspected of sympathy with the missionaries—and even on the road leading to the king's enclosure Mr. Ashe tells us that he saw the ghastly sight of a dissevered head and limbs lying in the middle of the pathway. Happily, Mr. Mackay's influence with the king was still sufficiently great to persuade him to send Dr. Junker, after a brief delay, upon his way to Bagamoyo. Arrival of Dr. Junker.

Then the missionaries asked leave to follow their guest, not only from their conviction that in the present state of matters they could do little good by remaining, but also as the strongest protest they could make regarding the horrible cruelties committed by the king or with his acquiescence. But this request M'wanga firmly refused. Mr. Ashe might go, and go he did; but Mr. Mackay was told that he must stay, and in Uganda this devoted pioneer of civilisation tarried for some months longer. Mackay was now the only Englishman at the king's capital, and for a time it was doubtful how long he would be permitted to remain as a representative of the once flourishing mission. It is, indeed, questionable whether the king would have been so anxious for his presence had he not been useful in mending his arms; for the Arabs continued relentless in their bitterness against the Christians, and worked upon the feeble mind of the king by representing that Mackay was in his country simply as a political agent. The Arabs' influence.

Then came the news of Stanley's expedition for the succour of Emin Pasha. This afforded them a chance of magnifying the force he had with him and of representing that he was marching on a mission of conquest.

Mackay, meanwhile, retired to Usambiro, a station on the southern borders of the lake (p. 60), and his place at the capital was taken by a fresh relay of missionaries, who were received by the king with almost as much distinction as his father had bestowed upon their predecessors.

The cup of M'wanga was by this time the atrocities to which their friends had been so recently subjected, and the persecution to which they were still at times liable at the hands of M'wanga's officials. He might, nevertheless, have continued undisturbed in his kingship had it not been for one of his usual outbursts of cruelty. By a cunningly-contrived plot he was on the eve of sending

"GOD'S ACRE," USAMBIRO, SHOWING THE GRAVES OF BISHOP PARKER, ALEXANDER MACKAY, AND OTHERS.
(*From a Sketch by Bishop Tucker.*)

nearly full. He had now filled the throne of Uganda for nearly four years, but his position, instead of getting stronger, had been gradually getting weaker. In spite of the majesty which in Uganda "hedges round the king with awe," his repeated acts of violence and rapacity, unredeemed by any of those generous impulses which, in spite of his cruelty, endeared M'tesa to the Waganda had rapidly alienated the loyalty of large numbers of his subjects. The "readers" were naturally slow to forget

M'wanga driven from the throne.

a number of the principal "readers" to an island in the lake, with the intention of leaving them to starve, while their enemies, who were privy to the conspiracy, brought away the canoes by which alone they could escape the cruel fate to be meted out to them. Tidings of the king's infamous trick, however, oozed out before he could carry it into execution. Then the Christians, in their turn, began to plot against their faithless king, being assisted in this conspiracy by the Mohammedans, who made catspaws of the "readers." Two armed forces now entered the country simultaneously by two different routes. Then, at the sight of the danger threatening him, M'wanga collected his pages and his wives, and fled unmolested to Magu, where, in the guise of a guest, he end, instead of increase, the anarchy that had seized upon Uganda. Some of the most mischievous chiefs were deposed, others pardoned, and the offices about the Court distributed

FORT OF KAMPALA, UGANDA, WITH SUMMIT OF MENGO AND HOUSES OF THE KING.
(From a Sketch by the Rev. Frederick Smith.)

became a virtual prisoner in the hands of the Arabs.

Meanwhile, the new king, Kiwera, an elder son of M'tesa, was enthroned without the loss of a single life; and for a time it almost seemed as if this peaceful revolution was to with considerable impartiality among the different sects. Thus, the post of prime minister was bestowed on a Roman Catholic; the next dignity in importance fell to a Protestant; while the Mohammedans received their due share of the patronage at the disposal of the new sovereign. Liberty of worship and of teaching was proclaimed, and there was a general gladness throughout the land when it was announced that a milder rule than had ever been known in Uganda was to signalise the *régime* then inaugurated. Christians now emerged from their places of concealment, and the new missionaries were busy from morning to night distributing to the people who swarmed round their stations the various books translated into Luganda and Kiswahili —the tongue of the Zanzibar coast. It seemed as if the day had just begun to dawn in the centre of the Dark Continent. Unhappily, this pleasing condition of affairs was not destined to last long.

The dawn succeeded by darkness. The new king proved to be a mere puppet in the hands of his chiefs; and the Mohammedan party, who had expected great advantage to themselves when they seated him on the throne, again began to contemplate the best means of getting rid of him for a more facile tool. Both they and the Pagan faction were dissatisfied at the large share of offices that had fallen to the lot of the Christians, and both determined not only to oust the king from the throne on which they helped to seat him, but to root out Christianity from Uganda. The native Christians, it was soon whispered abroad, were rebels, and were planning to make a woman Queen of Uganda in imitation of England, to which they were affirmed to be more loyal than to their native land. No sooner was the charge made, than those accused of this treasonable conduct were attacked and defeated. The missionaries, English and French, were placed under arrest, while their houses were gutted by an infuriated mob. And then, after being robbed of the few articles remaining to them, they were conducted down the lake, with this parting injunction—" Let no man come to Uganda for the space of two years. We do not want to see Mackay's boat for a long time to come. We do not want to see a white teacher back in Uganda until we have converted the whole of Uganda to the faith of Islam."

But just at the time when the new king was on the eve of being expelled from the position which he had occupied for so brief a period, his deposed predecessor, by the force of unexpected circumstances, was about to be restored to power by those very Christians whom he had persecuted. Mr. Mackay, hearing at his station of Usambiro (p. 60) that the king was in a woful plight among his Arab captors, invited him to take refuge with his old friend. This invitation the exiled sovereign could not then take advantage of; but later he managed to escape from the Arabs, and was received by the French priests at Bukumbi. The scattered "readers"

Murder of Kiwera, and enthronement of Kalema.

now began to imagine that M'wanga, tried in the school of adversity, was on the whole a better king for them than Kiwera in the hands of the Mohammedans. Accordingly, when the deposed ruler (after the fashion of his order) summoned all loyal subjects to rally round him, he found a considerable number of them at his back. Indeed, so far as Uganda was concerned, the road was almost open for the return of M'wanga. For the Arabs, dissatisfied with their puppet Kiwera, had deposed and murdered him; not, however, before the murdered king had assassinated two of his chief advisers, one of whom was Mujasi, who had been among the bitterest persecutors of the Christians. Kalema, the third son of M'tesa —the rest, in spite of their brother's supposed clemency, having been put out of the way—was now called to the throne, and promptly utilised the first few hours of power by murdering all his relatives who were unable to escape. M'wanga's attempt to regain power was not at first attended with complete success; for he was compelled to take refuge on the Sesse Islands, from whence he advanced up Murchison Bay, and established himself on the island of Bulinguge. From this point he despatched messengers both to the French and the English missionaries, begging their aid to recover his kingdom, at the same time professing sentiments of the utmost remorse for his past conduct and begging that bygones should be bygones. How far he was sincere time speedily showed. There was at all events a suspicious sniff of Pharisaism in the letter which the murderer of Bishop Hannington and the persecutor of the Christians sent to Mr. Mackay, "Formerly," he writes, " I did not know God, but now I know the religion of Jesus Christ. Consider how Kalema has killed all my brothers and sisters. He has killed my children, too, and now there remain only we two princes. Mr. Mackay, do help to restore me to my kingdom. If you will do so, you will be at liberty to do whatever you like. Sir, do not imagine that if you restore M'wanga to Uganda he will become bad again. If you find me become bad, then you may drive me from the throne, but I have given up my former ways and I only wish now to follow your advice."

The sixteen priests at Bukumbi declared themselves ready to accept the deposed king's professions of repentance, and the two Protestants considered it prudent to follow suit. M'wanga's second attempt to regain his throne was attended with greater success. The army of Kalema was defeated, and the reigning king driven into exile. Then, on the 11th of October, 1889, exactly a year after the expulsion of the Christians, M'wanga was escorted back to his kingdom by the very people whom he had persecuted and tried to drive out of the country. All that remained of the old mission-house at Natete, near the capital, was mounds of earth, overgrown with long grass and rank tropical vegetation. But another piece of land was given them on the hill of Mengo (p. 157), near the capital, a name that by-and-by became very familiar to English ears, and here a new house was built for them by the native converts.

Restoration of M'wanga, and the rebuilding of the mission-house.

History was now being made very fast in Central Africa. A new power was gradually spreading from the coast into the interior, and thus for the first time the restored king heard of the British Imperial East Africa Company. The

A new power in the land.

rise of this and other great sovereign companies, by which so large an area of Africa is now governed, will form the theme of another section of these volumes. Meanwhile it is impossible not to anticipate so far as to mention that, while on the island of Bulingugc, M'wanga learned that the representatives of this new force were at Kavirondo. It is extremely unlikely that the news gave him any great satisfaction. But, at that time eager to get assistance from any quarter, he immediately sent messengers to the Company's agents begging help from them, and in December duly received letters in reply, together with one of the Company's flags. This incident proved of the first importance in the events that were soon to crowd the history of Uganda; for, in accepting the flag, it was claimed that M'wanga had avowedly put himself under its protection, though it is likely enough that the king did not understand that this step involved any such consequences, or, more likely, was reckless what results it might entail so long as he could obtain the countenance of " the new white men." In his straits, he was careless of consequences.

But Kalema, though defeated, was not routed, and lay with his followers sufficiently near the capital to descend upon it when the opportunity seemed favourable. In the month of February, 1890, a large supply of guns and powder having arrived, he was again attacked and defeated, and M'wanga returned to Mengo in almost undisputed possession of all his old power. Politics now began to trouble the king more than warring sects ; for among his first visitors was Dr. Carl Peters, commander of a German East African expedition (pp. 59–64), who, in addition to his ostensible mission of trying to bring succour to Emin Pasha, was wandering about making treaties with any Central African chiefs who could be induced to put their cross to the documents which he placed before them. One of these papers was placed before M'wanga and, under the instigation of the French priests, who seemed to prefer any power in Central Africa to

Foreign politics.

the British, was duly signed by the restored monarch. The prime minister, with the Protestant chiefs, and supported by the English missionaries, entirely objected to this act on the part of the king, as he had already applied for aid to Mr. Jackson, the British was first the old Pagan party, the largest, but not the most powerful or the most aggressive. Then there were the Mohammedans, who were both numerous and audacious. The Roman Catholics were numerically the next most powerful, and finally there were the

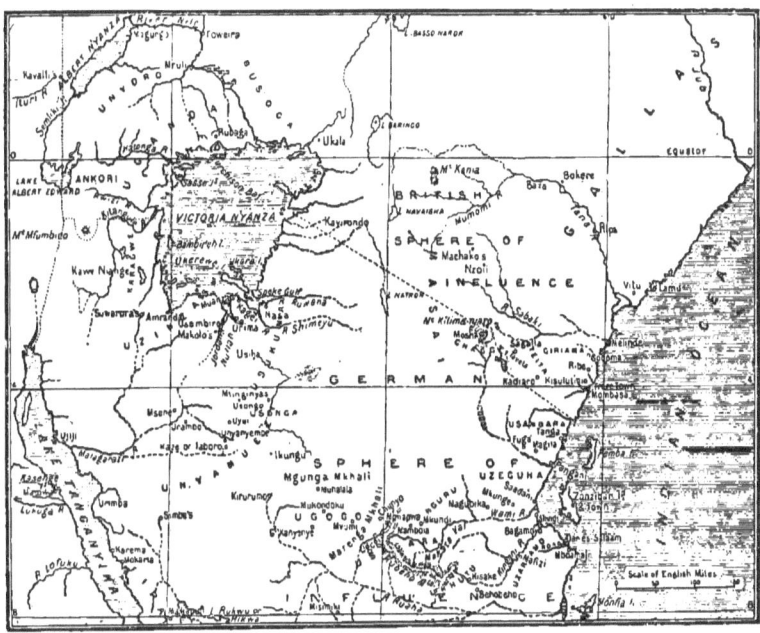

MAP OF EQUATORIAL EAST AFRICA.

East Africa Company's agent, who had sent him the flag a short time before.

The dissensions that followed this difference of opinion threatened so serious a breach of the peace that the English missionaries begged their followers to acquiesce in what had been done. About this period, however, the elements of anarchy that had been simmering for a long time in the country began to break out in undisguised hideousness.

Four religious—or irreligious—sects now divided up Uganda amongst them. There Protestants. The distinction between the creeds of the two Christian parties began however, soon to be lost sight of. The priests scarcely tried to conceal their political venom. One of them, indeed, had the imprudence to write a letter, which was afterwards printed, to the effect that the object that must now be aimed at was the extension of Catholicism and an unceasing warfare with the Protestants; but even when devoid of sectarian hate, they were unable to restrain the open display of it by their native adherents,

Protestant and Catholic were, however, terms heard less and less. It was the French party and the English party among the natives that daily became more and more pitted in bitter enmity against each other, and this politico-sectarian strife was, if not fostered by the priests, not discouraged by them.

From sour looks and angry words the different sects proceeded to actual riot and even murder. In short, Uganda was fast approaching a condition of anarchy, when there appeared on the scene a man who speedily produced order out of chaos and compelled the different parties to understand the meaning of *pax Britannica*. This man was Captain Lugard, who, in 1890, took possession of Uganda in the name of the British Imperial East Africa Company. But what happened then, and what followed his arrival and departure, must form the subject of another chapter; for now the missionary enterprise of Uganda merges into the history of its political relations.

The latest of the Central African missions is one founded by Dr. James Stewart as another Lovedale, and is a centre from which trained teachers, skilled in the arts of peace, may be spread all over the region between the great lake and the Indian Ocean. Though a long way from Uganda, it is necessary before leaving the African missions to say a few words regarding this experiment in the civilisation of Africa. The funds for beginning this work were supplied by a few North Country friends, for the most part connected with the Imperial East Africa Company, in whose territory it is situated. In order to establish the East African Scottish

The East African Scottish Mission.

NZOI.
(*From a Sketch by Bishop Tucker.*)

Mission, Dr. Stewart, whose labours in Nyassaland and as head of the Lovedale establishment in South Africa (p. 127) are so well known (pp. 131-134), made a journey into the interior which, not many years ago, when travelling in that direction was rarer, would have been of note in geographical annals. Nowadays, however, the route which he and his caravan followed, was the usual one by way of Mazere, Mwache, Taro, and Maungu to the river of Tsavo, the starting-point being Mombasa. The Tsavo—150 miles from the coast—which was reached on the 9th of October, 1891, is a river twenty to twenty-five yards broad and less than waist-deep in the dry season, and the first stream of any consequence between this port and the sea. Here the expedition changed their course and, instead of going by the direct road into the interior, proceeded parallel to the Tsavo till the Sabaki was reached. After this, they kept along its banks until Kibwezi formed their halting-place. Kilundi's village, where the missionary caravan formed a permanent camp, is distant about half a mile from what is known as Stockade No. 4 of the East Africa Company. The natives were perfectly friendly, eager for the expedition to remain, and, as an inducement, unusually liberal in their offers of land for building and cultivation. Finding no other site—and several were examined as far north as Machako's—the Kibwezi district was finally selected as the home of the mission. The soil is good and, though not excessively rich, easily wrought, while any quantity of limestone to be burnt into lime can be obtained on the spot. Nor is the situation without beauty. The snowy crest of Kilimanjaro is visible on a clear morning, while, by cutting some avenues through the jungle, the Ulu or Kiyulu mountain to the south-west, and the Mbwinzoi Hills in the north, will be seen from the doors of the houses. Finally the river, though not large and not without crocodiles, is full of fish of good size and fair quality, and affords a boundless supply of excellent water all the year round. Tea and coffee ought to grow well if the rainfall is sufficient. Cotton might also prosper, and the india-rubber tree —one species of which grows in the river valley—is still unknown by the natives as a source of saleable gum.

Land was accordingly bought and a treaty entered into with the chief for the erection of the necessary buildings; and at the date of the last accounts from Kibwezi everything promised well for a prosperous future in this new centre of civilisation, the five or six members of the mission finding the climate healthier than the Zambesi Valley and the lower districts of the coast of Lake Nyassa. Mosquitoes are absent, but the white ants, if not guarded against, are destructive to the timber of houses; while the black ants, Dr. Stewart adds, with the tolerance of a man who has had to bear with worse things than insect-bites, "may occasionally drive the occupant out for a few hours, generally in the night-time; but that is a mere temporary inconvenience, and not peculiar to the station." There is, however, a species of gad-fly which attacks man, though it is rare; but little fear need be entertained regarding the ravages of the few wild beasts in the country. Altogether, considering that Kibwezi is almost on the equator, it is comparatively pleasant and even healthy if common-sense precautions are taken. By-and-by out-stations will be formed; one as far distant as Machako's, eight days' travel northward, at a little over 5,000 feet above the sea, a second at Nzoi (p. 161), three and a half days' distant, and 4,000 feet above the sea, and others as circumstances may counsel. Perhaps, also, an entrance may in time be made into the Galla country, north of the Tana river; and, if the Mombasa and Victoria Nyanza Railway is ever made, it must pass so close to Kibwezi that this spot will become an important one in Central Africa.*

* Dr. Stewart's "Report on the Establishment of the East African Scottish Mission in the Territories of the Imperial British East Africa Company, 1891-92" (private circulation, 1892). For an opportunity of seeing this document, and for much other information, I am deeply indebted to Dr. Stewart.

CHAPTER VII.

THE HUNTER'S PARADISE: EARLY AND LATE: A CONTRAST.

The peculiar Plants and Animals of Africa—South Africa—Its Special Features—Changes brought about by Man—Decimation of the Great Game—Causes—Sportsmen—Colonists—Natives—Traders—Professional Hunters—Prospects of the Future—The Elephant—Thunberg—Sparrmann—Unfortunates Astray—A Bogged Herd and what befell Them—Great Bags—Rhinoceros—Black and White—A Legend of the Salt River—Numbers killed by Oswell, Vardon, and Others—What Sir Andrew Smith Saw—Hippopotamus—Its Confined Range—On Lake Ngami—Lions—Cape Buffalo—Giraffe—Zebra—Quagga—Wart Hog—Leopard —Cheetah—Antelopes—Species still holding their own in diminished Number—Koodoo—Lechwe—The Duke of Edinburgh's Drive—Species on the Wane—Klipspringer—Springbuck—What Gordon Cumming Saw—What is not now to be Seen—Blesbuck—Tsessebe—Hartebeest—Others Dying Out—Natal Redbuck—Bontebuck—Reedbuck—Pallah—Pookoo—Waterbuck—Eland—What Le Vaillant Saw—Cape Town in 1780—Apes on Table Mountain—Herds of Bontebucks—Hartebeest. Ostriches, and Zebras within a Week's Travel of the Capital—Buffalo Elephants at Plettenberg Bay—Hippopotamus, Buffalo, and Elephants at the Gamtoos River—A Hunting Costume—Lions, Jackals, Buffalo, and Guinea-Fowls at Algoa Bay—Gnu and Bustards at Little Fish River—Leopards and Lions at the Platté—Kolben—Paterson—Barrow.

THE animals, and, to some extent, the plants also, of Africa are for the most part peculiar to it. The continent constitutes the Ethiopian region of zoologists, though from the life characterising them its different areas are capable of subdivision. South of the Sahara there is, however, a certain similarity. But the desert fauna, which is extremely limited, graduates insensibly into that of North Africa on the European side of the Atlas Mountains. Here —in the Barbary States—the animals and plants are closely akin to those of Europe on the other side of the Strait of Gibraltar and the Mediterranean.

But it is in a very limited portion of South Africa that the most remarkable features of the life of the continent are found. Roughly speaking, its limits as a typical region are the narrow strip of territory limited by the mountain ranges which form the boundary of the Cape Colony and Natal, though, perhaps, in a wider sense it may be considered to include Mozambique. Perhaps the Kalahari desert and the Limpopo river, or even the Zambesi, form its most natural boundaries on the north. Into this triangle, which ends in the Cape of Good Hope, a most extraordinary collection of plants and large animals would seem to have been driven and, being unable to go farther south, to have huddled and developed here; and the farther south the country is examined, the more remarkable in character and variety do the *feræ naturæ* become. The flora alone is most interesting in the world, its Cape heaths, shrubby pelargoniums, proteas, many bulbous plants, euphorbias, welwitschias, thorny shrubs of the "stay-a-bit" type, stapelias, orchids, and a host of other species, imparting to this dry area features which would alone make it notable were not the quadrupeds that graze upon them of still greater moment in the popular eye. In no other part of the globe are there so many genera and species of plants congregated in the same space, and nowhere else are so many peculiar forms found. A similar richness and specialisation characterise its zoology, though animals not being so closely dependent on soil and climate as plants, there has been a greater intermixture of immigrants from the north than we find in the sister kingdom of Nature. Still its fauna is, to a marked degree, isolated—South Africa being, from the naturalist's point of view, closely akin to an oceanic island; though, from a geological point of view, there is no evidence that it ever held that relation to the rest of the continent immediately north of it. This peculiarity applies to the animals of all groups, though it is solely with the larger that the

The fauna of South Africa.

following chapters deal. Insects, fishes, reptiles—all have genera and species confined to this part of Africa; and though the birds do not present so many peculiar forms, some of them are very interesting. But the South African mammals are, though scientifically not perhaps so remarkable as some of the lowlier species, decidedly the most striking from the ordinary traveller's point of view.

presented was the enormous herds of great game. So common, indeed, was the spectacle, that it is only now, when animals then abundant are scarce or extinct, that we can realise what a wonderful sight was vouchsafed to the earlier explorers and colonists of South Africa. The American prairies of the writer's youth presented a scene comparable with what might have been witnessed almost anywhere

GAME IN SIGHT!
(From a Photograph by Mr. Fred Moir.)

There are more peculiar forms than in any other division of the Ethiopian region, though in extent it is the smallest. The golden moles, the elephant shrews, the long-eared fox, the *Lycaon* or hyæna-dog, the jumping hare (*Halemys capensis*), the aard wolf or Mona jackal (now getting very scarce below the Orange River), and the earth-pig, are among the best known of eighteen genera of mammals almost, or quite, limited to South Africa.*

However, to the traveller over South Africa fifty, or less, years ago—and even yet—the most amazing spectacle which the country

* Wallace, "Geographical Distribution of Animals," Vol. I., pp. 266-269.

in the Cape Colony not actually settled up, and everywhere in the native territories to the north. Several of these gregarious animals were peculiar to South Africa; but, unlike the species mentioned, the majority were common to most of the continent, though, with few exceptions, nowhere so abundant as in this confined end to the north of the Cape.

The most common of these animals were antelopes of many species, zebras, quaggas, and giraffes. The elephant, now approaching the close of its career in all parts of Africa, was frequently met with in the Cape Colony at a date well within the memory of men still alive, and the lion might be nightly heard

WHEN GAME WAS PLENTIFUL.

close by the fields of the settlers. But it was not in twos and threes that most of these beasts were seen. Valleys were full of them. The veldt was in places moving masses of these large game, and a hunter was in no way particularly lucky in killing three or four elephants in one day. Even in Livingstone's time we have seen that game was enormously plentiful in parts of the Cape Colony (Vol. II., pp. 170-174, 185-187) now traversed by railways; and many of the most notable exploits of Harris, Oswell, Vardon, Gordon Cumming, Baldwin, and even Selous, the last of the great African hunters, were performed in places where it would be now difficult to find the quarry which, in these comparatively late times, they slew in such numbers. The rapid decrease of the great animals of South Africa is one of the most regrettable, though, at the same time, one of the most inevitable incidents in the history of colonisation. The bison was killed off the American prairies by the deliberate slaughter of the "skin" hunters, whom the progress of railways enabled to reach their haunts. Mere sportsmen, and still less settlers or Indians, had little share in the extermination of the great wild ox: all they slew had scarcely any effect on its multitudes at the time of which we speak.

The South African decimation has been due to different causes. From the beginning of this century—earlier even—adventurous sportsmen have visited the region of which we speak for the purpose of hunting its great game.

SHOT BUFFALO.
(*From a Photograph by Mr. Ernest Gedge, by permission of the British Imperial East Africa Company.*)

Several of these hardy hunters helped in no small way in opening out the country, not only by sharing in actual exploration, but by the interest which their exploits among the wild beasts aroused in the minds of those who read their books. Yet huge as

Causes of the decimation of the South African fauna.

were the "bags" they made, it is doubtful if they seriously diminished the herds of game. The colonists were more fatal in their execution. They were on the spot and were always growing more numerous; and as the demand for food increased, or the market for hides and ivory came nearer, the denizens of the wilds had to pay the penalty. The "trek-Boers," or "emigrant farmers," living as they did in the remoter parts of the country, were most serious in this onslaught. Grazing and hunting were their chief pursuits, and their skill with the rifle was, and is, phenomenal. Then the natives obtained firearms, with the result that species which, like the elephant, they were rarely able to spear to death, or to capture in pits, or in the "hopo" (Vol. II., p. 174), fell in great numbers before their trade muskets, and still more rapidly before the rifles which by-and-by took their place.

About the same period the professional ivory hunter, who was just as frequently an ivory trader, penetrated regions beyond the boundaries of the Cape, or "old colony," killing all he could kill, and tempting the natives by the price which the hitherto almost unconsidered ivory, horns, and hides brought, to slaughter in any manner as many more as they could manage to do to death.

These were the main causes of the rapid decimation of the great herds of South African game. Compared with the people described, the sportsmen from Europe—the "hunters" proper, whose travels we are called upon to briefly notice—accomplished little of the destruction deplored. Among the elephants and lions, no doubt, a well-equipped "jäger" of the Gordon Cumming type did something to lessen their numbers. But the most determined of these were then seldom longer than a year or two in the country, and, with a few exceptions, the explorer *malgré lui* killed his game in a sportsmanlike manner. He wished amusement rather than tusks, or horns, or hides, and acted accordingly.

Be this as it may, in one way or another, singly or combined, the result has been so remarkable that we may profitably devote a few pages to noting the most salient facts about this destruction of South African animals, which forms so strange an episode in the story of the continent. At the same time, it must be remembered that, though the Cape of Good Hope and the regions immediately north of it are mainly concerned, much the same tale comes from almost every other part of Africa. Everywhere the natives have obtained arms, and wherever the explorer has gone he has been followed by the traders, shooting themselves and encouraging others to shoot. It is, indeed, difficult to draw any hard-and-fast line between the hunter by profession and the hunter by necessity. Mungo Park was not a sportsman, and from the lack of game most of those who penetrated from and to the north seemed to have been deficient in the most marked trait of their successors. But nearly all of the later explorers—Speke, Baker, even Livingstone—have been compelled to pursue great game for food, or to kill it out of self-preservation; and some of the former have, from love of gain or love of sport, penetrated so far into the outer wild, that beginning—like Petherick in the north, and Selous in the south—as traders or hunters, they ended as travellers, held in esteem wherever geographers most do congregate. As men—men with rifles and ploughs—multiply, the "provisional races," and the wild animals on which they prey, are doomed to retreat before them. It is possible, now that efforts are made to taboo gunpowder as an article of commerce, that the "beasts" may again be "more and more," and man, through the Hamburg gin, which is infinitely more lethal than villainous saltpetre, be "less and less." For the moment, however, the signs are all the other way.

In following the routes of travellers by no means remote, we have seen how abundant the elephant used to be. Chiefs did not know what to do with the rotting tusks, except, perhaps, like one of Mr. Rider Haggard's heroes, to fence their kraals with them. They know better nowadays; for the ivory trade, we

The elephant.

have learned (Vol. II., p. 139), is practically the slave trade "writ small," and the slave trade means war, murder, and kidnapping; so that it is almost with pleasure that we hear of travellers going to Tanganyika and back again without as much as sighting a tusker. This destruction, however, is not a modern incident. It began with the utter extermination of the herds which, less than twenty centuries ago (Vol. II., p. 227), wandered through the forests which then covered the region north of the Atlas Mountains; and, curiously enough, it next set in at the extreme southern part of the continent, a land, in the day when Pliny wrote, not even dreamed to exist.

Little more than a century ago the elephant roamed all over the Cape Colony. Thunberg, in his second journey into Kaffraria* in 1773, tells us that he met with a man who assured him that " in his younger days the elephant was very numerous" near Cape Town; that, in travelling to and from that place, one might kill such great numbers of them that he himself had often shot from four to five in a day, and sometimes twelve or thirteen; and that twice in his life, when he was out in pursuit of these animals, "he had shot with his own gun twenty-two each day." Sparrmann, a traveller of about the same date,† confirms this astounding tale; for, so writes this early voyager, " in the country near the Cape, elephants are sometimes seen in large herds, consisting of many hundreds, and in the more remote and unfrequented parts of the interior they are still more numerous."

But little by little, and latterly very fast indeed, with the hunter on their trail, they have retreated northwards and eastwards, though always in diminished numbers, and never able to find any safe retreat; until it is questionable if any have a permanent home in parts of the Cape Colony where, not many years ago, they were quite abundant. At the beginning of this century one of the earliest of the Dutch hunters stood at the Kuruman Fountain, and there collected sufficient ivory to enrich himself speedily. Sechele's country in Gordon Cumming's time—1846-49—was still plentiful enough in elephants to afford employment for many seekers after tusks, though most of that great hunter's exploits were performed in the hills about Shoshong, where game existed in quantities almost incredible to this generation. Livingstone saw elephants in extraordinary numbers along the Zouga river—now more generally called the Botletli—as late as 1849, and round Lake Ngami not less than 900 are mentioned as having been shot a year or two after his first journey thither. Baldwin had good sport there in 1858, but the trek-Boers of 1877-78 finished most of them in that region. Still following them up without mercy, the hunters have left very few along the Chobe river and Zambesi, where early in his "jäger" life Selous found them so numerous. A troop, partially preserved by Khama, the enlightened chief of whom we have already spoken (Vol. II., p. 178), still frequents the almost impenetrable jungle—so dense and thorny that even the elephant-hunter hesitates to enter it—between the Zambesi and Linyanti roads; but even there they will not always be permitted the immunity they at present enjoy.‡ Mr. Bryden mentions a strange event that happened a few years ago at Molepolole (Koloben), in Bechuanaland. A troop of nine or ten elephants, presumably from the northern part of the Kalahari or from the Botletli river, had by some accident strayed from their usual haunts, and were discovered on the hills near the town. But they never returned; for the entire population turned out, and in a short time every one of the hapless beasts—mostly cows and calves—were hunted down. A still more wanton case of destruction is related by the

---

* "Voyage au Japon par le Cap de Bonne-Espérance, les Iles de la Sonde," etc. (1796). In English 4 vols. (1795).

† "Voyage to the Cape of Good Hope towards the Antarctic Circle, and round the World, but chiefly into the Country of the Hottentots and Caffres, from 1772-1776," 2 vols. (Engl. trans.), 1785; another 2 vols., 1789.

‡ Bryden, "Gun and Camera in South Africa" (1893), p. 489; and Nicolls and Eglinton, "The Sportsman in South Africa" (1892), p. 59—both admirable works, to which the writer is under obligations for most of these facts regarding the modern range of South African animals.

same writer, himself one of the most successful of the hunters who fell on the dull days of South African venery. About fifteen years ago some Boer hunters—and many of the best of the professional ivory seekers are natives of the country, though, not being authors, their exploits are seldom known outside the immediate circle of their acquaintances —came upon a morass in the region between Lake Ngami and the Upper Okavango, in which they witnessed what was to them a welcome sight. This consisted of 104 elephants bogged and helpless. Many of the unfortunate beasts were calves, tuskless or poorly provided with these attractive features; but that did not matter to the Dutch "hunters." They were slaughterers, and not sportsmen: and before the sun went down the marsh was full of the carcases of elephants, few of which were profitable, and none of which could ever be utilised for food.

The result of this ceaseless massacre—inevitable, if undesirable—is that, with the exception of a few scattered herds in the least frequented parts of Matabeleland and Northeast Mashonaland, the impenetrable bush of the low-lying country near Sofala Bay is about the only part of South Africa where this great wild animal is now to be found in comparatively large numbers. The Colonial

WILLIAM CHARLES BALDWIN.

Government is trying to preserve it in some of the forests in the eastern provinces of the Cape. A permit to shoot a single specimen costs £20, and even then is difficult to obtain; but, as the elephants are seldom seen, payment is generally made in vain, the intended victim declining death on any terms. At all events, it is no longer to be pursued on horseback: the hunter who is ambitious of laying one low has to take to foot, and run the risk which a pedestrian suffers when the elephant reverses the *rôle* of hunter and hunted. In earlier times it was not thought anything extraordinary to kill sixty elephants in one hunting trip of four guns, as Baldwin did on

TWO-HORNED RHINOCEROS.

his last expedition—in 1860—to the Zambesi; and about the same date the famous Boer hunters, Jan Viljoen and Petrus Jacobs, slew in a single raid ninety-three elephants.

In the days when Harris and the earlier hunters took tithe of the South African game **Rhinoceros and hippopotamus.** the two species of rhinoceros which until lately frequented that region were so abundant as to be almost a positive nuisance to the sportsman in pursuit of nobler quarry. The black one* was gradually approached nearer and nearer, as the impossibility of the brute extricating itself became more and more evident; until, finding that their efforts to compass its death were ineffectual, a sage proposal was made to cut a hole in its almost impenetrable hide, and thus get at its vitals more readily. Here the story ends, as such a story should; and it would be spoiling the point to question its veracity, except that in the Dutch version the Englishmen are the heroes, while the

A CRITICAL MOMENT.

"very common in the interior," and the white species† "very common after passing Kurrichane." At one time, like all other South African game, the rhinoceros was found in the near vicinity of Table Mountain; and in connection with this fact an absurd legend is said to be preserved in the archives of the colony. Once upon a time, so runs the tale, some country-folk found a huge rhinoceros mired in the quicksands of the Salt River, not over a mile from Cape Town. Attacking it with all manner of improvised weapons, they

* *Rhinoceros bicornis* (p. 166). † *R. simus.*

slow-moving Hollanders are credited with the tale in its rival edition. Be it fact or fiction, it is certain that a rhinoceros will never more be seen near Cape Town or anywhere else in the more settled portions of the Cape Colony. A few linger in the Chobe river swamps and in the neighbouring Zambesi region. Until Mashonaland was overrun with prospectors it was quite common there. Some are still to be seen in Matabeleland, in the district which Lo-Bengula called his "preserve," while it is reported as frequent in the country about Sofala Bay; but it is now idle to search for the rhinoceros about Lake Ngami, where a few years ago it was abundant. They swarmed round every desert fountain and water-hole, and could be shot any night by the half-dozen. Oswell and Vardon, in Livingstone's time, killed eighty-nine in one season, Andersson upwards of sixty in a few months, and others a number not much less. The Dutchmen and Griquas also, as soon as they found a market for its hide, slaughtered it indiscriminately—the "rhinaster" not being a very difficult animal to bag—with the results described.

This, however, was the black species. The white one, if not extinct, is on the verge of disappearance, and before these lines are published it is probable that it will have gone the way of the quagga, at one time as abundant. If a few—and they must be few indeed—still survive, Mr. Selous is confident they are confined to a small tract of country in Northern Mashonaland. Even from there they would have vanished, had not the occupation of that country by the British South Africa Company kept all native hunters out of Matabeleland to the west of the Umniati river. In former times it wandered over most of South Africa, though early in this century it had retreated north of the Orange River, and tradition affirms that at a still earlier date it frequented the open wastes of Great Bushmanland also. By 1890, when Mr. Bryden was hunting in that region, this huge brute, sometimes standing six feet and a half high, and measuring between sixteen and seventeen feet in length, had disappeared from Ngamiland and the North Kalahari, one of the last refuges of the great game of South Africa; and there is no ground for believing that the white rhinoceros ever existed north of the Zambesi. Yet though on occasions active and swift, the species in question was as a rule sluggish and not so keen of eyesight as its congener, the black rhinoceros. Hence it fell an easier victim to the hunter, and when we consider the abundance of this beast not many years ago, the slaughter of it since the professional hunter began to penetrate its haunts must have been more than usually indiscriminate. Sir Andrew Smith, during his scientific expedition in 1835,[*] saw in one day's travel in Bechuanaland between one hundred and one hundred and fifty rhinoceroses, and in the same day one hundred giraffes, though that part of the country was never specially noted for troops of the latter animals.

The hippopotamus (Vol. II., p. 113) at one time swarmed in all the South African rivers. It is now extinct south of the Limpopo, or Crocodile, and, though a few are said to exist still at the mouth of the Tugela on the east coast, it is many a year since the last was killed in the rivers of the Cape Colony. Even the Botletli and Tamalakan, in which they were plentiful not long ago, are the homes of only a very few wary old animals, and in the Limpopo it is not until Selika's is past that any great number are seen. But in the Chobe and Zambesi they are still plentiful, and in Lake Ngami they may yet be seen in herds of twenty or more. Naturally cautious, emerging only from its strongholds to feed at night, Messrs. Nicolls and Eglinton are of opinion that the "hippo," still so abundant in intertropical Africa, may continue to haunt the rivers of South Africa long after the elephant and rhinoceros are mere legends of the country on their banks. It would, moreover, appear that this huge beast, so powerful in the water, and so helpless on land, is becoming extremely wary of the seeker after its hide for sjamboks or riding-whips. At all events, the Kaffirs, though better armed than of old, are much more afraid of an encounter with the "sea-cow." So marked is this that it is no uncommon spectacle to see herds passing unmolested up and down the open water in broad daylight right in front of Moremi's old town on Lake Ngami. In Andersson's day[†] they would have attacked

[*] "Report of the Expedition for Exploring Central Africa from the Cape of Good Hope, 1834" (1836): *Journal Roy. Geog. Soc.*, Vol. VI., p. 394 ; "Zoology of South Africa" (1849), etc.
[†] "Lake Ngami" (1856); "The Okovango River" (1861); "The Lion and the Elephant" (1873), etc.

them with spears and harpoons. At present, though not more pusillanimous than their fathers, the natives, armed with breech-loaders, choose the prudent part by closely hugging the shore with their canoes, dreading any chance of meeting with the "river-horse" in open water.

The lion in Sir Cornwallis Harris's time was "usually found among reeds in open plains, gregarious and very common" in the Cape Colony.* The hunter who comes upon its "spoor" in the colony nowadays can congratulate himself as a fortunate man—or the contrary; for even in the remoter parts of the Transvaal, about Delagoa Bay, and in British Bechuanaland, they are now very rare, so that the traveller in those countries may return without ever having heard their roar, supposed to be so dreadful, although in reality the lion roars only when he is feeling the joys of a full stomach. Still to a neophyte the music of a troop of the king of beasts around a hunters' camp is not reassuring. About the year 1877 lions were often sighted in troops below the mountains close to the Gold Fields, in Secocoeni's land, and in the "Kaap," a mountainous district to the right of the Lydenberg main road.†

The lion.

Along the Botletli, where they are still numerous, the presence of Burchell's zebra is a sure sign of the lion not being far away, and in the bushier parts of Ngamiland the incautious explorer may at times come upon them unawares. It would also appear that in Mashonaland—where until the pioneers of the Chartered Company arrived under the leadership of Mr. Selous in 1890, the sound of firearms had been comparatively rare—the lord of African animals is still to be met with, though possibly not in quite such alarming numbers as a recent party of visitors to that country were led to believe.

The Cape buffalo ‡ (Vol. II. p. 64), once so

* Harris, "The Wild Sports of Southern Africa, being the Narrative of an Expedition from the Cape of Good Hope through the Territories of the Chief Moselekatse to the Tropic of Capricorn" (1839).
† Aylward, "The Transvaal of To-day" (1878), p. 229.
‡ *Bubalus caffer* (pp. 165, 177).

common, is now getting very circumscribed in its range. The trek-Boers of 1878 drove them from the Lake Ngami region, where they were numerous. Now the only specimens in the Cape Colony are perhaps those preserved in the dense bush of the Eastern Provinces. Farther north they are still to be met with, and as soon as the Zambesi is crossed immense droves may be looked for along the course of that river up the Barotse valley.

Buffaloes, giraffes, and zebras.

The giraffe, when the European sportsman first entered the hunter's paradise, might be seen in troops on all the great plains of the interior, within easy reach of Cape Town. But nowadays it is not until the parched desert of the North Kalahari is reached that the sight of a specimen may be expected, and everywhere else this fine animal is getting so scarce that a specimen in a zoological garden is often a desideratum. In Matabeleland Mr. Selous found it and the buffalo plentiful about the year 1882, and there it is still seen, though in decreasing numbers. In Mashonaland proper it is very scarce, and into the country east of the Gwelo river, for some inexplicable reason, it never wanders.

Burchell's zebra,§ the "bonte quagga" of the Boers, formerly inhabited the plains beyond the Gariep, or Orange River, in immense herds; but, though still common, it is rarely seen until some way beyond Palachwe. The common zebra∥ (Vol. II., p. 228), at one time even more plentiful in the mountainous pastures of the Cape Colony, is now confined to some of the eastern districts, where it is strictly preserved. Otherwise it would soon share the fate which is rapidly overtaking Burchell's allied species, and in all likelihood has already befallen the quagga.¶ No harmless South African animal has been more cruelly persecuted than these characteristic species. They are so easily hunted to death that it is scarcely an effort to "bag" them, yet not only the Boers and the Kaffirs have slaughtered them in the most ruthless

§ *Equus burchelli.*   ∥ *Equus zebra.*
¶ *Equus* (Hippotigris) *quagga.*

manner, but English "sportsmen" have not been ashamed to boast of shooting half a dozen out of the herds of fifty or a hundred—seldom less than ten—in which Burchell's zebra is found consorting with ostriches, brindled gnus, and hartebeests. The quagga is already bush which it inhabits is more closely approached. The leopard ‡—the tiger of the colonists—is still met with in the Transvaal and Bechuanaland hilly country, but in Natal and the Cape it is not likely to survive long. The cheetah § is another species doomed to

IN SEARCH OF PREY.

altogether, or almost, beyond the hope of preservation. Out of the herds which at one time inhabited the upper portion of the Cape Colony not one has been seen for several years; for the animal commonly called "quagga" by the Boers and the traders, and other unscientific people imitating them, is really Burchell's zebra.

The wart hog,* the representative of the more northern wild boars, is also greatly on the wane, while the bush hog †— **Hogs and cats.** never common—is likely before long to disappear altogether from Matabeleland, Mashonaland, Natal, and the Eastern Provinces of the Cape, when the dense destruction in Natal and the "Old Colony," and the serval,|| if it was ever common in South Africa, is now extremely rare.

But it is perhaps the numerous species of antelope which have their home in South Africa that form the most characteristic features in its rapidly diminishing fauna. So amazingly numerous were some of them that even yet they hold their own, in decreasing herds, no doubt, but still plentiful enough to furnish "sport" to their enemies, or food to the natives, who either live in their country or form the camp-followers of the hunters, traders, and (farther north) of the explorers. Among the species

* *Phacochœrus œthiopicus.*   † *Sus larvatus.*   ‡ *Felis pardus.*   § *Cynælurus jubatus.* || *Felis serval.*

that are still common are the steinbuck,* ourebi,† grysbuck,‡ duiker,§ rhébuck,|| reedbuck,¶ nakong,** lechwe,†† sable antelope,‡‡ and koodoo,§§ which, in spite of the continual persecution to which it is subjected, is still found scattered in favourite localities throughout the whole of South Central Africa. Yet as far as Cape Colony, Natal, and Orange Free State are concerned, it is only preserved on a few farms in a semi-domesticated state. But in Bechuanaland, and other less frequented spots on the edge of the Kalahari, and on the Lake Ngami, its fine spiral horns may be often seen above the dense bush in which it takes refuge, or in the dry forest country, in which, owing to its capability of doing long without water, the koodoo has its natural home.

though still plentiful in the swampy margins of the Chobe, Mababe, and Tamalakan rivers. But even the marshes which it affects will not long serve to protect it from the natives, who eagerly hunt it for the sake of its hides, which are held in much esteem for making karosses,|||| or upper garments, which the bitter cold night of even a South African winter renders necessary. When large areas of the country are submerged, the lechwe, now a very timid animal, gathers in herds composed entirely of rams, which are driven into deep water and then, surrounded on all sides by canoes, are speared to death in large numbers. "Common" is, however, only a term of relative importance in speaking of South African, and indeed of

SHOT HARTEBEEST.
(From a Photograph by Mr. Ernest Gedge, by permission of the Imperial British East Africa Company.)

The lechwe, first seen by Livingstone during his expedition to Lake Ngami in 1849 (Vol. II., p. 191), has now become scarce in that region,

any African game; what is common to-day was infinitely more abundant a few years ago, and may before many years either be extinct or so rapidly on the wane that its

* *Nanotragus campestris.*
† *N. scoparius.*
‡ *N. melanotis.*
§ *Cephalophus grimmi.*
|| *Pelea capreola.*
¶ *Cervicapra arundinum.*
** *Tragelaphus spekei.*
†† *Kobus lechêe.*
‡‡ *Hippotragus niger.*
§§ *Strepsiceros kudu.*

|||| "Kaross," "kraal," and "assegai"—three words used universally in South and even in other parts of Africa to indicate respectively a skin cloak, a native village or cattle-fold, and a dart or spear—have no place in any native language. They are supposed to be a corruption of Dutch and Hottentot.

end must be simply a matter of time and that not of long duration.

In 1860 a hunt was got up for the Duke of Saxe-Coburg-Gotha and Edinburgh—then Prince Alfred—who had paid a visit to the eastern part of the Orange Free State. The hunters, Mr. Bryden tells us, still talk of the vast herds of game that were slaughtered to make this royal holiday in the African Republic. A thousand of Moroka's Baralong were impressed as beaters. A huge extent of country was surrounded, and, as in the old days of the "hopo," gradually closed upon until it was computed that 25,000 head of great game were in sight of the "sportsmen." " Black and blue wildebeests, Burchell's zebras, quaggas, ostriches, blesboks, hartebeests, and springboks were to be seen charging hither and thither in affrighted squadrons, and raising clouds of dust. The number of game slain that day ran into thousands—6,000, some people say; several natives were trampled or crushed to death by a charging herd of zebras, while others sustained broken limbs. Even at this distance of time it is probable that the Duke still remembers that wonderful spectacle on the Free State plains. Nowadays those plains stand bare and desolate. Even as late as 1882, when Vryburg was founded by the freebooters, and a few tents and huts represented the present capital of British Bechuanaland, hartebeests and blesboks were known to gallop right through the camp." This will no longer be a tale of Africa, any more than the story that the Eskimo in a Greenland settlement can shoot reindeer from their hut doors in a winter's snowfall, or that black-tail stags can be killed—as they were killed in 1863 by the writer—where the city of Vancouver now stands and within sight of the then dwindling town of Victoria.

Yet ten years later, the districts of Harrismith, Kronstadt, Rhinosterspruit, and Bethlehem—an area altogether of about 6,000 square miles—were, like the great middle veldt in the Transvaal, literally swarming with countless herds of antelopes, of nearly every species. "Quaggas"—Burchell's zebra, no doubt—were seen in troops everywhere, and the land was fairly overrun with wildebeests, or brindled gnus, blesbucks, springbucks, and other less gregarious species. But before six or seven years had elapsed most of them were shot off, or fell before a disease not unlike that which decimated the domestic cattle, aided, Mr. Aylward thinks, by the drought to which parts of South Africa are increasingly subject. Some of the Boers and other residents are true sportsmen; but the majority are mere skin- or pot-hunters, who have been known deliberately to cut the throats of thousands of large game which have got mired in the deep mud on the border of a river they had attempted to cross.

But with such senseless, such utterly reprehensible, slaughter as that shown in South Africa to amuse the royal midshipman, it need scarcely be a surprise that many of the antelopes have since that day been unable to withstand the unintermittent massacre of which they have been the victims. Among the species that are rapidly on the wane may be enumerated the klipspringer,* the "chamois of South Africa," as Messrs. Nicolls and Eglinton call it, which was at one time very numerous on the mountains around Cape Town and Simon's Town, and is said to be still occasionally met with there; but farther in the interior, especially in Bechuanaland, and on to the Zambesi, it is "fairly common," although only a shadow of what its numbers were in days not very remote. The bluebuck,† the springbuck,‡ the blesbuck,§ the tsessebe,|| the inyala,¶ the hartebeest,** the blue†† and black wildebeest,‡‡ or brindled gnu, the gemsbuck,§§ and the roan antelope |||| are for the most part extinct in the Cape Colony; and the few still found cannot—let them be protected as they will—long remain alive, except in a half-tamed state in a preserve,

* *Oreotragus saltator.*   ¶ *Tragelaphus angasi.*
† *Cephalolophus monticola.*   ** *Bubalis caama.*
‡ *Gazella euchore.*   †† *Connochaetes taurinus.*
§ *Damalis albifrons.*   ‡‡ *Connochaetes gnu.*
|| *Damalis lunatus.*   §§ *Oryx gazella.*
|||| *Hippotragus equinus.*

or on the farm of a more than usually intelligent settler. The springbuck (p. 185) is an example of the rapidity with which an antelope gets thinned by the hunters. When Harris wrote the now classical narrative to which every historian of the South African game must so frequently refer, this animal was "scattered over the plains in countless herds." Nor would it be any exaggeration to apply the same phrase to the vast multitudes which Gordon Cumming saw here twelve years later. The accumulated mass of living creatures which the springbuck—so called on account of its habit of springing or taking extraordinary bounds—forms on its greater migrations, this famous, and now only justly appreciated, hunter tells us, speaking of a time before 1849, "is utterly astounding"—and it took a good deal to astound the Laird of Altyre (p. 208)—"and any traveller witnessing it as I have, and giving a true description of what he has seen, can hardly expect to be believed, so marvellous is the scene. They have been well and truly compared to the wasting swarms of locusts, so familiar to the traveller in the land of wonders. Like them, they consume every green thing in their course, laying waste vast districts in a few hours, and ruining in a single night the fruits of the farmer's toil. The course adopted by the antelopes is generally such as to bring them back to their own country by a route different from that by which they set out. Thus their line of march sometimes forms something like a vast oval, or an extensive square, of which the diameter may be some hundred miles, and the time occupied in this migration may vary from six months to a year."*

The place where these thousands of springbucks were seen, with here and there a herd of black wildebeest, was not far from the town of Cradock, on the Great Fish River, in what is now one of the most thickly settled portions of the Cape Colony. The only flocks of springbucks now to be seen either there or in

* "Five Years' Hunting Adventures in South Africa" (1893 Reprint), p. 44.

the Orange Free State and Transvaal are on farms, from the owners of which permission to shoot them must first be obtained. Sir Charles Warren's expedition, which in 1884 drove out of Bechuanaland some intruders besides antelopes, all but exterminated the great herds which used to frequent the Salt pan at Groot Choiang, north of Vryburg; and though it is still fairly plentiful in the open and arid flats north and south of the Botletli river, in North Kalahari, on to the Zambesi, in Great Namaqualand, Damaraland, and portions of Ovamboland, its agility did not serve to prevent it from becoming all but extinct in the Protectorate mentioned. The blesbuck no longer ranges the plains of Lower Bechuanaland, the Transvaal, and the Orange Free State in countless thousands. The skin-hunter has made it very rare, though Sir Charles Warren's expedition is also blamed for its practical extermination in southern Bechuanaland. The tsessebe, or sassaby, is no longer, as in Harris's day, in "considerable herds" in Bechuanaland. North-west of Lake Ngami, in Khama's country, and in the remoter parts of Mashonaland, it is said to be still plentiful. But after a year spent in various portions of Bechuanaland, Mr. Bryden, one of the most scientific of recent sportsmen in South Africa (p. 176), tells us that he never saw even the "spoor"—that is, the track—of one. It is doubtful whether it ever frequented the Cape Colony: at all events, it is not now found there.

The same tale is to be told of almost every one of the species mentioned in the foregoing list. Thus the hartebeest (p. 173) is no longer to be seen in the Cape Colony, except on a couple of preserved farms: and it is only in Ngamiland, that remnant of the hunter's paradise on both banks of the Botletli, and in Great Namaqualand that it is to be met with in large herds. Yet in the first three or four decades of the century, the hartebeest roamed in prodigious numbers on every plain beyond the Orange River.

But if the species mentioned are fast on the wane, there are others which are getting so rare that before long they must—let the South African colonists protect them as they may—follow the white rhinoceros and the quagga. The Natal redbuck* is everywhere rare. The bontebuck † in Harris's day was not very common: yet it was still found in Zoetendals Vley, near Cape Agulhas, and was abundant in the interior. "Indiscriminate, wilful, and senseless slaughter has rendered it practically extinct." Indeed, it cannot now be classed among the wild game of South Africa, Messrs. Nicolls and Eglinton being acquainted with it only as the semi-domesticated inhabitant of a farm near Swellendam, in Cape Colony. The reedbuck, ‡ once found wherever reeds and water abounded, is now confined to some of the rivers in the north-eastern districts of the Transvaal, while in Bechuanaland it is practically exterminated. To see the rooibuck, or pallah,§ once so plentiful in Bechuanaland, the bushy country bordering the Limpopo must be reached, while the pookoo,|| the scientific name of which recalls Major Vardon, a famous sportsman of Livingstone's day, and the man who first made Europe familiar with the tsetse-fly (Vol. II., p. 67), then and for long previously much too-well known in South Africa, is now confined to a small area near the place where the Chobe joins the Zambesi and does not seem ever to have had a much wider range. The poor quality of its flesh will not save it from the natives, though possibly Mr. Selous' verdict ** that in flavour it is several shades worse than that of the

MR. H. A. BRYDEN AND FRIENDS ON TREK AT MOROKWENG.
(From a Photograph by Mr. Bryden.)

waterbuck, usually considered the most unpalatable of all the South African antelopes, may preserve it from the pot-hunter, though its comparative rarity will be its doom as a museum specimen. Finally, not to enumerate various antelopes too scarce or too slenderly marked to have obtained popular names, the waterbuck †† just mentioned, the kring-ghat of the Boers, is now rarely met with except in the more secluded parts of the northern Transvaal, and in the low country

* *Cephalolophus natalensis.*   ‡ *Cervicapra arundinum.*
† *Damalis pygargus.*   § *Epyceros melampus.*
|| *Kobus vardoni.*

** "A Hunter's Wanderings in Africa." p. 167.
†† *Kobus ellipsiprymnus.*

towards Delagoa Bay, in the Botletli country, and along the Zambesi. Even the eland* (Vol. II., p. 181), at one time found in troops all over the country, is not now seen until the North Kalahari is reached; and, in spite of the efforts of the Colonial Government to save it and sights as the earlier travellers witnessed. A more instructive study in the story of Africa cannot indeed be found than to compare the fauna of the best-known part of the continent—say, a century ago—as a hunter of

Le Vaillant: a story of the "ancien régime."

YOUNG COW BUFFALO CAUGHT IN A PYTHON'S COILS.

other species from destruction by means of protective laws, it is vain, even if it was desirable, ever to expect a return of the days when South Africa was the hunter's paradise and the antelope's hell.

No longer will the sportsman again see such

* *Orvas canna.*

that day saw it, and the mangled remnant of the magnificent herds of animals that are all that are left to his successors. Compare, for instance, the casual remarks of Andrew Sparrmann, the Swedish naturalist, Carl Thunberg, another pupil of Linnæus, and François Le Vaillant, a famous French ornithologist, who visited the Cape Colony before the close of the last century, and the jottings of the latest writers on the same country, whose works we have so frequently quoted in these pages. When Le Vaillant reached the Cape the *ancien régime* was beginning to hear the strange rumbles of that *débâcle* which was not only to end it, but to bring about a change of masters for South Africa. But in 1780 the old order had not changed, and the Dutch still possessed a small portion of what now constitutes Cape Colony and the other offshoots which have grown out of its expansion. Le Vaillant resided for nearly six years in the settlements—though his journeys did not extend beyond Great and Little Namaqualand, the Karroo and the mountains which enclose it, and the east coast as far as Kaffraria—in short, little more than the Colony as then limited. He travelled much as people still travel who are distant from railways and roads—by bullock-waggon (Vol. II., pp. 169, 180), attended by a swarm of Hottentots.

Perhaps he was a little more in fear of Kaffirs than travellers need be nowadays, and decidedly in more danger from the lurking Bushmen of the Sneeuwberg than has been the case for a great many years. But beyond the fact that Le Vaillant carried a monkey to keep him company and a cock to crow him awake in the morning, his outfit did not differ very much from that of the latest trader; but he saw Kaffirs where there are now white men, kraals where there are now towns, and traversed for days great tracts of country without apparently a human being where, at this moment, there are swarms of men—as swarms go in South Africa. Otherwise the genial French naturalist might have been "trekking" and "inspanning" and "outspanning" to-day among the Boers, most of whom, however, were actually, like Le Vaillant himself, Huguenot Frenchmen, who had adopted another land and tongue.

Yet there was one vast difference between the hunter of 1780 and those of more than a century later. This consisted in the amazing swarms of animals which everywhere met his gaze, and rendered the collection of specimens easy and supplied a plethora of food for his native followers. We can only glean a few jottings here and there.* Everything was very cheap in Cape Town—thirteen pounds of mutton being at times sold for sixpence, an ox for twelve or fifteen rixdollars—a Cape rixdollar was one and sixpence—and ten quarters of corn for about the same sum, and other things in proportion, though during the ensuing war forty-five rixdollars were given for a wretched bag of potatoes and two shillings sterling for a small cabbage. In those days Le Vaillant complains that the French were hated and the English so adored that when any of that nation took up their residence in a Dutch family "master, mistress, and even the children, soon assume their manners. At table, for example, the knife never fails to discharge the office of the fork."

After a century or more of Boer marksmen game was, he says, no longer to be found close to the Cape; yet at Saldanha Bay the leopard preyed on the flocks, while the lion seemed frequent not far from the capital. Apes haunted Table Mountain. A little beyond the River Bot rhebucks, nowhere found in large numbers nowadays, were met with in prodigious flocks, while in less than a week after leaving Cape Town on his journey along the east coast to Natal Le Vaillant's camp was within view of flocks of bontebucks: hartebeests, zebras, ostriches (Vol. II., 188), and other large game: all so tame that, had it not been for the dogs chasing them, it would have been easy to shoot a great number without alighting from the waggon. Every day, long before the settlements were left behind, bontebucks appeared in flocks of two thousand at least, and near the valley of Soete-Melk a herd

* "Voyage dans l'Intérieur de l'Afrique," 2 vols. (1790); "Second Voyage dans l'Intérieur de l'Afrique par le Cap de Bonne-Espérance." 3 vols. (L'an 3); "Travels into the Interior Parts of Africa by Way of the Cape of Good Hope: in the Years 1780, 81, 82, 83, 84, 85," English translation, 5 vols. (1790–96). In reality, though the author, who had passed his youth in Surinam and Holland, set out on his journey in 1780, he did not reach the Cape until the following year. The English version is indifferently executed.

of four or five thousand hartebeests, antelopes of all kinds, zebras and ostriches, hung within sight, afraid to approach a pond near which the traveller had encamped. The ostrich, it is needless to say, is now only domesticated in Cape Colony, though plentiful in a wild state in parts of the Kalahari, Namaqualand, and Damaraland. It is doubtful whether the spotted hyæna* still exists in Cape Colony, and the brown hyæna † is only to be heard of in the most unfrequented part of the country. But at Mossel Bay, now a busy part, Le Vaillant was alarmed every night by their howls, and had to keep large fires alight to scare these sneaking beasts from attacking their cattle. A little beyond Blettenberg, so called from a pompous Dutch Governor, who had caused a stone with his name engraven on it to be erected there—a bushbuck strayed into the camp pursued by nine "wild dogs," the Cape hunting species,‡ still sparsely distributed in the Colony. By-and-by the buffalo was seen, and close to the sea elephants were met with, one of which was killed--not without putting the hunter in peril of his life--while others were heard of in the neighbourhood. One herd, indeed, disturbed the camp the next night, and four more were added to the sportsman's trophies before he left the shores of Blettenberg Bay.§ At the Gamtoos river hippopotami were reported, and elephants and buffaloes were so common and so easily killed with the rude flint-lock smooth-bores of the period that the camp was filled with more provisions than could be consumed. Yet, miserable as was Le Vaillant's battery compared with the weapons of the modern sportsman, he rather piqued himself on his equipment. A beaver hat with broad flaps, after the fashion of the "Age of Sensibility," knee-breeches with jewelled buckles, and tied shoes, was, judging from a portrait handed down to us, his hunting costume

"Le sport."

* *Crocuta maculata.*
† *Hyæna brunnea.*
‡ *Lycaon venaticus.*
§ Or Plettenberg, as it is usually spelt.

The rest was quite in the style of the modern Gaul bent on "le sport." "I was completely armed," he tells us. "In the side pockets of my breeches I carried a pair of double-barrelled pistols; I had another pair of the same at my girdle; my double-barrelled fusee was slung at the bow of my saddle; a large sabre hung by my side, and a poniard or dagger from the button-hole of my vest. I could therefore fire ten times almost in a moment. This arsenal incommoded me considerably at first; but I never quitted it, both on account of my own safety, and because by this precaution I seemed to increase the confidence of my people. My arms, doubtless, appeared to them to correspond with my resolutions; and, full of this idea, each pursued his way with the utmost composure, leaving to me the care of defending them." A little south of the Zondag river, which falls into Algoa Bay a little north of where the thriving town of Port Elizabeth now stands, buffalo were common ; the whole country swarmed with guinea-fowls, and at break of day springbucks were seen in great multitudes. A little farther north, lions added their voices to the nightly concert of hyænas and jackals, and day by day troops of apes visited the camp. In the Klein-Visch (or Little Fish) river, a hippopotamus was killed, while gnus were tolerably abundant. Indeed, so plentiful was game in 1781 that notes upon its abundance, descriptions of visits from Hottentots and Kaffirs, and tales of the abominable cruelties of the Dutch settlers to the natives, form the bulk of Le Vaillant's narrative. Bustards varied his dietary, but as springbucks and other antelopes were always in view, food of the best description was never lacking. When the country, then known as Kaffraria, was entered, flocks of gnus, ostriches, springbucks, bushbucks, or other species were met with at every step. On his journey back again to Cape Town a flock of springbucks was met with which filled the entire plain. They were migrating from the dry rocky regions in the south for some woody, watered region in the north, and must have numbered many thousands: as many as fifty was a rough estimate of our traveller. Elands and rhinoceroses also were seen among the Sneeuwberg valleys. Lions and leopards were troublesome on the Platté banks, many of them following up the antelopes in their migrations, though so plentiful was game, even to within sight of Cape Town, that the beasts of prey had little need to exert themselves.

Throughout all Le Vaillant's other journeys to Namaqualand the same relative abundance of the now fast-diminishing game of South Africa is heard of. As a traveller, he glosses every scene over with a romance that has led this disciple of Rousseau and the Sentimentalists to be suspected of indulging in occasional deviations from strict veracity. But no doubt need be entertained regarding the truthfulness of his records of the vast herds of game seen towards the end of last century; for not only do Kolben*—in more scientific matters not a very accurate authority—Sparrmann, and Thunberg confirm him by their descriptions at an earlier date, but much the same tale is told by Lieutenant Paterson,† who in 1777 and 1778 made three expeditions into the Hottentot country north of the Cape, and one into Kaffraria, which Le Vaillant entered only a few years later. Neither of these travellers, nor Barrow,‡ who at a later period went over the same ground, were hunters; but all the African travellers have been, and had to be, more or less killers of wild animals, and could scarcely fail to see the amazing herds of animals that covered the country at the time of their journeys, of which those of Le Vaillant may be taken as fairly typical. They were not explorations in the strictest sense of the term, for they did not extend over any ground absolutely unknown; but as a hunter's picture of the early days of South Africa, when civilised man was beginning slowly to wrest the land from wild tribes and wild beasts, the dusty volumes of these old travellers will still repay perusal.

* "Account of the Cape of Good Hope," etc., translated by Medley (1731).

† "Narrative of a Journey into the Country of the Hottentots" (1789).

‡ "Account of Travels into the Interior of South Africa," 2 vols. (1801).

SHOT GRANT'S GAZELLE (*Gazella Granti*) OF EAST AFRICA
(*From a Photograph by Mr. Ernest Gedge, by permission of the Imperial British East Africa Company.*)

A GOOD BAG.
(From a Photograph by Mr. Ernest Gedge, by permission of the Imperial British East Africa Company.)

CHAPTER VIII

BEAST AND MAN: SOME CAMPAIGNS OF A LONG WAR.

Game and Travellers—Influence of a Change of Masters in South Africa on Exploration—Trutter and Sommerville—Cowan and Denovan—Campbell—Moffat—Visitors to a Pool—Rhinoceroses and Hippopotami—A Boy's Mishap—A Tale of a Man and a Lion—A Chief Devoured—Burchell and Others—Captain Alexander in Namaqualand—Traces of Le Vaillant—Baboons and other Wild Animals—Running down Zebras on Foot —Bushmen and Lions—A Plethora of Game—The Black Rhinoceros—Its Friend and its Enemies— Walvisch Bay and the New England Whalers—Game among Flocks—A Story of Men and Monkeys— The Land of Lions and Leopards—Captain Harris—Rumours of Lake Ngami—Journey from Port Elizabeth over the Snowy Mountains—Vast Herds of Springbucks—Moselikatse—A Landscape Alive with Game—A Natural Preserve—"Dar Stand de Olifant"—A Fairyland of Sport—A Landscape Black with Elephants—The Young One and its Dead Dam—The Hippopotami and Crocodiles of the Limpopo—An Unfenced Menagerie —A Pest of Rhinoceroses—Giraffes, etc.—Rustenburg District in 1837—A New Antelope—The Vaal River— The "Emigrant Farmers"—Nearing Civilisation.

It would not appreciably serve our purpose, which is to trace the gradual progress of the African hunters from the known into the unknown, and the rapid diminution of the wild animals which fled before them, to spend much space over the earlier explorers of the country now comprised in Cape Colony, Orange River Republic, Transvaal, and Natal. At a later date we may have occasion to revert to them whilst speaking of the colonisation of South Africa. But even during the Dutch occupation the exciting amusement which the vast swarms of animals afforded, and the abundance of food which they supplied tempted many enterprising travellers to penetrate into the then little-known Kaffir countries. Most of these explorers were either military officers or naturalists; but very few, if any, of them were, as might have been expected, of Dutch nationality. Thus Le Vaillant was a Frenchman, Sparrmann and Thunberg were Swedes, and Lichtenstein, though a native of Holland, was, like Kolben, of German extraction. Henry Lichtenstein * accompanied Governor

* "Travels in Southern Africa, 1803-6" (Eng. trans., 1812).

Janssen in his progress through Cape Colony to the Orange River just before it passed into the hands that now hold it. He was the first person to visit the Batlapings. This was in 1803–6. His descriptions are, like those of his predecessors, full of notes regarding the vast herds of antelopes—one of which (*Bubalis Lichtensteini*) bears his name —elephants, and other wild animals; but the greater number of South African travellers were, and have continued to be, English-men. Barrow and Paterson were of that nation, and no sooner had the Dutch lost their hold on the Cape than the missionaries took up their position in a land Some early explorers. where they had hitherto either been excluded or regarded with cold sympathy. In 1801, the Colony labouring under a scarcity of cattle, Messrs. Trutter and Sommerville "trekked" through the Great Karroo and across the Orange River as far as Lithako, in Bechuanaland, in order if possible to obtain a supply from the natives. They heard of the "Barrolongs," but were too terrified by the tales told them to penetrate their country. In 1807 Captain Denovan and Dr. Cowan, in attempting to traverse the Bechuana country to the Portuguese colony of Mozambique, were lost sight of, and, though their fate has always remained a mystery, they are believed to have died of fever in descending the Limpopo river. Other native accounts, however, insist that they were murdered in the country of the Wanketzens.

Campbell, one of the early missionaries was also one of the most active of those who reached the remoter parts of the Colony after it became a British posses-sion. Elephants and zebras had in 1812, the year when he arrived, suffered no diminution from what the travellers of the preceding century had to tell of, and fires had to be lighted at night to scare away lions and other wild beasts. On the shores of Burder's Lake —so named from the then secretary of the London Missionary Society—the missionary party shot nine "bucks," a quagga, and an ostrich, and on their way to the Orange River the journey was rendered exciting by the travellers' hourly risk of falling into the traps and pitfalls constructed by the natives for the capture of elephants and lions. Campbell's second journey, which began in 1820, was shared in by the celebrated Robert Moffat and his wife, the parents of Mrs. Livingstone, during which they reached Kurrichane, the chief kraal of the Marotsi people, and Kuru-man station, or New Lithako, the future scene of Moffat's labours, was established. In-teresting though this and other missionary journeys were, the plan of this volume, which

THE REV. DR. MOFFAT.
(*From a Photograph by J. Moffat, Princes St., Edinburgh.*)

is to trace the opening up mainly of unex-plored Africa, compels us to dismiss them with this brief notice.* In the Karroo The hunting and other now colonised districts adventures springbucks, quaggas, and ostriches of Robert Moffat. were extremely abundant. Halting by the borders of a pond in the Barolong country, not far from the village of Sebateng, Moffat had not long to wait before several lions came to lap the water. Then a buffalo arrived. It was succeeded by two giraffes and a troop of quaggas. The male leader of the herd, however, scenting danger, gave a

* Campbell. "Travels in South Africa" (1815–22); Philip, "Researches in South Africa among the Native Tribes" (1828), etc.

peculiar whistling signal, and set off at full speed without drinking. A huge rhinoceros was the next visitor, and, receiving a mortal wound, moved off without troubling the hunters. The white species* was in those days quite numerous, and considered so fierce that it feared no enemy but man, and when wounded or pursued not even him. The lion flew before the rhinoceros like a cat, and it has been known to kill even the elephant by thrusting the horn into his ribs. Hearing the approach of more lions, the watchers thought it better to make off; but on the way to the village at which they were encamped they passed by herds of other animals on the way to the drinking-place.

Gnus, springbucks, hartebeests, and ostriches crowded their path in countless numbers, and increased daily as the waggon trundled farther and farther away from the thinly-peopled settlements into the region where there were no settlements at all and, in places, almost no natives. In parts of Griqualand baboons were still disagreeably numerous, and even dangerous when a hundred or more of them were encountered in a narrow defile; for, if one was wounded, the others were safe to attack the hapless hunter and tear him to pieces. The hippopotamus also might often be encountered in the Orange River; but, from having been frequently hunted, was by no means so inclined to tolerate man's presence as in more remote waters. A native with his boy was hunting the animal in this river not long before the period of which we speak. Seeing one at a distance below an island, the man passed through a narrow stream to get nearer the object of his pursuit. He fired, but missed, and the hippopotamus instantly made for the island. Then the hunter, seeing his danger, ran to cross the river-banks: but before reaching it, the "sea-cow"

A hippopotamus adventure.

seized him and, it is said, severed the body in two with its monstrous jaws.

Lions were encountered almost hourly, and, among other scenes, an attack upon the giraffe was a common spectacle. One of these animals was lying browsing at ease under the shade of a camel-thorn-tree,† when a lion, approaching from behind, stealthily sprang upon it; but just at that moment the giraffe turned its head, and the lion, missing its aim, fell upon his back among the thorns. Next day its body was found transfixed by the sharp, spike-like prickles on which it had been impaled. At the Rhenish mission-station of Bethany, on the Modder river, where a lion is never seen nowadays, this characteristic African animal was so common that it would sometimes be met with in the outskirts of the village.

Lion stories.

A Kaffir from this place, visiting some friends at a distance, was horrified while resting near a small pool to see a large lion watching him from the other side. Unfortunately, the man had laid his loaded gun beyond his reach, and, at any sign of reaching for it, the lion roared in so menacing a fashion that the wretched Kaffir was glad to purchase neutrality by a cessation of this constructive hostility. The situation now became extremely painful—if not for the lion, at least for the man; for, putting aside the imminent prospect of being devoured, the rock on which he sat, exposed to the glare of an African sun, was so hot that he could scarcely bear to touch it with his naked feet.

But the enemy was inexorable. Any exhibition of an intention to seize the weapon was followed by a warning roar; so that the man had all day long to temper the almost intolerable heat of the rock by placing one foot on another, until by evening both feet were so roasted that he had lost any sense of pain. The lion seemed to have only recently dined; otherwise it is extremely unlikely it would have displayed such tolerance to its helpless *vis-à-vis*. At noon it walked to the pool to

---

* Dr. Moffat mentions that the Bechuanas distinguished four species; in reality, there are only two (p. 169), *Rhinoceros marelli* and *R. keitloa*, the distinction being based on the shape of the horns in different individuals.

† *Acacia giraffæ*: the Dutch settlers know the giraffe as the "cameel"—hence camelopard.

drink, looking round every few steps to watch the Kaffir, and, when he reached for his gun, turned in a rage, and was on the point of pouncing upon him. Then quenching its thirst, the vigilant brute came back to its old post. Another night passed, but whether the Kaffir slept or not he could not tell. All he knew was that it must have been at very short intervals, and with his eyes open; for he always saw the lion at his feet. Next forenoon the animal went again to the water, and while there, hearing apparently some noise in an opposite quarter, disappeared in the bush. The man now made a strenuous effort to seize his gun, but on attempting to rise he fell, his ankles being apparently without power. However, he got the musket, and crept to the pool to drink, determined, if the lion returned, to discharge the contents of his weapon into it. But it did not appear. Then, unable—with his toes roasted by the sun and the hot rock, and his legs flayed by the sharp-edged grass—to walk, he crawled along the nearest path on his hands and knees on the chance of some traveller passing that way. This hope seemed destined to disappointment, when a countryman came up and took the famished and crippled Kaffir to a place of safety, where he recovered, though he was lame for life (p. 188).

The lion was indeed in those days, and for many years afterwards, the king of the South African wilds. His presence had always to be calculated on; for at night the oxen would tremble at hearing his roar, and, if the traveller failed to keep his camp-fire burning, or his thorn stockade up, the chances were not very remote that, before many hours elapsed, he would be disturbed by that royal visitor. The progress of colonisation soon diminished his numbers. Yet in 1835-37 the lion was so abundant on the route between the Orange and Vaal Rivers that the "Voortrekkers," or emigrant Boers, are said to have killed as many as two hundred.

A Batlaping chief, chasing a giraffe, wandered so far from home that he had to pass the night in the bush without his tinder-box, which, in a day when lucifer-matches were unknown, was an essential portion of a traveller's equipment. The want of this implement cost him his life; for next day an attendant found the chief's horse killed by a lion, but scarcely touched, at the spot where they had encamped for the night. Of his master, however, nothing could be seen except his skull. Saddle, bridle, and clothes had all been devoured, while the traces around showed that a number of lions had revelled on the ghastly meal, which, for some reason, they seem to have preferred to any other, if, indeed, they had not been alarmed before the horse could be eaten.

As for less noble beasts, they were so numerous in the earlier part of this century that the good missionary does not think it worth while mentioning them, except casually. But all of the antelopes named in the preceding chapter, zebras, quaggas, ostriches, and elephants were still abundant even within the limits of Cape Colony as then circumscribed, while in the native territories, long ago absorbed into it, they were everyday sights.

A more scientific traveller than Moffat, whose contemporary he was, appeared in 1812 in the person of Dr. William Burchell, whose name is likely to live, for some time at least, in Burchell's zebra, a species which, as we have seen, is generally mistaken for the extinct, or all but extinct, quagga, and in the also extinct white rhinoceros which he discovered. He penetrated Bechuanaland as far as Chuë, one degree north of Lithako, to the country which he calls "Karrikarri," but which is more familiar as Kalahari, hunting the wild animals which were everywhere abundant in the route he took, and observing their habits with the eye of a trained naturalist. It was his intention to penetrate through the Kalahari desert so-called—though in reality it possesses many grassy spots, trees, and an abundance of juicy bulbed plants—to the Portuguese settlements south of the Congo. If he had succeeded in this design, Dr. Burchell would have anticipated

HUNTING THE SPRINGBUCK.

Livingstone by more than forty years. Less familiar, however, with the natives, and less fortunate in those who accompanied him, he failed to persuade any of them to go with him, the result of which is that this meritorious hunter is now almost solely remembered by the plants and animals brought back by him.* Among naturalists, however, Dr. Burchell deserves a high place, and, though the country traversed by him was only new to a very small extent, he is not without a reputation in the history of geographical exploration.

Under the British rule Cape Colony and the neighbouring countries were so rapidly ransacked by a host of travellers that we have been able to name only the principal of them. There were, for example, Thompson† in 1827, David Hume and Robert Scoon, two Scottish ivory traders in 1835-36, and Dr. (afterwards Sir Andrew) Smith in 1835-36, who penetrated far enough north to cross the Orange River nearly 400 miles from its mouth, and added considerably to our knowledge of the geography and zoology of that region. But it is unnecessary to recall the work of them and others in addition to the names already mentioned, since the tale they had to tell is pretty much the same as that of their predecessors, so far as the abundance of animal life is concerned. This region is now largely threaded by railways and roads, and the seat of a thriving population: but in those days the war between beast and man had still left the victory with the former. Few of the natives had firearms, and the Boers, keen hunters though they always have been, had up to that date scarcely affected the swarms of wild animals, elephants, perhaps, and lions alone excepted; for these were undoubtedly getting fewer, being killed whenever possible for profit, and in defence of the crops and the flocks, not to speak, as far as the lions were concerned, of the flockmaster also. But large portions of Cape Colony were still

little known, and regions just outside its limits were about as unfamiliar as Central Africa was until the last twenty or fewer years.

Among those who essayed to explore those regions was Captain James Edward Alexander, a Scottish officer ‡ whose good fortune it was to live so recently that he witnessed the settling and exploiting of a large portion of the country which he traversed in 1836-37. Leaving Cape Town, he slowly proceeded with the usual waggon and pack-oxen outfit up the western part of the Cape Colony, on the seaward side of the mountain ranges which guard the interior of that region, through the country now known as the Western Province, Malmesbury, Clanwilliam, and Namaqualand to the Kowsie or Buffalo River, which then formed the boundary of the colony in that direction. Crossing this stream, Captain Alexander continued in the same direction, across the Orange River, until, bending seaward, Walvisch Bay formed a limit to the northern course hitherto taken. The waggons were then driven eastward into the country of the Hill Damaras, through a region sufficiently indicated by the name applied to that branch of the mixed Hottentot and Kaffir races.

From Ni-ais, a kraal of these people and the Namaquas, Captain Alexander again turned southwards, taking a course roughly describable as about parallel with his northward one, but in general over a degree farther east, and arrived in Cape Town a little more than a year after having set out on this interesting journey.

James Edward Alexander.

‡ General Sir J. E. Alexander, K C.S.I., died at Westerton, Bridge of Allan, in 1885, at the age of eighty-two, after a distinguished career as a soldier and traveller in many parts of the world, which he had described in numerous works. It was he who, in the evening of his life, obtained the Khedive's permission to transport "Cleopatra's Needle" to England, and to his influence with Sir Erasmus Wilson the world is mainly indebted for saving that obelisk from being broken up. He was knighted for the journey he made in South Africa; but though it was performed under the auspices of the then newly-founded Royal Geographical Society, Alexander's name does not, strangely enough, appear among medallists of much less merit. But in 1837 there were giants in the land.

* Burchell, "Travels in the Interior of South Africa," 2 vols. (1822).
† "Travels and Adventures in South Africa," 2 vols. (1837).

Throughout the whole of his exploration he was seldom out of sight of big game. Even within Cape Colony large animals were so plentiful that the worthy Captain takes credit to himself for not attempting a feat of which he had heard some of his friends boast—namely, the "killing of four elephants in one day, or the same number of hippopotami with the same gun"; while Boers were more frequently seen in pursuit of steinbuck than engaged in avocations that might have been more lucrative, if less exciting.

At the Heere-logement, or Gentlemen's Quarters, he came upon the trace of a predecessor; for among other names carved on a tree overhanging the cave which has received that title was that of "F. Vailant, 1783," which shows that this traveller chose, like Shakespeare, to enjoy a variation in the orthography of his patronymic. The very names on Captain Alexander's map indicate the abundance of wild beasts. Here, for instance, on his route northwards are the "Lion's Mountains," and "plains with elands." Near the mouth of the Orange River, so full of hippopotami that it was dangerous to take a boat or canoe into the places where they were most abundant, "plains with leopards," "plains with lions," "plains with ostriches," "hills with springbok"; "lions, rhinoceroses, zebras, koodoos, springboks, etc.," "hills with baboons," and "plains with gemsbok," all appear among his memoranda before Walvisch Bay is reached. "Plains of brindled gnu" occurs on the way to the Ni-ais, while on the route back to Cape Town there is frequent mention of plains haunted by rhinoceroses, koodoos, hartebeests, ostriches, lions, and other animals now seldom or never seen in the localities where within the memory of man still living they were so common.

But of all the African animals of that day —more than lions and panthers, more than lurking Bushmen with their poisoned arrows —Captain Alexander says that baboons were most to be dreaded. This large dog-faced brute,* five feet in height, very strong, and covered with black hair, seemed to dread no animal except leopards, which prey on it. It lives on scorpions, spiders, lizards, bulbs, and gum, with which its paws are usually smeared. In the days of which we speak they could be seen almost anywhere in groups of a dozen or more, headed by a large male, the females bringing up the rear with their young clinging to their backs. In the morning they would descend from the holes in the rocks, where they had slept, to the cover of the trees on the river banks, where grows the juicy gourd called "naras,"† on which it, like nearly every other animal, feeds. Then its disagreeable "Quah, quah," is heard on every side, and, at the date of Captain Alexander's visit, the borders of the Orange River were not altogether safe to traverse; for this hateful brute never hesitated to attack a man, if he found him alone, or even to carry off a woman or child. If wounded, its ferocity knows no caution (p. 183): woe betide the unfortunate who encounters an enraged baboon.

Lions, the Namaquas declared, had been at one time more numerous; troops of half a dozen were not then so frequently seen as some years earlier. There were, however, no longer any elephants by the River Olifant, which had derived its name from their former abundance on its banks, and in the Namaqua country they had retreated several days' journey east of the Fish River. But lions, if less frequent than of old, were found everywhere, and of numerous shades from almost white to black, which led hunters to insist on there being several species in South Africa, whereas it is fully ascertained there is only one. The two species of rhinoceros were plentiful on the upper part of the Fish River: and zebras, spotted hyænas, giraffes, koodoos, gemsbucks, elands, hartebeests, klipspringers, springbucks, and other antelopes swarmed,

---

* The species referred to here and elsewhere in these chapters is *Cynocephalus porcarius*, Ishakma or Chacma.

† *Acanthosicyos horrida*, belonging to the Cucurbitaceæ.

brown hyænas, wild boars, jackals, being equally abundant. Game birds, such as bustards, of which there are four species, "pheasants"—as the francolins are called—and guinea-fowl could be had almost without the sportsman moving from his waggon. Unfortunately, however, venomous snakes were also so frequent that the traveller carried a little air-pump humbly feasting on the same carcase as the lion, these persecuted aborigines of South Africa have the art of frightening away a lion after it has eaten a full meal, leaving to them the remainder of the animal. " I live by the lions " was the boast of one of them : " I let the lions follow the game, kill it, and eat a bellyful. I then go near, throw about my arms

THE KAFFIR AND THE LION (*p.* 183).

to suck their bites, should any of the party get wounded.

In those days the assegai, or spear, was the native's main reliance; but so skilful were some of them that a man named Henrick and his son were able, when gunpowder ran short, to run down a zebra on foot, and spear the fleet animal as they came alongside of it. Yet it takes a good horse to overtake either a zebra or a giraffe. The Bushmen (p. 189) choose a less dignified part; for, like the little jackal, which may often be found

A swift runner and a lion's parasite.

and my skins; the lions go away grumbling, and I get what they leave. I never kill lions." Yet on one fateful day a lioness killed him. She was making a meal of a wild horse—many of which were at that time at large on the veldt—and he did not observe that she had whelps with her. Beginning to halloo in his usual way, she looked up, growled savagely, and, before he had time to retreat, she sprang at him and destroyed him on the spot.

At places, reputed to be "sharp for lions," Alexander used to lie down with a dustman's bell—we are speaking of the first year of Queen Victoria's reign—at his head, not for the purpose of summoning anyone to dinner, but with the intention of frightening the lions from approaching what might be theirs. And, indeed, it was only when game had temporarily left the country that this dreaded marauder became troublesome; for the warm hides, and roasting the livers for breakfast, a herd of the magnificent koodoo antelopes made its appearance. Then, before any of them approached within firing distance, a dancing flock of springbucks engaged attention, and anon two black rhinoceroses, covered with dried mud from the pools of the

WANDERING HUNTERS (MASARWA BUSHMEN), NORTH KALAHARI DESERT.
(From a Photograph by Mr. H. A. Bryden.)

at ordinary times man and oxen need not be attacked. Antelopes and zebras and giraffes were to be had for the taking; at the foot of the mountains especially these animals were rife. One day—and it was not a white-letter one— a cloud of dust ahead heralded the passage of a large troop of wild horses, some of which fell to the hunters' bullets. While the natives, for lack of water, were squeezing into their mouths the moisture of the half-digested grass in the horses' stomachs, cutting shoes from

A plethora of game.

Chuntop, in which they had been wallowing, tempted a shot; albeit, this thick-skinned brute will run away with a bushel of bullets in it, if they are fired at any other portion of his body except the backbone or behind the jaw. Finally, just to vary the programme, a female rhinoceros that had been wounded came snorting along with a furious rush, and, driving her horns under a bush, tore it up, covering herself with dust and gravel, all the time closely followed—as the black, unlike the white species, always is—by her offspring, occasionally ploughing the ground before her, and evidently bent on mischief. What might have happened can only be guessed at; for the hunters, wheeling to the right, doubled on the rhinoceroses, which, with their deep-seated eyes and limited field of view, cannot see except right before them. This afforded the opportunity for giving the dam a bullet as she passed and the young the chance, which they embraced, of disappearing among the bushes.

The black rhinoceros, though not to be attacked with impunity, is, however, not quite so ferocious as has been sometimes described, its "charges" being just as often a desire to escape some real or fancied danger as an exhibition of actual vengeance towards an enemy. Still, amiability is so far from being one of its virtues that, excepting the rhinoceros-bird (*Buphaga africana*), it has no friend in its native wilds; but this bird, seated on the brute's back for the purpose of picking the parasitic insects infesting its hide, acts as a sentinel, and, when any danger threatens, by flapping its wings and uttering piercing cries, warns its friend of the peril menacing both of them. When the rhinoceros and the elephant have a difference, the former avoiding the trunk of the latter, makes a dash at the latter's belly and rips it open (p. 183). As for the lion, it instinctively avoids the horned beast, and the Bushmen affirm that, although found in the same haunts, they give way to one another. Yet the hyæna, if hungry, will sometimes follow the rhinoceros and, by dint of its superior agility, bite it in the rear, until it falls and dies of hunger or from the attacks of an enemy so cowardly that a cow can successfully defend her calf against it.

In the Bull's Mouth Pass rhinoceroses, buffaloes, baboons, and other animals were plentiful in 1837. Indeed, they were so almost everywhere throughout the journey, although much of it lay over so dry a portion of country that the traveller often suffered severely from thirst, even within a short distance of Walvisch Bay, now the only portion of that region that has not fallen into German hands. But at the time of which we write the shore was entirely uninhabited by white men; yet the New England whalers even then frequented the bay for killing the animals from which it derives its name, the English whalers being heard of only at Angra Pequena; and elephants were reported at the mouth of the Swakop or Bowel River, a little farther north.

From Walvisch Bay, along the arid route eastward, game did not seem to be so abundant; though in the valley of the Humaris rhinoceroses and zebras often trotted in front of them, and too often the miserable inhabitants were destroyed by lions, elephants, and other wild beasts. Among the Damaras it was quite common to see their herds and flocks grazing in company with zebras and steinbucks, both of which could be shot by stalking them from behind an ox. When a lion killed any domestic animal, all the people of the village accompanied the owner of the property, in order to look on while he slew the marauder, so familiar had the Damaras become with lions and the like. They owned thousands of sheep and cattle, and every night, in order to protect them from lions, they were driven up close to the village, though not a season passed without men and oxen being killed by the most powerful, though not the most dreaded, animal of that part of Africa.

The natives were full of tales of encounters, and many of them bore on their persons ample evidence that these adventures were not quite imaginary. It may, however, be judicious to exercise some scepticism towards another story told by the Namaquas of a man who, not long ago, had brought up a young baboon and made it his shepherd. "It remained by the flock all day in the field, and at night drove it home to the kraal, riding on the back of one of the goats, which brought up the rear. The baboon had the milk of one goat allowed to it, and it sucked that one only, and guarded the milk of the others for the children. It also got a little meat from its master." The monkey held this office for twelve months, and then, unfortunately, was killed in a tree by a leopard, the hairy

Men and monkeys.

shepherd having apparently not acquired among his other accomplishments the art of shooting

Another anecdote quite as interesting, if true—and those who have the requisite faith may credit it—is of a little boy who was carried off by the baboons and kept by them for more than a year. When recovered the child was quite wild, and tried to run away to the baboons again. It was not for some time that he regained his mother tongue, and then only to praise the monkeys for their kindness to him. They ate scorpions and spiders themselves, but, seeing he left these dainties alone, they brought roots, gum, and wild raisins for him, and always allowed the boy, in acknowledgment of his superiority, to drink at the water pools first. If some of the stories of baboon-stolen children are true—and some of them unquestionably are—the captives' treatment is by no means always so humane.

On both sides of the Ukanip river huge fires had to be kept burning in order to scare off the large number of lions which roamed that country. Men were often snatched from their sleeping-places. Hence, in addition to fires and dogs, a watch had to be set at night; yet, in spite of all this care the ravenous brutes approached and killed one of the oxen.

Between the Hoons and the Kubieb river, where "much iron ore" was noticed, the country was uninhabited and entirely given over to lions, after which another track seemed to be equally the monopoly of leopards. The latter were even more destructive to sheep, sucking a little blood from twenty in a night, and if brought to bay sprang from one hunter to the other, and clawed their faces. This was avoided by the experienced covering themselves with their karosses and sitting down, the leopard in that case probably springing over them to pursue the fugitives.

Captain Alexander's journey was thus important, not only for the geographical points which he noted for the first time, but for the many natural history observations which were

A lion land and a leopard land

made and new species of animals and plants discovered.*

About the same time that Captain Alexander was engaged on his expedition along the western side of South Africa, *William Cornwallis Harris,* another British officer — Captain (afterwards Sir) William Cornwallis Harris, of the Bombay Engineers†—was hunting through Cape Colony and Bechuanaland to the Limpopo or Crocodile River in Zululand, returning by an unexplored route across the head of the Vaal River, where Moselikatse was at war with the "trek-Boers" who founded the colony of Natal. On this journey he heard, as Dr. Smith and others had, of the "great lake" in the north, which some ten years later Livingstone was to reach and render familiar to the world as Lake Ngami; but Harris's journey was not an exploratory one, in so far that most of the country over which he travelled was already more or less imperfectly known. He was a sportsman, and one of the most intelligent and successful of his order, who in following up the still abundant but retreating wild animals, penetrated and made known regions which before many years had elapsed were to be the homes of thousands and the scenes of flourishing mining and other industries.

But in 1836 Harris had little in view except the slaying of wild beasts; and these he found on the eastern side of the continent even more abundantly than his friend Alexander had discovered in the opposite direction. Nowadays it is a long voyage from Bombay to Cape Town which takes more than six weeks with a fair wind. Harris, however, was eleven weeks on board a "fast-sailing"

---

* "An Expedition of Discovery into the Interior of Africa, through the hitherto undescribed Countries of the Great Namaquas, Boschmans, and Hill Damaras," etc., 2 vols. (1838).

† In 1841—soon after his return from the expedition he made into South Africa—Major Harris, on the Royal Geographical Society declining to send him in search of Lake Ngami, was despatched to Shoa at the instance of the Governor-General of India. Having concluded a treaty of friendship with Sahela Selassye, the king of that country, he was knighted.—"The Highlands of Ethiopia," 3 vols. (1841).

East Indiaman before he reached Simon's Bay. Here the pictures which Dr. Smith painted for him of the vast herds of game in the interior fired the latest sportsman to be off. Cape Colony, at least in the extreme southern part, was, however, by this time getting thinned of the larger wild animals, and so Port Elizabeth, in Algoa Bay, was long to wait for game. Grahamstown had scarcely been passed before large herds of springbucks fired the ambition of the inexperienced dogs. From Graaff Reinet, then a picturesque little Dutch village, the Sneuwberg, a lofty range of mountains immediately to the north, was crossed by Sir Lowry Coles's, Pass during weather so cold that on the

PARTY OF GIRAFFE HUNTERS.
(*From a Photograph by Mr. H. A. Bryden.*)

selected by Harris and his friend William Richardson, of the Bombay Civil Service, as their starting-point for the interior.

It is scarcely necessary to describe their outfit and mode of travelling. The pack-ox and the lumbering Cape waggon, dragged by many teams of bullocks (Vol. II., pp. 169, 180), and driven by a Hottentot armed with a huge whip, who, in his turn, is preceded by the "voerlooper," or "boy" in advance, are now tolerably familiar to every reader of the literature of South African travel. Nor had they morning of the 5th September the mercury stood at 18° F., and the manes of riding-horses were decorated with icicles. But in Vogel Valley large troops of the gnu were seen for the first time, and soon the face of the country "was literally white with springbucks, myriads of which covered the plains" near Boksfontein. They were then on their way from one part of the country to another better grassed. These "trek-bokken," as the occasional immigration of countless swarms of this species of antelope

A migration of springbucks.

SHOOLI MUSICIANS.
(From a Photograph by E. Buchta.)

are called by the Dutch colonists, were, however, by no means welcome. To offer any estimate of the numbers would be impossible. Pouring down like locusts from the endless plains of the interior, whence they have been driven by protracted drought, lions have been seen stalking in the midst of this compressed phalanx, and flocks of sheep have not unfrequently been carried away by the torrent of life that has descended on the pastures through which it passes. "Cultivated fields,

was considered ample pay for a sturdy beast trained to the waggon.

At Kuruman, Mr. Moffat was visited and valuable information obtained regarding the travellers' proposed visit to Moselikatse, chief of the Matabele, Amandebele, or Abaka Zulus, as they were then called, whom he formed into a nation. This celebrated savage—father of the noted "King" Lo-Bengula (Vol. II., p. 178)—played havoc with the emigrant

Moselikatse, Chief of the Matabele.

AT THE FORD OF MALIKOE, MARICO RIVER.
(*From a Photograph taken for the Paris Society for Evangelical Missions.*)

which in the evening appeared proud of their promising verdure, are, in the course of a single night, reaped level with the ground, and the despoiled grazier is compelled to seek pasture for his flocks elsewhere until the bountiful thunder-clouds restore vegetation to the burnt-up country. Then the unwelcome visitors instinctively retreat to their secluded abodes, to renew their attacks when necessity shall again compel them." Trading seemed in those days to have been not unprofitable. Three fat oxen were bought at Campbellsdorf for a glaring red table-cloth, and a small canister of gunpowder

Boers who founded Natal and with the Bechuanas. He was the son of a chief who, being attacked and defeated by another tribe, took refuge with Chaka, the Zulu tyrant, predecessor of the still more terrible Dingaan, uncle of Cetowayo. Moselikatse (or Umziligazi), however, succeeded in gaining the favour of Chaka, who had just made a powerful nation of the Zulu tribe, and in process of time was entrusted with the command of an important post and a large number of cattle. With these he and his people fled to the north-westward. Every tribe on his way was "eaten up," and he soon became so formidable that his very name inspired terror throughout a vast extent of country. Having completely subjugated or destroyed every enemy from whose opposition he had anything to fear, he ultimately selected the country near the sources of the Molopo and Marico (p. 193) rivers—not far from the present Marico district of the Transvaal—for his permanent residence, and there at his then capital of Mosega, or at Kapain, a little farther north, he was residing in 1836, the terror of the surrounding nations.

On the way from Kuruman to Little Chúe, troops of ostriches were seen feeding on the boundless ocean-like expanse of country, the monotony of which was broken solely by clumps of bushes and ant-hills; and at Little Chúe, the extensive salt lake which bears that name was found surrounded by ostriches, springbucks, and other animals, attracted thither by the luxuriant "sour" grass, which the cattle refused to eat, and a small pond of water so intolerably alkaline that it was found impossible to purify it.

Acacia trees, gaudy with yellow blossoms, and perceptible at a distance by their overpowering aromatic perfume, formed the favourite food of hosts of giraffes, while small troops of quaggas and brindled gnus enlivened a landscape more pleasing than any which had immediately preceded it. In 1836 the quagga (which Harris is careful to distinguish from Burchell's zebra) was everywhere common, and seldom seen in company with the true zebra, which haunts mountain regions, while Burchell's species was generally followed by troops of the brindled gnu. The Chúe Desert, twenty miles across, was succeeded by a fine game country. Every hour brought the traveller into regions where hartebeest, quagga, and brindled gnu became more abundant. Near the Maritsani River (p. 197), troops of gnus, to be succeeded by first one herd and then another of zebras, sassabys, and hartebeests, poured into the valley from every quarter, until the landscape literally presented the appearance of a moving mass of game. "Their incredible numbers," this early hunter tells us, "so impeded their progress, that I had no difficulty in closing with them, dismounting as opportunity offered, firing both barrels of my rifle into the retreating phalanx, and leaving the ground strewed with the slain. Still unsatisfied, I could not resist the temptation of mixing with the fugitives, loading and firing, until my jaded horse suddenly exhibited symptoms of distress, and shortly afterwards was unable to move."

In many of the trees, thatched houses, resembling hay-ricks, were built. These the traveller imagined were shelters from the lions, many of which haunted the neighbourhood; but they were simply the habitations of large communities of the social grosbeaks (*Philæterus socius*), whose architecture forms one of the most interesting features in the ornithology of South Africa. On the Molopo River game was equally plentiful. To "pass under the nose of three rhinoceros" was not unusual, and lions were met with in troops of five or six, while other game was plentiful enough, in spite of the clouds of locusts, which ate up every green thing, and, in their turn, formed the welcome food of the wandering Bushmen. Moselikatse received the travellers with civility, not unmixed with a greed which, in the circumstances, had to be gratified. For his power was only limited by the fear of what might befall him if he behaved badly to white men. Yet how little that troubled him may be inferred from the fact that he had attacked several parties of "emigrant farmers" and traders, and had the murder of several of them, not unjustly, laid to his charge. On their way from Kapain to the Marico River the mazes of the shady parasol-topped acacias were filled with the same abundance of large game, guinea-fowls, and bustards, and a plain on the opposite side of the river was dotted over with trees, beneath which gnus, sassabys, and hartebeests were reposing. Giraffes were frequently seen crossing the level in little troops, and quaggas passed in such cavalcades that one of them would sometimes fall at each discharge of the rifle, affording, with the still more welcome white rhinoceros—which is not white—an ample supply of flesh to the lazy natives, who hung about in the hope of feeding without the trouble of hunting for their food. Groups of large deep pits for catching rhinoceroses were noticed. Each of them was dug at the end of a narrow path, cut through the bushes, and fenced with thorns—a sharp turning leading directly upon the trap, so that an unwieldy animal, being driven furiously down the avenue, could have little chance of avoiding the snare. The pits seemed to have been constructed as much for the sake of destroying the wild beasts as of catching them for food; for at the bottom of many of them the whitened skeletons of the animals lay, evidently on the spots where they had fallen alive and been left to starve to death and their carcases to rot.

On the banks of the Similakati, the fresh tracks of lions fired the eagerness of the hunters, not yet satisfied with slaughter, though the capture of two dogs, which had rushed to the river-side to quench their thirst, by a couple of enormous crocodiles warned them that an enemy even more cruel than the "king of beasts" had to be encountered by the unwary. Not content with devouring the dogs, these loathsome reptiles crawled out of their lairs at night, and ate up a portion of the leather of the waggon furniture, besides the shoes of the men, and would doubtless have disposed of the men also had they been accessible.

On the banks of the Bagobone River, in the Cashan—or Magalies—Mountains, the first traces of the elephant were seen in the shape of acacias torn up by the root, and hundreds of deep holes made by the heavy hoofs of these quadrupeds

A natural preserve.

"Dar stand de olifant."

during the time the ground was softened by the rains; and the perfect skeleton of an animal which had apparently died on the spot, and close by three lionesses lying asleep. A little farther on, the banks of the Limpopo were swarming with buffaloes, pallahs, Guinea-fowls, and ostriches; and the lions were so plentiful that a stockade had to be erected to protect the camp. The remains of an elephant calf devoured by them proved the boldness of the brutes, as well as the presence in the neighbourhood of tuskers, which the natives tried to drive out of their shelter by firing the long grass on the borders of the stream. Hyænas, wild hogs, jackals, waterbucks, rhinoceroses, and roan antelopes were equally plentiful. And such a superabundance of meat hung from every tree that it was hard to keep it from the flocks of obscene vultures that hovered overhead, or the more cunning hyænas, which, undeterred by the fate of those of their comrades that were slain, crept up at night to steal it or to hamstring the cattle. From darkness to daylight their dismal howls mingled with the bolder roars of lions—a melody with which the only surviving dog never failed to chime in.

The daring of the beasts in this part of the country showed that they had been very little disturbed. A white rhinoceros, not the most ferocious of its kindred, was even so irritated at being aroused out of its slumber that it made for the leading waggon, alarming the cattle by its loud snorting and hostile demonstrations, until a volley of bullets persuaded it to retire to a suitable bush, to be there despatched. From elevated places in the Cashan Mountains great droves of buffaloes could be seen in the valleys below, and in the narrow paths that were traversed an elephant, trumpeting in amazement at being interrupted, was a not infrequent fellow-traveller. At length, for the first time during these travels, the sportsmen saw a large herd lazily browsing on some grassy hillocks. A few minutes later the whole face of the landscape was "literally covered" with elephants. "Dar stand de olifant," the Dutch-speaking

Hottentot whispered. And at the smallest computation they must have "stood" to the number of three hundred. Every height and green knoll was dotted over with groups of old female and a calf were butchered; and during the storm with which the night closed in, troops of them passed close to the waggons after dark, their wild voices echoing

SHOOTING DUIKER.

among the mountains and sounding like trumpets above the tempest. Then, as Captain Harris lay awake, " heedless of the withering blast that howled without," he felt that his " most sanguine expectations had been realised," and that "he had already been amply repaid for the difficulties, privations, and dangers " encountered in coming " towards this fairy land of sport," where two cow elephants and a calf had been killed rather more easily than the same number of bullocks in a butcher's yard. However, Captain Harris acted only as many others did after him. He might, indeed, have killed many more, and takes credit to himself that one of his quarry was too old to be a mother, so that only one and not several elephants were lost to Africa by her death.

them, while at the bottom of the glen all that met the eye was a dense and sable living mass, moving among the trees, or majestically emerging into the open glades, bearing in their trunks the branches with which they protected themselves from the flies. All of them were females, many with calves following them, and, in spite of a volley fired into them from a safe place—for the hunter of those days was not without the instincts of a mere slaughterer—grazed for a time without apparently being aware of anything unusual going on. It was only when the first herd seen came thundering up the valley that they followed suit, leaving one of their company as a victim to the white man's craze for " killing something " which could be of no use even for food in a camp already over-supplied, and of little value to a wealthy sportsman whose trade was not the collection of tusks. Before many hours, three other large herds were passed, in which another

On returning to cut out the tusks of the fallen brutes, not one of the great herd seen the day before was visible. Only a solitary calf stood by the carcase of its mother, saluting her murderers with mourning, piping notes. Unconscious of how little any such attentions were due to them, the calf entwined its little trunk about the hunters' legs, demonstrating its delight by a thousand ungainly antics, as it enticed them to reach the body of its mother quickly. Already the corpse was swollen to an enormous size, and surrounded by an inquest of vultures, whose beaks had been unable to penetrate the tough hide. Little recked the young elephant of this unsightly scene. It ran round its mother's corse with such touching demonstrations of grief, wailing all the time and vainly attempting to raise her with its tiny trunk, that even the rude Hottentots were affected by the conduct of this affectionate compunction, and divested him of the idea that he was shooting, as he had so often shot before, a merciless tiger in Guzerat. Finding that its mother heeded not its caresses, the miniature elephant followed her tusks to the waggons. It died, however, in the course of a few days; as did two others, much older, that were afterwards captured, demonstrating the cruelty and wastefulness of life

ON THE MARITSANI RIVER.
(From a Photograph by Mr. H. A. Dryden.)

little brute. Then for the first time Captain Harris began to regret that, in firing at the herd yesterday, he had not felt greater that follows the slaughter of nursing-elephants.

The Cashan Mountains seem in those days

to have been what our hunter described them—a "fairy land of sport." Elephants were often observed climbing, with the agility of goats, to the very summit of the chain, until at length they stood out in bold relief against the blue sky. At the sound of a shot a tribe of pig-faced baboons would emerge from their sylvan haunts to display anything but sympathy with the intruder; and the lions took frequent advantage of stormy nights to visit the cattle-fold. At that time, too, the Limpopo was full of hippopotami, dividing the lordship of the river with the crocodile, which gave an alternate name to that stream, and all along that part of its valley visited by our travellers the country presented the appearance of a huge unfenced menagerie—the host of rhinoceroses that daily exhibited themselves almost exceeding belief.

"A fairy land of sport."

Not half a mile from where the waggons stood the white rhinoceros was so numerous that twenty-two could be counted in view, four of which had to be killed in self-defence. On another occasion Harris was besieged in a bush by three at once, and had some difficulty in beating off his assailants. Buffaloes in troops might also be seen from the camp, glaring with "malevolent grey eyes" under shaggy brows at the intruders on their domains, and at times charging with the fury which makes these beasts, if wounded, among the most dangerous of all the African animals. The roan antelope, or gemsbuck, will also at times charge viciously when unable to continue its flight, and being the size of a large horse, with robust, recurved, scimitar-shaped horns, its fury is not to be despised. This antelope is, however, so destitute of speed that it may be ridden to a standstill without difficulty: it is then that the exhausted beast turns at bay.

In those days every glade in the Cashan Mountains, not very far from where the capital of the Transvaal now stands, abounded with brindled gnu, hartebeest, sassaby, quagga, ostriches, and wild hogs. And among the sedge-bordered rivulets, the reedbuck, now extremely

Rustenburg in 1837.

rare in the Transvaal, was common, while in the mountain range and its grassy environs, klipspringers, rhébuck, ourebi, steinbuck, and duiker (p. 196) swarmed. But with the exception of the garrulous guinea-fowl, whose nightly cackle might be heard as they ascended the trees to roost, feathered game was comparatively scarce; a few bustards of different species, and sand-grouse—the "partridge" of the colonists—were about the only birds observable, from a sportsman's point of view. On the banks of the Limpopo, a buffalo was killed as it was swimming across, and a black rhinoceros, as it got pent up in a *cul-de-sac* formed by an old stone enclosure; while, to vary this amusement of slaughter, a troop of brindled gnus, being pursued by a rhinoceros, dashed into a defile in the hills, at the outlet to which, the "hunter" relates with some gratification, he stationed himself, and "disposed of two with each barrel."

As the party proceeded towards the junction of the Marico with the Limpopo game became scarcer, and the few miserable remnants of the Bakwarris, who had fled here from the fury of Moselikatse, were disinclined to hold any communication with the travellers. Even the offer of a pinch of "Irish blackguard" snuff, of which a plentiful supply was carried, failed to dissipate the suspicion of strangers engendered by much misfortune in these timid people, emaciated and even starving in a land so swarming with game as the country immediately north of them, and even in the close vicinity.

In going south-east from the Cashan Mountains, through a region characterised as "beautiful beyond description" in its flower-spangled meadows between rich stretches of grove and forest, herds of elephants were seen from the waggons, browsing in indolent security or bathing in the pellucid streams. Upon being attacked, they would rush, a hundred strong, down the ravines with upraised ears and swaying trunks, "trumpeting" wildly and levelling everything before them. Nor did scarcely a day pass without the party seeing two or three lions, which invariably retreated when disturbed. For, however troublesome they were found at night, none of the feline tribe, with very rare exceptions, showed at any other time the least disposition to molest their human visitors, unless, indeed, the latter commenced hostilities. It was in the Cashan Mountains that Harris added to his four hundred trophies the new species of antelope which has ever since borne his name. This is the sable antelope (*Hippotragus niger*), or Harrisbuck, no longer very plentiful, except perhaps in northern Matabeleland and in the low districts of the East Coast. In the region where it was discovered it is questionable if a single specimen now exists.

A new antelope: the Vaal River.

Passing the Vaal River (Vol. II., p. 168), rhinoceroses ceased to be seen. But elands and other animals akin to them were still abundant, and at places the river "literally teemed," to use Captain Harris's favourite expression, with hippopotami. Lions were also still so abundant that on the banks of the river thorn fences had to be erected every night to prevent them from attacking the cattle. So what with the roaring of the royal beast round the waggons, and the unceasing snorting of the "sea-cows" in the river below, the vicinity of the Vaal was, in spite of the solitude which then reigned over all the now busy region of graziers and gold and diamond diggers, by no means the place for a nervous man to enjoy a night's rest.

At the Saltpans, south of the tributary known to the natives as "Nama Hari, or Donkin River,"* vast herds of blesbucks licked up the crystallised inflorescences, and numbers of the gemsbuck were seen. This antelope Harris describes as a powerful and dangerous antagonist, charging viciously, and defending itself when hard-pressed with wonderful intrepidity and address. Its skeleton, he assures us, has "not infrequently" been found locked in that of a lion, the latter having been transfixed by its formidable horns in a conflict which has proved fatal to both

* Probably the Valsch of the later Dutch nomenclature.

combatants. Modern travellers, it may be added, have not been so fortunate as to see any of these struggles between the unicorn and the lion. No doubt they all fight viciously if brought to bay, though of their ferocity they wot not.

On the way southwards the emigrant farmers, who were on their way to found the first of their settlements outside of Cape Colony, encamped on the banks of the Calf River. It is needless saying that Englishmen were by this time no longer the popular persons with the Dutch they were in Le Vaillant's day. On the contrary, the Boers who had left the colony in dissatisfaction with the law freeing slaves—Hottentot, Kaffir, Malay, Negro, and sometimes Bengalee even—held Englishmen, their rifles, and their shooting in about equal contempt. Opportunities for disproving the Dutchmen's low opinion of the latter accomplishment were, however, still plentiful, though the gnu and the springbuck from constant persecution had become so wild that it was necessary to display a red handkerchief on the muzzle of the rifle to inveigle the former within range. In other parts of the country stalking (p. 200) was generally superfluous; but as the abodes of civilisation were neared the herds of antelopes became sparser, and invariably less easy to approach.

Nearing civilisation.

Captain Harris's journey may, however, be accepted as a typical one not only of the period to which it relates, but as excellently illustrative of the abundance of game in the part of the country over which it extended, namely, parts of what are now Cape Colony, Orange Free State, Bechuanaland, Transvaal, and Matabeleland. Besides skins and skulls of all the animals killed, he brought back elaborate drawings of the species interesting to sportsmen, most of which were afterwards published and, with his interesting narrative, form a classic record in the history of South African pioneering.†

† "The Wild Sports of Southern Africa, etc." (Bombay, 1838; London, 1839; Edition with many Plates, 1852). "African Views" (1838).

STALKING BLESBUCK BEHIND OXEN.

CHAPTER IX.

MAN AND BEAST: THE BEGINNING OF THE END.

Influence of Harris's Tale on the Decimation of South African Game—Early Traders—Their Ways of Life—Gordon Cumming—His History—Boers and Englishmen—A Hunter's Kit—Cumming's Journeys—Herds of Game in Bechuanaland—Meets with Moffat and Hume and Hears of "a Missionary named Livingstone"—Cumming's Various Journeys in Bechuanaland and into the Limpopo Valley—His Feats with the Hippopotamus—A Vision of Blesbucks—Return—Reception—Foolish Incredulity—Livingstone's Testimony—Oswell and Murray—Oswell's Exploits—The So-called Rhinoceros oswelli—The Kobus vardoni Commemorative of Major Vardon and the Antelopus roualeyni of Cumming—Lake Ngami and the Hunters and Explorers who Made for it—Galton and Andersson's Attempt to Reach it from Walvisch Bay—Andersson's Success—Green—Wahlberg—Hemming's Hunting Trip from Walvisch Bay to the Congo—The Chapmans and Baines—Baldwin and the Zambesi—Mysterious Initials—Decrease of Game in Ngamiland with Increase of Visits to Lake Ngami—Polson—Waddington and Aldersley—Selous—His various Journeys and Discoveries—A Hydrographic Problem, etc.

THE publication of Harris's account of the swarms of animals found on the outskirts of Cape Colony marks a distinct date in the history of the battle between man and beast in South Africa. It fired, in the first place, a host of professional hunters and sportsmen to take tithes of the vast herds of elephants that swarmed in the country which he had visited. Then, after the fear of Moselikatse and his brother chieftains had abated, the traders' wagons trundled not only to the remotest farms of the "trek-Boers," who had now begun in earnest those pioneer journeys into the wilds which form so remarkable a feature in the history of South African colonisation, and into the native territories beyond. Most of the professional hunters were Dutch; but some were Englishmen, more Scotsmen, while the traders of the region with which we are concerned were for the most part of British nationality. As a merchant, the Boer has never excelled; and in a bargain with a Scot the Dutchman usually fares as fares the earthen pot when it comes into collision with the brazen one. They carried—for though the trader is still a familiar personage in South Africa, railways The early and towns have greatly altered his traders. way of doing business—a little of everything; and the pedlar of the wilderness who, after he had outspanned his oxen on a Boer farm, was deficient in the capacity to persuade Mynheer or his vrouw to barter a few fat oxen for some of the commodities which he proceeded to "offload," could not, even with the large profits made in the business, long continue his peculiar calling. The life was a hard one, and not without perils; and, as his goods were generally paid for in cattle, his journey only finished when he had nothing more to sell. Then he sold the waggon or waggons—for the more affluent had often more than one—to his last customer, and returned in light marching order to the colony. Picking up his cattle on the different farms where he had left them, he had, by the time he reached Beaufort or Grahamstown, quite a herd to dispose of for the butchers' bills which usually took the place of cash, but which, as the holder discovered when they were due, were not quite so negotiable as current coin. Many of these men possessed an almost unique knowledge of the country, and when they extended their operations into the Kaffir countries, would have obtained a name among travellers had they taken the world into their confidence. But that is what they seldom did. They were not book-writing folk, and, indeed, were in no way anxious to reveal to their possible rivals the information touching hunting haunts, or those "new markets" of which they, like all people with something to sell, were in search.

We can, therefore, do little more than indicate, in general terms, the share these unlettered hunters or traders took in opening up Africa. They were not always pioneers; but they were often the first to follow the pioneer, and by inculcating the savage with a love of traffic, and teaching him how much he required for complete happiness, impelled him to labour instead of to fight. But as ivory was about the one article which the trader demanded, and the skins of wild beasts the only other goods which the barbarians had to barter, the fauna of South Africa suffered sorely in the operation. However, it was not until tropical Africa and the Arab traders' sphere of evil influence were reached that slaves and ivory became synonymous. In the Kaffir countries—and, it is needless to say, in the British colonies—the traffic in men and women was not known in the days of which we speak; and if the Boer liked to have a servant without paying wages, he did not acquire his

GORGE IN THE BAMANGWATO MOUNTAINS.
(*From a Photograph taken for the Paris Society for Evangelical Missions.*)

serf latterly by the very crude process of stealing him, or buying him from somebody who had stolen the merchandise.

However, of all the pioneers in the wake

of whom the hunters and traders followed, the most notable were the missionaries. Campbell, Moffat, and Livingstone were not hunters either by profession or by inclination, though they had often to be so by necessity. But they were pioneers, and wherever they or their colleagues established posts, the hunters and the traders followed them and made these stations the centre of their operations. For if some of the less generous of these slayers of wild beasts might have had the evil taste to sneer at "the missionaries," they always found it extremely convenient to take advantage of the respect which the natives had acquired for white men through the teachings of those despised apostles of the wilderness.

Among the earliest English sportsmen who made a hunting expedition after the model of Major Harris's was the celebrated Roualeyn George Gordon Cumming (p. 208).* He did not open up any new country. Nor, immense as his success was among the great game of South Africa, were his experiences in any special degree different from those of the hunters whom we have taken as a type of their class. But the vivid manner in which he described his adventures, and the courage with which he faced danger, have given this intrepid Scot an enduring reputation among those who warred with the beasts of South Africa before the struggle had begun to show signs of being with the man. Gordon Cumming, the second son of a Scottish baronet, was born on the 15th March, 1820, and after leaving Eton entered the Madras Cavalry. A few years later he joined the Cape Mounted Rifles, but soon resigned his commission to take part in the five years' hunting expedition which constitutes his chief claim on the memory of the world. His travels were made in the usual fashion, with ox-waggons, and his pursuit of game was usually on horseback, except when it was killed as it came to drink at the "fountains" or pools after dark. Endowed with enormous physical strength, indomitable animal spirits, and health that never failed him, the stalwart Highlander, tramping in a kilt and his shirt-sleeves at the head of his caravan, is a picture which old residents in the Cape Colony and Bechuanaland can still recall. Khama, Chief of Bamangwato (Vol. II., p. 177), was one of the hunter's "boys," and never wearies of describing the glorious days of long ago —he means 1843 and the years following— when the country swarmed with lions, buffaloes, rhinoceroses, and other game. Elephants roamed in profusion, being only disturbed by Cumming and a few other hunters on the Shoshong hills and in the valleys. Here the tusks were left to rot, and firearms were almost unknown among the tribesmen.†

Roualeyn George Gordon Cumming.

In those times the British were regarded by the Dutch settlers with even greater dislike than they are at present. Indeed, so jealously did the Boers look upon any attempts to penetrate what they called "onze veldt" ("our country")—the name they applied to all the vast territories beyond the Vaal River—that they fined a Mr. Macabe 500 rix dollars for presuming to recommend, in a letter written to one of the Cape papers, a route to Lake Ngami, then, like the lake itself, not known to the white man. The Transvaal authorities not only did this, but they went to the length of imprisoning the hapless correspondent until the fine were paid. It was, therefore, not a very favourable period for Cumming to penetrate northwards through the districts settled by these stubborn folk, so determined to exclude all not of their own blood from the outskirts of South Africa. But suspicion soon vanished after a few minutes' conversation with the genial Scot. For in some way they imagined the kilted jäger to belong, like themselves, to a nation who had been hardly used by the English; and when the impression was confirmed by a glass of something at the waggon-tail, the Boer left convinced that the people who drank such liquor and wore such

---

* He was the brother of Miss Gordon Cumming—so well known to the readers of travel in many parts of the world—to whom we are indebted for some notes on the famous hunter and the unpublished portrait on p. 208.

† Bryden: "Gun and Camera in South Africa," p. 257.

clothes ought to be permitted to go where they pleased.

As a specimen of the varied outfit a traveller required half a century ago—and, in the more out-of-the-way regions, still requires—we may note some of the contents of Cumming's waggons. Besides weapons numerous and good, he carried lead ladles of various sizes, a whole host of bullet-moulds—the era of cartridges and breech-loaders was as yet scarcely in sight—loading-rods, shot-belts, and powder-flasks. Three hundredweight of lead, fifty pounds of pewter for hardening the balls to be used in destroying the large game, ten thousand prepared leaden bullets, bags of shot of all sizes, one hundred pounds of fine sporting powder, three hundred pounds of coarse gunpowder, about fifty thousand best percussion-caps, and two thousand gun-flints, with greased patches and cloth for the same, completed his lethal outfit. Spare yokes, yoke-skeys, whip-sticks, rheims and straps, and two sets of spare linch-pins, were necessary to the traveller who should put a thousand miles between him and a saddler's shop. For provisions, the country was depended on to a large extent. Accordingly, the reserve consisted mainly of three hundred pounds of coffee, four quarter-chests of tea, three hundred pounds of sugar, three hundred pounds of rice, one hundred and eighty pounds of meal (maize), one hundred pounds of flour, one hundred pounds of salt, a keg of vinegar, several large jars of pepper, half-a-dozen hams and cheeses, two cases of gin, an anker of brandy, and half an "aam" (seventeen gallons) of the potent brandy known as "Cape Smoke," in addition to the simple cooking utensils required, water-casks, or "fagie," and tar to mix with grease for lubricating the waggon-wheels. To ingratiate himself with the natives, six dozen pocket-knives, twenty-four boxes of snuff, fifty pounds of tobacco, three hundred pounds of mixed beads, three dozen tinder-boxes, a hundredweight of brass and copper wire for wrist and leg ornaments, and two dozen sickles, were stowed in the capacious

A hunter's kit in 1843.

waggons, besides a good set of carpenter's tools. A gross of awls, a gross of sail-needles, fifty hanks of twine, two bolts of sail-cloth, two dozen gown pieces, 117 dozen Malay handkerchiefs, thread, needles, and buttons, ready-made jackets and trousers, several dozen cotton shirts, Scots bonnets and "cocker-nonys," a few medicines, some arsenical soap, and the ordinary detergent article were also included, in addition to £200 in cash.

This outfit was, more or less, that of all travellers bound for a long journey into the interior of South Africa who wished to be independent both of Boers and Bechuanas. To this day much the same impedimenta would be required. But naturally many of the articles are superfluous in a country now penetrated by the railway, and some of the lethal weapons would excite the derision of the modern sportsman, just as those of Harris were out of date in Cumming's day, and Le Vaillant's battery was quite prehistoric before the typical sportsman whose feats are recorded in the previous chapter set forth on his campaigns. A pickaxe and a spade were among the most important of Cumming's accoutrements, for a large portion of his shooting was done by the side of "vleys," or temporary water-pools, and other drinking-places, after dark. At that hour lions and other animals came to drink, and were potted with comparative ease and freedom from danger by the hunter, who lay concealed in a hole dug for his convenience. Gordon Cumming's first journey, taken in 1843, was to Kuruman, by way of Grahamstown and Colesberg, then a military station much in favour for the good shooting in the vicinity and the little pipe-clay in the garrison. We do not hear much of elephants or lions, or even of rhinoceroses, until the Vaal River was crossed. But when in Bechuanaland, the Scottish hunter was in his element. The antelopes, which had been plentiful throughout his entire trek from Grahamstown northwards, now swarmed, while lions and elephants afforded nobler food for his gunpowder. At Kuruman, Dr. Moffat

Gordon Cumming's journey.

was stationed, and here also he found David Hume, an old trader, who, after some early explorations of the country, had settled here by invitation of the missionaries. Of Moffat, Cumming had nothing but good to tell: "Together with a noble and athletic frame, he possesses a face on which forbearance and Christian charity are very plainly written, and his mental and bodily attainments are great. Minister, gardener, blacksmith, gunsmith, mason, carpenter, glazier—every hour of the day finds this worthy pastor engaged in some useful employment—setting, by his own exemplary piety and industrious habits, a good example to others to go and do likewise."

Hearing from Dr. Moffat that "a missionary named Dr. Livingstone, who was married to his eldest daughter," was stationed at and the civilisation he had introduced the attraction to the latter quite as much as the game that swarmed in the vicinity. But learning that there was an abundance of elephants in the Bamangwato country (p. 201), the hunter did not tarry long with Livingstone, who in those days was a personage entirely unknown to fame.

Ostriches, zebras, and the other characteristic animals of South Africa daily increased in number, until, by the time the party arrived in what is now known as Khama's country, the herds of buffalo, giraffe, pallah, wildebeest, and other antelopes were so numerous as to be almost incredible to anyone not familiar with the troops seen in the same country by Harris and the other forerunners of Cumming. It was in the Bamangwato Mountains that

£1,200 WORTH OF IVORY AT A TRADER'S STORE AT PANDAMATENKA.
(*From a Photograph taken for the Paris Society for Evangelical Missions.*)

Mabotza, in the vale of Bakatla, about fourteen days' to the north-east, Cumming made for that point, the missionary being, in this case, the pioneer of the sportsman, his first elephant was killed, showing the rapidity with which the large game of South Africa were already retreating from the more settled country. But in this region there were ample to make amends for those which had been exterminated elsewhere. Herds roamed the valleys everywhere, and a night Cumming set out, in March, 1845, on a second expedition, which brought him again into the Bamangwato country, where he soon bagged

ON THE LIMPOPO RIVER.
(From a Photograph taken for the Paris Society for Evangelical Missions.)

watch by a hole seldom failed to lay one or more lions low before break of day. Buffaloes, rhinoceroses, koodoo, leopards—every four-legged beast of the country—seemed to have their home in this favoured region. Even Harris's elysium in the Cashan Mountains was not thicker in great game. But as Cumming's experiences were very much those of his predecessors, it is not necessary to weary the reader with a repetition of his hunting exploits, until, his men refusing to go any farther, the waggons had again to be turned to "the colony"—though the country which he had travelled is now included either in that division or in the Bechuanaland protectorate.

After a short stay at Grahamstown, his fifteenth elephant, and found lions "too numerous to be agreeable," while to kill five rhinoceroses by the side of a pool as they came to drink was not regarded as a very extraordinary feat of venery. By the 2nd of February, 1847, Cumming was again in Grahamstown, laden with hunting trophies, and with ivory and ostrich feathers which he sold for "somewhere about £1,000," thus largely recouping the expenses of his different journeys.

A few weeks' stay in civilisation was enough for the intrepid hunter, who, on the 11th of March, started out on a third elephant-hunting expedition, taking this time, however, a short cut from Colesberg, across the Vaal River, through the territories of the Chief Mahura to the Merisani (Maritsani) River. In this journey he was successful; but it led him to a considerable distance away from and down the valley of the Limpopo River (p. 205), where immense herds of buffalo were met with, and pallah and waterbuck abounded. Here also, amid a host of crocodiles, the hippopotamus was seen for the first time, and an antelope discovered which he refers to as the Scrolomootlooque, or *Antelopus rouuleynei*, under the belief that it was a new species and deserved to bear his own name. It is now very scarce on the banks of the Limpopo, but is generally regarded as simply a smaller, more reddish-hued form of the bush-buck. Here Cumming had one of those reckless adventures which led untravelled critics to shrug their shoulders, and compare him with Waterton, who rode an alligator. Having wounded a hippopotamus, he dashed into the river to secure his quarry, reckless of the crocodiles that made it dangerous to drink at the edge, and of the "hippos," in no way disinclined to resent intrusion on their domain. "As I approached Behemoth," he tells us, "her eye looked very wicked. I halted for a moment, ready to dive under the water if she attacked me; but she was stunned, and did not know what she was doing. So running in upon her, and seizing her short tail, I attempted to incline her course to land. It was extraordinary what enormous strength she still had in the water. I could not guide her in the slightest and she continued to splash and plunge, and blow, and make her circular course, carrying me along with her as if I was a fly on her tail. Finding her tail gave me but a poor hold, as the only means of securing my prey, I took out my knife, and, cutting two deep parallel incisions through the skin on her rump, and lifting this skin from the flesh, so that I could get in my two hands, I made use of this as a handle; and after some desperate hard work, sometimes

A reckless feat.

pushing and sometimes pulling, the sea-cow continuing her circular course all the time, and I holding on at her rump like grim death, eventually I succeeded in bringing this gigantic and most powerful animal to the bank. Here the Bushman quickly brought me a stout buffalo-rheim from my horse's neck, which I passed through the opening in the thick skin, and moored Behemoth to a tree. I then took my rifle, and sent a ball through the centre of her head, and she was numbered with the dead" (p. 209).

As the river was full of "sea-cows"—little herds of from twelve to thirty being constantly in sight—the hunter need not have been so anxious; but it was his first, and at the time he did not know where another was to be obtained. Less fortunate, two of his horses were killed and consumed by lions, and a petty chief had to be flogged for imitating the lions' example. Immense herds of elephants gave variety to lion, buffalo, and sea-cow shooting. The latter seemed more plentiful the lower the Limpopo valley was descended, while the numerous lions became so fierce that one of the party was seized by the neck and killed before the brute could be driven away. As for elephants, a herd of one hundred was not uncommon, while black and white rhinoceroses were so frequent that they seemed not to have been much disturbed since the white hunters had first reached the Limpopo. The tsetse fly also now began to cause alarm for the safety of the cattle and horses. But with game so plentiful, it was hard to leave this charmed valley, where animals of all kinds were so untouched that herds of zebras and buffaloes, numbering three and four hundred, were everyday sights; and antelopes of many species were even more abundant than they were farther south. But by-and-by the tsetse became so fatal that the cattle died, and a messenger had to be sent to Livingstone's station for help to enable the party to return to Colesberg.

Cumming's last expedition was again to the Limpopo, and was as successful as any of its predecessors. Though game had in 1849 moved farther into the interior than where Harris had seen it, there was still plenty a short way from the settlements. Ten days after leaving Colesberg there was no lack of it, and close by the Vet River the hunter witnessed a sight which he declares to have been one of the most wonderful in all his varied experience among the wild beasts of southern Africa. Right and left the plain was one purple mass of graceful blesbucks, which extended without a break as far as the eye could strain, the depths of their vast legions covering a breadth of about six hundred yards. Soon after this great herd had disappeared, another, comprising thousands, passed. Zebras, blue wildebeests, hartebeests, buffaloes, and sassabys were still abundant, and both elephants and lions plentiful enough to prevent the hunter's eye from losing its cunning. But Cumming's experience on his last trip to the Limpopo determined him to make it his last. A Mr. Orpen, who accompanied him, was dreadfully torn by a leopard, while he himself was prostrated by a fever. Even his customary luck did not encourage him to tarry much longer in a country where he had already earned the title of "lion hunter," albeit many a sportsman before and after his day has quite as amply deserved that name. By this time his hunting trophies had accumulated to such an extent in Colesberg that it took nine heavily laden waggons to transport them to Port Elizabeth, where they were duly shipped, to the weight of thirty tons.

In England Cumming's narrative* aroused various feelings. All the schoolboys who read

The return of Gordon Cumming. it—and all the "rolling stones"— wearied to be off to Shoshong and the Limpopo region; and there before long several went to imitate their hero's feats. But the more critical, though quite as imperfectly informed people, who had never read Harris or Alexander, and did not know a bontebuck from a brindled gnu, were extremely sarcastic touching the hunting exploits of the Highland laird. He was likened to Bruce, to Mendez Pinto, and to a great many historical personages not supposed to be martyrs to the truth, while Cumming's unconventional ways quite shocked the dull Philistinish folk of 1850. His collection there was, however, no disputing. It occupied a prominent place in the Exhibition of 1851, and was shown in many country towns as "The South African Museum"; and until the famous hunter's death and its dispersal, formed a display of great interest at his house in Fort Augustus.†

In reality, there was little in Cumming's adventures to excite incredulity. Harris and his predecessors saw and slew quite as much game—or might have slain it, had they been more butcherly inclined—and in many parts of the country the wild animals were for years afterwards quite as numerous as in the districts scoured by the "Lion Hunter," if, indeed, they were not even more plentiful. No one nowadays questions Cumming's narrative. Other hunters have fully confirmed all that he tells, and among the most pleasing testimonies to his veracity are those of the natives. Colonel Parker Gillmore, who, under the pseudonym of "Ubique," has won a good name among the latter-day hunters of South Africa,‡ tells how he camped beside a "vley" where his predecessor had killed a great variety of game. "The old chief remembered him well, and when I informed him that I had seen the big Highlander many times in London and elsewhere, his wrinkled face became suffused with pleasure. But when I finally told him that the great hunter was dead, sadness seemed to overcome him, and he scarcely spoke another word, but soon after departed to his kraal, looking—possibly in my imagination —far less youthful and elastic in his gait. In many parts of this remote portion of Africa I have come across natives who well

---

* "Five Years' Hunting Adventures in South Africa" (1850; reprint. 1893), and, in a condensed form, "The Lion Hunter of South Africa" (1858).

† He died there on the 24th of March, 1866.

‡ "Days and Nights in the Desert"; "The Hunter's Arcadia"; "The Great Thirst Land," etc.

knew this mighty Nimrod—some even that have hunted with him, and one and all agreed that he was the bravest and most daring white man they ever knew. To them I have recounted the principal episodes which he narrates in his work, and which have been condemned by many of his countrymen as utterly improbable, nay, impossible—but one and all, without a single dissenting voice, attested to their truth.

"Sicomey, the father of Khama, now king of Bamangwato, when a fugitive at Matchuping's, told me of deeds performed by Gordon Cumming which, if possible, outrivalled those he has recounted in his work: and I have often thought that these were withheld from the British public for the reason that he had not authentic witnesses to produce who could endorse his statements."*

But it was not for some years after his return that Cumming received a testimonial to his truthfulness, from a quarter whence the world least expected it. When the hunter visited Bechuanaland, he received—we have seen—much kindness from Dr. Moffat and his son-in-law, Livingstone. Moffat was then a well-known man, but the name of the latter was strange to the thousands who, in 1857, became familiar with it as that of the greatest of African travellers. In his first book he bears warm testimony to the veracity of his much-maligned countryman. Letloche, about twenty miles beyond Bamangwato, was Cumming's farthest station north, and as Livingstone was frequently visited by the daring hunter, and heard from the guides who accompanied him verbal accounts of the adventures

* "Shooting," November 17th, 1886.

ROUALEYN GEORGE GORDON CUMMING.

not then published, he had no hesitation in characterising his severely criticised volume as an accurate description of South African hunting. "The native guides learnt," he tells us, referring to the sportsmen who preceded or followed Cumming, "to depend implicitly on the word of an Englishman for the subsequent payment of their services, and they gladly went for five and six months to the north, enduring all the hardships of a very trying mode of life, with little else but meat of game to subsist on —nay, they willingly travelled seven or eight hundred miles to Grahamstown, receiving for wages only a musket worth fifteen shillings. Only one man ever deceived them; and as I believed that he was afflicted with greediness to a slight degree of insanity, I upheld the honour of the English name by paying his debts." Before Cumming left Africa he met, at Colesberg and other places, with Mr. William Cotton Oswell and Mr. Mungo Murray, names before long—like those of Mr. Webb (p. 210) and Colonel Steele, two other South African sportsmen of about the same period—to be linked with that of Livingstone in the exploration of South Africa. Like Major Vardon, who also had (in 1848) visited the Limpopo, these sportsmen had made their head-quarters at the mission stations in the game country. Mr. Oswell (Vol. II., p. 225) had entered the Madras Civil Service early in life, but his health failing, he was, like so many others in like case, ordered to the Cape of Good Hope to recruit. This he did to such good purpose that he lived to the age of seventy-five, one of the halest of English country gentlemen.

Oswell and Murray.

GORDON CUMMING'S ADVENTURE WITH THE HIPPOPOTAMUS (p. 200).

He spent the best part of five years in Africa, hunting over tracts now the site of farms and towns, but at that time a haunt of wild beasts. When Livingstone determined to cross the Kalahari, until then supposed to be impassable (Vol. II., p. 183), Oswell and Murray returned from England in order to accompany him. They therefore deserved, and have always obtained, part of the credit due for the discovery of Lake Ngami, though, indeed, as nearly every traveller in Bechuanaland had for nearly half a century

W. F. WEBB.
(From a Photograph by D. Battenhaussen, Port Elizabeth.)

heard more or less accurate native gossip about this sheet, a less definite term than "discovery" would apply to their reaching the goal for which they set out. Oswell and Murray, indeed, bore the greater part of the expenses attendant on the journey; and, apart from the geographical results of their travels, they opened up a region which has ever since been the only one in Africa that bears any resemblance to the country which the earlier hunters saw in the Cape, Orange Free State, Bechuanaland, Transvaal, and in the Limpopo Valley.

Unhappily for the persecuted fauna of Africa, the last of these places of refuge was from that date invaded by an ever-increasing crowd of sportsmen. Oswell was the most modest of men. No persuasion could induce him to put on record any of his interesting experiences, though every trophy from Africa, South America, and other countries in which this valiant "Shikari" had pursued wild beasts, with which his house at Groombridge, near Tunbridge Wells, was decorated, recalled an adventure. It was Livingstone and his two friends who discovered the lechwe antelope (*Kobus lechee*) in the region near the Botletli River, where it is still common. The pookoo (*Kobus vardoni*) of the same country, though now extremely rare, bears the name of another sportsman who also died without putting the world into his debt.

The kuabaoba, or straight-horned rhinoceros (*R. oswelli*), is, however, not a permanent species (p. 183), but a variety of the black one. This is to be regretted, for the man after whom it was named deserved the fame which zoology has to bestow, albeit he played sore havoc among the African ferae. For years after he left Bechuanaland the natives and the professional hunters used to talk of the courage and skill with which he hunted the elephant. No such adept ever came into the country; and when the Kaffirs wished to flatter Livingstone, they would tell him that if he had not been a missionary he would "have been just like Oswell." For up to that date he was the only European who hunted without dogs. A few yelping curs easily distract the attention of the tusker and render him incapable of attending to man. He endeavours to crush them by falling on his knees, and sometimes places his forehead against a tree ten inches in diameter, and pushes it before him. The only danger to the hunter is, that the dogs may run towards him and bring the elephant along with them.

Oswell had been known to kill four large old males in one day, bearing in their jaws ivory worth one hundred guineas. His narrow escapes were many. When on the banks of the Zouga (Botletli), in 1850, he pursued an elephant into the dense thorny bushes on the margin of the river. As he followed it through a narrow pathway, he saw his quarry (of whose tail he had but got glimpses before) reversing the part of hunter and hunted. As the beast turned and rushed on him, he had no time to effect a passage. The hunter therefore tried to dismount; but in doing so he was thrown on the ground, with his face upwards to the elephant, which, being in full chase, still went on. Mr. Oswell, seeing the huge forefoot of the animal about to descend on his legs, parted them and drew in his breath, as if to resist the fatal pressure of the other foot, which he expected would next moment crush his body. Happily, however, the whole length of the infuriated beast passed over him, and he escaped unhurt. A similar experience is in the repertory of Mr. Selous. In both cases, it is perhaps needless to add that, as when Livingstone was thrown down by a lion, the length of time occupied by the incident seemed a good deal longer than it took in actual seconds.

The discovery of the character of the Kalahari, and of the multitude of elephants on the shores of Lake Ngami, soon brought numbers of hunters and traders on the scene, until the lake and the surrounding region became one of the best known of the Cape border-lands. Explorers also, in an age when inner Africa was far from the familiar field it is nowadays, began to think of a region then regarded with much the same feelings that the more northern lake-land was a few years later.

Lake Ngami and its hunters: Galton and Andersson.

Among these was Francis Galton,* still active in scientific work, but in 1850 only known as a young man anxious to effect an exploration from South-West Africa to the lake just discovered by Livingstone. He was not a hunter in the sense that the

* Francis Galton was born at Duddeston in 1822, and educated at King Edward's School, Birmingham. After studying medicine, he graduated, in 1844, M.A. at Trinity College, Cambridge. A visit to northern Africa stimulated him to undertake the expedition which forms his chief claim to rank among travellers. Since 1852 he has devoted himself to meteorology, the problems of heredity, finger-marks, and allied subjects, which, as a grandson of Erasmus Darwin, he may be considered to have a family claim to investigate.

word has been used in these pages. But his companion, Carl Johan Andersson, was both a sportsman and a naturalist. A Swede by birth,† though, it is understood, the son of an English sportsman who, under the name of "L. Lloyd," passed many years in Scandinavia, he came to England with a large collection of living animals and specimens, by the sale of which he intended to defray the cost of a journey to the hunter's paradise of South Africa, when he heard of Mr. Galton's intended journey and his willingness to permit him to join in it.

Their travels, which began in August, 1850, at Walvisch Bay, were intended to explore the Damara and Ovampo countries, the unknown districts between Namaqualand and Benguela, and, if possible, reach Lake Ngami from the west. This programme, owing to the disturbed condition of the region nearest them, was only partially carried out. Erongo, a curiously shaped mountain, was, however, visited and examined, and a new country, not seen by Alexander and their other predecessors, entered upon in March, 1851. Finally, in spite of the warnings received and the visible evidences they were constantly coming across of the Namaquas' ruthlessness, they reached Ovampoland, then almost entirely unknown. But any eagerness they felt to explore the Cunene River, or the lands towards the east, was thwarted by the peremptory refusal of the Ovampo chief to permit his white visitors to go farther than his capital. Accordingly, to Walvisch Bay they were forced to return. This was the last essay of Mr. Galton in African or other exploration, though his pleasant narrative‡ obtained for him one of the Royal Geographical Society's medals, which had been denied to Alexander and to Harris.

Andersson, however, could not bear to return without accomplishing the feat on which he had set his heart. In this he succeeded. He reached Lake Ngami, and

† He was born in 1827, at Elfsdalen, in Wermland.
‡ "Narrative of an Explorer in Tropical South Africa" (1853; new edition, 1892).

explored the Okavango River, now known to be connected with the Zambesi basin. Taking to hunting as a profession, he built a camp for himself and another celebrated sportsman,

FRANCIS GALTON.

Frederick Green, in Ovampoland. Being foolish enough to join in a war between the Damaras and Namaquas, he was rescued by Green, who found him lying wounded in the path of the enemy, and, after lying between life and death, rose a cripple, to begin his last journey in an ox-cart. Accompanied by Ericsson, a Swedish hunter, he reached the long-sought-for Cunene, but he was seized with dysentery and died, on the banks of the Ovakuambi, on the 5th of July, 1867. His grave is still pointed out by the natives, who have enclosed the last resting-place of the hapless Scandinavian by a hedge of thorns.*

Andersson found animal life abundant in all the country over which he travelled, and as a slayer of the elephant and lion he had scarcely a superior among his contemporaries. Meanwhile, however, Lake Ngami, by the multitude of wild beasts that

* "Lake Ngami; or, Explorations and Discoveries in South-Western Africa" (1855); "The Okavango River" (1861); "The Lion and Elephant" (1873); "The Birds of Damaraland" (1872); the two latter being posthumous.

surrounded it, had attracted more sportsmen than any other part of South Africa. As early as 1855, Green and Wilson, accompanied by the Swedish naturalist, Wahlberg, reached it and ascended the Botletli, while the lake itself was completely circumnavigated by the well-known hunter and trader, Chapman, who made several trips between it and Walvisch Bay.

Wahlberg was a Swede, who arrived in South Africa in 1838, and gradually extended his expeditions beyond Zululand on to the Limpopo, being for a time accompanied by Delegorgue, a French naturalist. In 1845 he returned to Sweden. But he was in Africa again in 1853, charmed by the thought that in the new country discovered by Livingstone he would have a virgin field for hunting and natural-history exploration. In Ngamiland, however, the Swede met his death. After many narrow escapes, he was trampled to death near the Tamalakan River, by an elephant which he had tried to stalk on foot. He was a skilful hunter, having within a few hours killed four elephants, besides wounding a fifth; but he was foolhardy, and met the fate which he

CARL JOHAN ANDERSSON.

had often foretold for himself. Many years later, Mr. Hemmings, an English sportsman, accomplished what Andersson and Galton failed in doing; for in 1884, accompanied by a Dutch hunter, this gentleman, without self-advertisement, or, indeed, ever publishing the fact, succeeded in passing from Walvisch Bay to the Congo at Vivi.

By-and-by, however, even Lake Ngami ceased to be very far in the outer wild; and, with the number of visitors intent on killing, the elephant and other game became not quite so plentiful as it was in the years immediately succeeding its discovery. Nor were the natives quite so simple. Accordingly, when Livingstone reported the Zambesi flowing through Africa farther to the north, the hunter and trader's "trek" began to move in that direction. Among the pioneers who essayed this journey were Thomas Baines and the two Chapmans in 1861. The first was instigated to undertake this journey from Walvisch Bay in the hope of meeting

Baines, the Chapmans, Baldwin, and the Zambesi.

Livingstone and clearing himself from the injustice done him (Vol. II., p. 238); while the Chapmans, who had already journeyed to and from Lake Ngami more than once, were travelling in the way of business. The route they took was tolerably well known, being the ordinary track by Elephant Fountain, Reit Fountain (Tounobis), and Lake Ngami,

CLEANING HEADS AFTER AN ELAND HUNT.
(From a Photograph by Mr. H. A. Bryden.)

and thence across the Tamalakan by Kounyara, Gerufa, and Daka to the Victoria Falls, where they arrived on the 23rd of July, 1862, less than sixteen months after setting out from Walvisch Bay on their leisurely journey.* Even then the game in the Ngami

* Baines: "Explorations in South-West Africa, etc." (1864); Chapman: "Travels in the Interior of South Africa, comprising Fifteen Years' Hunting and Trading, with Journeys across the Continent from Natal to Walvisch Bay, etc." (1868). James Chapman did not consider that his share in this and other expeditions had received that full acknowledgment which they deserved.

Lake land had begun to diminish. The first travellers had found it so abounding with herds of antelopes that they never thought of killing domestic cattle after reaching that country. The Botletli banks at that time teemed with elephants, and the deserted places of 1862 were then alive with other game. Now scarcely a buck was to be obtained without searching for it, and the labour of procuring food consumed much of the time that should have been devoted to other work.

Baines evidently believed that he and his companions were the first travellers who had visited the Falls since Livingstone discovered them in 1855; and he tells us that he read on a tree above the cataract "the letters D L 1855, and below them C L 1860, with the broad arrow of the Government cut beneath them." The "C L" stood, no doubt, for Charles Livingstone. But in 1862 there ought to have been on the tree "W C B" in addition; for two years before Baines and the Chapmans arrived, the famous hunter, William Charles Baldwin, had reached the Zambesi from Natal, and, he tells us, cut his initials "on a tree on the island above the Falls, just below Dr. Livingstone's, as being the second European" who had reached them, and the first from the East Coast. There can be no mistake about the locality; for Livingstone told Baldwin that it was "the only place from the West Coast to the East where he had the vanity to cut his initials." Again, to render this curious omission more puzzling, Baldwin assures us* that from the date of the discovery of the Falls "to this [1860], with the exception of Livingstone's party, no European but myself has found his way thither." Polson, a trader, tried in the same year to reach Walvisch Bay from the Zambesi with waggons; and a few years later the river was not only visited by hunters from Natal, but the continent crossed from the Falls to the West Coast. But, as these journeys were over the colonies, it has not been considered proper to include them among the passages from sea to sea

* Baldwin : "African Hunting and Adventure from Natal to the Zambesi," etc. (1862).

across the broader and less-explored region farther north.

Baldwin, whose name has just been mentioned, may be regarded as a pupil of Gordon Cumming; for it was that hunter's book which instigated him, after an unsettled life at home, to roam South Africa from 1852 to 1860 in search of the wild animals still numerous as late as the last-named year. His trips took him mainly into the "hinterland" of the East Coast, St. Lucia Bay, Zululand, the Amatonga country, Transvaal, Lake Ngami, and latterly, as we have seen, to the Zambesi. But even then English sportsmen were wandering very far afield; for on his way back Baldwin met Messrs. Waddington and Aldersley, who had pushed on from Angra Pequena, on the West Coast, to Lake Ngami, through Great Namaqua and Damara lands, and were then on their way to the Cape.

The hunting adventures of these and the other sportsmen of that epoch are full of interest. They found endless elephants and other large game to kill; but, after what has been already described, a narrative of what they did would prove somewhat monotonous. Accordingly, it is needless saying more than that what Alexander and Harris and Gordon Cumming saw, Baldwin and his successors, to the close of Selous' hunting career in South Africa, also saw and took part in, though every year to a less and less extent. The lions and elephants got fewer, and the vast troops of zebras and giraffes rarer and rarer and thinner and thinner. Even the blesbucks and the bontebucks ceased to migrate in their countless thousands; and it is certain that the latter-day hunters no longer found the rhinoceros a "perfect nuisance," while every animal, when not killed off the face of the land, retired farther and farther into the few retreats left in a much-ransacked, much-prospected, much-"trekked" over country. It would be idle, even were it possible, to recount the many sportsmen who helped to decimate the South African feræ. Few of them added anything to our actual knowledge of the region they travelled over;* most of them did not penetrate farther than the well-known hunting-grounds, and only a few of them considered it necessary to leave behind them a record of their slaughterings and adventures.

A hunter of different grade is the last of the great slayers of South African game whom we can find room to notice. This is Frederick Courteney Selous. A London artist's son, and a Rugby schoolboy, he could have little experience of sport or anything **Frederick Courteney Selous.** else when, on the 4th of September, 1871, he set foot for the first time on the sandy shores of Algoa Bay, with £400 in his pocket, a good battery in his boxes, and the weight of only nineteen years upon his shoulders. But he had read Gordon Cumming, Baldwin, and the literature generally of South African sport, and he was resolved to gratify his love of natural history by studying the ways of animals in their native wilds. It was only an after-consideration that resolved him to shoot them for the sake of a livelihood. Neither tall nor particularly robust-looking, the native chiefs readily gave him permission to hunt in their territories, smiling cynically at the idea of such a boy doing much execution among the elephants of their forests, while the lions were more likely to kill him than he was to do any harm to them. In those days there was still plenty of large game in South Africa, but not in the older parts of the colonies, or even in the Orange Free State and Transvaal, where the earlier sportsmen had found it so profusely. But outside these bounds, away in Bechuana and Ngami lands, in the Matabele country and in Mashonaland, by the Zambesi and across it on to the Manika plateau, it could be had in something

like its old abundance. Petrus Jacobs, the Boer hunter, who had killed, perhaps, more elephants than any man in Africa, was still at work, and Jan Viljoen and Hartley, the veteran Englishman, had not ceased exploits which ran those of "old Piet" and his son David very close. A host of other names might be mentioned among those of the professional ivory-collectors and English sportsmen who then (and subsequently) ransacked the country in search of game and amusement. Most of them are now under the inhospitable soil of

FREDERICK COURTENEY SELOUS.
(From a Photograph by J. Thomson, Grosvenor St., W.)

South Africa. But the boy who in 1871 looked so little likely to survive the perils of his calling, is in 1894 a more robust man than he was when the twenty years of a hunter's life were still all before him and the Geographical Society's medal was not even dreamt of as the reward of map-making in the intervals of more heroic occupations. Mr. Selous' earliest hunting was in Matabeleland, in the country formerly ruled over by Moselikatse and now—or until lately—by Lo-Bengula, a son after his father's heart; and for three years he remained in Zambesia without ever experiencing the slightest desire to exchange his free wild life for the comforts and restraints of civilisation.†

---

* An exception must be made, among those who have essayed authorship, in favour of Gillmore, Dryden, Eglinton, Nicoll, and my lamented friend, the late Mr. W. H. Drummond. For though they might not have explored any new country, their works are admirable contributions to field natural history. Drummond's "Large Game and Natural History of South-East Africa" (1875) is still, and must always continue to be, a valuable work.

† This outline of Mr. Selous' travels is gleaned from his papers communicated to the Royal Geographical Society, particularly that in the *Geographical Journal*,

ENCAMPMENT OF TRAVELLERS IN THE ZAMBESI COUNTRY: LESHOMAS SELLING NATIVE PRODUCE.
(*From a Photograph taken for the Paris Society for Evangelical Missions.*)

During this time he and his friend George Wood travelled over a great deal of country on foot, on horseback, and with a Cape waggon (Vol. II., p. 169). In this way they made the acquaintance of the splendidly watered plateau in which the Nwanetsi, Lundi, and Tukwi Rivers take their rise, and went as far south as the junction of the Ingesi and Lundi Rivers, not a great way from Mount Bufwa. All the country between Matabeleland and the Zambesi was hunted over during the dry seasons—and always on foot—as far eastwards as the Sanyati River, and westwards to the Victoria Falls, and up the Chobe (Kwando) to the Sunta outlet (Vol. II., p. 196). Game was plentiful enough in this then little-known

April, 1893, pp. 289-324. his "Hunter's Wanderings in Africa" (1881), and various personal data from other sources. His "Travel and Adventure in South-East Africa"—of which the outlines have been given—which appeared in the autumn of 1893, has also been consulted.

region—twenty-four elephants, besides other large animals, having been killed by Selous in the marshes of the Chobe, where a number of Masubia refugees from the tyranny of the Barotse chief Sipopo had taken refuge.

In 1876, after a visit to England, Selous was back again to his old haunts; but, finding a lack of elephants, he and Mr. L. M. Owen determined to cross the Zambesi to the neighbourhood of the Kafukwe and Loangwa Rivers, where they were confident their quarry would be found, following the course of the Zambesi to the place where the former stream joins it. Part of their route lay through the country of the Manansa tribe, an offshoot of the Makalakas, who had been driven with great slaughter from their homes south of the Zambesi during the incursions of the Matabele. They were a feeble, friendly people. The Batongas bore a worse reputation; but, as no white man had travelled among them since Dr. Livingstone, Charles Livingstone, and Dr. Kirk passed through their country in

1861, the memory of these visitors seemed to restrain their evil passions. Farther on, the land was devastated by war and slaving parties, Portuguese officials then (as now) carrying on the trade without the central Government nearer the coast having any power (or inclination) to check their infamous contempt of orders. By-and-by the four donkeys which were their sole beasts of burden died. Carriers were hard to obtain, and after crossing the Manika plateau* to Sitanda's village, elephants were as invisible as ever; and even the game on which they had to exist was so scarce at times they were almost

settlements of the traders and missionaries in Matabeleland, empty-handed so far as ivory was concerned, but with more geographical information than they had hitherto obtained.

In 1878, Mr. Selous and three companions had a better elephant season in northern Mashonaland. They also cut a new road from the Umfuli to the Sebakwe River, as the old hunting-road to the north of the Machabi Hills had become impracticable for waggons—the new route traversing a beautiful stretch of "high-lying, open, and well-watered country." Next year the region between the Mababi, Machabi, and Kwando Rivers, as far as Mai-ini's

CHARACTERISTIC PORTION OF SELOUS' ROAD.
(From a Photograph by Mr. Ellerton Fry.)

starved for food. Fever did its work, so that it was with great trouble that Selous and his companion could again reach the friendly

* Not to be confounded with the Manika country in South-Eastern Africa.

was hunted over. At that time buffaloes, lechwe antelopes, and other animals were very plentiful, though even then game had been driven beyond the more frequented part of Matabeleland. Yet less than twenty years before, the missionaries at Inyati, the most advanced station of the London Missionary Society, were often called by the natives to drive the elephants out of their cornfields. Buffaloes and rhinoceroses were continually seen going down to drink in the afternoon. Lions roared nightly round the house, and frequently quenched their thirst at a reedy pool not more than two hundred yards from the doorstep of the mission quarters. On this journey Selous crossed the Kwando during a very dry season, when the oxen had to pull the waggons for 120 miles without a drink or a rest. On the other side of the river they visited the site of Linyanti, the capital of Sebituane, the Makololo chief who was visited by Livingstone and Oswell in 1852. When the Makololo Empire fell to pieces (p. 6, and Vol. II., p. 194), on the death of Sekeletu, all of its old prosperity deserted Linyanti. Indeed, at the time of which we speak, the sole signs that it had ever been inhabited were a few fast-crumbling remains of a Kaffir town. Where, fifteen years previously, cattle had grazed and human beings had tilled the soil, herds of buffaloes and lechwe antelopes roamed; and in all the land—to use a native expression—"there were no lords but the lions." And with the buffalo had come the fatal tsetse fly which debarred settlement by a cattle-keeping race. The graves of Sebituane and Sekeletu were pointed out, and the Kaffirs of the party laid offerings on them, for the sake of obtaining help in the hunt from the spirits of these mighty chiefs. Their pale ghosts, however, refused to favour the new-comers; for they did not see many elephants, and one of the party lost himself and died of thirst in the desert country between the Chobe and Zambesi. At Linyanti a suggestive relic was noticed, in the shape of the tires and nave-bands of a waggon which had long since crumbled to decay. It may have been the remains of one belonging to Livingstone, or, more likely, to the unfortunate mission party which, with their wives and children, died here in 1861, with the exception of Mr. Price and two of Mr. Helmore's family. The Chobe and Machabi, it was noticed, rose steadily from the first week in June to the last week in September, when they began to recede. There cannot be any doubt of the Okavango—of which the Machabi is an outlet—and the Upper Kwando (Chobe) being connected nearer their sources; otherwise their waters would not rise and fall so steadily *pari passu*. Yet there are no snows to melt at the sources of these rivers, and the Zambesi, which rises in the same latitude, decreases steadily in volume day by day during the dry season, as, indeed, do all the South African rivers. "Besides the channels which still become annually filled with water from the overflow of the Chobe and Okavango river systems, there are many others which are now quite dry, but in which the natives say they used once to travel in canoes. Farther to the south-east, too, in the country between the Gowai and Nata Rivers, there are old river-beds, some of which are quite dry, whilst in others pools of water may still be found; and where such pools exist they are either permanent, or water may be obtained by digging when they are dry, which seems to show that water still runs in these ancient river-beds below the surface."

A hydrographical problem.

In 1880 Mr. Selous was in Mashonaland with Mr. Jameson, in after years the companion of Mr. Stanley on the Congo (p. 31). Together they traced the course of the Umfuli River to its junction with the Sanyati, proving conclusively that it did not run into the Zambesi, as was represented on all the maps published up to that date.

After a second visit to the country which was becoming less and less his home, Mr. Selous revisited Mashonaland in 1882. At that time much of this now comparatively familiar region was a blank to geographers. Mr. Baines had never penetrated beyond the River Manyami; and though Messrs. George Westbeech and G. A. Phillips, both well-known traders, had accompanied a Matabele "impi," or war party, to the sources of the Mazoe in 1868, their journey had not resulted in the addition of any documentary facts to our previous ignorance. Karl Mauch, a German geologist, after rediscovering the ruins of Zimbabwe (Vol. I., p. 8, etc.), had travelled past Mount Wedza, near the head waters of the Sabi, on through Mangwendi's country and down the valley of the Ruenya (or Inyangombi) River to Sena, on the Lower Zambesi.

Still, the country on each side of Mauch's route was, until Selous made Mashonaland his own particular country, very imperfectly laid down on the best maps. During 1882, 1885, 1887, 1889, 1890, 1891, and 1892, Mr. Selous was almost constantly travelling over the Mashona plateau, partly in his capacity of a professional hunter—though since 1882 he was oftener occupied in "filling-in orders" for museums than in slaughtering elephants or lions—and partly in the service of the British South Africa Company, whose pioneer force he led to the promised land. This portion of his labours, therefore, will be described later. But the work he did in the years mentioned helped largely to complete the approximately accurate map which has since been compiled from his sketches and those of Dr. Knight Bruce, Sir John Willoughby, Mr. Swan, and the late Mr. Walter Montagu Kerr. During 1882 Mr. Selous journeyed from the plateau of the Zambesi by way of the Umvukwe Hills to the north, and then down the valley of the Umsengaisi River to the Zambesi, which he followed westwards to Zumbo. In the course of this exploration he discovered that the Panyami flows into that great river some fifteen miles east of Zumbo, instead of to the west of that place, as had hitherto been supposed to be the case. In 1884 Mr. Selous met Mr. Kerr in the Transvaal, and travelled with him to Matabeleland. Thence Kerr "trekked" through Mashonaland to Chibinga, and on to Tete, and from that town to the Portuguese territory through the Makanga and Angoni countries right to the southern shore of the Lake Nyassa.* Mr. Selous, after parting with the young traveller who was so soon to end his promising career, started for the Mababi River, and piloted his waggon for three hundred miles across country, chopping his own road as he went, until at last he struck the old hunting-track from Bamangwato, Khama's town, to the Mababi, near the pool of Sode Garra. In 1888 he was in the Mashukulumbwe and Barotse countries† (Vol. II., pp. 200, 204, 205, 208, 209), and in 1889, tracing the Mazoe River to its source, which was found to be very far from where it was placed on the maps.

After a brief visit to England in the spring of 1889, Mr. Selous was again in Mashonaland, and in the following year guiding the British South Africa Company's pioneer expedition to that country over four hundred miles of road made through a wild country of forests, swamps, and mountains. Yet the eighty waggons were never delayed one hour by the road not being ready for them nor went a mile out of their way by the leader mistaking his route. This remarkable journey is reserved for another volume. "Selous' Road" (p. 217) will be the young Englishman's most enduring claim to a place in the chronicles of South Africa. The next two years were spent in the service of the Company, mostly in exploration, of which the most notable feature was a journey down the Revue to near its junction with the Buzi. A few months later he crossed the former river near Vumbi's town, and examined the country between the Pungwe and Buzi rivers in the unsuccessful attempt to find a waggon route to the Lower Pungwe which would be free from the tsetse fly. But all the lowlands were infested with this pest.

Mr. Selous was in 1893 once more "at home," looking back over his hunting days as something of the past. The great game has been exterminated in South Africa, except where forest and swamp protect it. We hear of it on the Zambesi, and in the remote regions near the great lakes, though in nothing like the

After twenty years.

* Kerr: "The Far Interior," etc. 2 Vols. (1886).

† "Journey to the Kafukwe River, and on the Upper Zambesi," *Proc. Royal Geog. Society*, 1889, p. 216.

quantity seen by the early hunters in the south. The campaign is about over, and man is the victor. Mr. Selous will perhaps be the last of the great hunters—the "mighty Nimrods" is the correct phrase, we believe, but the man who has best earned it objects to the title. In future there may be Nimrods, but they will not be mighty. Yet the latest of all the long line of South African hunters disclaims ever having wished to "make a bag." He shot for ivory and for specimens, not for the glory of a game-book; and it is his proudest memory that, with the exception of an attack made upon his camp by the Mashukulumbwe, led by a few rebel Marotse, in 1888, he never had any serious trouble with the natives. "During my twenty years' wanderings"—and the words are worthy of note—" I have been amongst many tribes who had never previously seen a white man, and I was always absolutely in their power, as I seldom had more than from five to ten natives with me, none of whom were ever armed. On the whole, therefore, I think I may say that the natives of the interior of Africa with whom I have come in contact have treated me well; and, on the other hand, I can proudly affirm that in my person the name of Englishman has suffered no harm in native estimation." This honest boast still holds good. For on the outbreak of the Matabele war, Mr. Selous, considering his place as a burgher of Mashonaland to be with his fellow-citizens, immediately left England for the scene of the trouble with Lo-Bengula. His knowledge of the country proved of the utmost service, and he was one of the few members of Major Goold-Adams's force wounded during the skirmishes on the road to Buluwayo. But this is part of another story.

NATIVE HUNTERS RETURNING FROM THE CHASE.
(From a Photograph taken for the Paris Society for Evangelical Missions.)

VILLAGE OF KITETU IN THE KIKUYU COUNTRY.
(From a Sketch by Bishop Tucker.)

CHAPTER X.

THE ENDING OF AN OLD ERA AND THE BEGINNING OF A NEW ONE.

The Hunter graduates into the Naturalist, and the Naturalist becomes Explorer—Dr. Emil Holub the Bohemian—Earning the Means of Exploration by Medical Practice in Kimberley—His Early Excursions—His Great Expedition beyond the Zambesi and its Pillage and Ruin in the Mashukulumbwe Country—One Result of the Journey—The Brothers James—Their Hunting Trip in the Soudan—Their Journey in the Somali Country from Berbera to the Leopard River—Count Teleki and Lieutenant von Höhnel—Their Ascent of Mount Kenia and Discovery of Lakes Rudolf and Stefanie—William Astor Chanler, the American Explorer of Africa—His Journey into the Masai Country—His Second Expedition with Lieut. von Höhnel—The Tana River—The Mackenzie River—The Lorian "Lake"—The Guaso Nyiri—Mountains which do not Exist—The Jombini Range—The People of the Country—Captain Swayne in Somaliland—Harar and its Changes of Late Years—Imé—Sport—Dr. Schweinfurth—His Early Years—His Journey through the Bongo, Dinka, Niam-Niam, Madi, and Monbuttoo Countries—His Discovery of the Welle—His Description of the Akkas, etc.—The Close of the Age of Loose Description—The Coming of the Scientific Travellers.

IN the preceding sketch little has been said of Mr. Selous' hunting adventures. The hunter had, indeed, almost imperceptibly graduated into the naturalist, and the naturalist into the explorer; and, though the experiences of every explorer are individually different, they have a kinship when the travellers journey in the same region. Otherwise we might halt longer over the expeditions of Dr. Emil Holub, a Bohemian physician* (p. 223), who made several journeys

* Born at Holitz on October 7th, 1847, and graduated M.D. in the University of Prague in 1872.

into the Cape border-lands in the intervals of medical practice in Kimberley. Indeed, until Dr. Holub received during his second visit to South Africa some help from his sovereign and the various scientific societies of his native country, the funds which he expended on these semi-exploratory, semi-zoological trips were earned by his medical practice among the diamond-diggers of what was in those times about the Ultima Thule of South African civilisation. Dr. Holub's enthusiasm thus forms one of the most interesting episodes in the story of the opening-up of

Africa. For, though his labours do not bulk large beside those of the explorers whose achievements form the theme of our earlier volumes, they were accomplished in circumstances which entitle their author to an honourable place among modern travellers. When the young surgeon left his native country in 1872, his aim was to win for Bohemians a place, however small, among those who had made the world more familiar with Africa. His outfit for that task was meagre in the extreme. Beyond his professional acquirements, and some knowledge of natural history, he had few scientific accomplishments to enable him to map his route or to record the features of the regions which he might visit. He knew no one in all the continent, and no one had ever heard his name. Worst of all, he had little money, and without money, or its equivalent in goods, the reader must by this time have learned, it is rather more difficult to travel in Africa than in England. In the former there are no casual workhouse wards, no charities, no hospitals, no hospitality which is not to be paid for in some form, and a remarkable scarcity of those simple souls who give for the asking. Holub intended to practice for fees, the liberality of which had amazed Holitz and its frugal folk; though, as the Bohemian "artz" did not understand either English or Dutch, his chance of finding patients in a country inhabited by Englishmen and Dutchmen seemed perilously small.

Dr. Emil Holub.

All this, however, Dr. Holub only knew when he landed at Port Elizabeth. When he bade good-bye to Prague, full of airy dreams of new lands—for all was new to him—and of the natural history collections with which he could fill the museums of Austria and Bohemia, he had been unable to obtain the slightest assistance either from the Government or the learned societies, which in a few years rained on him orders and diplomas with a profusion amazing to the British explorers who receive so few of these cheap rewards for work compared with which Dr. Holub's meritorious labours look very small indeed.

A few thrifty countrymen had lent him fifty-three pounds, on the condition that it was repaid in three months. But it was not until the inexperienced traveller found himself passing out of the Custom House, after paying duty on his guns, with three pounds in his pocket, that he began to realise that five hundred florins was not quite a fortune in that Africa with which he had little acquaintance except through translations of Livingstone's books.

This discovery was not the most pleasant of his life. Thanks, however, to the Austrian Consul, he obtained a few patients among the German families in Port Elizabeth; and, as soon as the means of moving were forthcoming, the doctor was on the road to the newer region of the diamond fields, or what was then known as Griqualand West. The citizens of Kimberley in 1894 may not quite realise what that city was in 1872, without railway communication with the outer world, without the electric light, and without any buildings which they could honour with the humblest epithet in the architectural vocabulary. At present they live in houses of brick or stone, and may—if the "blue" has been washing out well—dine sumptuously every day. When Holub intimated his intention of earning money enough out of their ills to make an African expedition, he had to affix his professional "plate" to a hired tent six feet by eight. This humble abode formed for months not only his bedroom and his consulting-room, but his dispensary, his laboratory, and the workshop in which he prepared his snakes and bird-skins and stored his collections. Very often, when a patient called on him in the middle of the day, the rays of the sun burnt so intolerably through the thin canvas roof that an umbrella had to be raised to protect both patient and practitioner; "and," he tells us, "it was similar when there was rain."

In this way he practised until February, 1873, working much and spending little, until he had saved what he thought enough for his first journey beyond the Colonial bounds.

This led him into southern Bechuanaland and the southern section of the Transvaal. In two months the doctor returned, in Kimberley parlance "dead broke," and resumed practice until in November of the same year he was off again on a second journey. This lasted for six months, and took the naturalist into more of the Bechuana country, as far north as Shoshong. But when he returned to Kimberley a second time impecunious, he found it not quite so easy to obtain patients ready to find him funds for a third trip. They complained that the "German doctor" was too flighty—too apt, just when he was understanding their constitutions, to disappear; while his rivals, of whom the number was daily increasing, were always prepared to prescribe without an ulterior thought of the lands that lay beyond the Vaal and the Zambesi.

However, by March, 1875, Dr. Holub was off on a third expedition, which lasted twenty-one months and took him into all the Bechuana tribes, or "kingdoms," as he calls them, and into the Marotse (or Barotse) country north of the Zambesi.

After this he went home, the conveyance of his huge accumulation of specimens taxing to tension-point the ever-slender resources of the enthusiastic traveller.* Hitherto, he had not explored any very novel territory, though his last journey had added very considerably to our minute acquaintance with the geography of a country which was soon to become a very well-known part of Africa.

Yet the energy with which he had endeavoured to ransack a wide region with the smallest of means marked him out for better things. Accordingly by 1884 he was again on his way, accompanied by his wife and

* Holub : "Seven Years in South Africa," 2 Vols. (1881); "Colonisationa Afrikas"; "Das Ma-Rutse-Ma-Bunda Reich"; Pelzeln and Holub: "Supplemente zur Ornithologie Süd-Afrikas"; Holub and Neumeyer: "Beiträge zur Erkenntniss der Kreideformation im Gebiete der Flüsse Zwartkop und Zondaug," and other papers. See also *Proceedings of the Royal Geographical Society*, 1880, pp. 166, 261.

provided with what he considered ample funds for a journey from Cape Town to Cairo. Unfortunately, however, like so many travellers who have been successful on small expeditions, Dr. Holub failed to do anything commensurate with the scale on which his new one was planned. This, however, was not due to any remissness of energy on his part or on the part of his courageous wife. After being delayed some months at Pandamatenka (p. 204), he passed beyond the Zambesi on the 10th of June, 1886, and began his journey in the Batoka (Batonga) country,

DR. EMIL HOLUB.
(*From a Photograph by J. Mulač, Prague.*)

penetrating in a northerly direction with a slight bearing to the east—crossing Selous' route of 1877–78 (p. 216) for a distance of 305 miles. All this region is described as covered with small trees, among which the tsetse fly abounds. The Luengue (Livingstone's Loangwa) tributary of the Zambesi he found flowed from the north-west, and not from the north, as its discoverer had inferred from native information; while he did not find the valley of the Zambesi bordered on both sides of its middle course by hilly country. Dr. Holub, on the contrary, saw on the north side of the river a vast extent of low-lying, marsh-covered land, where even in the coolest season the traveller is apt to contract intermittent fever. To the N.N.E. of the Batoka "Bashukulompo." This section of Africa is watered by the Loangwa, and is more elevated than that of the Batoka. The people inhabit-

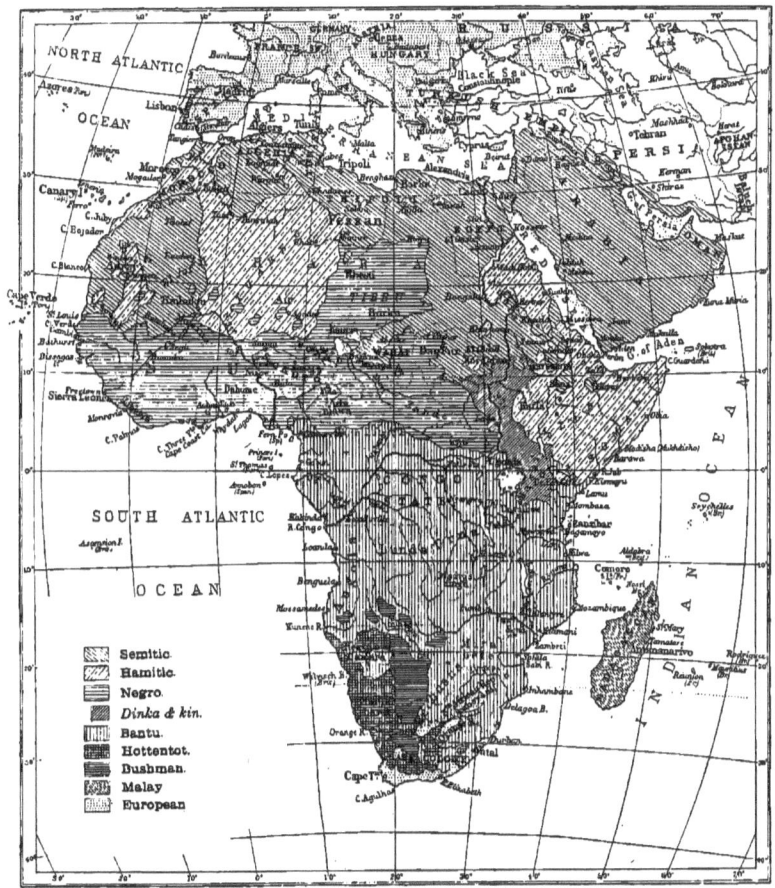

MAP SHOWING DISTRIBUTION OF LANGUAGES IN AFRICA. (By E. G. Ravenstein.)

country the Bohemian traveller explored the Mashukulumbwe territory—a region hitherto so unknown that on Livingstone's maps it is indicated from hearsay as the home of the ing it formerly dwelt in the lake country, but for the last two centuries they have been established on the northern affluents of the Zambesi. They are described as a fine race, with aquiline noses. The men twist their hair into a kind of chignon and are sparsely clad. The women wear trousers made of tanned hide, and shave their heads, and, from a widespread habit—which is shared by the men also—of knocking out their front teeth, have a sinister physiognomy not justified by their natural paucity of good looks.

Yet of all the features in Mashukulumbwe life the one that has proved most fatal to the happiness of these people is their possession of vast herds of cattle. In this kind of wealth they are probably richer than any South African tribe, every hut possessing on an average one hundred oxen. Otherwise they had little to recommend them from the explorer's point of view. Indeed, they wished to have nothing to do with him or any other white man, all they had heard of that class of people not being favourable. Accordingly, partly by threats and partly by cunning, they forced Dr. and Mrs. Holub to leave their country, though it was not until the explorer's camp had been attacked and pillaged, Oswald Zoldner, one of the party, killed, and the rest obliged to flee across swamps and rivers, more dead than alive, that they finally abandoned the hope of examining the Mashukulumbwe country more completely. This tribe has not redeemed their reputation, for two years later they raided Mr. Selous' camp. Even the Batongas, so civil when Mr. Selous first visited them, having become more familiar with and less afraid of white men, were no longer respectful to them. They behaved very badly to Father Teroede, who tried to establish a mission among them, and in 1888 murdered David Thomas, who founded a trading post on an island in the Zambesi. Still more recently a Portuguese party met the same fate.*

GROUP OF MASHUKULUMBWE.
(*From a Photograph taken for the Paris Society for Evangelical Missions.*)

* Selous: "Travel and Adventure in South-East Africa" (1893). p. 297.

When finally the Zambesi river was reached and succour obtained, Holub's expedition was so completely wrecked that any hope of continuing it had to be abandoned. With the exception of the explorer's note-books, everything was lost, and months of rest were found necessary to enable the plucky Bohemian and his wife to recover from their fatigues and suffering before trying to return to Cape Town. The crowning misfortune of the expedition happened on the 2nd of August, 1886. But long before Dr. Holub reached the territory of the Central Zambesi, which he named Albert Land, the party had met with a succession of unlooked-for mishaps. New men and a new policy no longer made his path so easy as on his former journeys, while to transport the baggage of a following which, besides natives, included six men of the Austrian Ambulance Corps, was a slower business than in the days when Holub travelled lightly equipped by choice and by necessity. Hence, almost from the time of his leaving Colesberg, then the terminal station of the South African railroad, his narrative is filled with tales of misfortune. In the Matabele country a fresh disaster befell the caravan, owing to the oxen eating a poisonous narcotic plant, the only antidote to which is tannin; and the malarial fevers of the deadly Barotse land and country in the vicinity of the Victoria Falls and Leshoma Valley (pp. 5, 6) cost the lives of two of Dr. Holub's companions. The tsetse fly could not always be avoided even by the precaution of travelling by night; and, unlike most other travellers who, coming from the east, brought their own porters with them, the Bohemians could not persuade any of the tribesmen through whom they passed to carry their burdens for any length of time; so that their route had necessarily to be a very zigzag one, as the pleasure of the different tribal chiefs and their people dictated.*

Apart, however, from the natural history and geographical notes made, and the information brought back regarding the various tribes of Kaffir-Zulu stock known as Ma- (or Ba-) toka, Mashapea, Ma- (or Ba-) rotse, Mabonda, Makalaka, Mankoga, and Mashuka, the news which he had to tell in the more southern country of the Mashukulumbwe and their great herds of cattle led to a curious and by no means fortunate result for these unfortunate people. For, in addition to being raided by the Barotse and neighbouring tribes, the tidings now reached the ears of Lo-Bengula, King of the Matabele. This chief, like his father, had become the terror of that part of Africa. He was the head of a nation of ferocious soldiers, so eager for bloodshed and plunder that it was only when he encouraged his people's warlike propensities he could keep control over them. Every tribe in their vicinity had been reduced to servitude by them. The poor craven Makalakas and Mashonas of Mashonaland had for years trembled at the sight of a Matabele "impi," or war party; while the industrious people of Khama (Vol. II., p. 177), that model chief, hid themselves in the swamps, where alone they were safe from the Matabele, eager to wash their spears in alien blood. Born and bred on the healthy uplands of South Africa, they fell victims to malaria, sunstroke, thirst, and hunger in the lowlands. So much was this the case that, in the raids in question, hundreds of the unseasoned warriors died. Thanks, however, to the protection of the British Government, Lo-Bengula found Bamangwato no longer the ready prey it was wont to be; and when the promoters of the British South Africa Company proposed to acquire the power of exploiting Mashonaland, "King Lo" would most likely have raised more obstacles than he did, had it not been, so Dr. Holub claims, that the latest white man's expedition had revealed

* Holub: "Von Capstadt in das Land der Ma-Schukulumbe. Reisen im südlichen Afrika in den Jahren 1883-87," 2 Vols. (1890); *Proceedings of the Royal Geographical Society*, 1888, p. 647, 1891, p. 373; and Kafka:

"Illustrierter Führer durch die Südafrikanische Austellung des Afrikareisen den Dr. Emil Holub" (Prague, 1892), a description of his African collection, with some notes on which the writer has been favoured by Dr. Holub.

to him another land swarming with cattle—the wealth of a South African tribe—which he might harass to his heart's content. Always suspicious of the whites, the king had become still more chary of trusting them since the British took possession of Bechuanaland and the Transvaal fixed its boundary between him and the native states. For, Dr. Holub tells a correspondent, the latter of these measures stopped his raids towards the south, and the former towards the west. "At a later period, when the Chartered South Africa Company took energetic action in the field of local politics, many persons who knew the king thought he would not submit to a pacific settlement. By giving in on this occasion, however, he proved himself to be a clever politician. The news which I brought south on returning from my second trip to the interior, as to the great wealth in cattle of the Mashukulumbwe tribes, reached the king's ears, and he directed his next expedition against this people, crossing the Zambesi for the purpose. That raid was a success, and Lo-Bengula, having thus discovered fresh woods and pastures new, in connection with which he considered the British Company no obstacle, showed a disposition to meet the overtures of the latter. In addition to this, his fears of the Dutch constituted a further inducement to come to an understanding with the British. It was an open secret that for years the Boers had been making preparations for trekking towards the north and north-east. Their most experienced men had, in the course of their hunting expeditions, visited the Matabele and Mashona countries and considered them suitable for settlement. Lo-Bengula, knowing the courage of the Boers in their fights with wild beasts and, further, that they were the best marksmen in South Africa, decided (against the noisy opposition of the young soldiers in his army) that the best policy was to come to an understanding with the Company."

Accordingly, in an indirect way, the Bohemian explorer's unfortunate expedition helped the South Africa Company to give Mashonaland to the British, and it is quite possible—the end is not yet—to involve the new lords of Mashonaland in more than one of those native wars which have marked the progress of colonisation in the neighbouring region.

Dr. Holub was essentially a "scientific traveller." Unlike most of the earlier explorers, when Africa was so unknown that merely to trace a track in it was merit enough, he had the ambition to bring back something more than a sketch-map, which, at best, is simply the means of localising facts about plants and animals, rocks and men, and climate. And it is to the credit of the Germans that, coming to Africa when, if we except Barth's

ROUTE MAP OF HOLUB'S JOURNEYS.

expedition (and that was actually an English one), opportunities for great discoveries were over, they inaugurated that more exact kind of exploration which is now demanded of the present traveller. But Holub was also a hunter, though one who, like most of the latter-day hunters of South Africa, graduated insensibly into the geographer and naturalist, since the disappearance of the great game no longer tempts to spend time in slaughtering it.

South Africa had, indeed, by this time become no longer the unhappy hunting-ground it had been so long. Sportsmen, if they wished to do great things, or to see a virgin country, had now to go farther afield.

Among these were the brothers **The brothers James.** F. L. and W. D. James (pp. 229, 230), two Englishmen who in a quiet way connected their names with a section of Africa. After a sporting trip in the Soudan *

* F. L. James: "Wild Tribes of the Soudan. An Account of Travel and Sport chiefly in the Basé Country, etc." (1883).

between Massowah and the Akbarah, during 1881 and two subsequent years, they succeeded, in company with Messrs. Aylmer, Lort-Phillips, and Thrupp, in penetrating part of the Somali country in the north-east angle of Africa. Their original intention had been to cross from Berbera to Mogadoxo. But the hostile disposition and uncertain temper

TRAVELLER'S FLOTILLA ON THE ZAMBESI (AT SESHEKE).
(*From a Photograph taken for the Paris Society for Evangelical Missions.*)

of the Somali tribes compelled the journey to terminate at the Leopard, or Shebelyi, River, the travellers being quite content that they escaped so well. Much of the area traversed had been previously unmapped and unexplored. But the great feat of the expedition, apart from its geographical features, was in taking a caravan of a hundred people and over a hundred camels across a waterless waste to the comparatively fertile region on the Leopard River. For thirteen days the camels travelled without a drink, and only once, at the end of the ninth day, was a little dirty fluid like liquid mud found to replenish the exhausted water-bags.

None of their predecessors had fared much

better in this vast territory, about the size of Spain. At various times vessels stranded on the Somali coast had been seized and their crews murdered or enslaved. The earlier explorers, like Cruttenden in 1848, did not aim at reaching farther than the mountain range some sixty miles from the coast, Burton (Vol. II., p. 51) being, perhaps, the first who penetrated farther. Hildebrant, Menges, Revoil, Sacconi, Panagiotos (who was killed), Haggenmacher, and Porro, who, with all his party, was murdered in 1885, are among the best-known of Messrs. James's predecessors. To be killed seemed, indeed, to be the fate of nearly every man who had hitherto ventured into Somaliland.* The young Englishmen escaped this fate, though one of them (Mr. Frank Linsly James) was soon to end his career on the continent of which he had essayed so successfully to be an explorer. A wealthy yachtsman, he had visited nearly every latitude from Nova Zemlaia to South America, and in 1890 was on the west coast of Africa, where, encountering a wounded elephant at Benito, about a hundred miles north of the Gaboon

WILLIAM D. JAMES.
(From a Photograph by J. Edwards, Hyde Park Corner, W.)

* F. L. James : "The Unknown Horn of Africa. An Exploration from Berbera to the Leopard River" (1883); and "A Journey through the Somali Country to the Webbe Shebeyli" (*Proceedings of the R. G. S.*, 1885, p. 625).

River, he was killed by the infuriated beast. A similar doom befell Mr. Guy Dawnay, another English sportsman, who in 1889 perished in East Africa from the attack of an angry buffalo, and Captain Faulkner, who, after accompanying Mr. Young on his Livingstone search expedition (Vol. II., p. 255), was killed by some natives of the Shiré on his return from a private hunting expedition in that country.

England had at one time almost a monopoly of travellers of this type—of men not scientific explorers by profession, or in any way compelled to live an unluxurious life. But by this time other nations, fired by the tales of the English explorers, began to yearn for a share of their glory. And so the names of Count Teleki (p. 234), and Lieutenant Ludwig von Höhnel, Teleki and von Höhnel. the one a Hungarian, and the other an Austrian naval officer, deserve a brief notice, even in chapters now beginning to be crowded with the names of travellers who

DATOKA TYPE.
(*From a Photograph taken for the Paris Society for Evangelical Missions.*)

have come too late to obtain the recognition they would have obtained a few years earlier.

Their expedition was essentially a sporting one; but sporting expeditions in 1887 were going much farther afield than South Africa; and, as the hunters had to pursue their prey into regions less known to the geographer, they became explorers in spite of themselves.

This was, indeed, the fortunate lot, and the wise choice also, of the two Austro-Hungarian travellers, whose work is less known in England than it deserves. The first attempt to ascend Mount Kenia, one of the snowy peaks of Central Africa, was not the least interesting portion of their labours. The altitude at which they stopped was 15,350

F. L. JAMES.
(*From a Photograph by J. Edwards, Hyde Park Corner, W.*)

feet, or about 3,000 feet below the summit, though later observations render the exact height they reached doubtful. As seen from the west, the mountain looks like a truncated pyramid surmounted by two rocky pinnacles, apparently the ruin of an ancient crater. In reality, the "spitze" is the central cone of a much-denuded old volcano of which the crater has long since disappeared.* Up to 8,500 feet the mountain slopes are densely wooded. Then follows a region of bamboo thickets, after which, at 10,500 feet, begins a region of mosses, within which grows the curious tree-ragwort (*Senecio*

* Gregory, *Geographical Journal*, Vol. II. (1893), p. 327.

Johnstoni). Beyond 15,000 feet is a zone of perpetual snow lying in patches. Hence the Masai name of the mountain—Doinyo Egere—"the dabbled peak." Up to the point reached by the climbers on the western side the slope is so gentle and gradual that a carriage-road could be easily constructed, and, no doubt, this will actually be done in the coming time, when Kenia competes with Kilimanjaro as an East African sanatorium; but the southern slope is less easy of ascent.

More important geographically was, however, the Austro-Hungarian officers' discovery of a great lake some three hundred miles to the north-east of Victoria Nyanza. This sheet had been rumoured for some years before under the name of Samburu. But it was now re-named Lake Rudolf, after the late Crown Prince of Austria. It is about 162 miles long, but not more than twenty in width. A second smaller lake to the north-east— Lake Stefanie—was found, like so many of the sheets subsequently proved to exist in this country, to be salt, owing to the absence of any outlet, the evaporation being equal to the amount of water received from their feeders. The land in the vicinity of these new lakes is bare and arid, and their borders and the banks of the river are scantily peopled by Gallas, who live by fishing.†

One expedition leads to another. One sportsman is fired by the exploits of a predecessor to try to imitate, if not excel, him; and wherever a traveller succeeds or, still more, fails, it is certain that before long a second will be ready to try what fortune has in store for him. Members of other nations besides the British were growing eager to offer themselves as sacrifices to the Moloch of African exploration. Hitherto the United States had taken little if any part in this perilous work. For, though Mr. Stanley was an American citizen during the entire period over which his travels extended,

† Von Höhnel : "Bergprofil Sammlung während Graf S. Teleki's Expedition, 1887-88" (1890) ; "Discovery of Lakes Rudolf and Stefanie" (Trans., 1894) ; and *Proceedings of the R.G.S.*, 1889, p. 408 : 1892, p. 532.

he was a native Welshman, and for the most part in the employment of Englishmen. A true son of the great Republic was, however, now to step into the vacant place. This was Mr. William Astor Chanler. One of the members of a wealthy family—as his "middle name" might indicate—he was still a Harvard undergraduate when he became "lord of himself, that heritage of woe." And a heritage of woe it seemed to the friends of Mr. Chanler when that affluent youth announced his intention of spending his twenty-first year on a hunting expedition to East Africa, in the land of that unamiable people the Masai. With one white man, his servant, George Galvin, and 180 natives, this programme was duly carried out in 1889, Kilimanjaro and the neighbouring regions being visited and explored. The experience thus gained, far from discouraging the young American, actually so whetted his appetite for pleasures more heroic than those of his years, that he returned to Europe with the fixed intention of devoting the next eighteen months in preparing for a much more serious expedition than that which he completed as an apprenticeship to African travel. He also persuaded Lieutenant von Höhnel to accompany him, so that some scientific results might be secured. His plan was first to reach Mount Kenia, and push thence to the southern extremity of Lake Rudolf. After this sheet had been thoroughly explored, the expedition would be directed towards Lake Stefanie, and through the six hundred miles of unknown country between these lakes and the Juba river. Thence, if so fortunate as to escape the ferocious tribesmen of this region, Mr. Chanler and his companions proposed to follow it to the sea, and along the shore to Lamu—a march in all of some three thousand miles, which it was estimated would take at least two years to accomplish. But it was not without imminent perils. It was in that portion of it which stretches from Mount Kenia to Lake Rudolf that Count Teleki lost a third of his caravan from thirst and disease, while the man who attempts to traverse the land of the Gallas and Somalis must remember that many tried it before him, and sometimes paid for the attempt with their lives (p. 229). Ruspoli, Revoil, Ferrandi, James, Bricchetti-Robecchi, Bottego, and others have essayed the exploration of Somaliland with varied success, and Von der Decken perished among the pioneers of exploration in this region. Chanler, however, entered it with a larger and more complete following than was at the command of any of his predecessors. He had, moreover, the unpurchasable advantages of youth, enthusiasm, the perfect health which does not always accompany five-and-twenty summers, and the disinterested desire to do what might very well have been left alone. His outfit was minutely complete, including even a search-light to show the position of the savages who attack by night, a wizard to impress them with "unequalled feats of legerdemain," and a dozen pairs of flesh-coloured gloves "to pull carelessly off his hands while conversing with African kings, and so impress them with the idea that he is skinning himself alive."* But such things were perhaps not calculated to impress African royalty in these days of unsophistication. Mr. Chanler, however, did not meet with all the good fortune he merited. Leaving, in September, 1892, M'Konumbi, on the coast of Witu, with a caravan numbering 185 men, 15 camels, 73 donkeys, 2 horses, 10 oxen, and 10 goats, Hameya, near Balarti, a station of the Imperial British East Africa Company, was reached more than two months later; but not before twenty men and five camels had succumbed on the way. The caravan marched in a leisurely way along the left bank of the Tana to Subaki, where it crossed to the opposite side. A small flotilla of twelve canoes carried some of the loads and food, though the Tana route was found so good that an ordinary trading party might accomplish the entire distance in the course of five weeks.

* Davis, "An American in Africa" (*Harper's Magazine*, March, 1893, where a portrait will be found).

From Engatana onwards provisions are plentiful, and there is no difficulty in obtaining water, if native guides are employed to point out the wells. Former visitors had left so bad an impression behind them that the Wapokomo, natives of the country, required considerable management before they were persuaded to establish friendly relations with the Europeans. The Somalis were less tractable, and a war party that had been ravaging the neighbourhood had to be driven off; but the Gallas of Korokoro were found to be very weak from the repeated attacks on the part of the Wakamba. Geographically, the journey was more fruitful in negative than in positive discoveries. Like Captain Dundas,* the brothers Denhardt, and various officers of the Imperial East Africa Company, who had previously surveyed the Tana river in a rough way, a careful search failed to find the "Galla" and "Friedrich Franz Mountains" of Dr. Peters,† who had travelled by much the same route. This is not to be wondered at, since neither this traveller nor his companion, Mr. Tiedemann, possessed any qualifications for adding to our cartographical knowledge, the Kaiser Wilhelm II. Mountains, with the Hohenzollern Peak, of which Dr. Peters presents so formidable a picture, turning out to be "low hills surmounted by gneiss tors." Otherwise their observations tallied with those of Captain Dundas, with the serious exception that Lieutenant von Höhnel considers the whole of the Tana should be put from eighteen to twenty miles farther to the west.

GROUP OF WAKWAFI.
(From a Photograph by Mr. Ernest Gedge, by permission of the Imperial British East Africa Company.)

* Gedge : "A Recent Exploration under Captain F. G. Dundas, R.N., up the River Tana to Mount Kenia " (with map), *Proceedings of the Royal Geographical Society*, 1892, p. 517. Mr. Ravenstein adds a summary of the history of its exploration. See also *Ibid.*, 1890, p. 120.

† "New Light on Dark Africa" (1891), p. 161.

Leaving their head-quarters at Hameya, the party made an expedition to trace to its source the Mackenzie river, one of the many Tana tributaries, and to investigate the reputed Lorian Lake. The Mackenzie was found to be a very shallow stream, swarming with game on its upper waters. The Guaso Nyiri (or Ururi), another stream, rushes over a mass of lava in its course in two currents, which form the "Chanler Falls," about fifty feet in height—its course below this spot being for two miles between sheer walls of black volcanic rock, poured out in comparatively recent times by some of the many extinct and dormant craters in this region. Here it is about eighty yards wide, but in flowing near the volcanic Marisi el Lugwa Zambo plateau, five hundred feet in height, rich alluvial soil borders each side of it, the river, however, dwindling as it passes across this plain until when last seen it was barely thirty feet wide and one to two feet deep.

The "Lorian Lake," one of the many discoveries or legends hoarded by traders and travellers of late years, is simply an extensive swamp filled with high reeds, though likely enough flooded during the rainy season. North of it the country is described as an undulating scrub-covered desert, so deserted that from Hameya to Lorian, only one native was seen, except on the Jombini Range. But during the wet season, when pasturage is more plentiful, the Marisi Plateau and its vicinity are probably visited by the Rendilé tribes, who have trading relations with the Jombini Range dwellers. Folds that had contained camels and goats—animals said to be plentiful on the range mentioned—and camps that had been inhabited by Wandrobbo were also noticed. The Jombini Range is, indeed, very fertile and thickly populated by Wamsara on its western slopes, while the Waembi keep to the eastern portion of the range, and pay more attention to agriculture than do their more warlike neighbours. They seem an offshoot of the Kikiyu race, but use many Masai and Mkambu words, and have adopted numerous Wakamba and Wakwari settled among them. The Waembi

STREET IN LAMU, EAST AFRICA.
(*From a Photograph taken for the Imperial British East Africa Company.*)

grow sweet potatoes, yams, cassava, beans, sugar-cane, and two kinds of millet; but they are fast destroying the forest with which the range was evidently formerly covered.*
In February, 1894, the remnants of Mr. Chanler's party returned to Mombasa from Daicho,

* *The Geographical Journal*, 1893 (Vol. I.), pp. 269, 533; (Vol. II.), pp. 367, 534.

north-east of Mount Kenia, after a visit to the little-known Rendilé country. Mishaps had befallen the expedition. The climate of Hameya proved fatal to all the camels, thirty-three of the donkeys, and several of the cattle and goats, so that it was with difficulty that the beautiful and healthy Jombini Range could be reached before the rainy season. Even then this could only be accomplished by throwing away much of the baggage, and loading the rest on the forty donkeys which had escaped the tetanus-like attacks of which the others perished. The loss of donkeys and camels

COUNT SAMUEL TELEKI (VON SZEK).
(From a Photograph by T. Heyman, Cairo.)

was not the only trouble of the expedition, for most of the porters had deserted, and Von Höhnel, wounded by a rhinoceros, was forced to return home invalided.

It will have been noticed with what steadiness the days of the hunter have been passing away. We find eager Nimrods hieing them to Africa and leaving it with more geographical notes than heads and hides and horns, simply because, finding their old haunts or the haunts of their predecessors exhausted, they had to seek new and necessarily more remote regions. In this way the Zambesi was reached, and then the lands beyond it, until the sportsman emulous of doing anything worthy of note broke ground on the east coast. But East

Captain Swayne: the last of the hunters.

Africa is not, and never was, so swarming with game as South Africa, and by-and-by it will be a forbidden region to the man ambitious of "making a bag," since the lords of that wide-stretching land have already passed ordinances touching the slaughtering of the great beasts, and will effectually prevent such massacres as go on, and have gone on, farther south. In the remote wilds, by Lake Albert Edward (p. 69), Emin Pasha and Lugard saw many elephants and rhinoceroses, though, so far as the elephants are concerned, this must be about the last refuge which they have found, and we have seen that at the head waters of some of the Tana tributaries (p. 233) the hunter might even yet realise the fearful journeys of the men of thirty, forty, or, still better, of fifty years ago.

However, as late as 1886, Sir John Willoughby and Sir Robert Harvey found all the sport they desired near Kilimanjaro and in the country between that mountain and Mombasa. The game killed was mainly elephants and rhinoceroses, though lions, leopards, Burchell's zebra, buffalo, eland, koodoo, the gazelles named after Grant (p. 180), Thomson, and Waller, and most of the antelopes with which we have become familiar in South Africa, occurred more or less frequently.* During the dry season the elephants live on Kilimanjaro, up to a height of 9,000 feet, but during the rainy months they descend to the lowlands, where they are killed by the natives with poisoned arrows. But no kind of game is as plentiful in that country as it was, and in places still is in South Africa. Nor can we credit the sportsmen who burst into this, until a few years ago, entirely unexplored region with adding greatly to the geography of the country, though their notes on the game, when they made any, or put them at the disposal of the world, are worthy of all praise. In the evolution of the development of Africa, the hunting expedition just

* Willoughby: "East Africa and its Big Game" (1889); Faulkner: "Elephant Haunts, etc." (1868); Lugard: "The Rise of Our East African Empire" (1893), Vol. I., pp. 492–544.

mentioned was nevertheless of importance to the opening-up of the continent. For Sir John Willoughby, charmed with the resources and the life of the land of which he had caught a few months' glimpse, returned to the east coast, and has ever since taken a prominent part in subduing Mashonaland for the purposes of British industry.

Even the latest hunting expedition which was planned for a campaign near Lake Rudolf has not altogether been energy thrown away. It broke up almost before it left the coast, from causes which we need not discuss. But one, at least, of its members made his way to Uganda, and has since helped to bit the refractory sectaries of that empire until they are prepared to recognise the inevitable, while Dr. J. W. Gregory, of the British Museum, who remained in the country, visited, in 1893, Lakes Baringo, Hannington, and others in the same great valley of subsidence, and returned by way of Likipia and Kenia, the geology of which he examined. The Aberdare Mountains turn out not to be a double range separated by the Ururi Valley, but a volcanic mass piled up near the edge of the Likipia escarpment. Dr. Gregory climbed Kenia three thousand feet higher than did von Höhnel in 1887. The latter's description he did not find quite accurate, nor was the topography of the mountain laid down with much nicety. Gregory also explored the glaciers and head waters of the Tana and the water-shed between the Tana and Athi rivers. But it is clear that the modern sportsman must seek game farther afield. The Mahdists have closed the Soudan, so that a journey up the Nile, or across country from Abyssinia —such as Bruce and Baker and the Jameses among others made—is no longer possible. But the land of Prester John is getting better opened, thanks to the Italian settlements on the coast; and since part of Somaliland is now recognised as British, and the East Africa Company is keeping the marches on the south, this once closed country is becoming accessible to sportsmen. The latest of that class of explorers in the Somali country,

perhaps one should say the pioneer sportsman, was Captain H. G. C. Swayne, R.E., who, early in 1893, went to Harar and Imé from Bulhar without mishap. Since Burton's day Harar has undergone several changes. More travellers than one have reached it,* and, after having been taken by the Egyptians in 1875, and again receded to its native Emir, this remote town, once the capital of an independent state, is governed by an Abyssinian Ras, or General. The population is, however, of the usual mixed character. Of the 37,000 people—the great majority women —about one-half are Harari, who closely resemble the Abyssinians, though they have imitated the Arabs in dress and manner. The rest are made up of Abyssinians, Somali, and Gallas, in whose country the town is situated. A large portion of its former prosperity has vanished, Tadjura and Berbera, about two hundred miles distant, having absorbed much of its trade in coffee, beads, cattle, and the dyestuff called "wars"; while the slave trade, which at no very distant date flourished exceedingly, has now, owing to the prejudice of the European nations who are so rapidly garrisoning the borders of this secluded city, either been discontinued or is pursued with great secrecy. At present the rulers of Harar are very well disposed to Great Britain, and in the city Captain Swayne found Count Salimbeni, the representative of Italy, who has established a protectorate over most of Somaliland—and several Europeans engaged in business—a state of matters very different from the day when Burton had to visit the place in disguise and remain in extreme retirement during his residence. Returning to Jig-Jiga, about halfway to the coast, Captain Swayne went on a shooting expedition to the Jerer Valley, and obtained a lioness, several rhinoceroses, and a couple of panthers as the reward of his labours, and near Segag, one of the camps of Captain Baudi, an Italian officer, who had gone to Imé three years before, a bull elephant was shot.

After passing through the Malingur tribe,

* Paulitschke: "Harar" (1888).

communication was opened up with some difficulty with that of Rer Amaden. Here Jama Doria, a minstrel or troubadour well known through all of Somaliland, came to the sportsman's aid, lending ponies and supplying him guides to go to Imé, 150 miles distant, while Captain Swayne's own caravan remained at Dambas Werer in charge of the friendly bard. At Imé, the Adone chief acted

NIAM-NIAM GIRL.
(From a Photograph by R. Buchta.)

as host, and balanka or waterbuck furnished entertainment to the sportsman's rifle. The Adone people are black, and, like everybody in this quarter except the Malingur Agaden, call themselves British subjects. Of the Abyssinians they seem to be very much afraid, all of them deserting their huts on the alarm spreading that Captain Swayne's little cavalcade was the advance guard of an Abyssinian force. The Malingurs live in the Tug Fafan Valley, and being in the great eastward path of invasion, were compelled to yield to King Menelek's troops; but the Rer Amaden were not so easily conquered, having from time to time inflicted great loss on the Abyssinians. The remains of a bivouac were pointed out where a large force of these people had been defeated only two or three years before.

Forests, consisting chiefly of tall casuarinas and evergreens, fringed both sides of the Webbe at Imé, and waterbucks were plentiful; but recent tribal wars had almost depopulated the country between Dambas Werer and Imé. Buffaloes and giraffes were heard of at the Gure Gallas; but the officer's leave approaching a close, he had to return for the time being to Aden, not, however, before being so unfortunate as to have material evidence of the presence of lions in the country. For at Durhi one of his men was carried off by a man-eating brute while riding alone in the jungle. Another was shot near Segag, and a large number of zebras of the species described in 1882 as $Equus\ grevyi$, though it is doubtful whether the finer and more numerous stripes characteristic of it are sufficient to separate it from the common $E.\ zebra$ found from one end of Africa to the other. They are, however, so numerous in this part of Somaliland that they form the favourite food of the Rer Amaden tribe. Captain Swayne's followers were rather unfortunate on this trip. Besides the lion's victim, one man had his leg broken by the fall of a camel; another, quarrelling with an Abyssinian, received the customary rejoinder of a spear-thrust; while a third was badly scratched by a panther which the party were following at night. Eight camels out of thirty were lost from the animals being unequal to the rapid marching, though two might have died from the bites of the "balanad" fly of Ogaden, or from that of the "dug," another poisonous insect, not, however, so deadly as the other. The return trip was by Milmil and the Habr Gerhajis country; but, getting his leave extended, Captain Swayne returned to survey the Gure Gallas country beyond Imé, though, "of course," the officer of Engineers tells us, his "main reason for those journeys is to open up new shooting grounds." *

In this meritorious extension of the work of the scientific branch of the Army there is, we venture to think, not much success to be looked for. There are now few wide areas of Africa of which the general characteristics are not known, and almost none of them swarm with game as South Africa swarmed with it in the palmy days with which the

* *The Geographical Journal*, 1893 (Vol. II.), p. 252, and 259 (map showing Captain Swayne's and Luigi Bricchetti-Robecchi's routes in the Somali country).

preceding chapters are concerned. The era of the hunter is over, and that of the great explorer is almost equally at an end. Hunting parties will still be organised to shoot whatever is to be shot in the regions off which,

NIAM-NIAM WIZARD.
(*From a Photograph by R. Buchta.*)

to use a homely metaphor, the cream has long ago been skimmed, and even " bags made " which may amaze a generation ignorant of the fortunes that befell the fathers of African sport. Indeed, at the moment of writing, the columns of the newspapers which concern themselves with the goings and comings of fashionable society intimate that a young nobleman has returned from a two and a-half years' hunting trip to the Zambesi country, where he had a fair share of the sport still to be had in no niggard amount in the less frequented parts of that region. And, no doubt, there will from time to time be similar adventures to record, in spite of the undeniable fact that the good days of the African sportsman are everywhere on the wane, and in some places gone never to return. Nor are the chances of the explorer as we have known him in the preceding volumes much

ROUTE MAP OF SCHWEINFURTH'S JOURNEY.

more promising. No great problems have remained for solution since Stanley's last journey, and it is difficult to indicate on the map any large stretch of country with the nature of which the geographer is still entirely unacquainted. There are, of course, plenty of huge spots crossed by rivers which continue to be indicated by a vague line of dots, and lakes out of number "laid down" in a manner equally unsatisfactory to the cartographer. To have explored these lacunae of the map would, at an earlier period in the history of African travel, have gained the adventurer much renown. But nowadays, so numerous are the travellers exploring different districts throughout the Dark Continent, the geographical journals can barely spare a few lines to the record of journeys which in extent and in results are not inferior to those of Mungo Park and the travellers who followed him. They have, moreover, now lost novelty. The accidents by flood and field which they have to relate are too familiar—almost too hackneyed—to command attention. As we approach nearer and nearer to our own times, the travellers, as a rule, demand less space. Their adventures are mainly of personal moment. Their results are what the student of current history is most interested in learning; while the excitement which imparted zest to the earlier expeditions is now, to a great extent, gone, since it is believed that, however much nominally new ground the caravan may traverse, the leader is quite likely to return without the story of any Gordian knot, or with the information that he found one only to untie it.

But if the world has fallen upon prosaic times, it is no longer content with the rough explorations of former days. So long as the traveller had a startling tale to tell, it was content to accept, although not altogether satisfied with, the crudity of his narrative. Now, however, it demands greater nicety in his descriptions, more accuracy in his maps, and a description of the races that will bear something like examination by ethnographers. Should the modern explorer make the blunders in botany, zoology, and geology which disfigure the volumes of the pioneers, even when these considered it necessary to touch upon such points at all, he would be apt to be pointed at by those who have inherited the traditions of Humboldt and of Barth. The latter was the first of the scientific travellers who penetrated Africa for any great distance, and Schweinfurth, his countryman, may claim to have been the second. In order to see the last of the hunters, we have somewhat anticipated events. We are now compelled to retrace our steps by a few years, so as to connect the eminent German savant whose name has just been mentioned with the new feature in African travel of which it is probable we shall not see the last for some centuries to come—namely, the time when a knowledge of geography more minute than that of old is demanded of those who wander in the wilds of Africa.

This traveller, who comes too late in the history with which we are concerned to find that space which, had the valley of the Nile been less known, would have been his right, may be regarded as the successor of Barth; for no traveller up to the time of his appearance—not even Roscher—had described the region over which he passed with the minuteness which that meritorious "erforscher" did. Dr. Schweinfurth was born at Riga on the 29th December, 1836, so that in being the son of German parents, though a subject of the Czar, he resembles Dr. Junker, who followed him as a traveller in the same region. During his studies at Heidelberg, Munich, and Berlin, he made botany a special study. He had been attracted to Africa by studying the plants collected in the Soudan by Baron von Barnim, who had travelled there with Dr. Hartmann in 1860, and fallen a victim to the climate, and it was as a botanist that in 1864 he made a journey up the Nile Valley and along the shores of the Red Sea as far as Abyssinia and on to Khartoum. But in 1868 he aimed at greater things, and, aided by a grant from the Humboldt Fund, again started for the Nile, with the intention of making his head-quarters at Khartoum, and thence, by accompanying the slave- and ivory-traders, of making his way into the remote parts of the river basin, and even beyond it to the westward. In those days, Jiafer Pasha was Governor-General of the Soudan. He was not, as even Egyptian Pashas go, regarded as a model ruler (Vol. II., p. 142); but the young naturalist had no reason to complain of him. For not only did he receive him with the utmost kindness, but by his letters

Georg August Schweinfurth

to the interior traders and the interest he was able to make with Ghattas (Vol. II., p. 146), the ivory-gatherer, sent the explorer most auspiciously on his way. From Khartoum to the mouth of the Sobat river was not a difficult voyage in 1869, especially when undertaken in the well-armed vessel of a merchant quite prepared for any contingency; and when at this port Mohammed Abu Sammat, the Nubian, begged the German traveller to consider himself his guest, "until he should

GEORG AUGUST SCHWEINFURTH.

have accompanied him to the remotest tribes," Dr. Schweinfurth was justified in considering his task half completed. Mohammed was a typical specimen of the Upper Nile merchant. Nominally engaged in buying ivory, he was in reality mainly a dealer in and a stealer of slaves. In pursuit of these branches of commerce he had virtually conquered regions large enough to form states in Europe.

Alternately fighting and bartering with the Shillooks, the boats of Schweinfurth's new friend reached the mouth of the Bahr-el-Ghazel, and landed on the Meshera, a group of islands inhabited by the Dinka. This deadly spot is the usual starting-point for caravans bound in the direction Mohammed's expedition intended to take, and here the naturalist had to wait for eighteen days, until Ghattas and his multitudinous horde of porters and other camp-followers arrived, to the number of five hundred. With these the march was begun, towards the end of March, from Ghattas' chief zereba to the country bordering the Dinka Dyor and Bongo territories. At this place, 1,545 feet above the sea, several months were passed, amid the utmost hospitality from all with whom he came in contact, until by the middle of November Mohammed's caravan again began to move. Crossing the Tondy, a tributary of the Bahr-el-Ghazel, and a host of minor rivers, December and January found him in the Mittoo country—a region of broad grassy plains, broken by huge stones of fantastic outline, and by thickets or single trees, with here and there an encampment of huts rising from a platform of clay "like paper cones on a flat table." These zerebas were often great villages (Vol. II., p. 144), full of cattle under Dinka servants, and everywhere presented so peaceful an appearance that it was difficult to realise that they were simply part of the great machinery of the ivory, which in almost every instance was synonymous with the slave, trade. In January next year a much more important journey was made into the Zandey, or Niam-Niam country (pp. 236, 237, 240, 241, etc.), then

NIAM-NIAM MUSICIAN AND WARRIORS.
(From a Photograph by R. Buchta.)

one of the chief hunting-grounds of the ivory-traders. The elephants that still swarmed were killed by the natives setting fire to the jungles in which they lived—the wretched animals huddling together and heaping grass over their bodies as a protection against the flames, until they fell suffocated by the dense smoke. Tall grass covered most of the region where trees did not clothe the soil, the villages of the natives occupying the open spaces which occurred at intervals. The Niam-Niam—a cannibal race the existence of whom had until then been known only by

NIAM-NIAM FARM: VISIT OF TRADERS.
(From a Photograph by R. Buchta.)

the reports of Piaggia, a roving Italian, who had passed a year amongst them,* and the Arab traders—are among the most savage of tribes. With the exception of a skin round their loins, they go entirely naked, a few stripes painted on their black skins serving in the way of decoration. From the Niam-Niam country that of the Monbuttoo—a race new to geographers—was next reached, and the acquaintance made of King Munza and his many wives. The capital of this monarch was some miles south of a river called the Welle, 800 feet broad, and deep in the driest season, which was found to flow to the west out of the area of the Nile basin. This was, perhaps, the most important geographical discovery of Schweinfurth's expedition, and for years afterwards formed one of the many problems in African hydrography. At first it was believed to be identical with Barth's Shari, which flows into Lake Tchad; but researches made by another German, many years later, proved that the surmise was altogether incorrect, the Congo being its destination. As a friend of M'bahly, or the Little One, the name by which Sammat was familiarly known to these people, Schweinfurth was speedily made at home with the Monbuttoo, though the dignity of King Munza did not permit him to meet the gaze of the white man until the latter had been sufficiently impressed with the magnificence of his King Munza of Monbuttoo. host. The latter was a portly being, whose person was profusely covered with copper rings, chains, and other gauds. His hair was done up in an enormous chignon, from the summit of which rose a huge copper crescent and a plumed hat made of reeds plaited into the shape of a cylinder, the whole ornamented with a profusion of red parrots' feathers. As in every African state function, the noise of horns and drums played a prominent part when Dr. Schweinfurth was first received by this self-important monarch,

* The only information left by Piaggia is what the Marquis O. Antinori collected from his verbal narratives, and published (as might be expected, with many blanks) in the *Bollettino della Soc. Geogr. Italiana*,1868, pp. 91-168.

and the rush to see the white man was so great that for a time it almost seemed as if he would be crushed by the ring of painted warriors. Munza was naturally quite as curious as his subjects; but *nil admirari* is in Africa, as in some quarters nearer home, regarded as the mark of a very superior person. Even the presents laid before him—objects which are seldom regarded with indifference—were merely glanced at and a few conventional questions asked of their donor. Emotion was evidently considered vulgar in the Monbuttoo court; for, whatever might have been the actual feelings of his Majesty, he did not permit himself to indulge in more than a furtive look. Professional jesters and singers then entertained the visitors, succeeded by a concert in which King Munza acted as conductor, his bâton being an instrument like a child's rattle, the whole winding up with a fervid oration by the king, which was understood to be a series of compliments to his guest, spiced, no doubt, with some to himself. Like all African chiefs, the wives of this potentate were many, and their greatest treat was to see their lord dance before them. Yet cannibals though the Monbuttoo, like the Niam-Niam, undoubtedly are, they excel in many arts. Their weapons of native iron, smelted in a rude though efficient furnace, are excellently forged. Their storehouses, filled with grain and other reserves of food, are capitally suited for the purpose to which they are put, and some of the wood-carvings executed by them are really artistic. The copper chains and other ornaments made by native smiths are also most ingeniously worked, and among specimens of their textile work Dr. Schweinfurth has high praise to bestow on their beautiful fabrics of woven grass.

It was among the Monbuttoo that the young traveller met for the first time with those Akka pigmies of whom so much has been heard in late years (p. 72), though he was not able to reach their country, described as about four days from Munza's capital. One of them, who had come on a visit to

Monbuttoo, was persuaded to accompany the traveller to Europe. Unfortunately, however, the little man died at Berber, so that it was not till some years afterwards that a specimen of this curious race of dwarfs made their existence familiar to the civilised world.

The breaking-up of Mohammed Abu Sammat's camp compelled Dr. Schweinfurth, very reluctantly, to return to the Nile, without visiting the head waters of the Benué, Shari, Ogowe, and Congo, near all four of which it was his firm conviction he had reached. As subsequent discoveries proved, this belief was not quite correct; but it is certain that he was only about 450 miles from the most northern point reached by Livingstone when he was necessitated by the lack of resources to leave to others the work he had so far accomplished with such unwonted completeness.[*]

To the last Jiafer Pasha was unwearied in his kindness; for when the traveller found to his dismay that all the stores he had left at Ghattas' zereba as a reserve had been destroyed by an accidental fire, the munificent governor replaced them by an ample supply despatched

[*] Schweinfurth: "The Heart of Africa: Three Years' Travels and Adventures in the Unexplored Regions of Central Africa from 1868 to 1871." 2 Vols. English Translation (1873); "Artes Africanæ" (1875), etc.

NIAM-NIAM TRIBESMAN.
(From a Photograph by R. Buchta.)

to Meshera. These were the last of Dr. Schweinfurth's great explorations in or on the borders of the Nile Valley. But they were not the only travels for scientific purposes which he lived to make in the region with which his name will always be honourably connected. Returning to Egypt in 1872, he founded, at the request of the Khedive Ismaïl, the Société Khédiviale de Géographie in Cairo, and was nominated its first President. In subsequent years he examined the natural history — the botany principally—of various districts bordering the Nile, and, as Director of the Egyptian Museums in Cairo, remained in that country until 1888, when he returned to Germany with the object of devoting the rest of his life to publishing the descriptions of the numerous collections he had made. It may be added that, in addition to many similar honours, Dr. Schweinfurth received in 1874 the Founder's Medal of the Royal Geographical Society "for his discovery of the Welle river, beyond the south-western limits of the Nile basin." This was his chief contribution to African hydrography, though much of the country visited by him, and especially Dar Fertît, was, practically, ground quite fresh to the geographer, though not to the slave- and ivory-traders.

THE GERMAN CONSULATE AT KHARTOUM DURING THE EGYPTIAN OCCUPATION OF THE SOUDAN.
(From a Photograph by R. Buchta.)

CHAPTER XI.

THE SCIENTIFIC EXPLORERS: BEYS AND PASHAS: NACHTIGAL AND JUNKER.

What Egypt has done for the Exploration of the Nile Valley—Nachtigal—His History, and how he reached the Nile from Tripoli—Murzuk—A Raid into the Tibesti Mountains—A Journey to Bornu—Lake Tchad—Borgou—Baghirmi and its History—Songhai and the Slave Trade—Villages in Trees—Fittri—Waday and its History—Excursion to Mangari and the Bahr-el-Salamat—Darfur and the Way Thither—History of Darfur—An Old Resident in Kobbeh—Browne's Travels a Century Ago—From Fasher to Khartoum—A Narrow Escape—Return to Europe—The Sheik Mohammed el Tounsy—Junker—His History—First Expedition up the Nile to Khartoum—To Sobat—Makaraka and Mundoo Countries—Bahr-el-Ghazel—A Second Expedition results in a Seven Years' Stay—Dem Suleiman—The Niam-Niam—Pagan Friends and Moslem Foes—Monbuttoo—The Wello and its Tributaries—The A-Barmbos Inimicable—Mambanga and Captain Casati—Bomokandi—Peoples—Held Hostage by a Monbuttoo Chief—Murder of King Munza by Arabs—The Settlement of the Welle—Makua—Shari—Moubangi Question—Echoes of the Mahdi—Reaches Emin—Retreats to Uganda through Unyoro—To Msalala with the Missionaries, and to Bagamoyo with Tippoo Tib—The Death of Junker.

AT the time Schweinfurth was exploring the Nile Valley and the country beyond it, Baker was engaged on his second expedition in the same basin, but in another direction (Vol. II., pp. 147-153). After this date little was done to examine this region by officials in the service of Egypt, and not a great deal by anybody else. For, with the exception of Albert Edward Nyanza, and its feeders and defluent, the broad outlines of the Nile system had been settled with the discovery of Albert Nyanza. Colonel Purdy-Bey examined in 1870, with the minute accuracy now regarded as necessary, the country between the Nile and the Red Sea, on the route between Mokattam and Suez, and Keneh and Kosseïr. These journeys did not add much to general geographical knowledge; but they were of value for the minute information they supplied regarding the topography and resources of that region, and indicated, with an exactness unknown in the old unscientific days which were before Schweinfurth—for the Commissioners sent by the first Napoleon confined themselves to Lower Egypt—the site of the Pharaohs' gold-mines, and the quarries of porphyry, and other valuable building materials

Egypt in Africa.

worked twenty-seven centuries before the Christian era. In 1873 Colonel Colston went

ERNST MARNO.
(*From a Photograph by Heinrich Graf, Berlin.*)

from Keneh to Berenice, and from that ancient port northwards to Berber. Next year the War Office sent Purdy-Bey into Darfur, Colston into Kordofan, and Mitchell, an engineer, to study the geology of the region between the Nile and the Red Sea, which enabled a better map to be drawn of Egypt than had hitherto been possible; while owing to the military stations established by the Khedive the country was explored with comparative ease to the borders of Borgou and Waday on the west, and Dar Fertit on the south. In 1874, also, Gordon became Governor of the Equatorial Provinces, with results which, we have seen, greatly enlarged our knowledge of the Upper Nile Basin; albeit Gordon, though an officer of the Royal Engineers, was never an enthusiast in scientific investigation. He did not encourage his subordinates to go beyond their duties, considering these quite sufficient for their energies. But it was seldom that he refused facilities to properly qualified explorers; and in Khartoum, with its consulates (p. 244), each charged with the interest of its nationality, the varied vagabonds who roamed in the interests of science found ample succour and advice. It was, however, under Gordon's orders that Chaillé-Long, his chief of staff, was sent up the Nile to Uganda (p. 143), discovering the so-called Lake Ibrahim, and proving, what had hitherto been only suspected, that the river which Speke had seen flowing out of Victoria Nyanza was the same that passed through the northern end of Albert Nyanza. Marno, a Viennese, helped to lay down the country between Lado and Makaraka, and in 1875-6 Gessi (Vol. II., p. 137) settled once and for all the origin of the White Nile and Albert Nyanza. The same river had, in 1874, been charted with more exactitude than before by Watson and Chippendale, officers acting under Gordon, and the navigation of Lake Albert been established by Gessi. Linant de Bellefonds (Vol. II., p. 287) charted the route between Gondokoro and the capital of Uganda, and Gordon himself surveyed, in 1876, the Nile between Foweera and Magungo, and the country between Foweera and M'rooli. About the same period

COLONEL CHAILLÉ-LONG.
(*From a Photograph by Lock and Whitfield.*)

the names of Munzinger Pasha, Mohammed Moktar Bey, and Abdallah Fendy—the two latter during the march of Raouf Pasha upon Harar (p. 235)—Mackillop, Ward, Abd-el-Razak Effendi, Durholz, Lockett, Field, Derrick, Dulier, Dennison, Diah, Kamzy, Magdy, and other officers in the Egyptian service, deserve honourable mention for minor contributions to the geography of the more remote parts of Egypt and its borders. The circumnavigation of Albert Nyanza by Mason Bey has already been noticed (Vol. II., p. 137), while several young Egyptian officers —Sabry, Samy, Nasr, etc., and more lately Prout, Pfund, Malini, and others—ascended the Nile to Dongola, and penetrated into the unknown south-east, and furnished the first detailed account of the route to Darfur. The reconnaissance of the northern frontier of Abyssinia by the officers attached to the expedition under Osman Pasha Refki was also of some scientific importance. But the rising in the Soudan soon confined any Egyptian surveys to districts not far from the Delta, and do not call for any notice in a work descriptive of explorations in unknown Africa. What has been briefly sketched* in the preceding pages may serve simply as a link in a narrative which, for reasons already given, cannot, as we approach the busy times we have now entered upon, be always strictly chronological. Egypt's share in the exploration of the continent of which it forms the oldest civilised section has, however, been of the smallest. The Nile Valley has been explored by foreigners, chiefly British at first, Italians and Germans latterly, though, indeed, its scientific surveyors have, like the rulers of Lower Egypt, always been of the most cosmopolitan description.

Schweinfurth, however, may be fittingly described, after Barth, as the first of the many scientific explorers who were so soon to flood Africa; and Nachtigal, another German, ranks next to him in date and status as a traveller of the newer and more accurate order.

Dr. Nachtigal (p. 256) was born at Eich-stadt, in the district of Stendal, between Magdeburg and Wittenberg, on the 23rd February, 1834.† After studying medicine at the Universities of Halle, Würzburg, and Greifswald, he served as a military surgeon until 1863, when a chest disease compelled him to seek a milder climate than that of Cologne, where he was stationed. Algiers was selected, and there he remained for a short time studying Arabic and the ways of those speaking it, until he was appointed physician to the Bey of Tunis. In this capacity he accompanied several little expeditions against revolted tribes, and in the course of these military excursions gained a useful familiarity with the language, habits, and general characteristics of North Africa bordering on the Sahara. This knowledge soon came in good stead; for in 1868 Dr. Nachtigal was chosen, on the recommendation of Gerhard Rohlfs (who had been offered the mission) to carry to Omar, Sultan of Bornu, the presents by which the King of Prussia intended to mark his appreciation of the services he had rendered to Rohlfs and his companions. Leaving Tripoli in February, 1869, Nachtigal arrived by way of Sokna, over a route along which we have accompanied more than one traveller, at Murzuk, then, as now, the "jumping-off place" to the desert beyond. Here he had to halt for some time until the caravan with which he was to travel was ready to set out, and thus had plenty of time to study the capital of Fezzan, the most remote province of Tripoli (Vol. I., pp. 240-2). Numerous trading caravans still pass through it to and from all parts of Central Africa—from 3,000 to 4,000 people being regularly engaged in the traffic that takes the route by way of Murzuk. The articles carried to the Soudan are Maria Theresa thalers—specially coined for this trade—calicoes, silk, velvet, woollen cloth, spices, glass-ware, trinkets, coral, amber, etc., while the

*Stone-Pasha, "Les Expéditions Égyptiennes en Afrique," *Bulletin de la Société Khédiriale de Géographie du Caire,* II• Sér. No. 7, 1885, p. 343.

† Dorothea Berlin: "Errinnerungen an Nachtigal" (1887); Franz-Pasha, *Bulletin de la Société Khédiriale de Géographie,* II• Sér. No. 7, 1885, p. 397.

goods taken in exchange are ostrich feathers, ivory, and slaves. But at the date of Nachtigal's visit, and not less since, the market for the last-named description of merchandise was no longer what it had been; so that to find any purchasers for their bondfolk the caravans have to diverge into the Moslem States, where they can be sold with less risk than in Tripoli and the North of Africa generally—albeit some slaves are disposed of surreptitiously. Add to this, the feebleness of the Bornu Government, and the refusal of the merchants to give credit, and the decay of the traffic to that region may be understood.

Thus far, Mademoiselle Tinné (Vol. II., p. 110) had accompanied Dr. Nachtigal, and with difficulty was dissuaded from joining him in a journey to Tibesti, the Tibbu country, a dozen days' journey south-east of Fezzan, with which he determined to utilise some of the involuntary delay that he was compelled to endure in Murzuk. Accompanied, accordingly, by four attendants (one of them, Mohammed el Gatrôni, a former servant of Dr. Barth), the German savant diverged from the straight route of his mission to visit the mountains of that region, particularly Tummo, Afafi, and Tarso, where he made many interesting observations on what was actually new ground, this upland district never having been up till then penetrated by any European. The heights mentioned extend to 8,000 or 9,000 feet above the sea, in the shape of a sterile, naked mountain clump, with a gigantic crater on its summit, and hard by a hot spring, which still further indicates the volcanic character of this desert "massif." In the valleys a little vegetation struggles for life and the only habitable spots are found.

Tibesti.

The scant population of these cultivable oases are ferocious nomads, from whom their first white visitor escaped with difficulty, reaching Murzuk in October, 1869, more dead than alive, worn out with hunger and fatigue, and impoverished by the loss of all his baggage.

After recovering, Dr. Nachtigal resumed his journey to Bornu, arriving at Kukawa, or Kuka, in July, 1870. From this point as his head-quarters many excursions were made into the Borgou country, in the north-east, and Baghirmi, to the south of Lake Tchad. This famous sheet of water has been many times visited since Denham, Clapperton, and Oudney first described it (Vol. I., p. 247). But Nachtigal examined it with such care that later explorers have not been able to add much to his data. During the dry season it possesses an area of about 10,000 square miles, but when swollen by the rains it spreads over a space fully four or five times as extensive. The eastern half of Tchad is really an archipelago of low islets inhabited by a race of semi-amphibious negro pirates, but the western portion of the lake is unencumbered. The sheet, in spite of no regular outlet being known to exist, is quite fresh, owing to the amount of water continually pouring into it from a number of streams, none of which, however, except the Shari—of which the Gribingi, Nachtigal's Bahr-el-Ardhe, is the upper part—is permanent, or of any great size. But during the wet season their united strength more than compensates for the evaporation during the rest of the year, the overplus escaping by a temporary river, which sometimes flows towards a low-lying basin three hundred miles towards the north-east.

Lake Tchad.

Borgou forms an oasis rich in dates, though so small that in no direction is it more than two days' march in breadth; and even that journey few care to take, for the Tibboos, who inhabit it, bear the worst of reputations as brigands. Baghirmi lies on the eastern frontier of Bornu, Lake Tchad and Waday adjoining it on its other sides, the entire area of the country being about 71,000 square miles, through the centre of which the Shari flows for a considerable portion of its course. The population is at present about a million and a half in number—of the Songhai type (Vol. I., p. 293)—and, though nominally Mohammedans

Borgou and Baghirmi.

and some civilised, still addicted to many of the grossest pagan rites. Low in stature, unpleasant in appearance, and prone to nakedness, the Baghirmi people are not an attractive race. Still, they are not savages. They are farmers, and grow great crops of durra and millet, which they dispose of for tobacco, pearls, and the cowry shells that form the currency of so many West and Central African

SLAVE-BOY OF DARFUR RESCUED BY GENERAL GORDON.
(*From a Photograph supplied by Dr. Felkin of Edinburgh.*)

countries. At Maseña, the capital—now abandoned for Bugoman on the Shari—a regular government of the Soudanese Moslem type had been for long established when Barth visited it in 1852. But at the period of which we speak the Sultan of Waday was at war with his brother of Baghirmi, the result of which was that the country was reduced to a state of complete vassalage to the former. The latest news (1893) is that some adventurers from Darfur, under a former slave of Zubeir Pasha, either on their own account, or at the bidding of the Mahdist Khalifa, had captured the capital, but were compelled to retreat before a large force sent against them by the Waday ruler.

At the time Nachtigal was a guest of the sovereign of Bornu, that once splendid empire had been so lopped of states once tributary to it that it was no longer so rich or powerful as of old. The Sheik Omar is described as a lettered man—as literature goes in Central Africa— amiable, honest, pious, and generous, but effeminate, and without the energy to rule a turbulent kingdom surrounded by rivals ready to take advantage of the slightest weakness on the part of anyone. At present the country may contain about five million inhabitants, though everything shows that Bornu is again a decaying state, with little chance of reviving under its present *régime*, albeit, rich in possessing a fertile soil, an abundance of horses and cattle, and a steady commerce with Kano and Nupe towards the west, which must always gives it a preponderating place among the Soudan States. In March, 1873, Dr. Nachtigal began to think that it was time for him to return home, since he had no idea when he left Tripoli of being so long on his journey. Instead, however, of taking the same route as that by which he had arrived in Bornu—which, it may be remarked, had been frequently traversed and has at least once since the date of Nachtigal's journey been tramped again * —he resolved to try one which until then had not, in part at all events, been the line of any civilised caravan. This was through the notorious state of Waday, in which Vogel had been murdered (p. 90; Vol. I., p. 302), from which Rohlfs had been repulsed, and on the borders of which—at Mao —Moritz von Beurmann had been done to death in 1863, in the course of a little-known expedition which he made in search of Vogel, to the country where Nachtigal then was.†

* By Monteil in 1892, who, though the first Frenchman to travel over it, did not go over any new ground.

† There were altogether seven expeditions fitted out with this object in view; but with the exception of Beurmann's, none of them accomplished anything.

Happily for the new adventurer into this den of assassins, the old Sultan, Mohammed Shereef, was dead, and though Ali, the new ruler of Bornu that the friendship of that kindly potentate now stood Nachtigal in good stead.

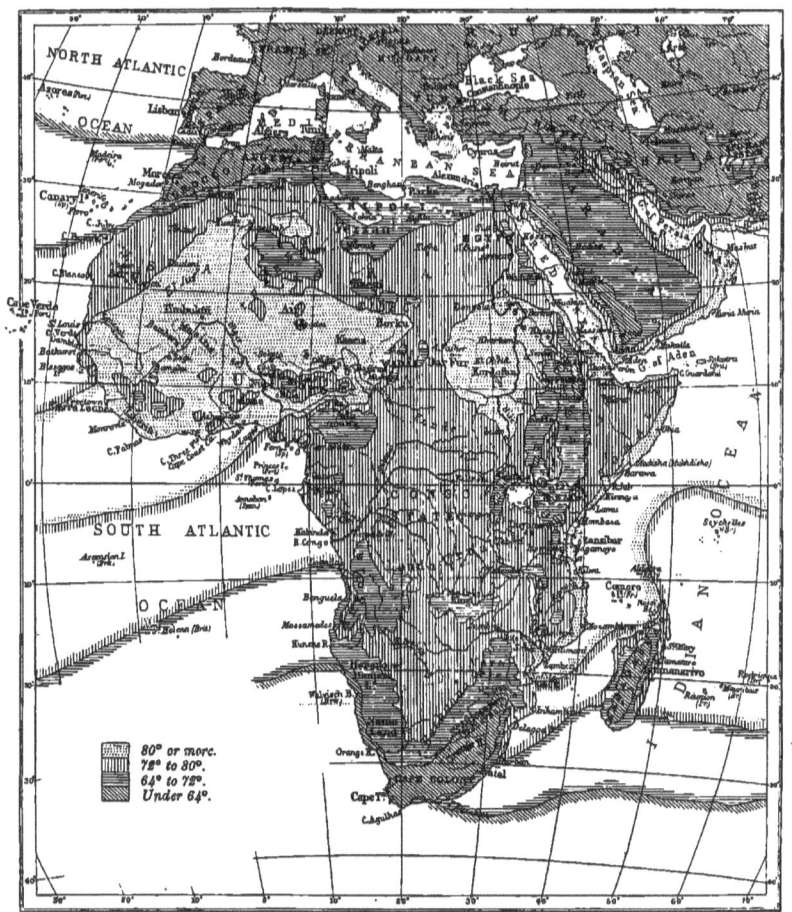

MAP OF THE ACTUAL MEAN TEMPERATURE OF THE AFRICAN YEAR. (*By E. G. Ravenstein.*)

sovereign, lacked a great deal in hospitality to vagrom men, he was an advance on his father, and on such terms with the

Before, however, setting out, he visited Songhai, once the centre of an empire, but now a small and densely populated state.

The natives go practically naked, and live in a much more savage condition than their neighbours; yet the country is rich in horses, goats, and poultry. Cattle and sheep are less plentiful. The horses do not exceed the height of ponies, but are tireless at their usual galloping pace. The goats are also of an unusually dwarfish size, but very fat; and, in lack of other domestic animals, the dog is reared for food, the flesh being looked upon as an article of luxury. All over the country the hunting of slaves goes on with great eagerness, and is attended with many of the horrors familiar to us as the concomitant of that traffic in other parts of Africa. Indeed, to use Dr. Nachtigal's words, it has changed an earthly paradise into an abode of demons. The beautiful shady woods, interspersed with fertile plains dotted with villages, are the ideal of peace and happiness, until a slaving party makes its appearance. Then all becomes ruin; the hamlet only a few hours before so perfect a specimen of sleeping tranquillity is only a heap of smoking embers. The men are corpses, and the women and children chained together on the march they know not whither. If they exhibit signs of weariness, a stroke of the hippopotamus-whip reminds the helpless wretches that they are now at the mercy of cruel masters. A sickly child is torn from its mother and tossed into the bush; and as soon as one of the women appears likely to give more trouble than will be repaid by her price in the slave-market, the inhuman monsters in charge of the gang promptly despatch her, or unloosen her from the chain, to fare as the hyæna will permit by the wayside.

Bornu, Baghirmi, Waday, and Darfur were in those days the chief markets for these captives, and, no doubt, still form their destination, since there is now no open sale for them in any of the countries of North Africa, except Morocco, where human beings are yet bought and sold, even before the eyes of the consuls, in the coast towns of that crumbling empire, or in the regular slave-markets of the interior. Twenty years ago a child of five, six, or seven years old was easily purchasable in Bornu for a shirt worth about three shillings, and the best slave seldom brought more than from fifteen to eighteen shillings. With human flesh so cheap, the stimulus of self-interest was almost lacking to the owner. One human being more or less scarcely mattered. The old were not worth their food. As for the others, strong or feeble, big or little, child or adult, sick or well, the only word ever addressed to them is "dyabki"—"Go on!"—followed by a blow of the whip; or the knife is drawn across the worn-out captive's throat with as little concern as if the murdered black was a sheep or a fowl. The savage folk thus preyed upon are naturally a feeble race without firearms, and, being regarded by the Mohammedans as simply "Kafirs," have not even the fallible protection against their persecutors which a common faith is commanded by the Koran to afford. To escape from their hunters, some of the tribes have built huts in the dense bombax-trees. Here they carry food and water, and even cattle, provided with which they are generally able to get an advantage over their enemies. Even bullets do little damage in the dense shelter, where the javelin-throwers cannot be seen, while the besiegers, in order to fire to any purpose, must come into the open, which the tree-dwellers take care to clear for a long distance around their arboreal strongholds.

At Waday, Nachtigal was kindly received by the Sultan, who in those early days of his reign seems to have been better inclined to strangers than he was a few years later (p. 11); for he not only permitted them to pass through his kingdom, but to explore the tributary state of Dar Runga. The chief feature of the country between Bornu and Waday is Lake Fittri, which forms the termination of the Batha River, just as Lake Tchad is the end of the Shari. Fittri is, however, a much smaller sheet than the latter, though the river flowing into it is nearly as large as the Shari. The region in the vicinity of this lake forms a small state of the same name; but during a large portion of the year it is almost uninhabitable, owing to the myriads of mosquitoes and other poisonous insects which torment man and his domestic animals, one of them, the "ter" fly, being dangerous even to horses. The inhabitants are the Bulala, the Kuka, and the Abu Simmin. The first, who form the dominant tribe, are of Arab origin. The Kuka, originally from Waday, have for ages been almost amalgamated with the Bulala, who speak the same language, and, from a physical and moral point of view, are practically identical with them. The Abu Simmin are, however, the true aborigines of the country—sprung, it is said, from a slave tribe, and now confined by their conquerors to a few villages on the shores and islands of the lake, where they live despised and oppressed. Yawa, situated a little way north of the embouchure of the Batha, is the capital, and here, at the date of Nachtigal's visit, the king resided. But his town is a poor one, and his country—dry and barren, without any of the umbrageous forests which give so pleasing an appearance to the shore of Lake Tchad—is a mere dependency of Waday.

This state comprises an area of about three thousand square miles, and close on three millions of people, though, if the vassal territories are included, fully two millions more must be credited to it. Its northern part is rather dry and correspondingly unfertile. But the north-east, east, and central regions are more hilly and watered by numerous streams, which form tributaries of the Botcha and the Batha, which, as we have seen, eventually unite to form the principal feeder of Lake Fittri. What commerce the country nourishes—and besides ostrich feathers, ivory, slaves, and manufacture of cotton cloth decidedly inferior to that of Bornu and Baghirmi, there is not much except a little indigo, wheat, and durra—is mainly in the hands of the traders from Bornu, and finds its way either to the

Waday.

north, over the desert, or through Darfur to Egypt. Slave-hunting, conducted entirely for the Sultan's profit, is still very brisk—the temporary check which it suffered from the half-hearted efforts of Egypt to prevent the traffic having been entirely removed when the Soudan fell into the hands of the Mahdists.

The Waday people form a mixture of many tribes, speaking several different languages. Of these, the Mabas, a people with a complexion varying from black to bronze, are regarded as the aristocracy, the Arabs, who are more numerous than in Bornu, not mixing much with the other races, and in general occupying an inferior position in native society. We first hear of Waday as a centralised state in the middle of the seventeenth century, when it was won to Islam by Abed el Kerim el Abassi, who at the same time put an end to the domination of the Tunjours. These people were evidently emigrants from Arabia before the time of Mohammed. But not in Darfur also, where they obtained the sovereign power, did they do anything to raise the civilisation, or the influence of their superior civilisation: on the contrary, they did much to degrade them to the level of the rudest Soudanese around them. Abed el Kerim, the dethroner of the old and the founder of a new dynasty, found from the first eager allies in the inhabitants of the north, who had no reason for loving the Tunjour Sultan Daoud. Accordingly, by their help he soon compelled the other tribes to embrace the new faith, and formed the present Mussulman state of Waday, with Wara as its capital, a distinction which it enjoyed until it was deserted for Abeshr within the last few years during one of those wars of succession by which this, like every other Central African kingdom, has been at times torn asunder.

The year 1873 had now arrived, and with it the fourth since Nachtigal had left Tripoli. Thanks to the mission on which he had been despatched, his long travels had been exceptionally prosperous, though the traveller had not gone

Darfur, and the way thither.

without his share of those fevers from which new visitors to inner Africa so seldom escape. Hitherto, so far as his journey from Bornu to Waday was concerned, he had been traversing what was actually or virtually ground fresh to geographers, and from this point to Darfur he would have the same good fortune. But just at the time when he was fain to leave Abeshr and its Sultan, whom—more of its internal dissensions, had virtually conquered it before it was formally united to the Khedive's viceroyalty, with the help of Egyptian troops.

It was these civil broils of which the echo had reached Nachtigal at Abeshr. Mohammed Hassan, the native king, was dead, and a war of succession had stopped all communication between El Fasher, the Darfur capital,

EUPHORBIA CANDELABRUM.
(*From a Photograph by Sir John Kirk.*)

fortunate than some of his successors (p. 11) —he designates as his "generous protector Ali," news, vague but not the less alarming, reached Waday regarding the condition of matters in Darfur.

In former chapters we have had a good deal to say regarding this ancient kingdom as a province of Egypt, and, since 1884, part of the Mahdist dominion. But in 1873 the country was still independent, for it was not until some time later that Zubeir, the slave-trader (Vol. II., pp. 141-2), taking advantage and the neighbouring sultanates. Then, while waiting for news, the rainy season arrived, and Ali, unwilling for his guest to run any undue risks in the unsettled state of the country, persuaded him to pass the days of involuntary idleness in a journey to Betcha, Kachemere, and Karanga, across the Batha, through the Kadjakse country to the Bahr-el-Salamat, a river which, after flowing through Lake Iro, joins the Shari to contribute its waters to Lake Tchad. This excursion, owing to the wet weather, took twenty days, though ordinarily the ground can easily be covered in ten or a dozen journeys. In the swamps near Mangari, the farthest

the insidious climate of Africa. It was, therefore, with gladness he received a message to the effect that for the time being—as events

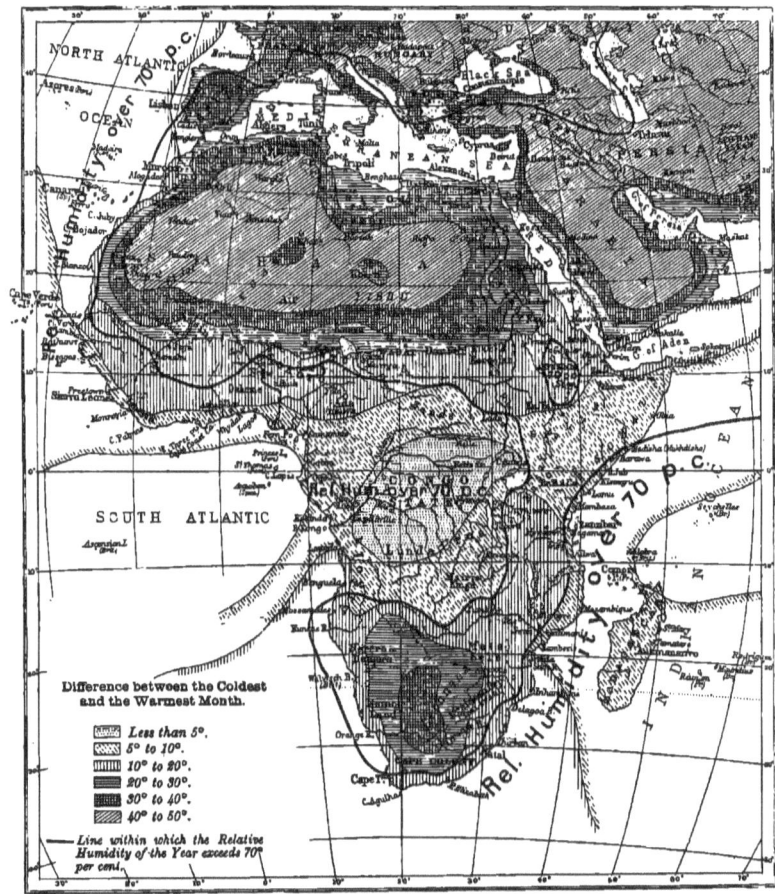

MAP OF THE MEAN ANNUAL RANGE OF TEMPERATURE IN AFRICA. (By E. G. Ravenstein.)

point to the south which Dr. Nachtigal had reached, malarial fever still further weakened a constitution which for a long time past had begun to be affected by

Mangari.

afterwards proved—the Darfur succession had been amicably settled. He would fain have gone beyond Dar Runga, which Ali had permitted him to visit—though at that season the route to it was simply one vast swamp—to examine the many streams which traverse the country, and even to reach the Welle of Schweinfurth, then, and for many years subsequently, one of the rapidly decreasing mysteries of African hydrography. But he was too anxious to return to civilisation while his waning strength allowed, to permit those temptations of travel to detain him any longer.

Accordingly, on the 17th of January, 1874, he bade good-bye to Abeshr, and started on the journey between that hot town and the capital of Darfur, through a country inhabited by gangs of border robbers—the Massalit—who admit the authority of neither of the two sultanates, which they plunder with troublesome impartiality. A guard of several hundred horsemen accompanied each caravan to the frontiers of Darfur, crossing, about halfway, the River Asounga, which river is in the tributary state of Dar-Tama (p. 11), and eventually finds its way through the KiyaandAzoum, which as one stream flow through Soula to the Bahr-el-Salamat. Beyond the Asounga, the route lies for the most part along the broad beds of streams, or rather torrents, nearly all of which rise on the northern side of the Jebel Marra —or Marra Mountain. Three journeys past the Asounga, the River Kadja is crossed, but, though not broader, it is deeper than the former; and then two days farther on, Tineat, the residence of the chief of Dar Fea—at that time named Hanefr—is reached.

Like all the heads of departments this magnate bears the title of "Shertaya." His district is threaded by a river of the same name, which, after a short course, is lost in the Bare, in its turn a tributary of the Azoum. Indeed, all the country west of Darfur is rich in brawling torrents flowing full during the rainy season, and correspondingly contracted after the rains are over, until in the dry months many of them are waterless. On the third or fourth day after leaving Tineat, the caravan with which Nachtigal travelled halted at Kabhakia—none of the "wadys" crossed being deeper than from a foot and a half to five feet. Kabhakia is situated at the base of the Marra Mountain, which, though not measured, appears to be about 4,000 feet in height.

All the way from Lake Tchad to the point where the Marra Mountain was crossed, at a height of over 3,000 feet, the country had been gradually rising, but beyond that dividing land it gradually fell until El Fasher was reached, the capital of Darfur, which stands about 2,000 feet above the sea-level. The vegetation along the course is rich, the margins of the streams being shaded by shrubs and trees common to the country, such as acacias (*A. nilotica*), the haraza, the *Zizyphus spina-Christi*, and various species usually found in similar situations. In the country away from water, the scarcity of arboreal vegetation gives it a steppe character, and on the slopes of Marra the fine *Euphorbia candelabrum* is the tree

ROUTE MAP OF DR. NACHTIGAL'S JOURNEY.

which most frequently strikes the traveller's eye (p. 252).

The third day after leaving Kabhakia, Kabeh is reached. This was in 1874 a populous centre, almost exclusively inhabited by Jellabas, and in after days, like the place just mentioned, was occupied by an Egyptian garrison until the Mahdist revolt swept away that dubious pioneer of civilisation in the Nile Valley, on the western edge of which Nachtigal now stood.

Then came another long day's ride, and El Fasher, the capital of Darfur, was entered. Here the weary explorer might have fairly considered his task near its end; for, if not in a place of absolute safety, he was so close to the borders of the Khedive's country that the suspicion which had all along dogged his footsteps ought now to have disappeared. But, unfortunately, this was not the case. A Christian was possibly not regarded as so villainous a fiend as he was in the fanatical sultanates farther west; but the proceedings of the Egyptians in the east had not rendered the name of Turk any more dearly loved than of old. For ages Darfur had been threatened by Egypt, and Gordon had gone so far as to insist on its annexation, along with Kordofan, as essential to the suppression of the slave trade. The treacherous Governor of Dar Fea had already despatched a courier to the capital, warning his master that a stranger, either Turk or Christian—and in either case equally dangerous—was on the road. To Sultan Ibrahim's credit, however, he refused to listen to the perfidious proposals of this chief to kill the suspected traveller before he was capable of doing any mischief. How Nachtigal might have fared had he been left friendless and moneyless in this distant stronghold of Islam it is hard to say; for the people were not friendly, and the Sultan only civil. Luckily, however, letters arrived for him from Egypt containing ample means to continue his explorations, and a request from the Khedive to the ally whom he was even then preparing to deprive of his kingdom to do all that lay in his power to assist the traveller. Whatever may have been Ibrahim's secret thoughts, he obeyed most loyally this semi-mandate of Ismail Pasha; for not only did he grant his visitor permission to go where he wished, but appointed certain individuals to afford him all the information he desired.

Darfur was in those days very little known, but it was by no means a *terra incognita* to European travellers. Indeed, as early as 1793, at the very time that Mungo Park was making his celebrated attempt to penetrate West Africa, William George Browne—a private gentleman of Great Tower Hill, London, and Oriel College, Oxford—fired by the fame of Bruce's travels, had crossed the Libyan Desert from Assiut with the Soudan caravan to Darfur, intending to return by way of Abyssinia. In 1793 all that Europe knew of a country which in the course of the next century became tolerably familiar, was from its being mentioned in the information collected from traders by Ledyard (Vol. 1., p. 173). The people inhabiting it were reported to be more tolerant of Christians than even the Egyptians themselves, to whom, moreover, the Furians were extremely obsequious. Browne also heard at Assiut that they made slave-hunting raids along the banks of the Bahr-el-Abiad, which he conceived to be the true Nile, and imagined that by accompanying one of these expeditions he might be able to traverse at least five degrees of unknown country.

Darfur: an early resident.

In two months Kobbeh, then the capital, was entered; but the first European to reach the country in which Dr. Nachtigal was so reputably received found that his troubles grew upon him. The merchants with whom he had travelled dispersed, leaving the Furians to make what they could of the white-faced wanderer they had brought with them, who wished to go on slave-hunting expeditions, and yet did not deal in that description of merchandise. He was, moreover, evidently an infidel, in spite of his occasional conformity, and they even affected to trace in him certain marks of inferiority distinguishing the Kafir from the Believer. As for the colour of his skin, never having seen a European before, they set it down as due to disease and judged accordingly.

Browne had engaged an old Cairo slave-broker to manage his money transactions in Darfur, where every kind of business was done by barter. This person, however, proved his evil genius; for he took the opportunity of a quarrel with him on the way to steal a

GUSTAV NACHTIGAL.
(From a Photograph by Adolf Halwas, Berlin.)

number of valuable articles, and then, in order to shelter himself, instilled into the Sultan's mind so strong a prejudice against the new-comer that he was refused an audience, and ordered to live at Kobbeh in the house of a creature of the treacherous slave-broker. Fever and dysentery attacked him, and his property was seized on a trumped-up charge of having committed a vile offence. At last the Sultan was forced to interfere in case the property of his own subjects in Egypt should be attached in reprisal. But even when Browne was admitted to his levee, he was received with the most pointed contempt, and never permitted to address the potentate, who sat on a splendid throne, and was hailed as "the buffalo, the offspring of a buffalo, the bull of bulls, the elephant of superior strength,

the powerful Sultan Abd-el-Rahman-el-Raschid."

Securing the friendship of the Melek of the Jelals, or foreign traders, the traveller was treated with more kindness, and permitted to earn a little money as a doctor. Still, he was not allowed to go on any journey, though he collected much accurate information about Borgou—which Nachtigal visited nearly eighty years later—Sennaar, Kordofan, Baghirmi, and Zanfara. At last it almost seemed as if he was to be kept a lifelong prisoner in Darfur, the death of the Melek not helping to render his virtual imprisonment any the more agreeable. The jealousy between Darfur and Borgou prevented the hapless Briton from passing to the latter, while the insurrection which just then happened to be raging in Kordofan was equally against the visit of any strangers to that kingdom. It was even doubtful if Egypt were practicable by the way he had come; for the Darfur Sultan detained the caravans while he attempted to negotiate with the Mameluke Beys, who then governed that country (Vol. II, p. 28), a monopoly of the Soudan trade. But by-and-by, a caravan setting out for the Nile, the merchants, afraid that it might be seized by the Egyptians if Browne were kept a prisoner, persuaded the Sultan to permit him to leave with it. This was done, and in due time he arrived at Assiut, after an absence of nearly three years, during which he had narrowly escaped death by disease, poison, or open assassination.*

Browne was the first European to reach Darfur. He saw the state before it had lost a great deal of its ancient importance. Nachtigal, whose reception was so much more hospitable, was the last traveller to visit the country as an independent sultanate. For the

* Browne published, in 1799, his "Travels in Africa, Egypt, and Syria, from the year 1792 to 1798." He is believed to have perished in 1813, during an attack on the caravan with which he was travelling in Persia. But his fate was never ascertained with certainty, and, owing to the unattractiveness of his literary style, the achievements of this meritorious traveller are now little more than an echo—a something of the long-forgotten past which concerns the historian alone.

LOWER CONGO CHIEF IN ROYAL "ROBES."
(From a Photograph by the Rev. R. D. Darby.)

terror of annexation to Egypt, which had been so long the ever-present terror of Waday and Darfur, was, all unconscious to the German explorer, about to befall the latter.

The history of Darfur, so far as history has preserved any memorials of it, begins with the Dadjo kings, who are said to have reigned in the Marra Mountains, and of whom a traditional

History of Darfur.

sultanate that he reigned as far east as the banks of the Atbara.

After the usual civil broils and murders we come to Abd-er-Rahman, surnamed El Raschid, or the Just, who was ruler when Browne visited the country, though that traveller experienced little of his supposed justice. The king had been selected by the people out of the usual line of succession,

CAMP OF WANDERING ABYSSINIANS.
(From a Photograph by Dr. G. Schweinfurth.)

list is preserved. Then came the Tunjur dynasty, one of whom, Dali or Dalil, was the real founder of the Furian kingdom. His penal code, the "Kitab Dali," still extant, shows that at the time it was compiled Darfur had not entirely accepted the dicta of the Koran. Suleiman the Red, who reigned from 1596 to 1637, was a great warrior and saint, and his grandson Ahmed not only completed the Mohammedanising of the State—albeit the Tunjurs are still not professedly Mussulmans — but encouraged immigration from Bornu and Baghirmi, and so extended the

being simply a poor priest noted for his learning and piety. It was he who, in 1799, sent an address of congratulation to Napoleon, then campaigning in Lower Egypt, and in return received two thousand black slaves from the general of a Republic which had just decreed the manumission of the bondmen throughout its own territory. During Abd-er-Rahman's reign the capital was transferred from Kobbeh, the nominal capital, to its present position, which, even in Browne's day, was the royal residence. His son, Mohammed-el-Fadl, lost Kordofan, and Mohammed-el-Hassan, the third of his forty sons, who succeeded him, spent most of his reign in expeditions against the Rizigat Arabs. Dying in 1873, old and blind, his son Ibrahim speedily found himself at war with the armies of the slave-traders, who by this time had begun to make themselves masters wherever they went. The principal of these bandits was Zubeir Pasha, of whom we have already had much to say, who defeated and killed Ibrahim in the battle of Menowachi, a short time after Nachtigal left. His uncle, Hasseb Alla, tried to recover the loss then sustained; but, Egypt interfering, he was captured by the Khedive's tropps, and, more fortunate than some of Ismaïl's victims, sent with his family to pass the rest of his days, in the dignified position of a pensioned king, *en retraite* at Cairo.

These events succeeded each other so rapidly that at the time of Nachtigal's visit they were scarcely even imminent. Egypt had long cast an avaricious eye on the rich copper, iron, antimony, and lead mines of the Darfurian hills, and had openly connived at the raiding of the flocks and herds which went on by armed slavers fitted out in the Soudan. Yet it was pleaded by Ismaïl Pasha that his annexation of Darfur, and the other kingdoms bordering the Nile Valley, was necessary in order to crush the man-hunting and man-selling which went on within their bounds. This excuse would most likely have availed Dr. Nachtigal very little had the invasion of Darfur taken place whilst he was at El Fasher. The chances, indeed, are that he would either have been killed by the infuriated people, as an Egyptian in disguise, or held as a hostage, in which circumstance his lot would have been even worse. Luckily, however, he was at El Obeid —afterwards familiar as the first capital of the Mahdi (Vol. II., p. 159)—before he met the army of Ismaïl Pasha Ayoub, Governor-General of the Soudan, on its march to Darfur. From Kordofan it was comparatively easy in those days to reach Khartoum. Yet Nachtigal found the journey hard enough. Before he entered the metropolis of the

From El Fasher to Khartoum.

Soudan he was almost too ill to travel, and poorer even than when he had started on his eastward journey from Bornu. For he had been robbed of everything, until he was nearly naked, his entire wardrobe consisting of a flannel shirt and an outer cloak, or "libade." But at Khartoum he was among friends, and on the 22nd of November, 1874, arrived at Cairo on board a special steamer, which the Khedive had despatched up the Nile for his convenience. Ismaïl Pasha was, indeed, so pleased with the energy shown by the German doctor that he offered him a place in the Egyptian Government. Anxious, however, to reach Berlin, he was forced to decline this mark of favour, though the delicacy of his health did not permit him to face the cold north for nearly a year later.* Indeed, he never quite recovered; for, though destined to inaugurate a great work for Germany and Africa, in describing which we shall meet with him again, this intrepid traveller was in a few years doomed to an early grave in the land with which his fame is linked. When he did reach Berlin, Europe was not niggard of its honours. Among other rewards of a similar character, he received the Founders' Medal of the Royal Geographical Society for having explored "the previously unknown region of Tibesti and Baghirmi, added much to our knowledge of Lake Tchad, and returned by a route previously untrodden by Europeans, through Waday and Darfur to Upper Egypt." The German Government— full of enthusiasm over the share Germans were taking in African exploration—gave

* Nachtigal: "Sahara und Sûdân : Ergebnisse Sechsjähriger Reisen in Afrika," 3 Vols. (1879–89) ; *Bulletin de la Société de Géographie de Paris* (1876), pp. 129-155, 255-277, etc. etc. Before reading Dr. Nachtigal's exhaustive account of the Central African kingdoms, it will be instructive to peruse the "Voyage au Ouaday" of the Sheik Mohammed Ibn-Omar-el-Tounsy, Réviseur en chef à l'école de médecine at Cairo, who, to some extent, anticipated Dr. Nachtigal. The sheik, though not a geographer, was a most intelligent man. His journey was made in search of his father Omar, and, though completed in 1803-4, was not published until 1851, when MM. Perron and Jomard translated it into French. His "Voyage au Dârfour," also translated by MM. Perron and Jomard, appeared six years earlier.

Dr. Nachtigal the refusal of the Consulate-Generalship to Tunis, and subsequently of the Minister-Residentship at Tangier. The first of these posts he filled for a short time, and the second he did not live long enough formally to accept. But this is anticipating our narrative by nearly ten years; since it will not be till 1884 that the traveller to whom we have just said good-bye need again form one of the characters in this Story of Africa.

If Nachtigal's journey may be regarded as immediately due to the stimulus imparted to Central and North African exploration by Barth, Rohlfs and Schweinfurth, the scientific travels of Junker were avowedly advised by the last-named explorers, whom he met for the first time at a Geographical Congress in Paris soon after the return of Nachtigal from the Nile.

Dr. Wilhelm Junker was born at Moscow on the 6th of April, 1840; but his parents were Germans, and in Germany he received most of his scientific education, and graduated as Doctor of Medicine. At first Darfur was the country to which his attention was directed, and it was with the intention of exploring it under the protection which he believed the Egyptian occupation would afford that he went up the Nile in 1875. His objects were mainly natural history collection and observation; and, with this in view, he examined part of the Libyan Desert, and the country from the Natron Lakes to the Fayoum. In February, 1876, he travelled up the Khor Baraka, of which the higher parts alone had at that time been explored by Europeans, and, after visiting Kassala and Kedaref, reached the Blue Nile at Abu Haras, and in June arrived at Khartoum. In those days no hint which the Egyptians could interpret had been given of the terrible turmoil which in a few years was to overwhelm the Soudan; and, under Gordon's auspices, any part of the vast territory could be reached with comparative safety. Sennaar was accordingly visited with Romolo Gessi, and an excursion made up the Sobat River as far as Nasar, preparatory to setting out for Darfur. But, on returning to Khartoum, Junker found that not only had that country been already stripped of any geographical novelties by the explorations of various Egyptian officers (pp. 245–6), but that the anarchy attendant on the passing away of the old rule before the new one was fully established rendered the autumn of 1876 an unfavourable season for his work.

The Upper Nile country was, therefore, fixed upon as the scene of his future labours, and at Lado, accordingly, he duly arrived

DR. WILHELM JUNKER.
(*From a Photograph by Maull and Fox, Piccadilly, W.*)

as the guest of the man destined in future days to be famous as Emin Pasha. Taking this post as his head-quarters, the Makaraka and Mundoo country (pp. 28, 29, 55, 261) was examined, the northern part of the Bahr-el-Ghazel province penetrated, and a journey made as far south as the Kibali River, now known as the principal tributary of the Welle. By the close of 1878 Dr. Junker was back to Europe in ill health, but laden with valuable collections and notes, only part of which his too-early death permitted him to give to the world. Africa, however, possesses charms too irresistible for most of those who have once looked upon her beauty—a gift more fatal to her lovers than to herself—and so, by 1879, Dr. Junker was off once more to the Nile, little imagining that seven years would elapse before he could again see Christendom. A full examination of the Niam-Niam or Zandy country, and the solution of what was now beginning to be known as the Welle-Makua problem, were the main tasks which he set himself to perform; but on the endless

Junker's second visit to Africa: a seven years' journey.

compass bearings only. He did not make any astronomical observations, being in the main an ethnographer and naturalist. From Khartoum he again worked his way up the Nile and Bahr-el-Ghazel to the Meshera-er-Rek, and thence to Dem Suleiman (Vol. II., p. 144), whence he turned south into the country of the notoriously cannibal

EL KHATMIEH, A SUBURB OF KASSALA.
(From a Photograph by Mr. Berghof.)

tramps backwards and forwards which he took in the years to come we cannot follow him closely. Much of the ground he travelled over was not new, though not a little of it was entirely fresh to geographers, while a large portion of it had never before been examined by a traveller of competent scientific knowledge—not even by Emin, who, indeed, did not make many actual explorations. Junker, however, did not give himself out as a geographer, and, in spite of his many accomplishments, the chief materials for a map which he brought back were elaborate

Niam-Niam. Thanks to the influential support which Junker had received owing to Gordon's goodwill, but not a little also to his considerate treatment of the natives (falling in with all their rules of etiquette, displaying unwearied patience, and preferring to travel with porters alone rather than risk the friction which an armed escort is apt to arouse), he obtained a friendly reception from Ndoruma, one of their most influential chiefs. Under the protection of this kindly man-eater, Junker built himself a zereba, or camp, and penetrated first and last as far as the Welle, and the country of the people whom Schweinfurth called the Monbuttoo, but who in their new visitor's probably more correct orthography are described as "Mangbattu." Here, again, the barbarous folk entreated him hospitably. Proceeding southwards and eastwards of the Welle, he reached a place called Mabub or Zereba Ali, where Schweinfurth had crossed his newly discovered river in 1870, and went on to Tangasi and Niangara, a little beyond his predecessor's farthest point. Then, after exploring various tributaries of the Welle, he returned to his friends at the Monbuttoo village.

In January, 1881, again turning south, the almost for the first time, Junker found himself among enemies, from whom he was glad to escape to the A-Madi on the other side of the river.

Meanwhile, Emin, having formed a station near Mambanga, south of the Welle, Dr. Junker went there to visit Captain Casati, journeying from thence to the Upper Bomokandi, an important tributary of the Welle, the route leading for most of the way through primeval forests. Vast undulating regions, rising at times into hills, or even into mountains, and again merging, as in the Bahr-el-Ghazel territory, into wide alluvial plains, are, however, the prevailing characteristics of the country

Character of country traversed.

MUNDOO WARRIORS
(*From a Photograph by R. Buchta.*)

country of the A-Madi, who occupy a bend of the Welle, formed the object of his exploration. Taking a route westwards, the Welle was crossed once more near the mouth of the Kumbala, and the territory of the A-Barambo tribe entered. But now, over which Junker had hitherto travelled. Throughout this huge empire of black men streams out of number flow either into the Nile or the Congo; the "divide," or watershed between those two great rivers, being a broad plateau or elevation. Civil war and anarchy had torn asunder almost every tribe or nation. The Niam-Niam, once a powerful confederation, were split up into parties continually at feud with each other, and, exhausted by internecine wars, lived in a condition of distrust and uncertainty. The Monbuttoos were in no better case. They, too, had lost unity and power since King Munza, Schweinfurth's friend (p. 242), had been murdered by the Arab slave-raiders. Cannibalism was only kept in check by the lack of material on which to exercise it, and not only did the Arabs hunt for captives, but tribe plotted mischief against tribe, for the sake of obtaining dead men to eat or living ones to sell to the camps.

The suspicion everywhere engendered by the state of things soon affected Junker; for after visiting Mamballe and the River Bomokandi, localities mentioned by Miani and Potagos, a Greek traveller, who had tried in a vague, unsatisfactory way to obtain some acquaintance with the less-known parts of the Nile Valley, he fell ill, and with difficulty after a march through an unexplored country reached the Nepoko. This river he believed to be identical with Stanley's Aruwhimi, a supposition partially correct, as it is a tributary of that well-known feeder of the Congo. Indeed, he nearly overlapped Stanley's route in 1886; for he struck the Nepoko about forty miles north of Ugarrowa, a place very familiar to the readers of the Emin Relief Expedition literature (p. 40). The Monbuttoo chief, A-Sanga Mombele, now insisted on detaining his white man as a hostage for the good behaviour of some of his friends among the Egyptian slaves and soldiers, so that before he could return to Tangasi, in July, 1882, he had suffered great privations. Ill, in want of goods to pay his way and to obtain the coarsest provisions, which were hard to procure among a people where charity is an extremely rare virtue, Junker returned to the zereba of Zemio, another Niam-Niam chief, where Bohndorff, his German assistant, awaited his arrival.

Evil days.

Instructing his sole European companion to make his way back to Europe by the Bahr-el-Ghazel,* Junker set out on another journey through the west Niam-Niam district, from which he did not return till May, 1883, having reached the Welle, near Ali Kobbo's zereba, close to the farthest point which Van Gele, a Belgian, attained from the west seven years later. Up to this date Junker, trusting to native information, had shared the belief of Schweinfurth, its discoverer, and other travellers, that the Welle was the upper reaches of the Shari, which, we have seen, is the principal feeder of Lake Tchad. But after he came upon the river, first at its confluence with the Werre, and, later, lower down at Abdallah's zereba, it was impossible any longer to doubt that it was a tributary of the Congo. This conclusion had, indeed, been already arrived at by Mr. Grenfell, when he had passed the Zongo rapids of the Mobangi (p. 126), which river it is now universally accepted as being, although several of the less essential links in the course have still to be traced.†

But by the time Junker had returned to Zemio's, the worst news he had heard yet had drifted to that remote African camp; for the tidings came that the Mahdist rebellion was spreading far beyond its place of origin, and had already crept to the Bahr-el-Ghazel province. After several months' delay, Junker set out in the hope of being able to catch one of the steamers which still came to the Meshera (p. 239). Fortunately, Lupton Bey (Vol. II., p. 157) kept his friend well abreast of the hopes and fears which racked the mind of that unfortunate Governor. Then, when a messenger arrived with a letter saying that all the military posts north of Ganda had been captured by the Mahdists, and that Lupton dreaded the worst, Junker, on receipt of the news, determined to return to Zemio's

Echoes of the Mahdi.

---

* Bohndorff was, at a later date, in Weissmann's service (p. 22).

† Wills. *Proc. of the Royal Geographical Society*, 1887, p. 285 ; Potagos : "Dix années de voyage, etc." (1885).

zereba, and, under the protection of the cannibal chief, make his way to Lado, where Emin and Casati then were.

Here, he arrived in January, 1884 (p. 26), and for the first time became aware of how narrow an escape he had from falling into the hands of the Mahdi. For on the 2nd of May, Lupton was compelled to surrender, and soon after Karamallah, the victorious general, sent, as we have seen, a demand to Lado for the Europeans there to appear at the rebel seat of government. There is, therefore, little doubt that if Junker had persisted in his original intention, he would, like Slatin and Lupton, have been doomed to long years of slavery among the fanatics who in a short time were to reconquer the entire Soudan. Indeed, as we now know (p. 27) that Emin and his officers had determined to abandon the Equatorial Province without resistance, it was only the accident of the Mahdists not making an immediate advance that prevented the calamity which he had avoided at the Meshera from befalling him at Lado.

But Junker had no intention of submitting so tamely and determined to retreat up the Nile to Albert and Victoria Nyanzas, and thence, if necessary, to Zanzibar, thus just reversing the route which Speke and Grant had taken in happier days. Meanwhile, no attack occurring, Junker returned to Lado from Dufli, where he had his temporary quarters.

The story of what happened afterwards has already been told in outline (pp. 25–30). In the doubts and fears and dangers of those times Junker had his full share. However, still expecting help from Khartoum, **A retreat to the Indian Ocean, via Unyoro and Uganda.** he held on, and it was only when the news came that Khartoum had fallen and Gordon was dead, that the intrepid Russo-German determined to delay no longer his attempt to return to that civilisation which he was convinced was rapidly coming to an end in the Soudan. We know how he reached Uganda in 1886, after being detained at Kabba Rega's owing to the war between Unyoro and Uganda,

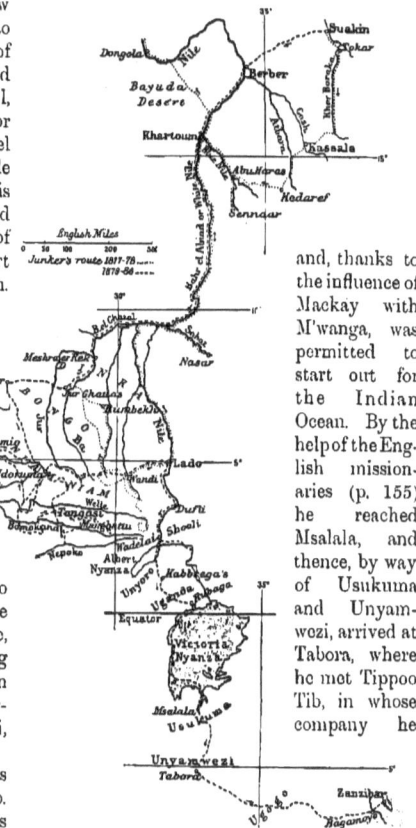

MAP OF DR. JUNKER'S ROUTES.

and, thanks to the influence of Mackay with M'wanga, was permitted to start out for the Indian Ocean. By the help of the English missionaries (p. 155) he reached Msalala, and thence, by way of Usukuma and Unyamwezi, arrived at Tabora, where he met Tippoo Tib, in whose company he arrived at Bagamoyo on the 29th of November, 1886.

Dr. Junker's labours cover a large field. They are more valuable for the scientific contributions to the history of the people, the plants, and the animals of the country

SHOOLI VILLAGE.
(*From a Photograph by R. Buchta.*)

SHOOLI MUSICAL INSTRUMENTS.
(*From a Photograph by R. Buchta.*)

traversed than for actual discoveries in geography. Yet they are not without this merit also; though crossing and recrossing as his lines do the tracks of previous travels, the critic who judges an explorer's work merely by the lines of his route being distant from those of any other will do but scant justice to the admirable researches of this patient man of science, who accomplished much on slender resources, without any display of force or the loss of a single life by violent means. The Makaraka country was, to a large extent, a mere name to geographers, until Junker familiarised us with it; and, though the Niam-Niam and Monbuttoo races had been introduced to ethnologists by Schweinfurth, they were for the first time fully described by his successor. The Momfu, Mabode, A-Bangba, Mangballe, Maigo, Mege, A-Bissanga, and other relatives of the Monbuttoo, were in like manner Junker's especial people; and besides the Upper Nile tribes, on his way to Uganda he passed through the Shooli (pp. 264, 265), and a host of other races, none of whom he left without examining their ways and their persons in a way that was unknown to the earlier travellers of the non-scientific order. Unfortunately, the privations of the last years of his life in Africa undermined a constitution never robust, and before those best able to judge were fully aware of how much the world was in his debt, Wilhelm Junker died at St. Petersburg on the 16th of February, 1892.*

* For the facts relating to Dr. Junker's career we are indebted to an obituary notice by Mr. Ravenstein, in *Proceedings of the Royal Geographical Society*, 1892, p. 185, where references to most of his writings will be found. His travels, or at least a sketch of them, appear in an excellent English translation by Mr. A. H. Keane— "Travels in Africa during the Years 1875-78," "Travels in Africa 1879-81," and "Travels in Africa 1882-86" (1890-92). There are some slight condensations in the English version, and the omission of some maps, which are more than compensated for by additional notes and illustrations. Papers on Dr. Junker's travels appear in *Bulletin de la Société Khédéviale*, II° Ser., No. 12, pp. 629-658, and in *Proceedings of the Royal Geographical Society*, 1887, pp. 399-420, to which the reader may be referred.

SHOOLI WARRIOR.
(*From a Photograph by R. Buchta.*)

CHAPTER XII.

THE INTERNATIONAL EXPLORERS: "ONE TRAVELLER RETURNS."

An African Renaissance—The Fresh Departure of the Belgian King—The Brussels Conference and what came of It—Much Talk and Small Results—A Catalogue of Failures—The Elephant Expedition—The Action of Great Britain and the Royal Geographical Society—A List of Unexplored Routes—Ways and Means—The Selection of a Region to be Explored and its Explorers—Keith Johnston and Joseph Thomson—They Start into Africa from Dar-es-Salaam—In the Coast Belt—Dull Days—The Rufiji River—Behobeho—Death of Johnston—Thomson Goes On—Wakhutu and Mahenge—Zuluised Race of Robbers—To the Central Plateau—A Delightful Gateway and a Depressing Moorland—A Curious Grievance—A Mutiny—Lake Nyassa—Tanganyika and the Lukuga Outlet—Ujiji—Attempt to reach the Atlantic—Failure—Peace with Honour—Wurua People—A Voyage down Tanganyika in the *Calabash*—The Homeward Journey—Lake Leopold—Murder of Carter and Cadenhead—More Belgian Fiascoes—Chief Simba—Arrival at Bagamoyo—Results of Expedition—Contrast of Thomson's Expedition with those of the Belgians—Some African Illusions—Failure to find Minerals or Elephants—A Coal-hunting Venture.

BUT while Dr. Junker was so far in the centre of Africa that only faint echoes of his wanderings reached Europe, events all-important for the future of that continent were in progress. For years before the date at which he set out for the Upper Nile Valley the eyes of the civilised world had been more and more directed to the "land of black men." The travels and death of Livingstone had surrounded with a sort of halo the regions into which he had introduced his readers, and Stanley's visit to Uganda had been the beginning of a great work in that country and elsewhere. The expeditions of Burton, Speke and Grant, Baker, and Cameron had ended in the annexation (not always to civilisation) of vast regions still devastated by the slave-hunters. This interest was heightened by the tales brought back by the German explorers, whose additions to our knowledge have been already noticed; and in 1876 we were waiting almost daily for news of Stanley, who had left Victoria Nyanza, to emerge, by a route west of Tanganyika, on the Atlantic coast. This was the geographer's concern in the exploratory renaissance which, ever since Livingstone's transcontinental journeys, had been more and more notable. But the merchants were also casting longing glances on these fertile regions swarming with millions of people, and wondering if realms, of old fabled to be so rich, had

An African renaissance.

not something in store for them also. New markets were what the trader yearned for, as, one after another, he saw the old ones closing and the customers of former days becoming his rivals in a more fiercely competitive era. And, above all—for its influence has ever been all-powerful in the opening up of Africa —the "religious world"—though it must not be inferred that the rest was irreligious— permeated society with a half-formed conviction that the white man was far in arrear of his duty if he permitted the black man to learn the blessings of civilisation by means of the Arab slave-dealer from one side of the continent and of the Hamburg gin-sellers on the opposite shore. It was with motives thus fired by philanthropy, greed, and a love of science, that the regeneration of Africa began. For it was in 1876 that the ideas which had been churning in so many minds took shape in the epoch-making scheme of the King of the Belgians.

It is likely enough that, without his taking the lead, something would have been done; but it might not have been done so well or so quickly, and certainly, had Europe been left to itself, it would not have been done in the same way. It is idle now to look back on the mistakes which were made, or on the high hopes then aroused, so soon destined to be disappointed. But, though much of what followed was inevitable, it must be admitted that no one else could have undertaken what Leopold II. did, without arousing more jealousies and suspicions. He was the sovereign of a small country without colonies or dependencies, and, by the terms on which it stood in relation to the Great Powers, debarred from running counter to the declared policy of any of them. Its neutrality in the broils of its neighbours, and its lack of a navy, or of an army capable of playing more than a peaceful part in any international trouble, pointed to the Belgian ruler as the most fitting person to take the initiative in the new departure. Hence, while Belgium had not hitherto furnished any African explorer, in a few months it was to be the starting-point of a great many, and to provide a literature on the theme of one section, large in, amount, if not of corresponding importance.

Accordingly, when the king issued invitations for a conference at Brussels on the affairs of Africa, the 12th of September, 1876, found a full gathering of delegates assembled. Many of them were men of eminence in various callings, and several—like Mr. (afterwards Sir William) Mackinnon, Sir Bartle Frere, Colonel Grant, Captain Cameron, M. Duveyrier, Sir Fowell Buxton, Dr. Nachtigal, Dr. Schweinfurth, and Dr. Rohlfs—familiar with various parts or interests of the country. Great Britain, Belgium, Austria-Hungary, France, Germany, Italy, and Russia were represented. Several nations, like Spain, Denmark, Sweden and Norway, Turkey, Holland, and Portugal, though more or less directly concerned in the affairs of Africa, expressed their doubts as to the utility of the gathering by neglecting to send delegates; and the semi-civilised States of the African continent, like Tunis, Morocco, Liberia, Madagascar, Zanzibar, and Egypt, were not invited. Otherwise it is improbable that Ismaïl Pasha, after the enormous sums he had spent ostensibly in the civilisation of the Nile Basin, would have omitted an opportunity of seeing what concern the latest Kafir congress

The Brussels Conference, September, 1876.

had for him. What was the fundamental idea actuating the king in summoning this conference is a question neither polite nor useful to inquire. At the time when he was entertaining his guests so sumptuously at the gathering over which he presided, various rumours were afloat. Belgium, it was, for instance, affirmed, was anxious to acquire a convict settlement; and, in the light of events that afterwards occurred, the Cassandras who talked in that way are inclined to think that they were not far wrong as to the motives at work. But though the Brussels Conference was really the first step in the founding of the Congo State—and the Congo State the beginning of that scramble for Africa which in a few years, was to be the scandal and the pride of Europe—in 1876 Mr. Stanley was between Tanganyika and Nyangwé (now a Congo station), and the extent—the very existence, indeed—of the vast territory through which he was soon to descend was unsuspected. The son of Leopold of Gotha and the grandson of Louis Philippe of France has never been accused of insensibility to the interests of his country or of himself; but, so far as the Brussels Conference was concerned, there is no reason to accuse him of ulterior motives. At that time he was comparatively young, full of vigour, and eager to distinguish himself in one of the few walks in life which the constitutional monarch of a little kingdom, the theme of many treaties, was able to take. His only son was dead, and he was now willing to devote part of his fortune to the regeneration of Africa. The suppression of the East Coast slave-trade was, indeed, about the only item laid before the meeting in advance. Hence, it was quite likely that all the king wished was that the delegates should either suggest plans themselves or homologate those which were simmering in his own mind.

A more systematic exploration of Africa, conducted in a more methodical way, by the well-planned co-operation of the different civilised nations was the outcome of the three days' deliberations of this congress. National committees were to be formed in the different countries in aid of the common object all of them had in view, to collect subscriptions, and to send delegates to the Central or International African Association, having its seat in Brussels. Then the members of the Conference, having established a geographical millennium on paper, went home: some honestly to attempt the carrying out of the objects aimed at, others to plot privately in favour of plans altogether incompatible with international comity. One of the chief resolutions of the Conference had been in favour of founding stations, extending across Africa, where the different explorers might find aid and succour without requiring to make their way to the coast—such stations to be unarmed posts whence the light of civilisation would irradiate the darkness around.* These, Belgium, which was perhaps the only country represented that really believed in the project, began to establish. The first route on which the posts were determined to be placed was that between Tanganyika and the East Coast. But the Belgian officers selected for carrying out this project were, like so many of her explorers made and not born, singularly unfitted for the task assigned them, or—*post hoc propter hoc* —unusually unfortunate in the mishaps of travel which befell them. The earlier attempts with a train of ox-waggons failed, owing to the cattle dying of the tsetse fly bites. On the death of Captain Crespel and Dr. Maes, its principal members, MM. Wauthier and Dutrieux were sent to

ON THE ISLAND OF CHISUMULU, LAKE NYASSA.
(*From a Photograph by Mr. Fred Moir.*)

A catalogue of failures.

* Banning: "Africa and the Brussels Geographical Conference" (translated by R. H. Major, 1877), p. 104.

supply their places. The former also succumbed to the climate near Lake Chaia, about eighty miles south-east of Kazé, or Tabora (Vol. II., p. 262); so that it was not until 1880 that Karema, on Lake Tanganyika (p. 288), was founded by Captain Cambier. For the first time a laudable effort was made to employ elephants as beasts of burden, so as to avoid the cost, trouble, and the ofttimes impossibility of obtaining porters. Elephants, we know, had, in the earlier history of Northern Africa, been tamed,* and Asiatic ones had formed part of the British expedition into Abyssinia; but their use was quite unknown in modern savage Africa, and since the early ages of the Christian era the African species had not been domesticated. Accordingly, though plans for forming "keddahs" for elephant catching and taming were among the many projects of that period, the first animals had, naturally, to be imported from India. Four, the gift of King Leopold, set out on their experimental journey under the guidance of Captain Falkner Carter, an Irishman with some Persian experience. But, unfortunately, either through the new arrivals not being properly managed, or not being

* In addition to the references already given regarding the ancient domestication of African elephants, see Cust. *Proc. of the R. G. S.,* 1882, pp. 381, 382; and Lugard: "East African Empire," Vol. I., pp. 491-498.

acclimatised—for they were not affected by the tsetse flies—or too heavily worked and too poorly fed,† with one exception—an animal which had not been burdened—they all died

ZANZIBAR BEACH.
(*From a Photograph by Mr. H. M. Stanley.*)

before reaching Tanganyika. A costly experiment thus failed, and was not resumed, much to the loss of African civilisation. For, though railways may in time penetrate the continent, porters will for many years be the chief means of carrying goods over a great part of it, where camels, horses, mules, and donkeys cannot live. One elephant will carry as much as fifteen of the loads (sixty pounds) borne by Zanzibar "pagazzi," though, of course, the risk of fifteen loads having to

† Rankin. "The Elephant Experiment in Africa." *Proceedings of the Royal Geographical Society,* 1882, p. 273.

be abandoned by the death of one animal must also be taken into account.

Karema (pp. 147, 288) was, indeed, established by the Association; but owing to ignorance, or worse, the well-meaning plans of King Leopold ended in almost nothing being done by it for civilisation or for the better knowledge of inner Africa. The national committees, however, did something to redeem the inefficiency of the International Commission, although in the end the fine sentiments about disinterested aims rendered the plan so grandiosely formulated at Brussels a butt for cynics and the satirists of poor human nature. Committees were formed in Germany, Austria-Hungary, Spain, Portugal, France, Holland, Italy, Russia, Switzerland, and the United States, in addition to that in Belgium, which, in some respects, was identical with the Central Association, of which it, like the others, was nominally a branch; albeit the fact of their not sending representatives to the Congress proved how doubtful were their views regarding its *bona fides*. By June, 1877, the Belgians had subscribed 287,000 francs, in addition to 44,000 francs a year. Two years later the capital had risen to 600,000 francs, the greater part of which was a gift of the king, while the only nationalities that had forwarded even small contributions were the Germans, Austrians, Hungarians, Dutch, and Swiss, the two latter, however, taking no part in the subsequent toil and turmoil. This fact alone is very eloquent as to the opinions entertained regarding the Brussels scheme. What came out of the work of the different committees we shall see by-and-by.

Of these the least noisy was undoubtedly that founded in Great Britain. The Royal Geographical Society, with which **Great Britain and the Brussels Conference.** it was practically identical, after receiving the confidential reports of its representatives at the Brussels Conference, came to the conclusion that, apart from the fact of its charter debarring it from entering upon any undertakings not strictly geographical, the exploration of Africa could be best advanced by those interested working independently of any international association, while maintaining friendly relations with it and the committees who thought otherwise. As circumstances proved, this fear of trammelling travel with obligations such as those implied by the Brussels Conference was well founded. For, while not a great deal of scientific value came out of that gathering, what did was largely due to English effort. A subscription, to which the society contributed liberally, was started by a special committee appointed by the council to "administer the African Exploration Fund." At the same time, it was intimated that the committee did not propose to confine their operations to the furtherance of expeditions under their entire control. They were willing to consider the propriety of assigning a grant in aid of any well-considered enterprise, so long as it seemed likely to secure good geographical results. Their aim, as announced, was to collect and diffuse the latest geographical information; to procure its early discussion before the Royal Geographical Society; to point out the more immediate desiderata in African geography; to prevent waste of effort in desultory or unimportant explorations; and to turn the large resources of the society in books and instruments, and especially in the willing services of its Fellows who were authorities on African matters, to helpful account. Altogether, £3,989 was subscribed, rather more than one-half being drawn from the society's funds.

The question then came to be, how best this modest sum could be utilised. Seven routes to the interior were suggested. Most of these have been explored, between 1877 and the present moment; but as an authoritative *précis* of how unknown Africa stood at that comparatively recent period, it may be useful to reproduce the information then laid before the committee charged with its consideration. The first line was from the gold-fields of South Africa—in other words, from the Transvaal, past the south end of Lake Tanganyika to Unyanyembe. This line would cross the Zambesi above Tete, and

Ways.

would connect the farthest point reached by Thomas Baines (17° 30′ south latitude, and 30° 30′ east longitude) with Livingstone's route in 1866-67. In its entire length it extended through twelve and a half degrees of latitude, and it led along the high land that separates Lakes Bangweolo, Nyassa, and Tanganyika— a comparatively healthy hilly country from 4,000 to 6,000 feet above the sea-level. It was considered of much consequence that the character of the people and the products of the land, as well as the physical features of the whole of the country traversed by this route, should be fully ascertained. If all these proved to be favourable to the undertaking, a line of overland telegraph might be opened from Cape Town, through the gold-fields to Unyanyembe, and thence in time to Egypt and Europe, a projection which was again mooted as late as 1894.

The second route—namely, along the eastern face of the Coast Range, between the Zambesi and the Equator—was only known at intervals, where it had been crossed by a few travellers, mostly at the same "passes." The contours of the range would, therefore, have to be explored either from the sea-face or from the plateau side, with the view, first, of determining the points where the range was nearest to the sea, as it was of material importance to get quickly away from the unhealthy coast to more elevated regions; and secondly, with the view of finding the most convenient lines of access to the interior.

The third route was from the east coast to the north end of Lake Nyassa. Portions of the district to be traversed by this route had been visited by Dr. Roscher and Baron von der Decken (Vol. II., pp. 66, 240), and, more recently, by Bishop Steere (p. 136). There appeared to be a natural highway across it, by which slave-caravans had travelled for many years. A route from the east coast to the north end of Nyassa was regarded as an important main line, whence connections might hereafter be made with the south end of that lake, and with the south end of Lake Tanganyika.

The fourth route was from the north end of Nyassa to the south end of Tanganyika. Livingstone crossed this route in 1872; but beyond this we were, in 1877, almost entirely ignorant of its nature, except that it would connect two great lakes, on one of which a missionary station was already established, and it would solve many vexed geographical questions, one of which was the real distance between the lakes. It was considered important to learn the capabilities of the country for a waggon-road to connect Tanganyika with the anticipated trading depôt at the north end of Nyassa. This is now known as the Stevenson Road. It will have been noticed that the Zambesi, and its principal tributary, the Shiré, had ceased to be included in this programme. But by this time the labours of the missionaries had made even the affluents of the latter—the Ruo, with the Zoa Falls (p. 273), among others—familiar ground. The fountain-head of the Shiré was now the starting-point for explorers.

A fifth route, considered promising but costly and perilous, was from the coast opposite Zanzibar to the south end of Victoria Nyanza, and thence to the north end of Tanganyika. The Church Missionary Society had that very year established a station at M'papwa, two hundred miles from the coast, and their parties for Karagwe and Uganda were expected to be at their destinations by midsummer. The experiences of the Rev. Roger Price, of the London Missionary Society, in the year 1875, had shown that the tsetse fly did not injure cattle on the route to M'papwa; and Mr. Price reported so favourably upon the physical features of this portion of the country, that a large party had started with bullock-carts, in which they were to proceed to Ujiji (p. 137). It was proposed, however, to explore a nearer way to Victoria Nyanza than that by M'papwa. The western third of the route, extending from the south point of Victoria Nyanza to the northern end of Tanganyika, had not then been traversed by Europeans, and lay across the high land that was believed to divide the Nile from the Congo.

Of the sixth route—namely, from Mombasa by Kilimanjaro to the south-east shore of Victoria Nyanza—little was known, except through the travels, reports, and hearsay of Dr. Krapf, Baron von der Decken, and the Rev. Mr. Wakefield, one of the oldest of African missionaries, and Mr. New; and even none of these gentlemen had penetrated farther than Kilimanjaro. It had, however, probably fertile. Speke had strongly recommended a route from east to west at one degree north of the Equator, but the one mentioned seemed to possess equal advantages, besides being shorter. At that date the Tana had been ascertained to be navigable for a hundred miles, and to be seven feet deep at fifty miles to the east of Mount Kenia. "It is said," the committee tell their

KILIMANJARO, FROM MOSCHI, SHOWING SNOW-CLAD PEAK OF KIBO.
(From a Sketch by Bishop Tucker.)

been a long-established caravan-route to the great lake.

The last route to be considered by the committee was from Formosa Bay by the Tana—or Dana—River and Mount Kenia to the north-east shore of Victoria Nyanza. The line passed through a mountainous country, and therefore, though only two degrees south of the Equator, was recommended as in all likelihood not subject to malaria or to any great heat. The district it traversed was reported to be well watered and subscribers, in words which read strangely, considering what has been ascertained in the interval (p. 233), that "the Samburo people to the north employ camels and horses; if this report be true, the explorer or trader would be independent of porters. This route has many recommendations; the famous Mount Kenia, capped, like Kilimanjaro, with snow, lies on the way, and the earlier portion of the journey might be made by water." All this sounded, a few years later, like very ancient history: it is now almost platitude,

FALLS OF ZOA ON THE RIVER RUO, A TRIBUTARY OF THE SHIRÉ.
(From a Photograph by Mr. Fred Moir.)

In addition to these specific lines of exploration, and in connection with a trunk-road across the continent, efforts, it was thought, ought to be made to explore the great extent of unknown country to the north of the Lualaba, so as to connect Equatorial Africa with Darfur, with Lake Tchad, and with the valley of the Ogowé.

The committee indicated to their travellers convenient places of rendezvous — such as Ujiji, on Lake Tanganyika, and Nyangwé (Vol. II., p. 272) on the Lualaba—"in the respective dominions of the Cazembe, the country traversed in Africa, supposing the party to return to the place whence it set out. In through journeys the rate had in many cases been nearly twice as great. The aggregate length of the seven specified routes was about 7,700 geographical miles. Consequently, the cost of filling up in an outline manner the great lacune in African geography would, on a rough estimate, amount to about £11,000. The following table gives these data in a very widely approximate form; but it may serve as a contribution to the story of how Africa was opened up, and

Means.

ROUTE.	APPROXIMATE DISTANCE IN GEOGRAPHICAL MILES.	COST, IF RECKONED AT £1 10s. PER MILE.
		£
1. Gold-fields to Unyanyembe, and back	2,000	3,000
2. East Coast Range, Zambesi to Equator *	1,400	2,100
3. East Coast to North of Nyassa, and back	500	750
4. North of Nyassa to Tanganyika, and back †	400	600
5. Zanzibar to Lake Victoria and Tanganyika, and back	1,600	2,400
6. Mombasa by Kilimanjaro to Lake Victoria, and back	900	1,350
7. Formosa Bay by Kenia to Lake Victoria, and back	900	1,350
	7,700	£11,550

Kassongo, and the Muata Yanvo. Nyangwé, as being at present the most advanced post of African exploration, is especially important as a depôt."

Other measures were suggested to be carried out when favourable opportunities occurred, such as placing "a steamer on the Congo above the Falls for purely exploratory purposes"—a scheme carried out so long ago (p. 118) that the recommendation has by this time taken its place among the earlier chronicles of the renaissance of African exploration —or exploitation.

The cost of despatching a well-equipped exploring expedition from England was in 1877 calculated at £1 10s. for each mile of the manner in which the ways and means were provided.‡

As it was impossible with the funds at their disposal to compass any exploration which cost half of the sum named, the committee resolved on devoting their efforts to the third and fourth routes—namely, those from Dar-es-Salaam, a few miles south of Zanzibar, to the northern end of Lake Nyassa, and thence to Tanganyika, and backwards to the east coast. In those days African travellers were not so numerous as they afterwards became. All the available men could, indeed, be easily reckoned up; and it so happened that among the usual crowd of volunteers

Keith Johnston and Joseph Thomson.

* This is a through route, but its cost is estimated at a single rate.
† If conducted independently from Lake Nyassa, and not in connection with Route 3, the cost would be increased.
‡ These particulars are, in addition to private sources of information, derived from the various papers and reports issued by the committee, and from Sir Clements Markham's exhaustive "Fifty Years' Work of the Royal Geographical Society" (*Journal*, Vol. L., pp. 81-82).

none with local experience which was sufficient to overrule other objections presented themselves. Accordingly, neither of the two men selected had ever been in Africa, though one of them had compiled an excellent textbook on the continent where he was so soon to rest. This was Keith Johnston (p. 275), only son of the eminent Scottish geographer of the same name, who eagerly accepted the command of the new expedition. But, if not a practised explorer, he was, perhaps, the most expert geographer who had ever entered Africa. For he was a trained chartographer, and, though only thirty-two, had already proved his capacity by work done in several of the great map-making establishments of England and the Continent, by acting as Assistant-Curator in the Royal Geographical Society's Map Room, by several books and atlases of which he was author, and by eighteen months' field labour on a Government Survey of Paraguay. In private life "Keith Johnston Secundus," as Livingstone, who had a good opinion of the geographical acumen displayed in his "Lake Regions of Central Africa" (1870), called him, was loved for his singular unselfishness, his firmness in what he considered duty, and entire absence of anything like self-assertion. German thoroughness distinguished all his labours, whether in the closet or in the field; while his well-knit frame and perfect health seemed likely to bear him well through the toils of an African journey. In 1871 he had, indeed, volunteered for the Livingstone Relief Expedition of that year (Vol. II., p. 263), and high hopes were entertained of his future career as an explorer. His companion, Mr. Joseph Thomson (p. 285), was in the still happier condition of having all the world before him. A native of Thornhill, in Dumfriesshire, he was a mere youth when he was accepted as Mr. Johnston's assistant; but, as the young Scotsman's later career as an African traveller proved, the right man generally appears when he is wanted. In this case, the countryman of Mungo Park and of Livingstone was, in spite of the doubts expressed at the time, admirably fitted for the duties he had undertaken. In the University of Edinburgh he had acquired a sufficient acquaintance with geology and other sciences, and what he lacked in experience was amply compensated for by an equable temper and a robustness which it took many a year of African swamps to shake. When to this was added a native shrewdness, in which the *suaviter in modo* was always at the right time admirably tempered by the *fortiter in re*, little was lacking to make up the ideal explorer he afterwards became.

KEITH JOHNSTON.
(*From a Photograph by C. Henwood, Chiswick.*)

At Zanzibar the services of Chuma, Livingstone's faithful servant (Vol. II., p. 281), In the coast belt: dull days. and of Juma, who had crossed Africa with Cameron, were secured, and an experimental trip was made to Usambara, a district on the mainland, for the purpose of detecting any oversights of equipment before it was too late. Accordingly, when, on the 19th of May, 1879, the party made for the interior at Dar-es-Salaam, its prospects were decidedly of the best. In all, it consisted of 150 men. The first few days led through Uzaramo, along those raised sea-beaches which form so characteristic a feature of East Africa. Now the way led through dense shrubberies, anon among tall cocoanuts, mangoes (p. 276), jack fruits and bananas, which clothed the hollows and river bottoms. Less happily, the route would for hours lie through swamps, or along paths cut into deep ruts by the rains, which fell for weeks at a stretch, until the Rufiji or Kingani River was reached. But, as a river, this stream turned out to contain about as much sand as water. To add to their gathering troubles, Mr. Johnston caught the fever which ended his career on the 23rd of June. Had he been persuaded to take rest, he might have recovered; but his mind was set on reaching Behobeho, or Berobero, 120 miles inland from Dar-es-Salaam, so that, though he daily grew worse, he insisted on being carried for a fortnight through the swamps and along the great scrubby desert across which the way to that goal took, in horrible pain from disease, the jolting of the porters, and the intense heat of the tropical sun. At last Behobeho was reached, on the other side of a great uninhabited desert covered with acacia thorns, where sign of life is seldom seen, and near the lower flanks of the mountains that border the great interior plateau. But it was too late, and poor Keith Johnston now lies in a lonely grave, a martyr, five weeks after he entered Africa, to his eager desire to ransack the continent with which. theoretically at least, he was so well acquainted.

Death of Johnston.

Had Mr. Thomson now turned back, or at least halted until he could have communicated with London, his youth and inexperience might well have justified this procedure. However, determined to carry out the task assigned to his dead companion, he did not even wait to consult the Geographical Society, but pushed on in the hope of doing something, if not everything intended when the expedition set out. He was then, just twenty-two, responsible for work in which, he was well aware, few had succeeded. Fortune, however, favours the brave, and it favoured the young Scotsman in a pre-eminent degree when, with his foot on the threshold of the unknown, he resolved to go forward and do his best. On the 2nd of July, Mr. Thomson accordingly resumed his journey—though at the time ill with the fever which had already more than once attacked him. The valley of the Mgeta, along which his course lay, is bounded by low carboniferous hills on the left, and the high mountain ranges that form the edge of the great central plateau on the right. These heights, by acting as condensers of the fleeting clouds, produce almost perennial showers, which nurture a rank vegetation in the marshy tracts. As might be expected, this rotting mass creates malaria and other diseases, the effects of which are evident on the Wakhutu natives. A more miserable, a more apathetic race does not exist in Africa. All day they would gather around the explorer's camp in crowds, sitting with their poor, ill-fed, withered bodies doubled up, gazing at the strangers with idiotic, lack-lustre eyes—looking, Mr. Thomson tells us, like so

Wakhutu and Mahenge.

MANGO FRUIT.
(*From a Photograph by Sir John Kirk.*)

many slave-gangs resting on their way to the coast, with all hope of life and liberty flogged out of them. In the Ukhutu country the dreaded Mahenge were encountered—thanks to the young traveller's tact, without any mishap, though so terrified were the porters thousand. Nor does the wonder cease when it is found that, in reality, the Mahenge are as cowardly as the tribes on whom they trample. Owing to their being armed like the Zulus, offshoots of whom are found far beyond the Zambesi, it has been supposed that they are

EAST AFRICAN WATER VEGETATION, INCLUDING THE MAGNIFICENT BLUE WATER LILY
(*Nymphæa stellata*, var. *Zanzibarensis*).
(*From a Photograph by Sir John Kirk.*)

that at the very name of these people they were prepared to throw down their loads and take to the bush. The Mahenge had until then been little, if at all, known. Their country comprises a very acute angle formed by the junction of the Rivers Ruaha and Uranga. But, as most of it is uninhabited, the robber race, who are to this day a standing terror to their neighbours, and have depopulated regions twice as big as that which they occupy, do not number more than four allied to that remarkable stock. This is, however, a mistake: their nearest affinities are to the Wagindo, Wanindo, and Wapangwa, who live south of the Rufiji.

Until a great wave of Maviti robbers passed across this region, they were, though vastly superior in physique and intelligence to the Wakhutu, not otherwise widely different from the people around them. But some of the Maviti, who are a Zulu tribe settled north of the Zambesi, remaining behind among the Mahenge, the latter speedily learned the former's method of warfare; and, having learnt it, adopted at the same time their arms and the marauding purposes to which they apply them. Yet, though the Maviti costume strikes terror into the faint hearts of the tribes upon whom they have been taught to prey, the Mahenge have little of the Zulu spirit. They dress in lions' skins; but the skins cover curs, notwithstanding.

Leaving Mgunda, the way led through a rich valley depopulated by the rovers they had just parted from, and, crossing the Ruaha, entered the Mahenge country. Here they were treated reasonably well, and were even popular, being regarded as a gratis sight, in much the same light that a party of Mahenge would be in an English village.

The expedition had now reached the comparatively healthy plateau of inner Africa, and could congratulate itself on having crossed a belt which has always proved most trying to the unseasoned traveller. Its progress henceforth was more agreeable, though very slow, owing to the steepness and slipperiness of the mountain-paths, and bad guides, by whose stupidity the expedition was hard run for food. Moreover, as a long-continued spell of rheumatic fever proved, Mr. Thomson was still far from having arrived at an African sanatorium. Even the beauty of the country lost half of its charm to a man so weak that he was, at frequent intervals, compelled to lie down to rest until he regained sufficient strength to creep on. Still, the sound of mountain torrents splashing along beds bordered by trees and ferns, the air heavy with the odour of flowers, forest clumps hoary with lichens and mosses, through the branches of which cool winds sighed, formed a cheering change from the dank marshes and depressing deserts left behind. Even the driving mist, which at times enveloped all in a clammy mantle, was not a repulsive sight to the Scottish traveller; for it reminded him of his native "haar" and that sea-ghost all in grey which rolls northwards from the Solway. "Now and then," as he told the geographers on his return, "a group of savage natives crowned some lofty eminence, and watched our progress through the half-veiling cloud as we wound our way along rocky dell, or deep down in gloomy valley, appearing and disappearing amongst the trees. These were charms which no amount of fever could blind us to, which acted as a solatium to all our troubles, and fascinated us with a boundless sense of liberty."

Even after the expedition was fairly on the plateau, the fever did not desert Mr. Thomson. At times he would be so feeble as to fall down helpless; and for a week memory so entirely failed him that, had it not been for his practice of noting down everything at the time, his diary would have been for that period an entire blank. The interior, however, proved as disappointing as the mountains through which access to it had been obtained formed a striking contrast to the region that had preceded them. For miles and miles ahead, as far as the eye could see, there stretched a bleak moorland, unrelieved by hill or dale or forest tree, varying from four to five thousand feet above the sea-level. The best parts of it consisted of grassy, undulating stretches rising into rounded ridges, to fall away into rounded valleys, monotonous in form or colour, but for the occasional occurrence of a patch of shrub, a grotesque baobab (p. 280), or an equally singular euphorbia. Not a sign of life was to be seen, with the exception of the "parson crow," a tawny vulture, or, it might be, a herd of cattle; while from morning to evening a sharp wind blew unopposed by sheltering hill or forest, causing the Zanzibar porters to light fires to warm themselves at midday.

The people of Uhehe are scattered in villages which stud this African upland at wide intervals, as the country is poor, and the chief food supply is the lean kine pasturing on the cold, clayey soil. But they are "a fine-looking race of gentlemanly savages," who either dress in nothing, or roll themselves in a winding-sheet of twelve yards of calico. They treated the white man with all the respect due to him, never saying anything unpleasant, except indirectly. Even in the important matter of "hongo"—customs, tribute, or blackmail, call it what you will—the Uhehe folk were delicate; and when the chief was offended at a breach of etiquette, the only notice he took of it was to absent himself for a week—a welcome spell of leisure which Mr. Thomson utilised for writing and despatching letters to the coast. Poor food and little of it, cold winds and rheumatic pains, are not, even at the best of times, were gratified the expedition would be wrecked, Mr. Thomson pocketed his principles, and promised that, since this was the desire of their hearts, they should never be denied, whenever necessary, an ample allowance of the hippopotamus-whip.

Marching through Ubena, a second and higher plateau was reached on the 10th of September, though this upland flat is so cut up by streams that it looks, to the inexperienced eye, like a series of mountain ranges from six to nine thousand feet high. This tract extends around the north and east sides of Lake Nyassa, half-way to Tanganyika, and

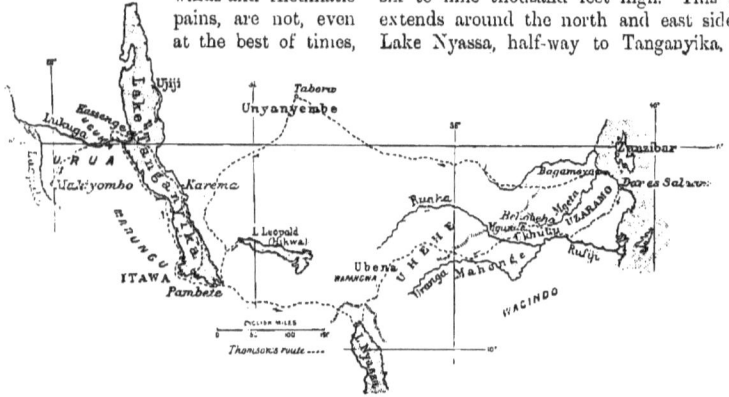

MAP OF KEITH JOHNSTON'S AND JOSEPH THOMSON'S ROUTE IN 1879-80.

inspiriting. But it was not these miseries which most depressed the porters. They had a grievance; and this grievance grew in time so intolerable that the whole caravan, with the exception of six, laid down their muskets, and intimated their intention of risking death or slavery by returning unless the wrong was righted. For it seems that their young master, anxious to practise a more humane kind of discipline than the traditional rough-and-ready way of keeping a gang of African porters in order, had fined them for misdemeanours, instead of inflicting the more summary punishment of flogging. To this the men objected. They wished to be "kourbashed"; and, as it seemed only too probable that unless their wishes around Lake Hikwa, Rukwa, or "Leopold" —a sheet of fresh water which Mr. Thomson discovered to lie about a degree east of the southern end of Tanganyika.

Lake Leopold reached.

Sir H. H. Johnston, who visited this sheet in November, 1889, found that it extended much farther to the south-east than had hitherto been supposed. The existing lake is, however, a shrunken vestige only of a much greater extent of water, as the level plain, fifteen to thirty miles in width, and almost flush with the water, shows. On the east side only, high mountains rise abruptly from the shore, the whole basin being, however, girdled by a wall-like range. The chief feeders of the lake are the Songwe, a poor, muddy stream, and the

Saisi, a large river. The approximate level of the sheet is 2,900 feet; but, owing to the rapid evaporation, the waters are brackish and almost undrinkable. It swarms with crocodiles, hippopotami, and fishes, while buffalo with singularly fine horns, elephants, zebra, many species of antelopes, lions, hyænas, and immense numbers of guinea-fowl, as exist anywhere in this part of Africa. They are few in number, and have "dark, sooty skins, prognathous jaws and thick lips, with small heads and shrunk-up, withered bodies." Their houses are mere human pig-sties; and, like the Warua of the Congo country, they cannot look anyone straight in the face, but deal in asides. A few days more, and

GROTESQUE BAOBAB.
(*From a Photograph by Sir John Kirk.*)

francolins, and ring-doves haunt its unlovely shores. Hunger, thirst, a scorching wind, a blazing sun, venomous flies, and the Wa-ungu, who, owing to a drought which had lasted two years, lived by hunting and rapine, are indeed poor recommendations to it. Even the Arab slave-hunters have deserted it.*

The people of the plateau just mentioned are Wapangwa, Wanena, and Wakinga—races about as degraded specimens of their stock

* *Proceedings of the Royal Geographical Society,* 1890, pp. 226, 227.

Lake Nyassa was seen in the distance, four thousand feet below the plateau on which the expedition was encamped.

On the shores of this fine sheet the caravan seemed to have arrived in a promised land, and with joy they tramped northwards, until, on November 2nd, 1879, they came in sight of Tanganyika. The work undertaken for the Royal Geographical Society's African Committee was now finished. Mr. Thomson had been just in time; for, while resting at Pambete, he was joined by Mr. James

Stewart, from the Free Church mission station on Lake Nyassa (p. 133). Suffering from fever, Mr. Thomson might well, with an easy conscience, have returned with his countryman; but when he looked at the broad expanse of this inland sea, he was seized with an irresistible longing to explore the Lukuga outlet of the lake which Cameron had discovered

<small>Tanganyika and the Lukuga outlet.</small>

confirmed by the exceptionally heavy rains of 1877-78 raising the lake so rapidly that when Captain Hore visited the place in 1878 he found the Lukuga flowing freely out of Tanganyika. Accordingly, leaving the majority of his men in charge of Chuma, Thomson started along the western side of the lake—a journey not hitherto attempted, owing to the difficulties which the mountains presented—and

UGUHA PEOPLE, WEST OF TANGANYIKA.
(From a Photograph by Mr. Fred Moir.)

four years before (Vol. II., p. 277), and had followed for about four miles. He then found it blocked up by vegetation, but observed a decided current setting out of the lake, and was told by the natives that it reached the Lualaba. In 1876 Stanley travelled about five miles beyond Cameron's farthest point, and found that a sand-bar cut off all connection between the lake and the basin of the Lualaba, but predicted that a small rise of the lake would be sufficient to sweep away this barrier.* His prescience was

* "Through the Dark Continent," Vol II., p. 52.

found the voluntary task he had undertaken the hardest piece of work he had hitherto attempted; for the tropical rains had now set in, and with them the thunderstorms which so often accompany the wet season in that part of Africa. The way was bad as bad could be, and the unfriendliness of the chief of Itawa, who kept the traveller prisoner for a time in his gruesome, skull-decorated town, did not add to the delights of this journey. But evidently thinking that a white man who could laugh in the midst of the excited warriors of the place was not "canny," he was let go, only to find himself, a little farther on, the object of great concern. For the excitable natives of Marungu mistook the little caravan for a party of slave-traders. "They used to gather round us in great crowds, and in the maddest excitement, yelling and shouting like demons, brandishing their weapons, as they danced round us, now running away with fierce war-cries, and then, in their excitement, rolling about on the ground as if in convulsions. If they had been on red-hot plates they could not have raised more commotion." These people live very miserably, and, like most mountaineers, are troubled with goitre—an unsightly disease which does not trouble those dwelling by the borders of the lake. To add to his hardships, fever again seized on the explorer; but just when so depressed with the malady that he could have walked with the most philosophical resignation into the lake, he received a new lease of life when, on Christmas Day, 1879, he beheld the Lukuga bearing the drainage-waters of the Tanganyika away to the Congo and the Atlantic. For six days he advanced down the river's course, until he reached a hill from whence he could see the great plan of the Lualaba spread out before him. There could be no mistake that the river was the outlet of the lake; for at that time he did not know of Captain Hore's previous visit. There was no barrier such as Stanley saw; and, with a current which swept along so swiftly that a canoe could not paddle against it, and which could only be crossed with difficulty, it was hard to think that this was the same river the course of which Cameron could only doubtfully trace by the motion of floating straws. It now rushed along between clearly-cut banks, and in a deep channel. In 1882 Major Von Wissmann visited the same place. At that date the Lukuga still flowed out of the lake, and so it did during his second visit in 1886, though the level of the lake had fallen four feet.* In the autumn of 1892 M. Delcommune traced the Lukuga to the so-called Lake Lanji; so that the character of the one outlet of Tanganyika is no longer open to question. However, as the fluctuations in the level of the lake exceed sixteen feet, a time must come when the Lukuga shall no longer be an outlet, unless, indeed, by that time the level of the lake be regulated by building a lock across its debouchure. At present all the great African lakes are falling in level, owing to climatic changes (Vol. II., p. 253), and partly also to geological influences, local and general, though, it is possible, the amount of water in them may sink and rise in certain recurring periods.†

At Kassenge, or Mtowa, Mr. Thomson's party found a station of the London Missionary Society established by an expedition that had left Zanzibar by the caravan route a month after he had bid good-bye to the same place, and had shown amazing energy, in spite of the death of their leader, Dr. Mullins, on the road to the lake. Crossing to Ujiji in a slaver's dhow, the care of Captain Hore soon restored Mr. Thomson to health, and enabled him to obtain from the wreck of the Abbé Debaize's great caravan —one of the abortive Belgian ventures (p. 287)—enough of goods to help him return to the Uguha country (p. 281), determined to trace the Lukuga to the Atlantic, or at least to its confluence with the Congo. But after pressing along its untrodden banks for a week (as already mentioned), the men broke into open mutiny, on the ground that they were being taken into the Manyema territory, where, as was not improbable, they would all be eaten up by that nation of cannibals (p. 71). The Wurua, the people of Urua, the country where he turned back, are, however, a thievish set of rascals. They would tear the clothes off the men's backs, and for the entire time they were amongst them neither life nor "Peace with honour."

---

* "Unter Deutscher Flagge," p. 229. and "My Second Journey through Equatorial Africa," p. 225 ; *Geographical Journal.* Vol. I. (1893), p. 357.

† Sieger, *Globus*, Vol. LXII., No. 21. Tanganyika, at the date of Captain Stairs's measurement (1892), was 2,693 feet above the sea-level.

property was for a moment safe. It was, indeed, only by good luck that the expedition managed to reach Kassenge again in a very woebegone condition, stripped of everything, the leader riding, as became a defeated traveller, who had lost everything but honour, on that meek animal, the mission donkey.

Happily, Captain Hore was at Kassenge with the *Calabash*, and in her, after a pleasant sail down the lake, Mr. Thomson and the members of his caravan who had accompanied him reached the place where he had left the main body in camp with Chuma. From this spot there was now nothing for it but to return to the coast. This was duly accomplished, with some adventures, and not without geographical profit; for it was during this journey that Lake Leopold was discovered. A few days were spent at Unyanyembe, and then the route was resumed until Bagamoyo was reached by the middle of July, with—what is, we believe, altogether unprecedented in the annals of African exploration—the loss of only a single man out of the 150 who had set out more than fourteen months before.* It was, indeed, the proud boast of the traveller, who had now gained a reputation which future years and further exploration only enhanced, that, in spite of much provocation, he had never pulled a trigger in offence or defence. He had traversed 2,830 miles of country, and of these upwards of 1,300 were over entirely new ground. He was the first to reach Lake Nyassa from the north, to journey between Nyassa and Tanganyika, to march along the west side of the latter, and to pass for sixty miles down the Lukuga. Lake Leopold had also been visited for the first time, and some light thrown upon a variety of geographical subjects, such as the Rivers Ruhua and Uranga, the mountainous regions north of Nyassa, and the interesting question relating to the drainage of Tanganyika. All this had been

* Thomson, "Journey of the Society's East African Expedition" (*Proceedings of the Royal Geographical Society*, 1880, pp. 722-742); "To the Central African Lakes and Back," 2 vols. (1881).

accomplished on little over £3,500, which must be considered moderate when it is remembered that Cameron's expedition cost four times as much, and Stanley's a great deal more. Yet nobody was killed, nor did anybody desert or behave in the improper manner which has become stereotyped in the story of Africa—facts which, if they detract from Mr. Thomson's merits in the eyes of the swashbuckler who measures his success by his butcher's bill, place him on the same high plane reserved for Livingstone and the few other travellers who have made their names good introductions for those who follow them.

Mr. Thomson's success, in spite of his inexperience, contrasted markedly with the monotonous tale of failure which befell the Belgian expeditions that <small>And Dispeace without it.</small> were making for or had reached Tanganyika about the same time. At Karema he had visited the International Association's agents—Captain Carter, of the abortive elephant expedition, a "jolly Irishman," and his colleagues, Captains Cambier and Popelin. In a few months Carter and Cadenhead, of the same service, were to be murdered on their way to the coast, about four days' journey from the north end of Lake Leopold —it was at the time generally considered, by a premeditated attack to which the "friendly and sagacious Mirambo" (Vol. II., p. 262) was privy. The redoubtable Simba is, however, believed to have been the murderer. Yet, it is contended, the misfortune was more an accident on the part of one of his war-parties than a deliberate crime. This is doubtful. He had long been a thorn in the side of the Belgian and French mission parties, though he received Mr. Thomson with great hospitality. Three days' march from Simba's, Cadenhead was met on his way to join Carter, and, on the following day, Messrs. Rogers and Burdo, two other Belgians, trying in vain to reach Karema. They had lost two gangs of porters, and did not seem to know what to do. In those days the agents of the Brussels International Association were scattered over half of Africa, and, so far as the Belgian expeditions were concerned, in a state of helpless inefficiency. Their goods and their porters littered the road, and at every village these incapable "explorers" formed the native butts. Mr. Thomson, who could not well be a prejudiced, and was, undoubtedly, a competent witness, looked upon the entire scheme, so far as it had proceeded, as little better than a farce. The paper plan had been good, but the officers selected to carry it out quite unfitted for their task. "These men," he declared in 1881, "have gone out professedly on a mission of 'peace and goodwill,' and have only succeeded in making every tribe they have come in contact with their mortal enemies. The so-called stations have been simply centres of disturbance. The Europeans have been lowered immensely in the eyes of the natives: and a barrier, which it will require years to sweep away, has been raised against the very interests they had been appointed to advance. Expedition after expedition has been despatched, only to arrive at its destination exhausted and worn-out—if, indeed, it has not found itself compelled to halt half-way.

ZANZIBAR.
(*From a Photograph by Mr. H. M. Stanley.*)

Such a pitiable spectacle has never before been seen in all the wide field of African exploration. Not a station has been fixed which deserves the name, not a traveller assisted (the would-be helpers themselves required to be helped), and not a single desired object attained." Mr. Thomson had, indeed, no great opinion of the commercial exploitation of Africa; for, so far as his experience went, there was little to exploit except slaves and ivory, an opinion also shared by Sir Samuel Baker. But slavery it was, of course, one of the objects of the international explorers to crush; and, after tramping to the great lakes and back again, Mr. Thomson left Africa without as much as seeing an elephant. He was

Some African illusions.

SOME AFRICAN ILLUSIONS.

continually hearing of districts where tuskers swarmed; but invariably he learned on arrival that this was long ago, and that the plenty was then in some other locality many days ahead, so that in the end he had to gain his acquaintance with the characteristic African animal by a visit to the Zoological Gardens. Another illusion vanished before Mr. Thomson completed his journey, and that was its mineral wealth. In South Africa there is abundance of this; but though gold is obtained on the west coast, and there is a talk of diamonds elsewhere, the deposits outside the settled part of the continent are still very shadowy. In Central Africa, besides the staples already mentioned, there was a marked absence of anything "worth trading for." No doubt unscientific travellers—and the explorers of this part of the continent had been, for the most part, ill-acquainted with geology—had, by their offhand remarks, led the world to believe that this was the actual El Dorado. "One traveller, for instance, hears of much iron being worked in a mountain, and concludes that it is probably a mountain of iron: another observes some nodules in the soil, and concludes that all underneath is iron. He sees a black rock in a precipice, and calls it coal: a white one, and he calls it chalk, until people have come to look on Central Africa as the future hope of the world. This has not been my experience, and I have now gone over a considerable area. Nowhere have I seen a single metal in a form which a white man would for a moment look at as a profitable or workable speculation. There is, no doubt, a considerable abundance of iron in many parts, but very little more than sufficient to supply the simple wants of the natives. Coal I saw none, and my researches would

JOSEPH THOMSON.
(From a Photograph by J. Thomson, 70a, Grosvenor St., W.)

lead me to believe that such a thing does not exist over the wide area embraced by our route."

This kind of talk had fired Seyed Bargash, Sultan of Zanzibar, with the notion that rich coal-fields existed on the banks of the Lujende tributary of the Rovuma River (Vol. II., p. 244). He even went so far as to engage Mr. Thomson to examine the district. But though he made a journey to the place where the supposed coal had been reported, and in other directions, he had to return without being able to report this source of wealth in the Zanzibar dominions, though an inferior lignite, of no economic value, has been found near the coast.*

Mr. Thomson received at a later date—namely, in 1885—the Founders' Medal of the Royal Geographical Society. It is, however, quite as interesting to record that his native followers were not forgotten. A handsome sword, with a silver medal, was presented to Chuma, who, with most of Mr. Thomson's men, had returned from taking part in Captain Phippson-Wybrant's ill-fated expedition to join their old leader in his abortive search for coal in 1881. A second-class sword and a silver medal fell to Makatubo, the "headman" next in rank to him, and a bronze medal and certificate of conduct, bearing the Consul-General's seal, were given to each of the 150 rank and file, who, in such expeditions, are usually not even accorded the immortality of a line of print—unless, indeed, when they desert, plunder, murder their master, or get flogged.

* Sir John Kirk seems, however, more sanguine than Mr. Thomson (*Proceedings of the Royal Geographical Society*, 1882, p. 65). See also, for a description of the Masai and Rovuma country, Maples. *Ibid.*, 1880, p. 337; and Last, *Ibid.*, 1890, p. 223.

CHAPTER XIII.

INTERNATIONAL EXPLORERS: MANY MEN AND MANY MINDS: THE END OF A DREAM.

The Views of the International Association Alter with Stanley's Descent of the Congo—A Tale of Folly—The Belgian Station of Karema—A Castle in Africa—The Italians—Antinori—Chiarini—Cecchi—Bianchi—Licata—A Fictitious Expedition—Portugal's Share—France—De Brazza—Largeau—Debaize—The Barrel-Organ as a Geographical Instrument—Missionaries—Père Duparquet—Germany—Pre-International Association Explorers—The Day of Small Things—West African Travellers—Schütt—Büchner—The Muata Yanvo—An Equatorial Potentate—Lenz—Rohlfs—Mechow—Pogge—Wissmann—The Bashilange—Reichard—Kaiser—Böhm—Evil that Good might Follow—A Tale of Misfortune and Death—Flegel and Others—Giraud—The Austro-Hungarians—Magyar's Semi-Fabulous Adventures—The English Explorers—Elton—Erskine—Phippson-Wybrant—Lord Mayo—Lieutenant O'Neill—Johnston—Thomson—Masailand—Something Happens, and the Story of Africa Enters upon a New Phase.

THE International Association was not long destined even to affect the guise of being the visible sign of international comity. For almost as soon as it had got into a semblance of working order, even before Mr. Johnston and his companion had entered Africa, Mr. Stanley had emerged from it on the opposite shore (Vol. II., p. 311). His vivid letters had already played a leading part among the factors at work in the Brussels Conference. But no sooner had he landed in Europe in the early days of 1878 than the tales which he had to tell of the vast flood of the Congo and its tributaries rolling through a rich land peopled by black people, led the International Association to concentrate itself more and more on this great waterway into the continent. Naturally, also, as the leading spirits of that body were always Belgians, its new aims became, little by little, more Belgian and less international, until, passing through various stages, the Congo Free State, under the sovereignty of King Leopold, was about all that remained of the airy schemes of international co-operation, without a thought of territorial aggrandisement, which were conceived in the autumn of 1876. However, that period was still a few years distant. In 1878 the various committees continued to talk—but not quite so loudly, nor with a shout so unanimous—of the self-denying clause, as in the short-lived "era of good feeling." They still sent expeditions out; yet these expeditions were, with a few exceptions, not of any great importance, and conducted with a half-heartedness which was but a forecast of the blatant disregard of old pledges which was so soon to be the beginning of a fresh departure in the history of savage Africa. The subscriptions which came in from the various committees, never at any time very lavish, now grew smaller, until the International Association ceased to exist even in name, and the scheme of international exploration resolved itself into every nation working for its own hand, and, latterly, for its own benefit.

It is, nevertheless, necessary, in order to maintain the continuity of this narrative, to note briefly what was done under the semblance of the Brussels Conference before that unsubstantial gathering had ceased to exert any influence on the immediate fortunes of the continent which it was intended to enlighten. So many men were now in Africa, and so many expeditions of minor moment engaged in various projects, that it is difficult to arrange them chronologically. These explorations crossed and recrossed each other and those of an earlier date, and were frequently simultaneous, especially in the halcyon days of the international scheme. We may, therefore, most profitably touch upon them under the heads of the various countries whose African committees were understood to direct them under the inspiration of the Brussels Congress.

Belgium was decidedly the most enthu-

A tale of folly.

siastic of the countries concerned. Yet it was noticed that, from the first news of Stanley's descent of the Congo, the Belgians confined their exertions almost exclusively to the west coast. Their misadventures in East Africa had, indeed, been sad enough to discourage any further enterprise in that direction, apart from the fact that already, as we know now, there were too pronounced suspicions of annexation in the air to permit those who had "interests" at stake to dissipate their energies. However, besides an expedition under Mr. Stanley to found stations on the Congo beyond the falls of that river—of which we shall have more to say when the founding of the Congo State comes to be described—the International Association, which, financially speaking, may be described as King Leopold, continued to despatch explorers from the eastern side of the continent, though, unfortunately, without any better success than had attended their predecessors. But the deaths of Captain Crespel and Dr. Maes from fever, followed by that of Lieutenant Wauthier, if they did not end the efforts of Belgium for the exploitation of Africa, effectually damped the ardour of its sovereign for expeditions in that direction. Henceforward, the energy which emanated from Brussels found a better outlet along the Congo and its tributaries.

The folly which characterised the entire proceedings of the Belgians in East Africa was not quite abandoned in the Congo valley. Yet, under the chastening tuition of misfortune and of English tutors, the worst of their early inexperience did not bring such disaster in its train as at the period when the road between Bagamoyo and Tanganyika was littered with the *débris* of Belgian expeditions under the International Association flag.

Karema: "un château en Afrique."

Officers, weary of the monotony of a garrison town in Flanders, dandies from the Allée Verte, and braggarts from everywhere, were ready to offer their services, which were too frequently accepted. Few of them seem to have had the slightest notion of what was expected of them; and what amazed Thomson and other travellers who met these gentlemen, even when no longer in the callow stage of novitiate, was their utter ignorance of even the elements of African geography. The English explorers had been reared in a sort of atmosphere of traditions; and, if necessarily deficient in the knowledge which these traditions embodied, they generally arrived on the scene of their labours well acquainted with what had been accomplished by their predecessors. The Belgians were, to the last, supremely unfamiliar with the literature of that exploration in which they had begun to take so prominent a part. They did not seem to have as much as read the translations of Livingstone or Stanley, though aiming at posturing in the salons of the Place Royale as their compeers, by dint of a fruitless promenade to the great lake and back again. What Thomson saw at Karema aptly illustrates the evil which was wrought by ignorance in Brussels and folly in Africa. Karema, it may be remembered, was the first of a series of what were intended to be great civilising centres. In order the better to serve this laudable purpose, it was built on a hill, 150 feet above Tanganyika, inaccessible from the lake, surrounded by a marsh and an uninhabited jungle, the haunt of mosquitoes and other insect pests. The nearest inhabitants on the north were the banditti of Kawendi; on the north-east, Simba was, at the time of their arrival, a name of terror to all peace-loving people; while, to complete the circle of robber-chiefs around this centre of civilisation, situated in a swamp and surrounded by a desert the notorious village of Makenda lay to the east of it. To add to its inconveniences as a place of trade, Karema is quite out of the line of the trading caravans: and, when the traveller whose description we are narrating saw it, was so hungry a spot that, with the exception of Indian corn, not a scrap of food could be obtained within miles of it. Fowls, sheep, goats, or cattle had all to be brought at great expense either from Ujiji or from Unyanyembe.

After reading the Utopian talk in the

Brussels Conference about the stations, of which Karema was the first—and, in that quarter, the last—being unmilitary and unarmed, the visitor was amazed to see a place sufficiently defended by marsh and water, intrenched by a system of fortifications on the latest principles of military engineering. Trenches, and walls and forts, curtains and demilunes were being formed with such

(white man), he significantly taps his head."

To complete this tale of folly, the chatellans of this African Agapemone had managed to arouse feelings of implacable hatred in the minds of their thinly scattered neighbours. Not a black man—who was described at the Brussels Conference as quite weary for work— would raise a finger to help them; so that all

KAREMA FORT, NOW A ROMAN CATHOLIC MISSION STATION.
(From a Photograph by Mr. Fred Moir.)

rapidity that one might have imagined that the languid creators of all these visible signs of truculence were so many General Brialmonts strengthening an African Antwerp against an European army on the march, instead of a possible attack from a few feeble villagers clothed in beads and nakedness. "Perhaps once a week a wretched native may be seen wandering past. He gazes with puzzled wonder at all this incomprehensible digging and building, goes home, calls his friends about him, and then, uttering pityingly the one word, 'mzungu'

the labour done on the Karema fortifications had to be performed by Waswahili brought from the coast, who, naturally, held themselves at a high price.

Yet this was not the most extraordinary of the Belgian blunders. After being decimated by disease and desertions, attacked here and plundered there, the international party who were responsible for this extraordinary Light in a Dark Place, heard, when almost at their wits' end, as well they might be after wandering about for two years like lost sheep, of a place called "Karema." It had been described in glowing terms by Mr. Stanley as admirably suited for such a station as that which they had set out to found. So to Karema they begged to be conducted; but though the situation did not come up to expectation, they consoled themselves for this disappointment by abusing the optimist opinions of the Anglo-American traveller. It was only on consider that their duty was done so long as they managed to live in reasonable comfort until recalled or promoted, the result was, in their opinion, immaterial. Having arrived there after so much trouble, the International Association agents had no intention of going any farther. They were even disinclined, in spite of the very object for which the station

DWELLINGS AT ACRÜR, ABYSSINIA.
(From a Photograph by Dr. G. Schweinfurth.)

the Englishmen pointing out that what Mr. Stanley had described was not Karema at all, but Massi-Kamba, twenty miles south of the place so called, to which the natives naturally led the Belgians, that they realised the cardinal blunder that had been committed. Yet, had they taken the trouble to look around them for a few leagues, many spots more suitable would have been discovered. As it was, a worse could have been with difficulty fixed upon. However, the white garrison of the Karema station seeming to was founded, to succour one of the Roman Catholic missionary parties, the remnants of which—one blind, another mad, and all starving—arrived at Karema on their way to join Père Denaud at Ujiji. Indeed, had it not been for the indignant protest of Mr. Carter, who, though lacking much in the way of discretion, seemed the only energetic member of the expedition, the poor priests would have received the cold shoulder from these incompetent representatives of civilisation. It may be added, that the three captains placed a more implicit faith in villainous saltpetre than apostles of peace ought to have done. They seemed to imagine that every black man was thirsting for blood, and, in accordance with that axiom, never stirred from the door of their huts without being armed to the teeth. As for treating porters by any other method than the lash, they ridiculed the very notion, in spite of the unanswerable fact that the whip had not succeeded in their case.* And what Karema was, on a smaller scale was Mpala, another station subsequently founded on the opposite, or western shore of Lake Tanganyika. Both are now in possession of the Roman Catholic missions (p. 147).

The Italians were less enthusiastic, and from the first confined their efforts to a circumscribed region in the north, where the heat of the climate scarcely affected a people reared on the hot shores of the Mediterranean. The Marquis Antinori left for a four years' exploration of Abyssinia, and thence on to the Equatorial Lakes. But though he reached Lechi, the capital of Shoa, after having narrowly escaped assassination between Zeila and Harar, and experienced many difficulties in crossing the Hawash, the Italian explorer was not destined to reach Victoria Nyanza or its sister sheet, Albert Nyanza, from that direction. His labours did much, however, to attract the Italians' attention to the acquisition of part of Abyssinia, and of a semi-protectorate of that kingdom (pp. 289, 292).

The Italians: Antinori, etc.

Chiarini and Gecchi, who left Shoa in 1878 with the intention of proceeding through Kaffa to the African Equatorial Lake region, were no more successful. For, though they reached Kaffa, they were treated as spies, and ill-used in Chera, a small district tributary to the King of Shoa, the result of which was the death of Signor Chiarini and the return of

* Thomson : "To the Central African Lakes and Back," Vol. II., pp. 185-193. A more appreciative, if less critical, account will be found in Count d'Ursel's "Les Belges au Tanganika," *Bul. Soc. Roy. Belge Géog.*, Vol. XVII. (1893), pp. 75-96, and in Wauters' "De Bruxelles à Karema : histoire d'une colonie belge " (1884).

Captain Gecchi. Gustavo Bianchi and Professor Licata were more fortunate in a journey which they made to the interior of Abyssinia, and thence to Assab, on the Red Sea, at the cost of the Italian Africa Society (formerly, "Il Club Africano di Napoli") and of Signor Rocca, an enlightened Naples banker. But this, like other Italian travels in North Africa, soon drifted into a reconnaissance of the Italian acquisitions in that quarter: and hence passes from our purview. To Italy may also be credited the expedition across Africa of Matteucci and Massari (p. 10), the African experiences of Casati, so frequently referred to, and even the more or less official work of Miani, Gessi, and their predecessors on the Upper Nile (Vol. II., pp. 104, 137, etc.). But we are afraid that Italy can claim no share in the apocryphal journey which the "Marquis Maurizio di Buonfanti" and "Dr. Van Flint," an American, were said to have made by way of the Niger to Timbuctoo, and thence back again to Lagos, in the years 1881-83. Indeed, we should not have thought it necessary to mention this romantic expedition had it not appeared in a geographical magazine and for a time imposed upon the world. It now seems that the entire story was a fabrication of the Damberger and Adams order (Vol. I., pp. 219, 238), as fictitious as the adventures which Bishop Berkeley invented for Gaudentio di Lucca, though without the literary charm that redeems the absurdity of that imitation of Utopia and Gulliver.

The journeys of Serpa Pinto and Capello and Ivens (pp. 2, 19) may be accepted as the Portuguese share in the international scheme. Portugal had, in an age when she had more energy than nowadays, made many important explorations in Africa, at present almost forgotten ; but the ventures just mentioned ended her contributions to African geography in modern times. Thenceforward, what little her officers did—and Serpa Pinto's after-labours were of this kind—was dictated solely by political considerations, though in reality it is to British travellers that we owe almost every-

Portugal : Pinto, etc.

thing regarding the less familiar portions of the Portuguese possessions in Africa. Whatever might have been their opinion of the aim of the new departure, the French were early in the field. Lieutenant Count Savorgnan de Brazza, a naval officer, with Dr. Ballay and M. Marche, in command of seventy soldiers, was ordered to proceed up the River Ogowé until their eastwards march reached Albert Nyanza or the Niam-Niam country. Dr. Ballay arrived at a point two hundred and fifty miles distant from the Gaboon, in spite of the misfortunes that befell the party in the loss of their instruments by the upsetting of canoes; and, worse still, by the unfriendliness of the Osyeba people, who were smarting under some wrong done them during a previous visit from white men. M. Marche had to return home invalided; but after many mishaps his companions succeeded, by April, 1877, in reaching the Pombara Falls, where the Ogowé, flowing from the south, becomes so insignificant a stream that it was not considered necessary to follow it any farther. M. de Brazza now resolved, in spite of the sufferings they had endured and their diminished stock of provisions, to direct his expedition into the still more unknown country to the east, out of the basin of the Ogowé, which had hitherto been followed. The region they were now to traverse was, at the time they penetrated it, devastated by famine and drought, so that hunger and thirst were added to the many other miseries of African travel. After crossing a water parting, they reached a stream, which, on being followed up, brought them to the Alima, a large river hitherto unknown, flowing eastward, and, without doubt, a tributary of the Congo. The inhabitants, like the majority of the people dwelling in this portion of Africa, proved to be extremely hostile, devoted to war and pillage, so that the explorers were attacked at every village they passed, and even pursued for long distances by canoes, in spite of the retorts which the savages received at the mouth of the Frenchmen's rifles. Leaving

France: De Brazza, etc.

this inhospitable river, they took a northern course, crossing on the way several streams all flowing in an easterly or south-easterly direction. One of the largest of these was the Likona, on the equator, at thirty miles north of which M. de Brazza found it necessary to retrace his steps, arriving at the Gaboon on the 30th of November, 1878, after an expedition which had lasted, with many interruptions, for nearly three years.

This exploration was not only important geographically, but had a direct bearing on the action of France in that scramble for Africa which she did so much to precipitate; for, soon after his return to the Gaboon, M. de Brazza again penetrated Africa, and established, by order of the French Committee of the Belgian International Association, the first civilising station on the Ogowé. But, it may be added, though this was nominally under the committee in question, it was, in reality, at the expense of the French Government—a circumstance which did not escape notice during the growing suspicion which was now encompassing the "international" exploration of Africa. This station he founded at the mouth of the Bassa, a tributary of the Ogowé, giving it the name of Franceville. Leaving M. Noguez in temporary charge, M. de Brazza then traversed the Leteke country, arriving in four days at the Alima, discovered by him on a former expedition. He was then close to the Bateke plateau, 2,600 feet above the sea, which lies between the Alima and the Mpaka, another affluent of the Congo, and is inhabited by a large and peaceable population, who live by the cultivation of this fertile upland (p. 293). Aided by these friendly folk, the French explorer descended the Lefini, which Mr. Stanley had named the River Lawson, to Pulobos, in the centre of the country claimed by the warlike Ubangis, or Apfurus, who had given that traveller so warm a reception both on his first descent of the Congo and on his more recent voyage up it in the interest of the Belgian Association. After a "treaty"—the validity of which formed before long a subject of hot contention, and which it is doubtful if the savage members of the "high contracting parties" quite understood the import of, except that they got many gaudy pocket-handkerchiefs—the chiefs ceded the entire territory of Meuma, or Ntamo, on the banks of the Congo, not far from Stanley Pool, to their most recent visitors. Brazzaville, a new station, was then founded, the French flag hoisted, and a small party left as more material proofs of the enlargement which the Republic had undergone during the last few hours.*

M. Largeau, who had already journeyed in North-West Africa (p. 89), was assigned the command of an expedition from the Mediterranean to Assini,

* De Brazza and Ballay, *Bull. de Soc. Géog. Paris* (Feb., 1880), pp. 113-143; Marche, *Rev. Géog. Internat.* (1877), No. 25, pp. 273-276; "Trois Voyages dans l'Afrique occidentale," etc. (1879), and *Tour du Monde* (1878), Nos. 936-8; Ballay, *Bull. Soc. Géog. Constantine*, t. IV., No. 2, p. 98; *Comptes rendus, Soc. Géog. Paris* (1885), p. 279, etc.

on the Gold Coast, exploring on the way the Jebel Ahaggar, in the Touareg country, and visiting Timbuctoo. In this project he was, however, disappointed; for, after penetrating a comparatively short way into the desert, M. Largeau had to return, pillaged of his stores and outfit by the wild nomads of these wastes. He endeavoured to organise another expedition for the exploration of the Agar plateau, to which no European had penetrated; but the support he met with was, unfortunately, too small to defray the cost of the undertaking. Accordingly, chagrined at the lack of appreciation which he received, this unfortunate explorer abandoned Africa and African exploration.†

Missionary enterprise, we have seen, was not neglected by France (pp. 146-148), though it is not uncharitable to say—the fact, indeed, being almost openly avowed—that anxiety for the African's moral reformation veiled

† Gros: "Nos Explorateurs en Afrique," p. 71.

ABYSSINIA: CALL TO PRAYER.
(*From a Photograph by Dr. G. Schweinfurth.*)

but thinly designs which, if undertaken under any other guise than that of religion, would have aroused the susceptibilities of Europe. Among these the most important expedition was that of the Abbé Debaize, towards the expenses of which the French Chamber voted £4,000. Its outfit was very complete and original; for, among other novelties, it comprised a barrel-organ, by the strains of which it was supposed the savage breast would be soothed into a condition of unwonted amiability. But the practice of the Africans did not coincide with the theory of the Abbé, who, after a mortifying experiment, had to abandon that terrible instrument and take refuge with the British missionaries on Tanganyika. Unfortunately, the good priest soon fell a victim to the climate; but not before he had become so convinced of the honesty and business capacity of his hosts, that by his will he left to them the arrangement of all his affairs. Lieutenant Giraud's journey, which, though stimulated by the new departure, was not actually connected with it, will be noted farther on (p. 301).

Nor was the ordinary organisation of the Jesuit and other African missions neglected in the unconcealed efforts at political aggrandisement for which the French African Committee were using the renewed ardour in exploration. The Uganda and Tanganyika missions we have already noted; but, reckless of the deadly climate of the Zambesi valley and the neighbouring region, the Jesuits had by the year 1882 settled in every locality which offered any promise of success. Nine of these devoted missionaries succumbed in the years 1880-82; yet, undeterred by the fate of their predecessors, others quickly arrived to fill their places. In the latter year they had occupied Buluwayo (or Gubuluwayo, to give

Duparquet: the Jesuits.

the capital of Matabeleland its proper orthography), Pandamatenka (or Patamatenka), the great trading centre south of the Zambesi (pp. 7, 15), the Tati gold-fields, Seshcke, on the Upper Zambesi, Tete, Mopea, near the mouth of the Shiré, and Quilimane. These

BATEKE CHIEF AND SON.
(*From a Photograph by the Rev. A. Billington.*)

stations were, of course, independent of those founded by the French Protestant Evangelical Society or by other Roman Catholic orders. Père Duparquet, for instance, made a most interesting journey from Walvisch Bay to Omaruru and from Omaruru to the Ovampo, in South-West Africa (p. 211). Contrary to the statements of previous travellers, the region between the two latter was found to contain a large population and to be covered with extensive forests and tracts of pasture-land, the coast-lying tracts alone being arid and sandy. During the rainy season the tribes scatter over a wide area, but concentrate in the dry months near springs and permanent water-holes. The Kaoko Range, on the southern side of the Cunéné, was actually a series of beautifully wooded plateaux, the reputation of which had already reached the outer world; for a party of "trek"-Boers from the Transvaal were met with in the very heart of the mountains. The Ovampo Valley, where there were many British and Portuguese traders, Père Duparquet, the first Frenchman who had ever visited it, describes as exceedingly fertile: "a veritable garden, watered by mountain streams full of fish," are the words in which the enthusiastic Frenchman chooses to characterise a region not esteemed quite so highly by previous explorers.*

These may be described as the last semblances of international exploration by the French African Committee; for the stations founded by M. de Brazza were soon handed over to the Government, and then any pretence of disinterestedness disappeared. The rift within the lute was now become too loud to be neglected by the most optimist of listeners.

Germany, no more than Belgium, possessed many men of African experience; but she took up the task better equipped than the Flemings. For just as France was stimulated to "seek," as M. Challemel-Lacour put it—"compensation abroad for losses at home," so the victors of Sedan were impelled to espouse great ideas by the fact that Germany was now a great country. It is doubtful if the German African Committees were ever actuated by any more disinterested motives than the explorations on which they entered than the idea that, late though the Fatherland had come into the field, it might, perchance, find

Germany and exploration: some early travellers.

* "Les Missions Catholiques," cited in *P.R.G.S.*, 1880, pp. 586, 628, 629; 1881, pp. 43–46; *Bull. Soc. Géog. Paris*, Nov., 1880, p. 459; Lima, *Bol. Soc. Geog. Lisbon*, 1880, p. 7; Nogueira, *Bull. Soc. Géog. Paris*, 1878, p. 72; 1879, p. 259.

in the vast unoccupied continent some space for those colonies without which there was a growing belief national greatness must be a kind of *bourgeois* prosperity. For many years prior to 1876, German travellers had been probing hither and thither in Africa. Barth, though in English employment, was a German of the Germans; and long before Rohlfs and Schweinfurth and Nachtigal had conferred distinction on their native land, Von der Decken, Roscher, and Otto Kersten had been exploring, or attempting to explore, East Africa, and publishing works on the importance of Germany acquiring a footing there, which were forgotten until, a quarter of a century later, the feverish struggles which agitated the scramblers for Africa in 1884 caused them to be recalled.

Minor explorers of German origin had been preparing the public mind—before the Brussels Conference gave a stimulus to exploration, though, perhaps, not in the way it intended —for the seeming sudden impulse it received a few years later. Carl Mauch, a gold prospector more than a geographical explorer, had as early as 1866–72 been working north as far as Matabeleland and the Zambesi; and about the same period Fritsch, by his researches, was making Bechuanaland and the Dutch Republic of South Africa better known than they had ever been in Germany. There was even an Africa Society in those seemingly remote days; for it was under this "Afrikanischen-Gesellschaft in Deutschland" that, in 1874–76, the Loango expedition was at work along the coast from which it took its name;† and Güssfeldt, Pechuel-Loesche, Pogge, Falkenstein, and Lenz were exploring various reaches of the western African rivers and the region behind the coast-lying lands. Lenz, who was afterwards to distinguish himself by a journey to Timbuctoo (Vol. I., p. 307), had penetrated as far into the interior as a waterfall beyond Longu, on the River Mani, where his stores failed him, and the explorer began to suffer severely from dropsy. Pogge made, in

† "Die Loango-Expedition," by P. Güssfeldt, J. Falkenstein, and E. Pechuel-Loesche (1879–82).

1875, a most successful journey to Musumba, the capital of the Muata Yanvo, the suzerain of the Cazembe (Vol. II., p. 253). His farthest point was Inshabaraka, beyond which he was prohibited from travelling. By attaching himself to a native caravan, Dr. Pogge obtained much information regarding the countries between the Kasai and the Kwango, and was the first educated European to reach Musumba, which lies many days to the north and west of Cameron's line of march. Contrary to current belief, he pronounced the Kasai a feeder of the Congo, though he erred in considering the Lualaba a member of the Ogowé system.* Bastian had, in 1857, gone from Ambriz through the old Congo kingdom to San Salvador (p. 120), and in 1874 organised a more important expedition to the "hinterland" of Angola; and, not to mention lesser contributions to the unfolding of the nature of these pestilent lands, Edward Mohr, who had been chosen to succeed Pogge, in 1876 fell a victim to fever at Melanje, while exploring the country south of the Congo; though, indeed, like more than one explorer whom it suited treacherous cowards to remove, there has always been a suspicion of his death having been compassed by poison.

Turning to East Africa, Dr. G. A. Fischer, who had spent many years on the coast, and Messrs. Denhardt were despatched by the Hamburg Geographical Society, in the winter of 1876, to penetrate, by way of the Tana, to Mount Kenia, taking with them carrier-pigeons in order to communicate more readily with the coast—an experiment which, however, did not succeed. Dr. Hildebrandt, a naturalist, was also commissioned to reach the great lake; but, following simply in the footsteps of Krapf, he did not get beyond Kitui, in Ukambani, from whence he returned laden with scientific facts and specimens. In the same year Dr. Erwin von Bary started with the object of reaching Timbuctoo; but, owing to the disturbed condition of the Touareg country, did not reach farther than the hot springs of Sebarbaret—that is, about one hundred and fifty miles south-west of Ghat.

All this, it must be remembered, was either before the notable Brussels Conference—from which we date much of the modern history of Africa—or before the **Schütt and Büchner.** plans of that gathering had been properly put to the test. As a first step towards this end, the German Society for the Exploration of Equatorial Africa, founded in 1873, and the motor in most of the explorations noted, coalesced with the German African Society, which had come into existence in 1876, to form the Berlin African Society as a branch of the new International Association. Yet even then, on the ground that it had practical commercial objects in view, the society received from the Imperial Government £5,000 in aid of its operations. In 1878–79, Otto Schütt was sent out with instructions to reach the capital of the Muata Yanvo,† a task in which Max Büchner succeeded in 1881, both travellers adding slightly to our knowledge of the country intervening between Musumba and the coast; though, as Pogge had already visited the potentate in question, commercial relations, rather than geography, were the objects in view.‡

Dr. Büchner, however, made excellent scientific use of his six months' stay in the Muata Yanvo's "Court." Shanama, **The Muata** or Naoësh, a Gatt, the fourteenth **Yanvo.** holder of the title, lives at Kawende, a place of 2,000 inhabitants, consisting of a number of hamlets scattered through a fertile valley—the name "Musumba," usually applied to it, really meaning no more than "the town." The Muata, who inhabits a huge, conical-roofed building on the spur of a hill in the centre of his capital, is very much like other African chiefs, though Dr. Büchner is inclined to join issue with those who pronounce him cruel. During his long residence in Kawende he saw no people whose noses

* Pogge: "Im Reiche des Muata-Janvo" (1879).

† "Reisen im südwestlichen Becken des Congo" (1881). He went as far as the Chikapa River.

‡ The narratives of these travellers are, for the most part, contained in the *Mittheilungen der Afrikanischen Gesellschaft in Deutschland* for the years concerned.

had been cut off or ears cropped; and during the whole of that period he knew of only three executions—two of the victims being people accused of "aggravated magic," and the third, one of the royal harem, for misconduct. It is, however, admitted, that, were it not for the influence of the Lukokesha, the number of capital punishments would be greater. This personage is the successor, not the descendant, of the wife of the first Muata Yanvo of the reigning dynasty. She has her own court and territory, and exercises so powerful a sway in the country as to be practically co-regent. Her argument for more clemency is that there are already too few men in Lunda to admit of many being killed for crime. Yet the most is made of those who are; for their skulls are stuck up at the entrance to the Royal Hall of Audience. This chamber is very large, and at the end of it stands a clay throne covered with a leopard-skin, on which the Muata sits to receive homage and deliver judgment. He is described as a finely-built though ugly individual, not unintelligent, and at times amiable, though his eyes are, as a rule, piercing and venomous. "His teeth project like the tusks of a boar; his beard is limited to a few bristles on the chin. The royal forehead was shaved, but the remaining hair was elaborately dressed and ornamented with parrots' feathers. A blue cloth of flannel, fastened round the waist, was the only article of dress worn by the king, and left the upper part of the body exposed. A string of beads, with an amulet, and a copper chain were worn round the neck, and rings round the legs and arms. Most conspicuous amongst the ornaments was the 'rukanu,' a stout bracelet made of human sinews, which is worn on the left wrist as an emblem of royalty. One lackey held a sunshade, a second assiduously plied a horse-hair fan, and a third kept close at hand ready to cover over the royal expectorations with earth. Courtiers and royal favourites knelt in front of the throne; Moari, the chief queen, sat behind it, and the Lukokesha, an elderly lady with bloated face and thick lips, was enthroned some distance to the left, in the midst of her women. A 'kabula,' or royal gate-keeper, armed with a two-tongued whip of ox-hide, kept order amongst the surrounding crowd, but never interfered with the prowling curs, which were allowed to circulate freely amongst

LOWER CONGO CHIEF IN "CORONATION ROBES."*
(*From a Photograph by the Rev. R. D. Darby.*)

* The "sceptre" is an elephant's tail; the dress is made of grass and ornamented with cowry shells; and the chief's face is daubed with camwood and whiting.

it." It may be added, that Dr. Büchner found the Lukokesha embarrassingly well-disposed to the white visitor, the royal lady, as in Dr. Pogge's case, insisting on his sitting beside her and sharing in the potations on which she was rapidly getting tipsy.

The Muata Yanvo rules a territory about the size of Germany, and receives the allegiance of three hundred chiefs and two million people; though his power is threatened by the Kioko, famous as smiths, elephant-hunters, and men-stealers, who are gradually spreading from the Upper Kwango northwards, and already hold considerable territories as far as is ordered to deposit his goods with the Muata, who despatches messengers throughout the country to collect the slaves and ivory wished for in exchange. It is next to impossible for a trader to obtain permission to transact business directly with the people; and, perhaps, as they are reputed to be cannibals, the privilege would be of dubious value. Even Dr. Büchner, after trying in vain to pass beyond the boundaries of Lunda, was forced to return to Malanje, where, on the 8th of February, 1881, he met Pogge, Wissmann, and Von Mechow.

On the plateau, which, as usual, was

CUTTING TIMBER IN A LOWER CONGO FOREST.
(*From a Photograph by the Rev. R. D. Darby.*)

Kasai in lat. 7° S. But the commerce carried on in this large area of country is very insignificant. Whenever a trader arrives, he reached after crossing the barren, waterless plains, covered with scanty grass, baobabs, and candelabra euphorbias (p. 252), and the coast belt of mountains, it rains from September to April, though seldom in excessive amount. During the wet season the temperature rises to 81°, but during the rest of the year the mercury sinks at times so comparatively low as to make a warm blanket comfortable. Throughout his entire journey, Dr. Büchner never saw an elephant or a lion; the rhinoceros and giraffe were quite unknown to the natives, and the zebra was so scarce that a strip of its skin was looked upon as a curiosity. Nor does the crocodile appear to exist in that part of Africa—the only large game at all common being the hippopotamus.*

Lenz, as we have seen, journeyed to Timbuctoo, while Rohlfs and Stecker succeeded in penetrating the Sahara as far as the oases of Kufra, from which they were repulsed (p. 90). Major von Mechow led another expedition under the African Society, though mainly fitted out by the German Government, as far up the Kwango as lat. 5° 5′ S., when the crew, frightened by the reports of imaginary cannibals, refused to go any farther (p. 126).

Lenz, Rohlfs, Mechow, Pogge, and Wissmann.

Pogge and Wissmann, who was afterwards to distinguish himself in Africa (pp. 12, 23, 24), originally intended to found a permanent station at the Muata Yanvo's capital. Dr. Büchner's tidings determined this expedition to proceed from Malanje northwards into a country still untrodden by scientific travellers, though, like so much "newly discovered country" on both sides of Africa, quite familiar to the ubiquitous Portuguese traders. At the Kioko chief Kimbunda's, they heard that war had broken out between him and the Muata. In spite of the chief's jealousy at any white man poaching on his particular preserves, the expedition passed along the left bank of the Chikapa, beyond the limits of Lunda, until, after forty-four days, the travellers found themselves at Kikasa, on the banks of the Kasai. Thence the expedition visited Munkamba Lake and the Lubi. Their progress from this part has already been traced in Lieutenant Wissmann's journey across the continent, Dr. Pogge, according to previous arrangements, turning back at Nyangwé (pp. 12–15).

The people of the Bashilange or Tushilange country, who are divided into numerous tribes, proved extremely kind to the strangers. At one time a war-like people, they have fallen victims to the smoking of Indian hemp, or "bhang,"† a drug now used from one side of Africa to the other. This hemp-worship, as Wissmann calls it, began, so far as the Bashilange are concerned, about the year 1865, and rapidly the Bena-Ramba, or "Sons of Hemp," found more and more adherents. As the craze for the narcotic spread, the old people who opposed it—the Chipulumba, or Conservatives—retreated to the more remote parts of the country, where they were pursued by the Sons of Hemp, and many of them slain. This common bond of union led to the tribesmen who used the drug having more intercourse with each other, making laws, and largely ceasing their intestine broils. But they soon became more feeble, and before long the Kioko, a wandering race (p. 297) much given to trade, war, and the chase, taking advantage of this degeneracy, made successful inroads on the Bashilange country, and profited by the extensive stores of ivory and gum it contained. Guns were imported, and so highly prized at the price of a tusk apiece that the owners became at once great men. Soon the Kioko were the virtual masters of entire regions, under Kassongo and Kabassu-Babu. The first account they ever had of white men was as late as 1874, when a Portuguese negro arrived and pretended to be a son of the king of that until then unknown race. It was this scamp who acted as Pogge's and Wissmann's interpreter. Even then so simple were the Bashilange that

The Bashilange.

---

* "Mittheilungen der Afrikanischen Gesellschaft in Deutschland," edited by Dr. W. Erman (1882); *P.R.G.S.*, 1882, pp. 678–685; Büchner, *Sitzungbericht der Ges. für Erkunde zu Berlin*, February, 1882; Bastian: "Die Deutsche Exp. a. d. Loango-Kuste" (1874-75).

† The "Kif" of Morocco, where it is much more generally smoked than tobacco.

Pogge was received as the spirit of Kassongo, who had died some time before their arrival, and his companion as that of Kabassu-Babu, a name which clung to him for years; and, as such, their influence became paramount, the brother of the late Kassongo following his "spirit" as far as Nyangwé.* Yet, in spite of their hemp-worship, the Bashilange are one of the most tractable, prosperous, and intelligent races in Equatorial Africa. The Luluaburg station of the Congo State is now in their country; and such has been their eagerness to ape every bit of civilisation exhibited to them that they are rapidly becoming civilised. All kinds of crops suitable to the climate are grown. They have burnt their idols, abolished the death penalty and the ordeal drink, make strong cloth, with pretty patterns, from the fibre of *Raphia nitida* palm, and fabricate every part of a gun except the barrel. They have begun to build two-storied houses of clay, try to dress in European fashion, to construct tables and arm-chairs, and to eat with knives and forks off a plate. They ride bulls, and make use of a hammock for travelling, though chiefs alone are allowed this luxury. All this, it must be remembered, has been the work of a few years only with a people who had so little idea of civilisation that, in 1874, a negro could persuade them into the belief that he was a son of the white man's king. If only they could learn to work, instead of making their women do so, and abjure the practice, which was once universal, and is still carried on secretly, of selling their female children for slaves, the Bashilange would rank as one of the few triumphs of European "culture" in the Upper Congo country.

On leaving Wissmann, Dr. Pogge returned to Bashilange Land, where he remained until November, 1883, cultivating the soil ceded to the station of Luluaburg established by him. No news coming from the outer world, he returned to the coast by a long detour northwards before crossing the Kasai, during which he discovered the

* Wissmann: "Through Equatorial Africa," p. 314

confluence of the Lulua with that river. Then, marching southwards as far as Kikasa, he reached Malanje on the 2nd of February, 1884. Here he had the pleasure of meeting Wissmann, who, since they had parted at Nyangwé, had crossed Africa, visited Europe, and was now again in Africa, leading a second expedition into the interior, which ended in another transcontinental journey (p. 23). It was, however, Pogge's last; for he had scarcely reached São Paolo de Loando before he died of inflammation of the lungs. This meritorious explorer was not only one of the most successful of the German travellers, but one of the most accomplished of a singularly well-equipped company. Born in Mecklenburg in 1838, he had visited Natal, Mauritius, and Bourbon in 1864, before he made his mark by joining the great expedition under Homeyer and Lux, which had been prepared in 1874 for the purpose of opening up relations with the Muata Yanvo. He was only permitted to join the party on the condition of paying his own expenses. But the return of the leaders, invalided before they had proceeded far on the way, gave Pogge the chance which so often occurs to African travellers, though not always with such success as befell Lander, Barth, Thomson, and the ill-fated Mecklenburger.

Up to this date £22,000 had been spent on these explorations. Güssfeldt's expedition cost £10,530, and though it made no great show on the map, was rich in scientific observations, the Germans being, almost to a man, admirably trained in the school of Humboldt. The second was less expensive—£4,459 clearing its bills. The African Society and its agents having meanwhile gained experience since those 'prentice days, the next four expeditions did not Flegel, Kaiser, Böhm, absorb more than about £7,000. Reichard and Giraud. Yet the African Societies did not falter in the work they had set themselves—or been set by the Government—to perform. It is, indeed, difficult to keep count of all the travellers who about this period began to overrun Africa, more especially on the upper waters of the Congo. Thus, Kund and Wolf, and Tappenbeck were continually coming across the routes of Wissmann and Pogge in that region, or co-operating with them, either in the Government employ or in the service of the Association which had now, under a new name, taken up the work of the old international one, and was concentrating its efforts on the Congo Basin. It is, perhaps, therefore at Kakoma, and afterwards at the more healthy position of Gonda. Nevertheless, as the "tembos," or buildings, were erected, and the rice-ground in the vicinity cultivated by the chief's slaves, we fear this detachment of international agents were not greatly concerned regarding one aspect of the morality they were to introduce into dark Africa. Dr. Reichard, indeed, actually defended slavery,

KILIMANJARO: ANOTHER VIEW OF KIBO, FROM MOSCHI.
(From a Sketch by Bishop Tucker.)

not undue suspicion to suggest that even then the German Chancellor was meditating acquisitions in that quarter. By-and-by we may have occasion to notice the activity of Flegel up the Niger and Benué during 1882-84, which, while it added to our knowledge of these regions, was not without ulterior objects. Nor, while concentrating most of their efforts on West Africa, did the Germans neglect the opposite side of the continent. Under an East African Society, Böhm, Kaiser, and Reichard were penetrating in the direction of Tanganyika and the upper waters of the Lualaba, building a station first on the feeble ground that the captives, if they obtained good masters, were really better situated than in freedom. The corollary to this is, of course, that so good an end justifies the means by which it is obtained—slave-raids, murder, theft, and kidnapping—in order that the victims of these curses of inner Africa may, by some chance, be better housed and better fed than at home! Reichard was, however, an exaggerated specimen of the swaggering type of explorers who then, and subsequently, were sent by Germany to diffuse the blessings of civilisation in Africa.

In the meantime, while the Disha, or female

chief of Gonda, was temporising, after the usual custom of the country, Drs. Böhm and Kaiser attempted an exploration of the west side of Tanganyika. The disturbed state of the country, owing to the wars of Mirambo and Simba, prevented much from being done beyond giving the travellers an opportunity of calling at the to Karema, from whence he returned by way of Nyassa and the Shiré.

Reichard * and Böhm were not much more successful after starting afresh on the 1st of September, 1883. They reached the Lualupa and advanced into Msiri's country, whom they found engaged in a war against Katapana in Urua. It was this chief who, a few years

MOUNT MERU, FROM MOSCHI.
(From a Sketch by Bishop Tucker.)

Karema station, where Captain Rammacker died soon after this date (1882)—the last of the Belgian explorers sent into East Africa. This station before passing into other hands served to shelter Lieutenant Giraud, of the French Navy, who in 1883-84 attempted to cross Africa by a new route, namely, from the coast south of Zanzibar, between Nyassa and Tanganyika, past the southern end of Tanganyika to Lake Bangweolo, and thence down the Lualaba-Congo to Stanley Pool. But, being plundered on the Luapula and at Cazembe's, he was compelled to beat a retreat later, had so fatal an experience with the whites, who coveted the copper-mines in the Katanga country. He had, indeed, little cause to have a high opinion of European civilisation; for the new arrivals actually offered to help him in his warfare as the price of being sent on their road. This bribe was, however, refused. Meanwhile Dr. Böhm died, and Dr. Reichard was permitted to visit Katanga and to explore part of the

* Also spelled "Reichardt" (p. 18). He was one of the most strenuous, though not one of the most judicious, advocates of German colonisation in inner Africa.

Lufira. When at last permitted to leave Msiri's capital of Kimpatu, he found every league of his progress a struggle against cold, wet, hunger, and the savages who attacked him with poisonous arrows whenever they imagined a favourable opportunity had offered itself. Roots and mushrooms were for days at a time his only food. All his collections had to be abandoned, and with difficulty travel through a region west of Kilimanjaro towards Lake Baringo, a semi-mythical sheet of water, first heard of by Speke and Grant, but still unknown to Europeans; but when only six days' march from the point at which he aimed his porters refused to go farther. The Masai warriors blocked the way, in consequence of which he had to return. Starting again in 1882 in

LAKE NAIVASHA.
(From a Sketch by Bishop Tucker.)

Mpala, on Tanganyika, was reached on the last day of November, 1884.* Msiri's behaviour both to Giraud and the German travellers was not good; but how far the latter were to blame has already been indicated on the chief's own authority (p. 18). It is sad to add that Dr. Kaiser, after visiting Lake Leopold, died of fatigue on its shores—some will say from a chill caught by a too-protracted bath in its waters—and was buried there by his negro followers in October, 1882.

In 1881 Dr. Fischer (p. 295) made an important journey from Pangani into the Masai country in East Africa. He had hoped to

* *Proc. Roy. Geog. Society,* 1885, pp. 540, 603.

a northerly direction, through Paré, Arusha, and Sigarari, he returned in a more westerly direction round Lake Naivasha (p. 302) and the Natron Lake to the volcano Donyo Ngai, and thence over the plain of Ngaruka to Mount Meru (p. 301), on the southern slopes of which the Wakuavi dwell. But Naivasha was his nearest approach to his goal. The Masai were troublesome; but, as the lives of those killed in self-defence could be paid for by blood-money, all terminated pleasantly—for the living.†

Neither the Hungarians nor the Austrians

† Fischer: "Das Masai-Land" (1885); *Proceedings of the Royal Geographical Society,* 1884, p. 76.

had, up to the period of Oskar Lenz's journey across Africa (pp. 21–23), taken much share in the exploration of that continent. Both this expedition and the still more important one under Teleki and von Höhnel (p. 229) may, however, be claimed as "Königlich-Kaiserlich" contributions to the flood of international travels. But, though they were undoubtedly stimulated by that scheme, neither was under its control, nor, indeed, undertaken, until the pleasant plans of the Brussels Conference had become very much matters of history. But Austria-Hungary is not on that account to be refused all credit for opening up the dark places of Africa. We must not, for instance, forget her self-denying missionaries (Vol. II., pp. 111, 159), one of whom, Father Ohrwalder, escaping with two nuns, brought, after long waiting, the first accurate news of what had been going on in the Soudan during the dark years succeeding its closure to civilisation. Nor can we neglect, before leaving for good and all the subjects of the Empire-Kingdom as African explorers, a Hungarian who, having the making of a traveller of note, may be recalled to the memory of a world that has forgotten if, indeed, it ever knew him. This was Ladislaus Magyar. The name looks fanciful, considering his nationality. Yet though much about Magyar is dashed with romance, he is understood to have been lawfully entitled to his patronymic. How he came to Africa is not known, but before the year 1849 he was in the Angolese province of Benguela, the husband, under a ceremony more or less binding, of a native "princess," having, like Schimper, the German botanist, who married in Abyssinia, where his family still reside, resolved to throw in his lot with the country in which he had settled.

Ladislaus Magyar: a romantic tale.

At that time little was known of the interior. Bowdich had in 1819 discovered the upper reaches of the Ogowé, and though Tuckey's expedition had three years earlier ascended to the Falls of the Congo, with much sacrifice of life from the climate, he returned uncertain whether that great river was or was not identical with the Niger (Vol. 1., p. 265). Before 1849 Magyar claimed to have gone from Ambriz across country until he struck the Congo, passed beyond the cataracts which had stopped all previous explorers, and traversed much of the region south of the river. Settling at Bihé (Vol. II., p. 281) in the barbarous magnificence of a black slave-owner, his wealth continually increasing through the man-hunting raids of his negro father-in-law, Magyar, by his own account, journeyed in 1852 as far south as the Upper Cunéné, returning through a desert and uninhabited region to the supposed source of that river in the Galangue Plain, between two and three degrees south of the Equator. The fall and banishment of his father-in-law suddenly cut short the Hungarian's career of prosperity and compelled him to return to earn a scanty subsistence in the town of Dombe Grande in Benguela, where he died in November, 1864, leaving an account of his wanderings which has since then been published, but, like the narrative of Paul du Chaillu's travels in Equatorial Africa about the same period, has been undeservedly treated with incredulity.* The latter, we shall learn in the course of a future chapter, did actually add something to our knowledge of the ethnography and geography of the country behind the French colony of Congo-Gaboon, while Magyar picked up much information about the country as far as Nyassa and Tanganyika, and, indeed, had he travelled no farther than did the Portuguese traders, he must have seen a great deal of country at that time quite unknown to the outside world.

All this is, however, only a parenthesis: it

* "Ladislaus Magyar, Seine beabsichtige Rückkehr nach Europa und sein dreibändiges Reisewerk," Petermann's *Geographische Mittheilungen*, 1858, p. 170; Hunfalvy: "Ladislaus Magyar, Reisen in Süd-Afrika in den Jahren 1849 bis 1857" (1859), a German Translation from the Magyar (1857); also a MS. Abstract of Magyar's Travels, by Mr. H. Rónay, in the Royal Geographical Society's Library. Sir Richard Burton accepted the substantial accuracy of Magyar's narrative and had, we understand, prepared an annotated translation of it.

LAKE JIPE, NEAR KILIMANJARO.
(From a Sketch by Bishop Tucker.)

has nothing to do with the vanishing International Association and its scheme of exploration on the basis of disinterestedness and a millennial reign of brotherly love. This project, we have seen, never did much in the way of stimulating English exploration, though exploration, private and unsubsidised, went on as of old without much regard to Brussels and its abortive plans. Amongst others a word is due to the good work done by Captain James Frederick Elton, who, after a stirring career with the British army in India and China, with the French forces in Mexico, as a private traveller in South Africa (where he passed from the Tati gold-fields to the Limpopo), as a Government agent in Zululand, and assistant political agent at Zanzibar, settled down as

The English again: Elton and others.

British Consul at Mozambique. But "settling down" was not one of Elton's strong points. He had already made an interesting journey between Dar-es-Salaam and Quiloa or Kilwa, and now his official duties and his private inclinations led him to embark on numerous journeys by sea and land. One of the most important of these was one which, early in 1877, he undertook into the interior from Mozambique to the Makua country east of Nyassa, up the River Lurio to the cataracts of the Bomba, and down again to Ibo—four hundred and fifty miles of the way being performed on foot. His last exploration was begun in March, 1877, in company with four other Englishmen. Striking across the

THE CRATER LAKE CHALA, ON KILIMANJARO.
(From a Sketch by Bishop Tucker.)

mountainous country which closes in Lake Nyassa on the north, they succeeded, in spite of native opposition, in reaching the Ujiji and the Zanzibar caravan-road at Usekhe, in Ugogo, where the leader of the expedition died on the 13th of December, 1877, in his thirty-seventh year, of malarial fever, or, by other accounts, of sunstroke brought on by privation and exposure. His four companions—Messrs. Cotterill, Rhodes, Hoste, and Downie—having laid their dead friend under a baobab tree, crossed in their northerly march Rufiji (the Ruaha of Speke) to Mpwapwa, and thence by the ordinary route to Bagamoyo.*

Another Englishman who about this period finds a place in the ranks of explorers was Mr. St. Vincent Erskine, who made several journeys into Umzila's country—that is, into Gazaland or southern Mozambique, a region now tolerably familiar.† In 1868 and the next seven or eight years, the country between the Pungwe and the Limpopo was laid down by him more accurately by means of astronomical observations than at any former period, and its resources examined minutely enough to have a powerful influence on the future of East Africa.

Captain Temple Phippson-Wybrant was a worse-fated victim of the African fever which has always raged fiercely, but in 1880 attacked his high-spirited countrymen like an epidemic. During his military service he had seen a little of South Africa, and life in Kaffraria had been so attractive as to determine him to fit out, at his own expense, an expedition to explore the then almost unknown country between the Zambesi and Limpopo rivers. His well-equipped party consisted of about a hundred natives under the celebrated Chuma

WATERFALL ON KILIMANJARO.
(From a Sketch by Bishop Tucker.)

* Elton and Cotterill: "Travels and Researches among the Lakes and Mountains of Eastern and Central Africa" (1879); *Journ. Royal Geog. Soc.*, 1878, pp. cxxxiv., ccii., etc.
† *Journal Royal Geog. Soc.*, 1875, p. 45; 1879, p. 25, etc.

(Vol. II., p. 281) and four Europeans. But scarcely had the adventurers left the settled country—four days' journey from Umzila's—when fever attacked them, among the first victims being the leader, who died on the 29th of November, 1880, on his thirty-fourth birthday. The rest of the party returned to the coast, and the expedition came to nothing.

Adventurous Englishmen were now turning up in all parts of the continent, sometimes as serious explorers, at other times travelling and enduring hardships for the mere pleasure of rejoicing in fresh scenes and novel excitements. Thus in 1882 the Earl of Mayo made a journey of over five hundred miles across the Sierra de Chella, from Mossamedes to the Cunéné in South Africa. The country was much what it was in Andersson's day (p. 211), but traders and settlers were by no means so rare as at that date. "Trek"-Boers from the Transvaal had made their homes in the Portuguese territory and the Roman Catholic missionaries had established themselves on the Cunéné banks. These pioneers had doubtless followed in the hunters' train, and the latter had been so successful that Ericsson, who had been an assistant of Andersson (p. 212), had at that time sixty waggons in the field, each waggon with sixteen or more yoke of oxen, with a dozen or so of European and native hunters, all engaged in collecting ivory, ostrich feathers, and other products of the wilderness, such as skins of the antelopes that abound there. At that time this firm of hunters and traders had a capital of not less than £200,000 embarked in this picturesque commerce between the Orange River and the Cunéné. *

There were still (as we have seen in another section of this work) great African journeys to be accomplished. But, unless very far from the coast, they were apt to cover comparatively little new ground; or, the new ground was in such detached areas that the traveller, in passing from one patch to another, was apt to cross and recross the tracks of his predecessors. Still, in the intervals between one spell of professional duty and another, Lieutenant O'Neill, R.N., during his term of consular duty in East Africa, managed to make so many actual contributions to exact geography that, in 1885, he received the Patrons' Medal of the Royal Geographical Society as a testimony of their appreciation of his "thirteen journeys of exploration along the coast and in the interior of Mozambique during the previous five years." In one of these he reached Lake Shirwa, and discovered the more northerly Lakes Amaramba and Chiuta; and, in another journey, explored a new and direct route from Blantyre to the coast. During his stay at Blantyre, the Scottish Mission near the Shiré was raised by him to a notable position in Africa. For Mr. O'Neill—a skilful astronomer—fixed, by an extensive series of lunar observations, the position of this post. This was a great service to explorers; since there are, perhaps, not half a dozen places in the interior of Africa even approximately near to their proper position on the map; and, apart from the observatories, not another at which explorers can adjust their chronometers. Blantyre's position on the globe is, however, so accurately ascertained as to have obtained for it acceptance as a meridian from which longitudes can be calculated with confidence. Mr. O'Neill possessed, however, another characteristic which, fortunately for the readers of travel-books, is almost as rare as good longitudes, and that was an extreme dislike of notoriety. Careful corrections of old maps and accurate surveys of new country were all that the modest consul aimed at bringing back from his journeys. And to this day he cannot be persuaded to write the book which, until recently, was as inevitable as the medal —which he obtained, and the Order—which has still to be offered him. A few brief papers in the geographical journals are the sole records of his achievements.†

Lord Mayo.

Henry Edward O'Neill.

* *Proceedings Royal Geog. Soc.*, 1883, p. 472.

† *Proceedings of the Royal Geographical Society*, 1881, pp. 632, 713; *Ibid.*, 1885, p. 616; *Ibid.*, p. 372; *Ibid.*, p. 130; *Scottish Geographical Magazine*, 1885, p. 337; *Ibid.*, 1885, p. 125, etc.

About this period also Mr. H. H. Johnston, an artist and naturalist, who had already made a voyage up the Congo, taken part in Lord Mayo's journey (p. 306), and visited other parts of coast-lying Africa, began to be a well-known name in the continent where, before many years elapsed, he was to occupy a leading place. At a time (1884) when the snowy Kilimanjaro (pp. 300, 305, 308, etc.) was not so frequently climbed as it was in after-days, he resided on it for several months, engaged in studying, under the direction of a Committee of the British Association, the animals and plants of that remarkable mountain.* Several years afterwards Mr. Johnston received a signal mark of his Sovereign's favour in the form of a K.C.B.

Sir H. Hamilton Johnston

But the most important of all these latter-day journeys, which may, by a stretch of charity, be understood as having, in a way, owed their initiation to the Brussels scheme, has been reserved for the last. This was Mr. Joseph Thomson's expedition across the Masai country to Victoria Nyanza, organised by the Royal Geographical Society, which was, with the exception of his previous one (p. 274), the only English expedition despatched avowedly as part of the work sketched out by the International Association. The region between the east coast and Victoria Nyanza was selected for exploration, and Mr. Thomson's commission instructed him to ascertain, if possible, if a practicable route existed across the Masai country to the lake, to examine the unknown country about Kilimanjaro and Kenia, the snow-covered peaks whose existence had been doubted only a few years before, and continue his route to the great lake. The journey was a difficult one, mainly because the Masai tribes lay in the way. These people —insolent and warlike to a small party,

Joseph Thomson in Masailand.

cowardly and predatory in the presence of a large one—had hitherto prevented any exploration in their country. They had driven back the pacific Krapf and Rebmann, and when Von der Decken and Thornton, after visiting Jipe Lake (p. 304) and Kilimanjaro, attempted to enter their country, they were met on its borders by thousands of these dreaded warriors and compelled to return to the coast. This disaster, Mr. Thomson suspects, was not caused without the machinations of Sadi-bin-Ahedi, the caravan-leader, whose little ways had lost nothing of their knavery in the course of the next twenty years. New had climbed to the snow-line of Kilimanjaro and discovered its wonderful crater-lake Chala (p. 304). But as he also was accompanied by Sadi, neither on this nor on another expedition a few years later did he manage to proceed any farther. Indeed, mainly, it is said, through the plots of this rascally Arab, he was plundered of everything, and died on the way back, broken down in health and spirits. It has, we are aware, been affirmed that the unfortunate missionary was poisoned by his Zanzibar guide. But as this atrocity is laid to the charge of Sadi by Mandala, the Moschi chief, who robbed the traveller and, by his own confession, was only prevented by his mother from killing him, we may dismiss this crime from the long category more justly credited to this oft-execrated individual (Vol. II., p. 263).

Since Thomson's day "a many men" have visited that country, not taking into account the American lady who rafted round the crater-lake of Kilimanjaro and received black kings in a court dress and scimitar. But, excepting Hildebrandt, a German naturalist (p. 229), the explorers mentioned completed the list of those who had gone farther than the threshold of the region † which the

---

* Johnston: "The Kilima-Njaro Expedition," etc. (1886). Sir Henry Johnston visited Kilimanjaro after Mr. Thomson had done so; but as he left before that traveller returned to the coast, his expedition has for convenience' sake been noticed here.

† In 1882 Mr. J. T. Last, a lay missionary, who during his long residence at Mamboia made useful surveys and ethnological researches in Masailand, visited the Masai living beyond the borders of the Nguru country, at that time only known by hearsay (*Proceedings of the Royal Geographical Society*, 1883, p. 517).

young Scot was about to penetrate. As for the region lying beyond, nothing was known by direct observation, geographers having to be content with the rough itineraries of Sadi and other traders, compiled by the Rev. Mr. Wakefield, a veteran East African missionary, who, in 1861, established the United Free Methodist Mission among the Wa-Nika and Galla tribes at Jomvu,

A retrospect.

his way to Lake Victoria, having been compelled to return after reaching the volcanic country around Lake Naivasha, half as big as Lake Zürich, and 6,500 feet above the sea (p. 302). This sheet is surrounded by splendid pasture-lands. Yet, though fed by two small rivers and, like so many lakes in this section of Central Africa, without outlet, its waters are said to be pleasant to the taste, and

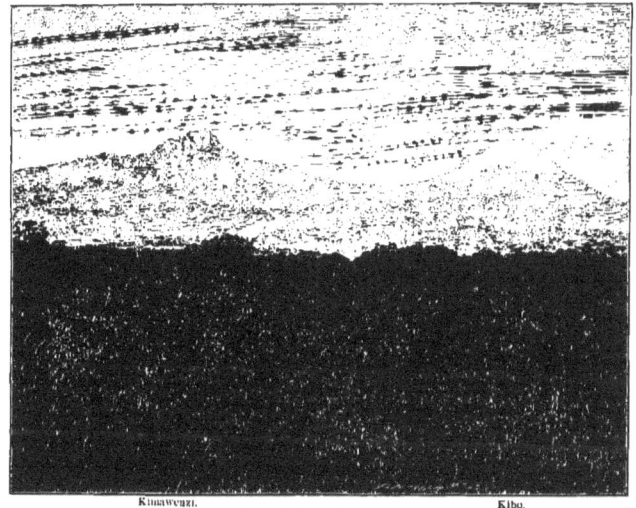

Kimaweuzi.   Kibo.
THE KILIMANJARO RANGE.
(*From a Photograph by Mr. Thomas Stevens.*)

near Mombasa, and at Ribe and Ndara, some miles inland (p. 131), and by his labours had added to our knowledge of the "hinterland" of the region in question. With £3,000 to pay his way, and Martin, a Maltese sailor, to help him, Thomson undertook to do (and did) what had been found impossible by so many experienced predecessors. He learned, indeed, by rumours on the road, that Dr. Fischer, sent by the Hamburg Geographical Society (p. 295), had started ahead of him. But the German traveller, though he penetrated the Masai stronghold, did not, we have seen, go far on

abound with hippopotami. Crocodiles, however, were not observed.

No wonder, therefore, that Mr. Stanley gave Thomson the significant advice before leaving England, "Take a thousand men or make your will!" But between the 15th of March, 1883, and the 2nd of June, 1884, the period during which he was engaged on his task, though there were times when the former alternative would have been desirable, and the latter was only too probable, the explorer had never occasion to kill or be killed—his invariable tact enabling him to go where a thousand men could not have gone with safety.

Patience, it is true, was often tried; but his motto was—

"Chi va piano va sano;
Chi va sano va lontano."

"He who goes gently goes safe: he who goes safe goes far"—so that with 140 men all told, most of them the veriest offscourings of Zanzibar, he had again the satisfaction of completing his mission without bloodshed. The Masai were all that rumour had painted them (pp. 311, 312). Cowardly in the face of a superior force, they were the terror of their feebler neighbours, and bore so bad a name that the Gallas, cruel, immoral, and barbarous though they are, regard it as a mortal insult to be compared with this race of black men. Yet the only criticism a successor in the same country could offer on Thomson's management of his expedition was that he should

The Masai and their country.

have resorted more frequently to violence, albeit, Dr. Peters, the German traveller, who makes this absurd commentary, in spite of his love of firearms, failed to do as well as the Scotsman without them. After an unsuccessful start, in which, however, he reached Kilimanjaro, and ascended it about 9,000 feet, he

HILL OF NDARA, BETWEEN KILIMANJARO AND THE COAST.
(From a Sketch by Bishop Tucker.)

returned from Taveta in order to get a few more men and replenish his diminished store of goods, starting again in July from Mombasa. The Masai were not friendly, marauding bands doing their best to intercept him, in default of Dr. Fischer having escaped their clutches; and the local chiefs never lost an opportunity of fleecing the traveller in their power, Muhinna and Sadi-bin-Ahedi, whom he had engaged as guides and interpreters, maintaining their reputation as traitors.

By the middle of July, his caravan strengthened by that of a trader, the explorer was again in the Masai country, by a route that lay along the eastern side of Kilimanjaro, through a beautiful stretch of pasture-land, the neighbouring snows of the mountain-top tempering the air to coolness, though it lies in the depths of burning Africa. As the expedition marched northwards, the ground rose into a broad flat ridge of 5,000 feet high, swarming with game, rhinoceroses especially being so numerous that there was at times danger from those that boldly burst across the line of the caravan. Buffaloes were also numerous. On one occasion an old bull tossed a donkey into the air, nearly killed two men, and was intent on more mischief when a bullet stopped its mad career. Over the ridge the route lay across the plain of Ngiri, the dried-up bottom of a lake that had occupied this region when Kilimanjaro was an active volcano, and they were glad to hear from a few elderly Masai that the warriors of that part of the country had all left on a marauding expedition. The scene from this vast flat Mr. Thomson describes as weird in the extreme. Most of it is a grassless expanse, varied with a few sheets of water and some scraggy trees and bushes. Natron and saltpetre cover other tracts, their brilliancy, as the sun shines upon them, being remarkable. The giraffe browses among the bushes, the zebra and the wildebeest gambol over the grassier spots, and other animals appear in such abundance that the wonder is how they manage to subsist in such a desert. In the morning the mirage elevates the game phantom-like, till they appear to be moving high in the atmosphere, "a marvellously beautiful effect is produced by the heated air rising from the sands, giving a curious wavy motion to the black and white stripes of the zebra, reminding one somewhat of the electric advertisements to be seen about railway-stations at home."

At the base of the Donyo Erok el Matumbato, where the volcanic country ended, the Masai, and with them misery, began to appear. Day and night these most arrogant of

From the Ngiri Plain.

African savages kept the caravan continually on the alert, until the strain was almost too much to bear. When they were not threatening open violence, they were begging or stealing, so that every camp had to be surrounded by a fence of thorns. Compared with indignities heaped upon the travellers, and necessarily submitted to, the laughing yell of the hyænas, the cries of jackals, and the roar of lions outside the stockade at night were welcome; for then their human tormentors had for the most part gone to sleep. Beyond Donyo Erok stretches a sterile desert, at the base of the Kapté plateau, the perpendicular escarpment of which grows dark and threatening over the plains.

Space will not permit of our following Mr. Thomson march by march in the midst of Wakikuyu and Masai, past pleasant places where food was plentiful, over deserts where the animals fell dead for want of water and lions followed in troops to prey upon them, past the great extinct crater of Donyo Logonot rising 3,000 feet above the surrounding plain—every day the scenes different, though, unfortunately, not with a corresponding change of fortunes, until Lake Naivasha was a welcome sight. Here, after ten days of plundering, the expedition had literally to bore its way through the Masai. But while Martin, the Maltese sailor, went on with the bulk of the party to Lake Baringo, Thomson, making his way out of the great meridional trough with its string of charming lakes, ascended a lofty, misty, Scots-like plateau, occupied by great numbers of Wakwafi, a tribe of Masai (p. 232), and covered with splendid forests of firs, heaths, and Cape Calodendrons. Then the traveller tramped over hills and treeless plains and the fine Aberdare Mountains, nearly 14,000 feet high (p. 235), continually annoyed by the Wakwafi until Kenia, shaped like a sugar-loaf, was reached. Unable to spend much time in examining this interesting peak (p. 230), owing to the tireless persecution of the tribesmen, a forced march

An Alpine Africa.

was made to the Likipia mountains, from which, from a height of 8,000 feet, the Baringo Lake presents a magnificent spectacle as it lies glittering below in the great trough or valley of subsidence, which extends from Naivasha. Of all the scenes witnessed by him in Africa, Mr. Thomson declares this to be the most magnificent.

EL-MORAU (OLD MEN) OF THE MASAI TRIBE.
(*From a Photograph by Mr. Thomas Stevens.*)

Crossing the Kamasia Mountains, the Elgeyo precipices were ascended from a narrow valley, and the shelterless plateau of Guas-'Ngishu traversed until Kabaras, in Kavirondo (Vol. II., pp. 80, 92), was reached. Then, for the first time since leaving Taveta, the expedition revelled in fowls and eggs, Indian corn, sweet potatoes, ground nuts, and other good things strange to the Masai country. The Wakavirondo proved to be a pleasant people—as the people of this region go,—formed by the coalition of two different races, the one in the north belonging to the Waswahili races, while the more southerly tribes clearly belong—their speech betraying them—to the Upper Nile stock.

On the 10th of December Thomson had the pleasure of drinking the waters of Lake Victoria some forty-five miles east of its outlet. But here the general good fortune of this admirable explorer deserted him. Stores began to get exhausted, and fever to fasten itself on the leader of the expedition. He therefore wisely determined, instead of going to the Nile, to turn back, through the more northern district, for the sake of visiting Elgon, or Ligonyi (Vol. II., pp. 84, 93, 96), a splendid mountain that almost reaches the snow-line. The chief features of Elgon are the vast caves that honeycomb the mountain. Numbers of them contain whole villages, with their cattle. But, as the fact of their extending far into darkness shows, this could not have been their original intention. Mr. Thomson considers that they are artificial and, since the material of which those he examined consists is a very compact volcanic conglomerate, that they must have been mines at a very remote period. On this assumption some attractive theories have been formulated (Vol. I., p. 10). But later investigations show that they occur in the lava, as well as in the conglomerate, and are probably not artificial, but merely vast blow-holes in the mountain, which is an extinct volcano, with a crater eight miles in diameter, and from 1,500 feet to 2,000 feet in depth. The cave-dwellers inhabit the southern side of the mountain, which is 14,000 feet high, the northern side being populated by a wretched tribe akin to the Waelgumi, still farther north. With the exception of a few Wanderobbo, they are the only inhabitants of this mighty mountain, which, by the way, has a base 150 miles in circumference.*

After narrowly escaping death from a wounded buffalo, Thomson set out for the coast by way of the base of the lofty Chibcharagnani range, Elgeyo, Kamasia, and Njemps, where a halt was made to enable him to recover from the tossing he had suffered at the horns of the infuriated bull. Dysentery

* *The Times* (London), May 29, 1893.

now added its misery to the other misfortunes that had begun to gather. Yet Baringo Lake — an inland basin 3,000 feet above sea-level, but not salt—was examined, an elephant was shot, and many fresh geographical facts were collected.

But before Naivasha was reached, walking became impossible, and even riding on a donkey, without assistance, an **Homewards bound: an** effort too much for his strength. **accumulation of troubles.** Luckily, the Masai were tolerable; and by the time Ulu was passed, the expedition was among friendly natives. Still weak, the lack of goods with which to buy food compelled the party to push on with all speed, with meat or without it, and often in sore need for want of water; until, on the 26th of May, they encamped at the base of Ndara (p. 309), and, on the 2nd of June, 1884, emerging from the wilderness, were greeted by their friends at the mission-station of Ribe.*

* Thomson: "Through Masai Land," etc. (1885); *Proceedings of the Royal Geographical Society*, 1884, p. 690.

Thus ended a remarkable expedition, and with it, also, an era in the history of Africa. For by the time Mr. Thomson emerged from the continent, a very notable, though not unexpected, event had taken place. This was the "Scramble for Africa." All pretence of disinterestedness in exploring had been thrown aside; the struggle was now to exploit the continent, every nation for itself. Then began the partition of the Black Man's Land, after which nearly every exploration was, more or less, connected with Chartered Companies and Spheres of Influence. However, the country which was divided up among the European nations who had, eight years before met with so many protestations of philanthropy on the lips of their delegates, was only what had not been already seized. Before, therefore, considering the new partition of Africa, it will be necessary to glance at the old one—in other words, at the colonies which had for centuries been carved out of the continent.

MASAI WAR PARTY.
(*From a Photograph by Mr. Thomas Stevens.*)

www.ingramcontent.com/pod-product-compliance
Lightning Source LLC
Chambersburg PA
CBHW030739230426
43667CB00007B/767